I0762729

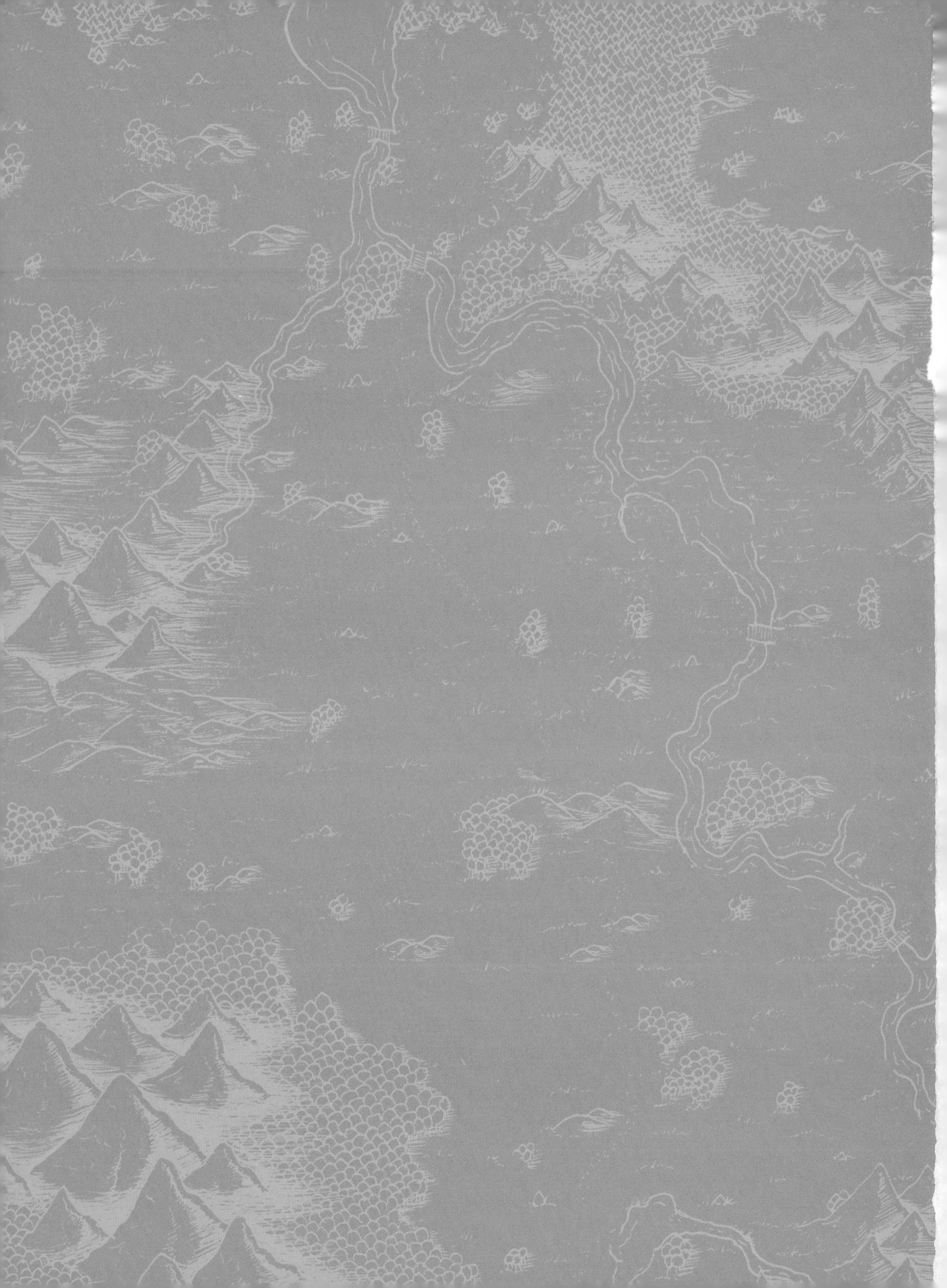

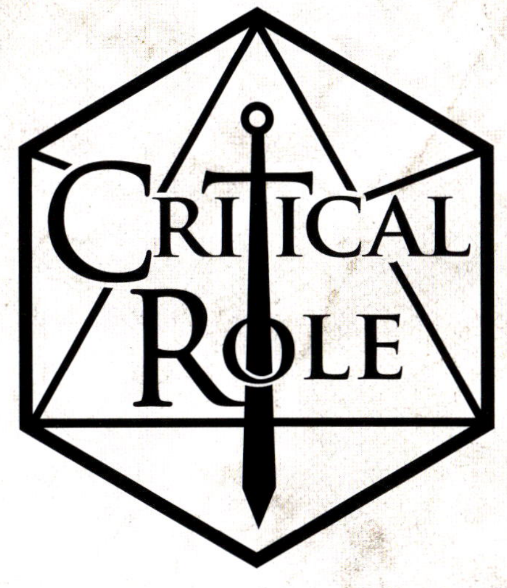

The Armory of Heroes

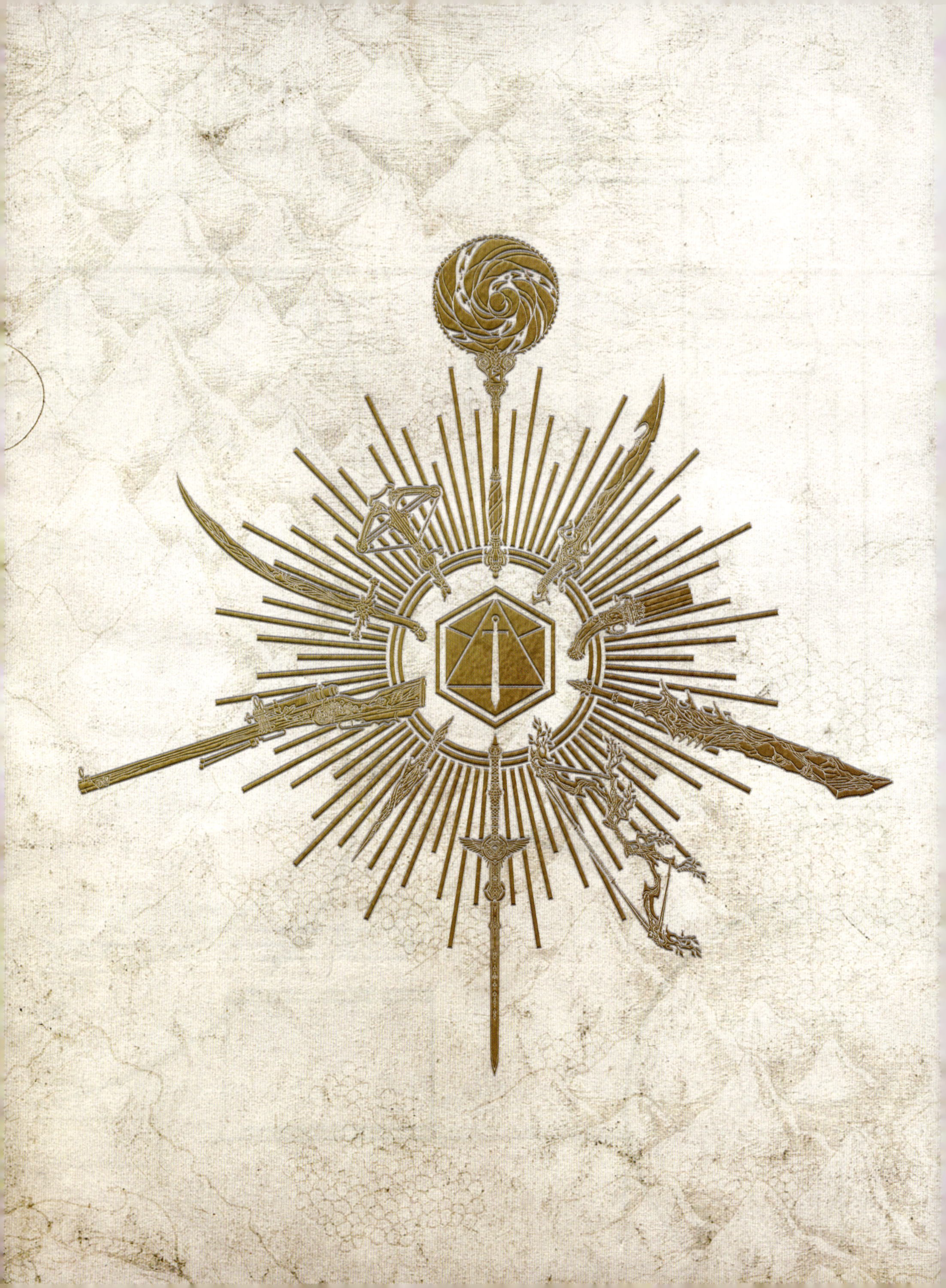

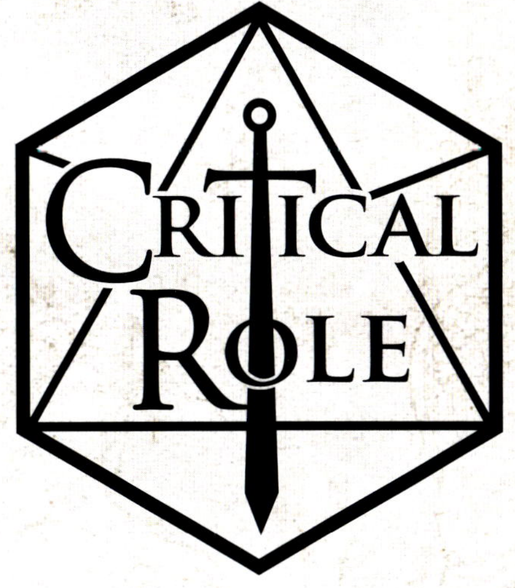

The Armory of Heroes

By **Martin Cahill**
Illustrated by **Ana Fedina**

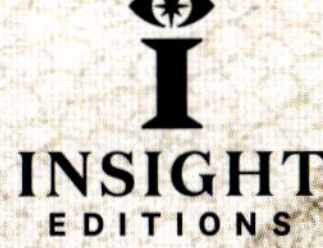

SAN RAFAEL • LOS ANGELES • LONDON

Contents

Mighty Nein

The Ring of Brass

Introduction

Dearest Reader,

If you're reading these words, it means you and I have something in common: we both share a deep love of Exandrian history. And if you're anything like me, you share a deeper love for those who shaped that history, molding that eternal clay which sits upon an ever-spinning wheel.

Those hands did not just belong to the gods, who in their primacy and betrayals shook the foundations of Exandria, but mortals as well. It is expected, Calamity or no, for history to yield to the touch of the divine. It is something rarer entirely to see all the ways in which mortal hands and mortal will, their drive, not only worked upon the history of Exandria but defended our world from dangers innumerable and devastating.

Professor? You're waxing again.

Ah! Yes. My colleague is correct. I shall leave these grander thoughts for my thesis-in-progress and get to the heart of the matter. For now, I must introduce my co-writers! Tallulah?

Much appreciated, prof! Name's Tallulah Fontaine, bard extraordinaire, ordained in the holy church of formidable bastards by the holiest of ne'er-do-wells, the one and only Dr. Dranzel! What I lack in ugly, I make up for in bawdy, blush-worthy ballads of the lewd and lecherous. But that's a side gig; a big green, half-orc lady has to eat, don't she? Most times, I'm gathering intel for the Golden Grin, still formidable bastards, but on the side of the decent and kind. When I heard this lovable egghead was gathering information on Exandrian heroes, I had all sorts of things to add.

Thank you, Tallulah, yes. You do know I can't hear your flute through this enchanted document, yes? It's just picking up the notes—regardless! Oren, would you care to introduce yourself?

Very well. I shall keep this brief. I am Oren Keth'Kaylis, a drow officer of the Kryn Dynasty and agent of [redacted]. While I often play the role of saboteur or intelligence, it also falls to me to keep record of the Dynasty and the Bright Queen's history with the rest of Exandria. When word reached me through my agent in [redacted] that Professor Dawnscale was conducting research into a number of high-value targets with history to the Kryn, I offered my assistance.

Wow, Oren, such talent, imbuing that much stiff upper lip through paper. Teach me your ways..

Bicker off the page, please, friends! To introduce myself, I am D'Rishk Dawnscale, Second Provost to the College of Arcane Histories, Keeper of Keys, and have been with the Cobalt Soul for nigh on thirty years after my escape from an unfortunate, near-fatal chapter beneath the heel of the Iron Authority of Tz'Arrm. My focus of study has always been the Age of Arcanum. But as I noticed similarities between the heroes of yesterday and the champions of today, I could not help but wonder at a culmination of all of them in one place! With the aid of Tallulah, whose ear for music catches tales as easy as tunes, and Oren, whose depth of research and commitment to truth often put me to shame, I believe we have done exactly that.

Together, we have catalogued the arms and armory of Exandria, and those heroes whose hands and hearts and minds wielded them against impossible odds.

Vox Machina is a name you probably hear a lot. Nine Hells, you probably see Vasselheim kids playing in the shadow of the Earth Titan, arguing over who gets to rage and be Grog or no, you can't be Keyleth, you aren't tall enough, and so on. You've probably heard "The Champion's Dark Sorrow," "Enter Meat Man," or "Grey Lady's Favor," at any number of taverns in Tal'Dorei. You've seen rifles on the shoulders of Whitestone soldiers, and you've seen a number of new temples to the Everlight. Hell, if you live in Wildemount, you've probably even heard of the ridiculous but effective Darrington Brigade. Vox Machina, for all they didn't wish for history's recognition, got it anyway. And their legacy lives on across the breadth of Exandria to this day.

The Mighty Nein do . . . not have that record of acclaim. Nor do I believe they would care for it. In fact, a few might actively despise it. As with Vox Machina, they did not wish for acclaim, and for the majority of them, would have been quite happy to live quietly on the fringes of the world. Fate had other plans but fate only works if other components are present. Heart. Empathy. Justice. Care. Even love. Fate alchemizes these constituents, and when they are put together, heroes are born. Though I have it on personal authority the Nein would cringe from that description. And if you asked any number of them why they faced the evils they did, why they put themselves between danger and Wildemount, horror and Exandria, why stop a war? The answer would be the same, I can imagine. "Because someone had to try." May we all be so courageous to try in such a manner when faced with that level of challenge.

And I have the honor and heartbreak to add to these two groups of champions. The head of my order has deemed it time to finally write about a long-lost company of heroes and their terrible fate. Here, you will learn of the noble Ring of Brass and their sacrificial role in the Calamity. A shadow council comprised of mages, merchants, bureaucrats, defenders, and engineers, each dedicated to the safety of Avalir, one of the flying cities of legend. Because of these six, all present at the crescendo of the Age of Arcanum and the start of Calamity, Exandria did not experience total annihilation. And though we lost the ancient continent of Domunas from the death of Avalir, the rest of Exandria was given a chance to live. Because of them.

You will see in what items we could recover, and what knowledge pulled from the earth, that though little is remembered of this Age, there is a common theme that connects the Ring of Brass across time to Vox Machina and the Mighty Nein. Yes, they all found and made use of items of great divine will and tremendous magic power. Yes, they were in their own way, families. But what unites them most is that when Exandria needed them, they answered.

And for that, across the Ages, we are grateful.

Maybe that is the true purpose of this tome, all this research . . .

Not just a cataloging, a taxonomy, or a knowing.

Nor just tales told, songs sung, and stories celebrated.

All these and more, let this tome be gratitude bound in vellum. Let it be a deep and sincere thank-you across time. Let that thanks echo through the halls of memory. Let it be a guide for those youths of Exandria, who even now, may find themselves drawn to the open road. Who wish to put themselves between innocents and ruin.

Learn from these heroes as we have. If we can at least do that, then they will always be remembered.

And if they can be remembered, I know all three of us will count this tome a true success.

Thank you so much for reading. Thank you for being here with us. We hope you enjoy every moment of your time with these heroes of Exandria.

We certainly did.

With sincerity,

Second Provost of Arcane Histories,
Professor D'Rishk Dawnscale

First Balladeer of the Golden Grin, Tal'Dorei Chapter,
Tallulah Fontaine

Agent of [redacted] Captain of [redacted] Officer
Oren Keth'Kaylis

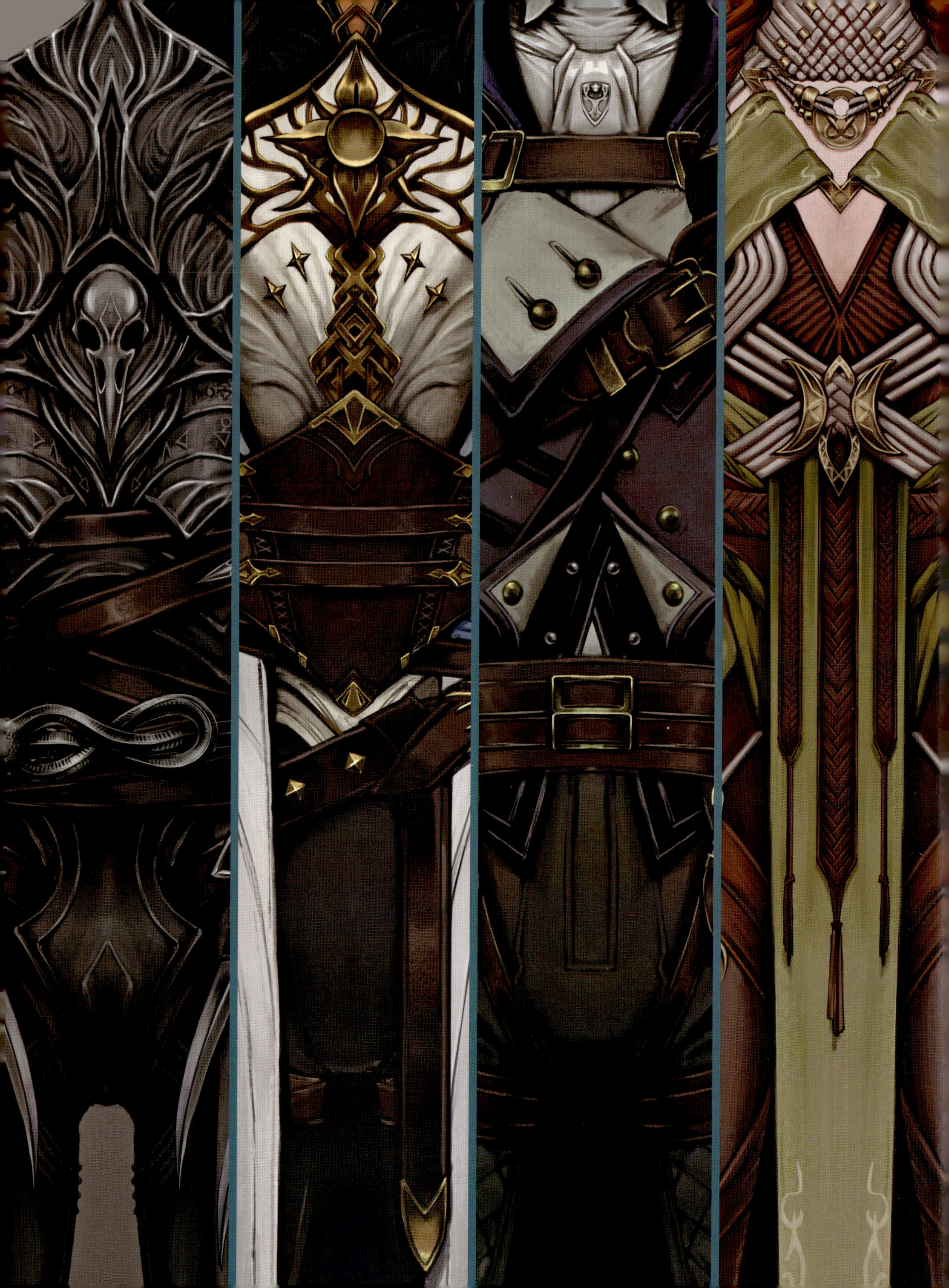

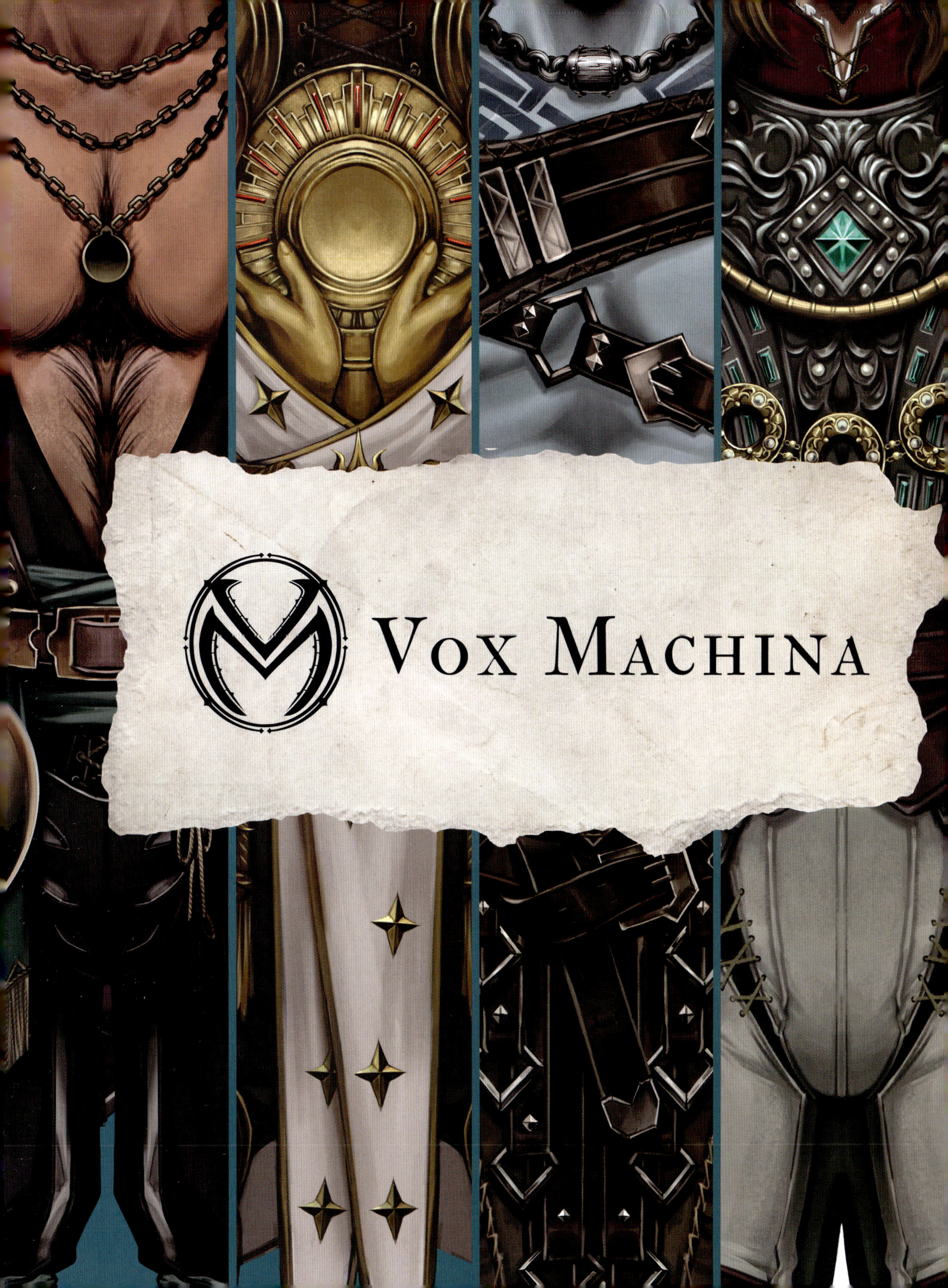
Vox Machina

Vox Machina

"Vox Machina, eh? Yes, yes, I remember them. At this point, who in Exandria doesn't? But I knew 'em way back when. Even trained the infamous Scanlan Shorthalt! What, you think talent like that just appears? Only with his daughter, Kaylie. Anyway, ah, Vox Machina. Knew 'em when their biggest concerns were warm beds, decent ale, and enough gold to afford either, though hardly ever both at the same time. I've seen mercenary companies come and go, people pulled together by chance or fortune, and after some time, they drift apart. But Vox Machina?

Yes, they came together by chance and fortune, but it was fate that bound them, tight as a stitch. And oh, it was tested, that bond. You can see it across the length and breadth of Tal'Dorei, starting from the heights of Whitestone, where they fought Lord and Lady Briarwood, the undead who usurped and took over Lord de Rolo's old home. You can see it across Emon, Westruun, and Mount Gatshadow, even Issylra and Wildemount, where the scars of the Chroma Conclave have healed but not faded; the legacy of dragons is made of stronger stuff.

You can see it across the planes, from Exandria to the Shadow Realm, from Elysium to the Fey Realm and back; Vox Machina could not afford to rest as they hunted the Whispered One, preventing his ascension to true godhood. Heroes, the lot of them, though that was never the point. They didn't put their necks on the line for glory. Any asshole can find glory. No, Vox Machina . . . they'd tell you they started as a bunch of shits, and they'd be right to say so. They were. But time after time, the call came, and they answered. They put themselves between harm and the world. And for that, we can only be grateful.

I know they all have fancy titles and stuff now, but they'll always be Vex, Vax, Grog, Pike, Percy, Keyleth, and Scanlan to me. Taryon? Oh, right . . . right! He was there, yeah. Well, he was pretty great, too! Not too bad for a buncha slap-dicks, huh?"

—TALLULAH FONTAINE, QUOTING DR. DRANZEL AFTER A MEETING OF THE GOLDEN GRIN

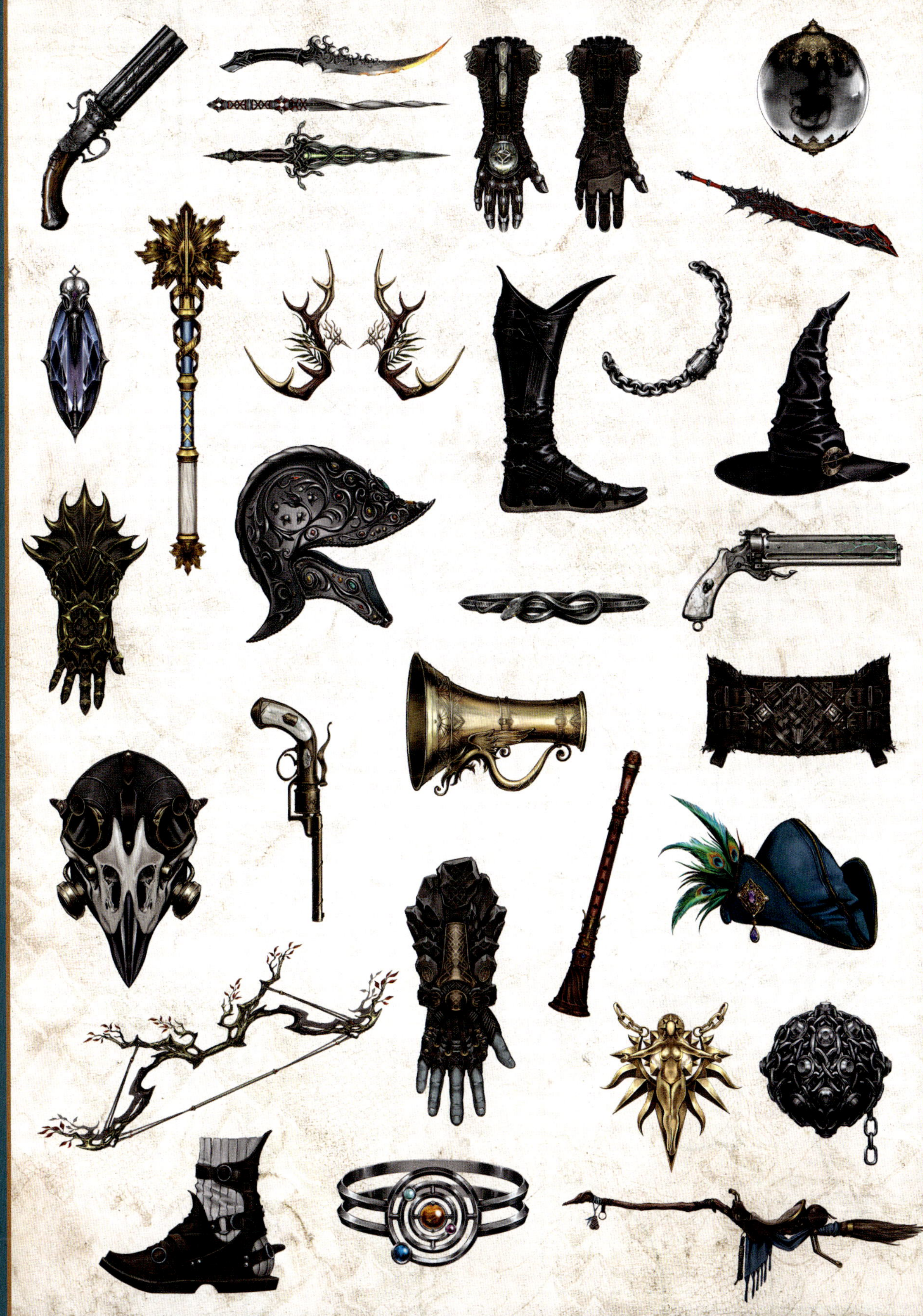

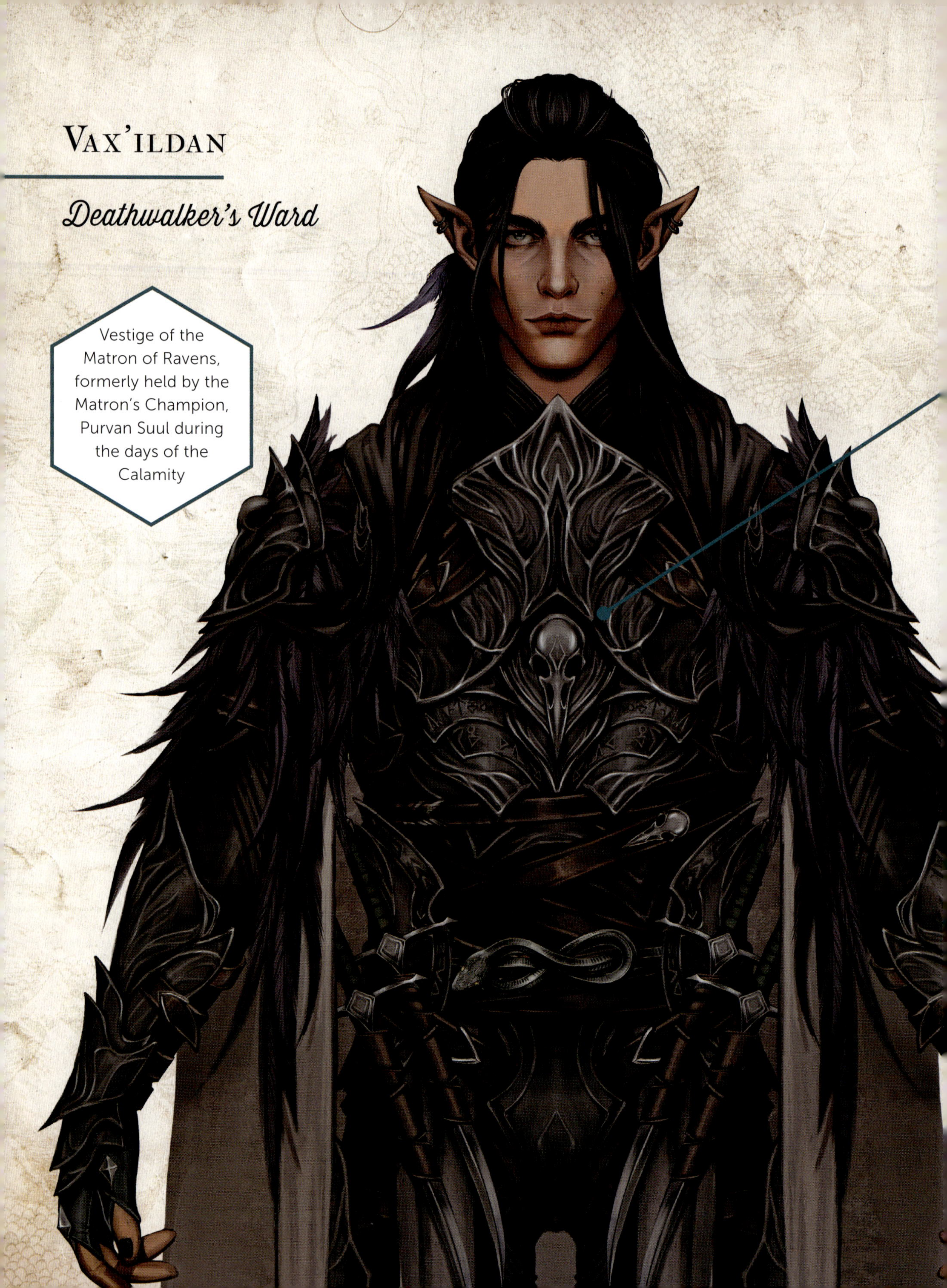
Vax'ildan
Deathwalker's Ward
Vestige of the Matron of Ravens, formerly held by the Matron's Champion, Purvan Suul during the days of the Calamity

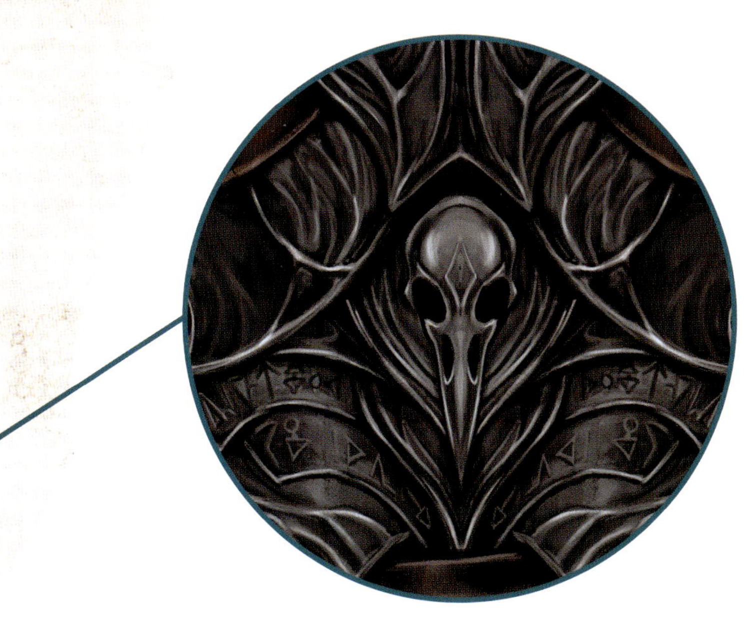

"In my research, I have found an ancient prayer from the first bearer of the Vestige. In Purvan Suul's own words:

**'Now I become Death, Her shrouded soldier
In Her cold embrace, naught may bring my end save Her
And on the swift wings of Her children
Will I bring Her cold, tender touch
To those that would evade it.'**

A striking prayer from one of the first champions of the Matron of Ravens. I can only imagine the awesome and terrifying vision he made, clad in the leather and feathers of the Deathwalker's Ward. Why, to some, it must have looked as though death Herself had arrived."

—Oren Keth'Kaylis

Found in a tomb at the bottom of a lake in Othanzia, the Deathwalker's Ward is a Vestige meant to repel death from its wearer, even at times granting the gift of flight for a short time.

However, armor crafted to repel death asks for payment in kind. Percival set off a trap where the Deathwalker's Ward was sequestered, and Vex'ahlia, twin sister to Vax'ildan, was caught in the blast of necrotic energy. With her life in the Matron of Ravens's pale hand, Vax'ildan stepped forward, demanding that he be taken in his sister's stead. And so, Vex'ahlia was saved as Vax'ildan entered his service to the Matron of Ravens, Her armor fitting him like fate.

From that day forward, he was granted the strength of the Deathwalker's Ward, whose many runes and enchantments gifted resistance to the damage he'd receive throughout their adventures against dragons, the undead, and more, at times even staving off death itself. He wore it for the rest of his time as a mortal man and took it with him into Her service after mortal life. Even in his service beyond death, it is said he is armored in her embrace still.

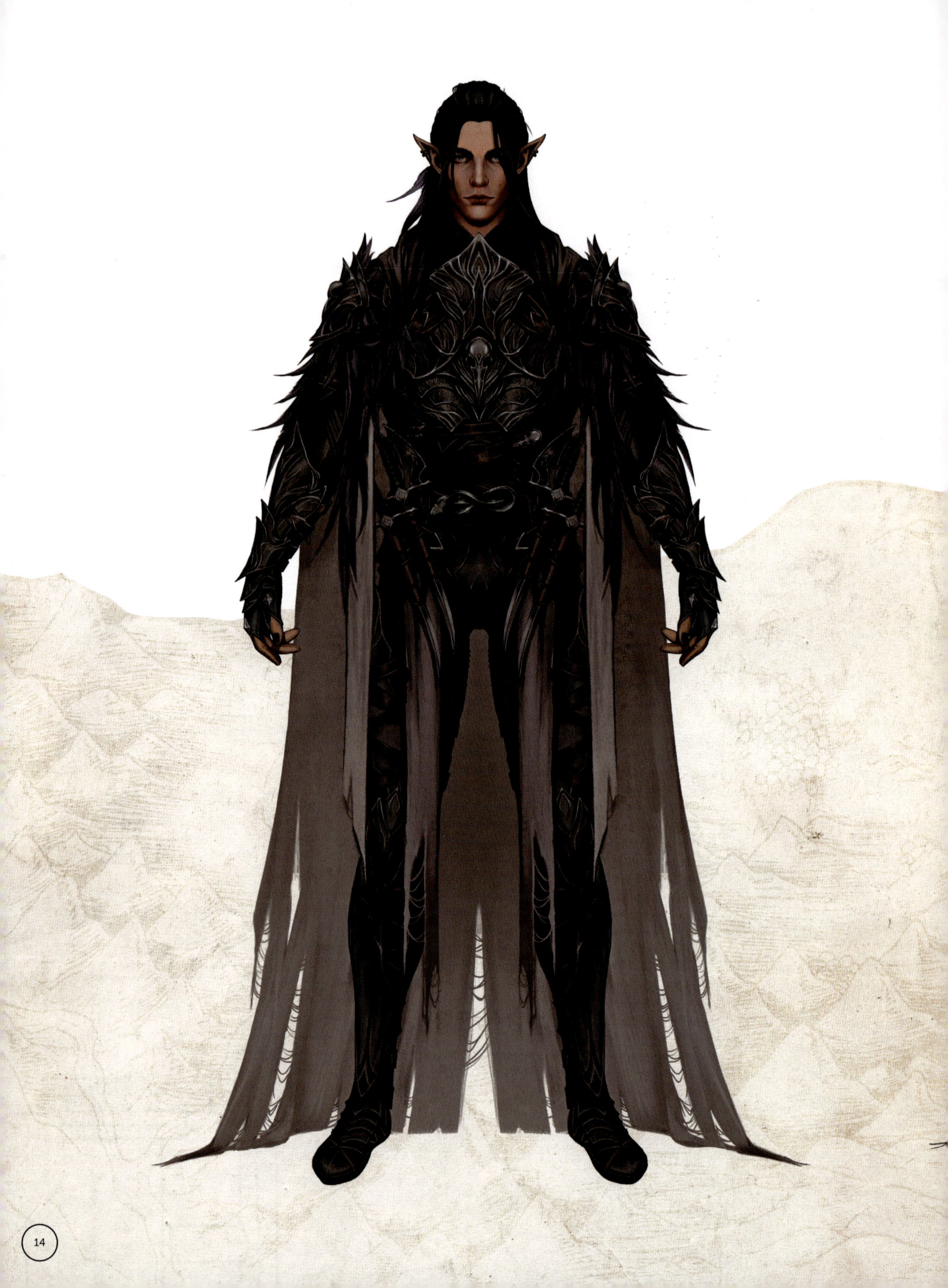

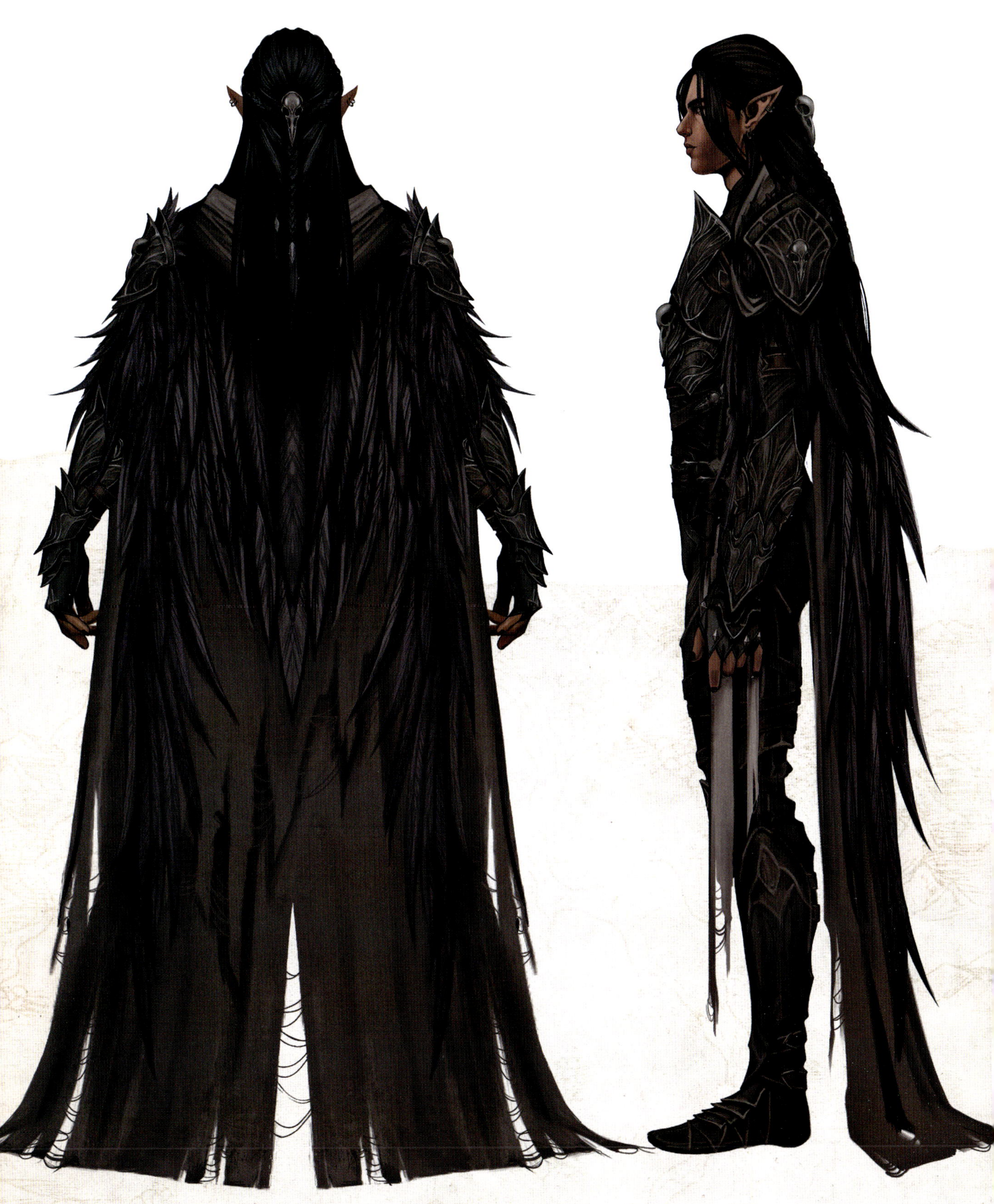

Simon

Slender and shaped like a garter snake, this belt could be removed and, with a word, turned into a real snake. Gifted to him in a youthful adventure, Vax'ildan named it Simon after a young child in Westruun whom Vox Machina helped. Often used for espionage, distractions, or entertainment, Simon the Snake was frequently called upon by Vax to help the stealthy thief sneak past this guard or that—and Simon was never more useful than when he was scaring others into missing Vax entirely.

He was almost lost within the Palace of the Sovereign when Vax infiltrated it in search of the Briarwoods, but the snake was recovered thanks to the ever-charming Vex'ahlia.

Simon would later go on to become Kynan Leore's for a time, a young mercenary whom Vax helped pull back from darkness. Eventually, Simon ended up in the hands of young Velora Vessar, little half-sister to the twins, a gift to her from Vax when he helped call her back to life.

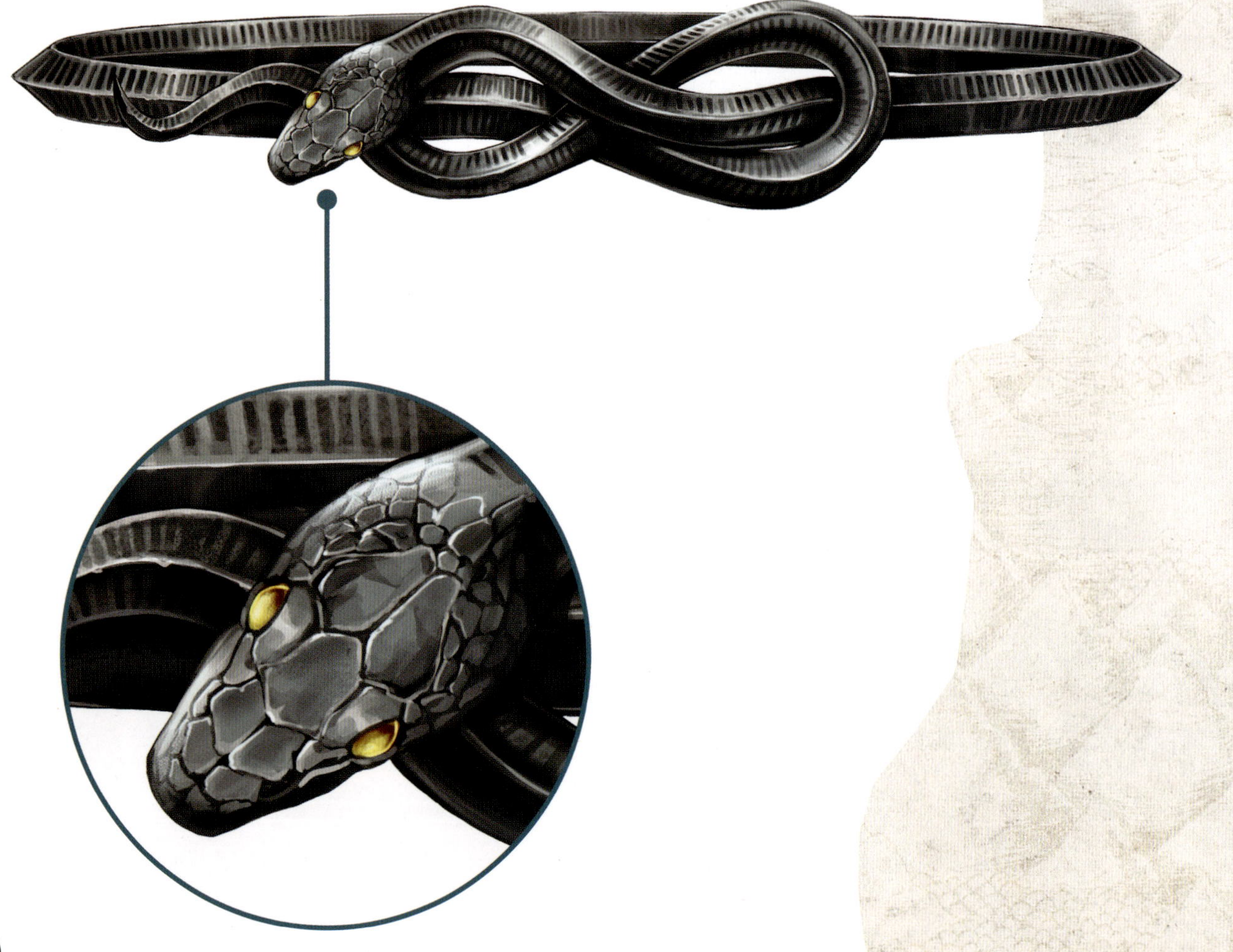

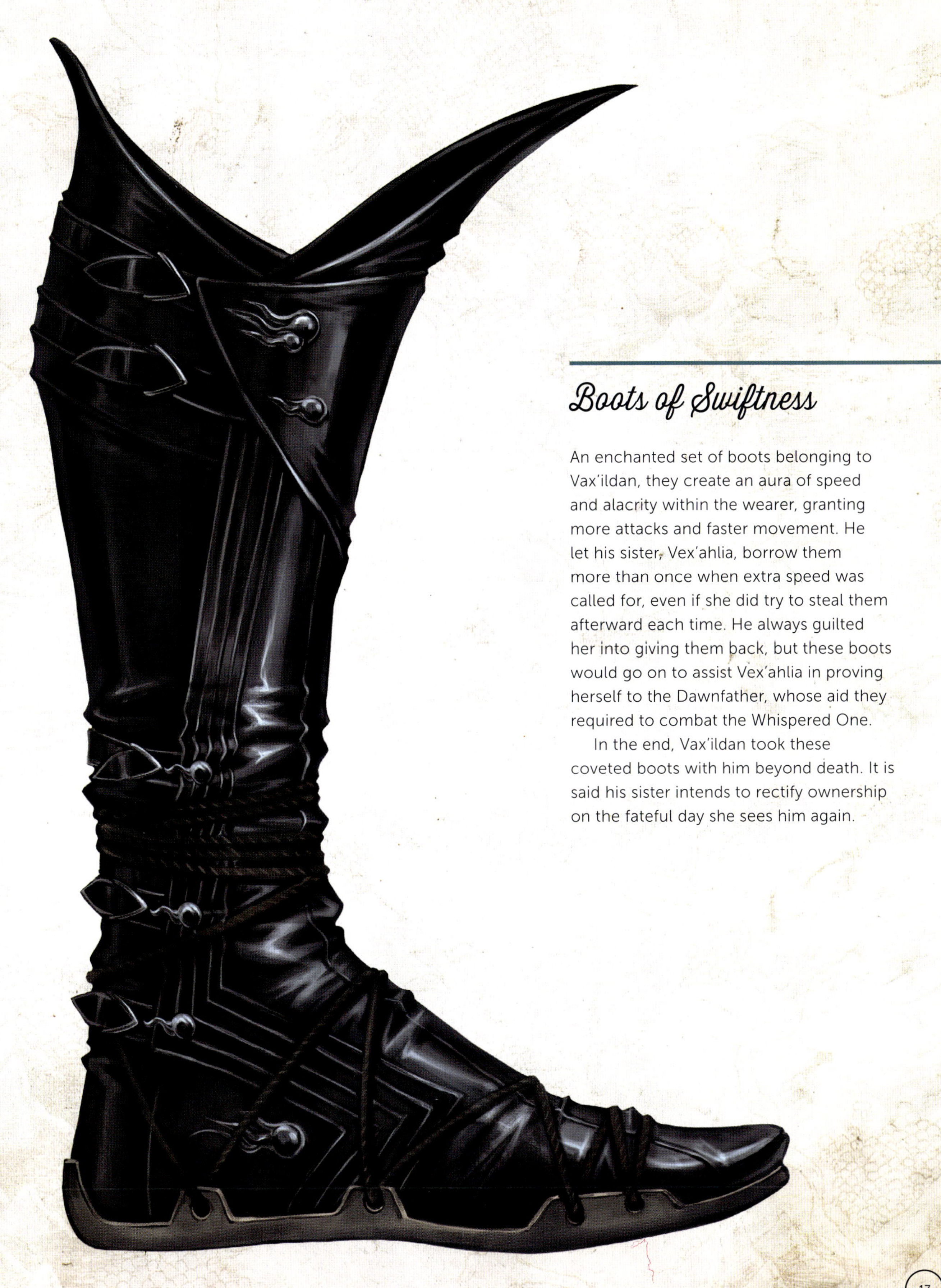

Boots of Swiftness

An enchanted set of boots belonging to Vax'ildan, they create an aura of speed and alacrity within the wearer, granting more attacks and faster movement. He let his sister, Vex'ahlia, borrow them more than once when extra speed was called for, even if she did try to steal them afterward each time. He always guilted her into giving them back, but these boots would go on to assist Vex'ahlia in proving herself to the Dawnfather, whose aid they required to combat the Whispered One.

In the end, Vax'ildan took these coveted boots with him beyond death. It is said his sister intends to rectify ownership on the fateful day she sees him again.

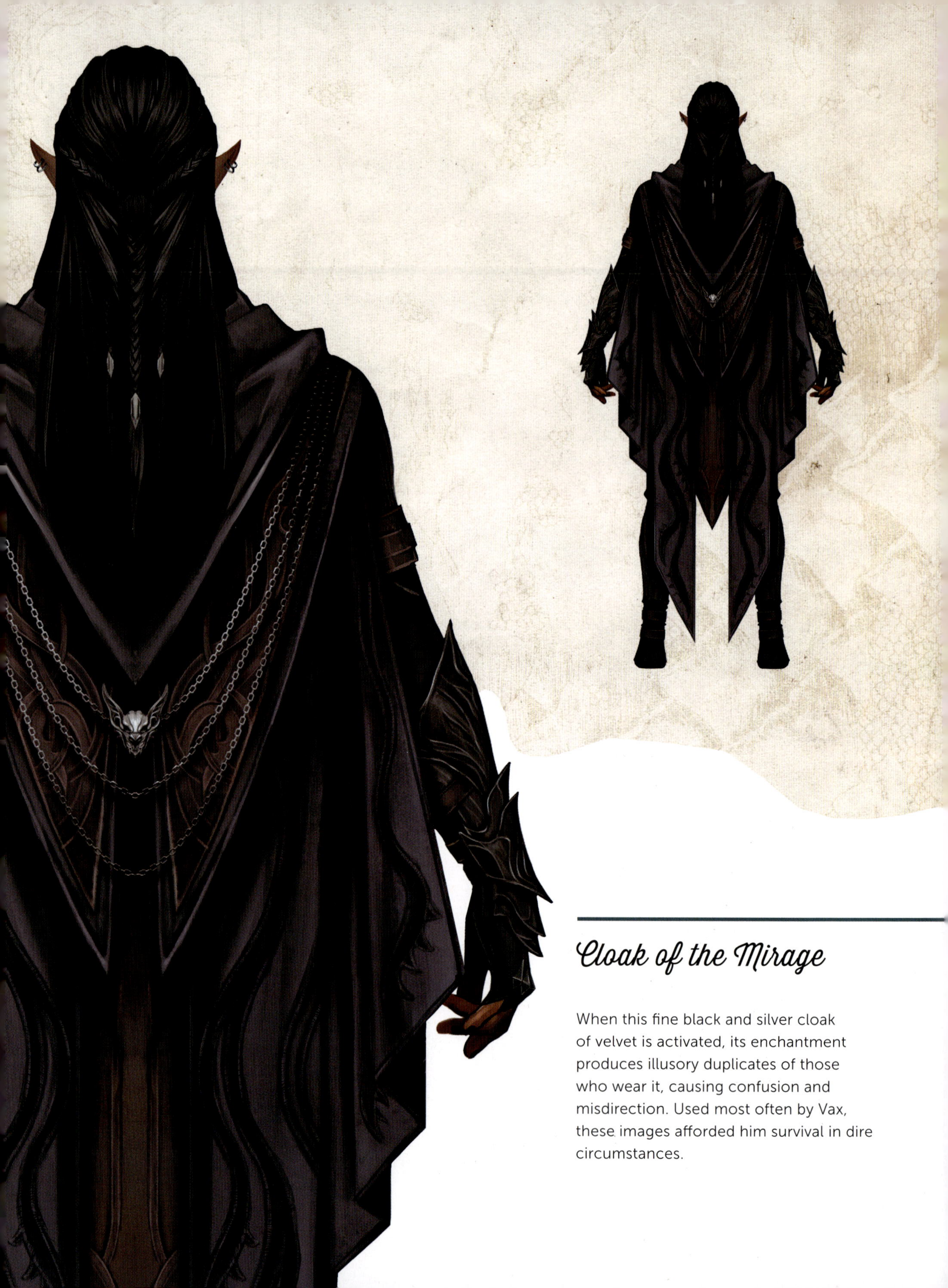

Cloak of the Mirage

When this fine black and silver cloak of velvet is activated, its enchantment produces illusory duplicates of those who wear it, causing confusion and misdirection. Used most often by Vax, these images afforded him survival in dire circumstances.

"How one gathers any tangible material from that darker, weirder place beyond the Astral Sea is beyond my expertise, but it was a time of Calamity; I suppose that motivates everyone, even gods, to get creative. It changed hands often throughout its time on Exandria, from divine assassins to mercenaries to mortal heroes, ending up where it seems it was destined all along. Taken into the divine realm by the passing of the newest Champion of the Matron, it is said the blade still speaks when used; a whisper of a prayer, or name, as her champion strikes out from the dark."

—D'Rishk Dawnscale

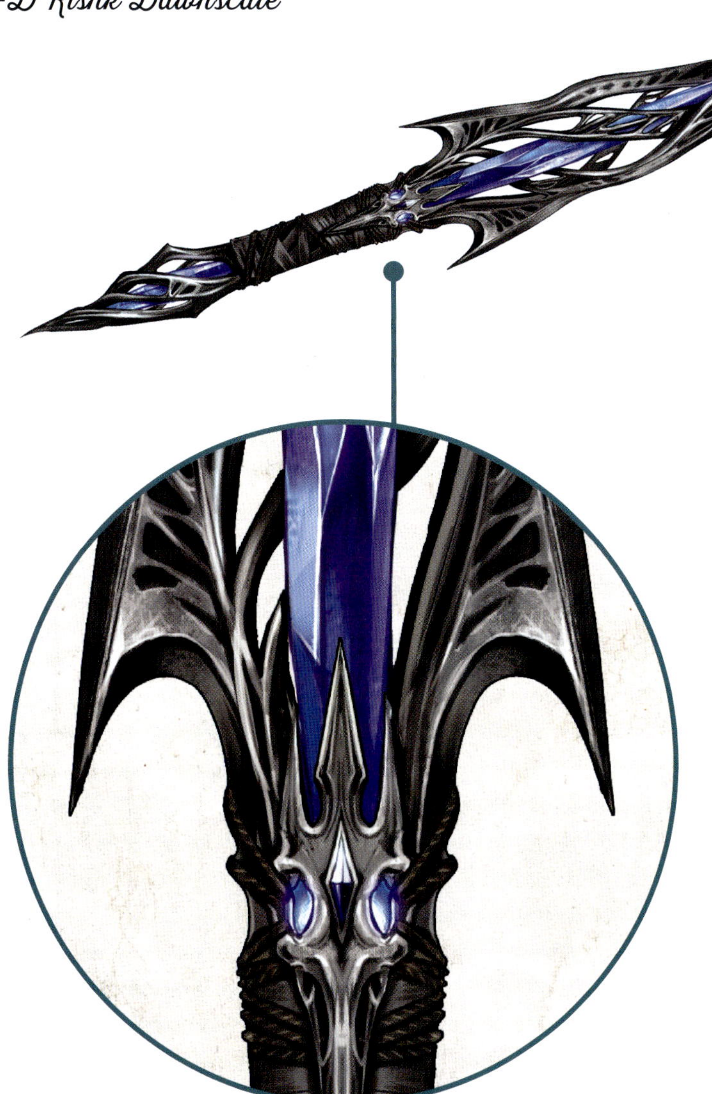

Whisper

A silver dagger forged from mercurial metals found in realms beyond, Whisper is a Vestige of the Calamity, crafted in the maddening dark of an unknowable realm. After being recovered by the rogue scientist Dr. Anna Ripley and gifted to her would-be assassin, Kynan Leore, the blade passed into the possession of Vax'ildan. Vax's speed and stealth were aided by the dagger's bending of shadow and form, making the speedy assassin almost impossible to track across the battlefield.

Used in the final desolation of the Cinder King, the voices of countless dead were drawn to Whisper's reality-piercing point and were used to impale the elemental dragon's fiery heart. Until his last breath and beyond it, it is said the Matron's Champion still wields the quicksilver blade, using it to bring the enemies of his goddess into her endless shadow.

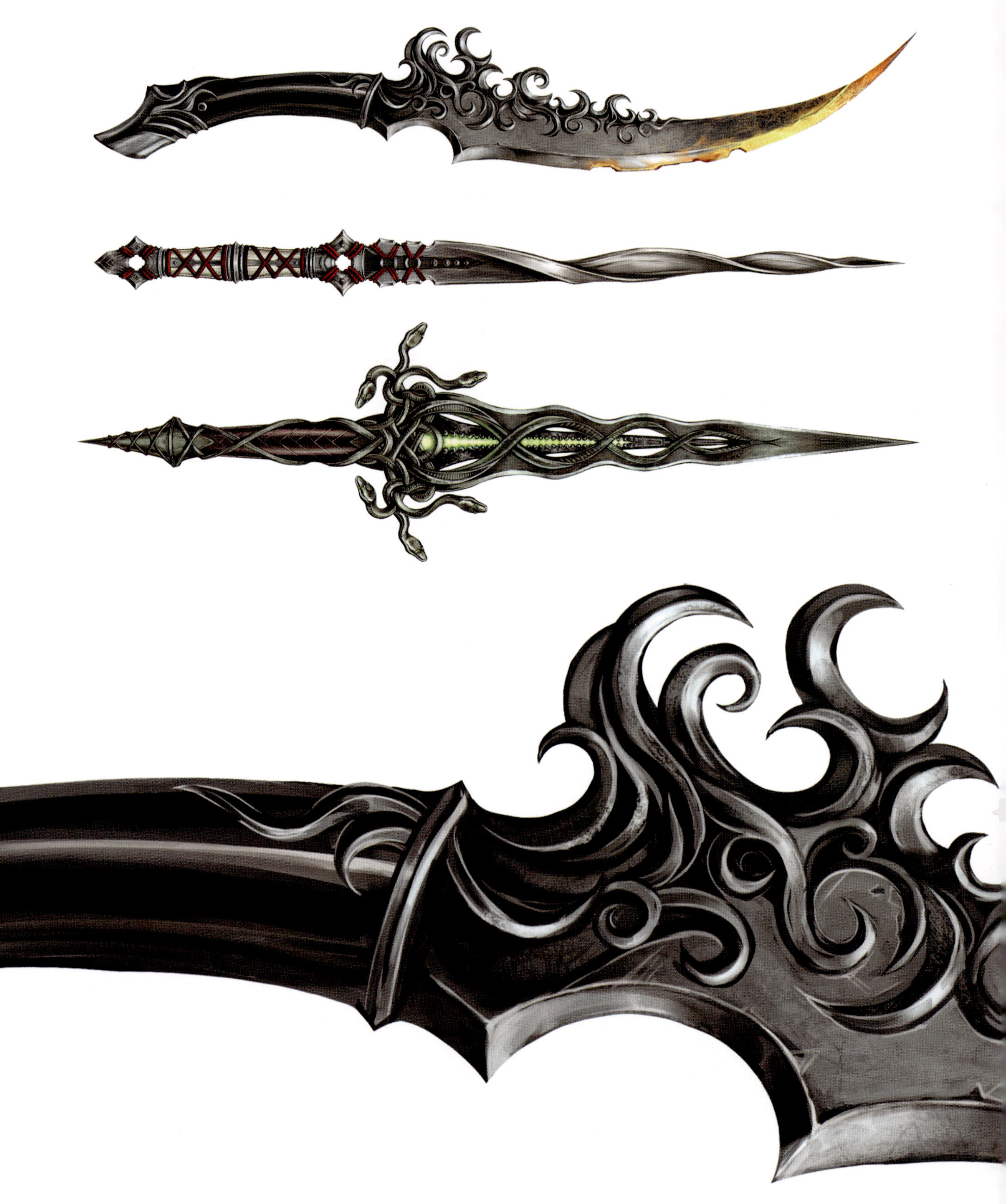

Dagger, Dagger, Dagger (Flame Dagger, Life-Eater, Poison)

Vax'ildan's signature weapons prior to acquiring Whisper were three magical daggers: one of flames, another of necrosis, and another of pure poison. He found these early on the road with his twin and added them to a bandolier of common blades, impressing mercenaries of the Clasp with his quick hands and natural dexterity. With three times as many chances to damage opponents, Vax'ildan used his speed to his advantage, and with his belt of recall, the blades would always find their way home to him, usually with a red token of their strikes coating their steel.

"The speed of these will make ya stagger!
Hear the cry o' 'Dagger, dagger, dagger!'
Enwreathed with flames, poison, and death
Vax'ildan with daggers three,
Will rob you of your final breath!"

—Tallulah Fontaine, stanza from "The Ballad of the Twins of Byroden"

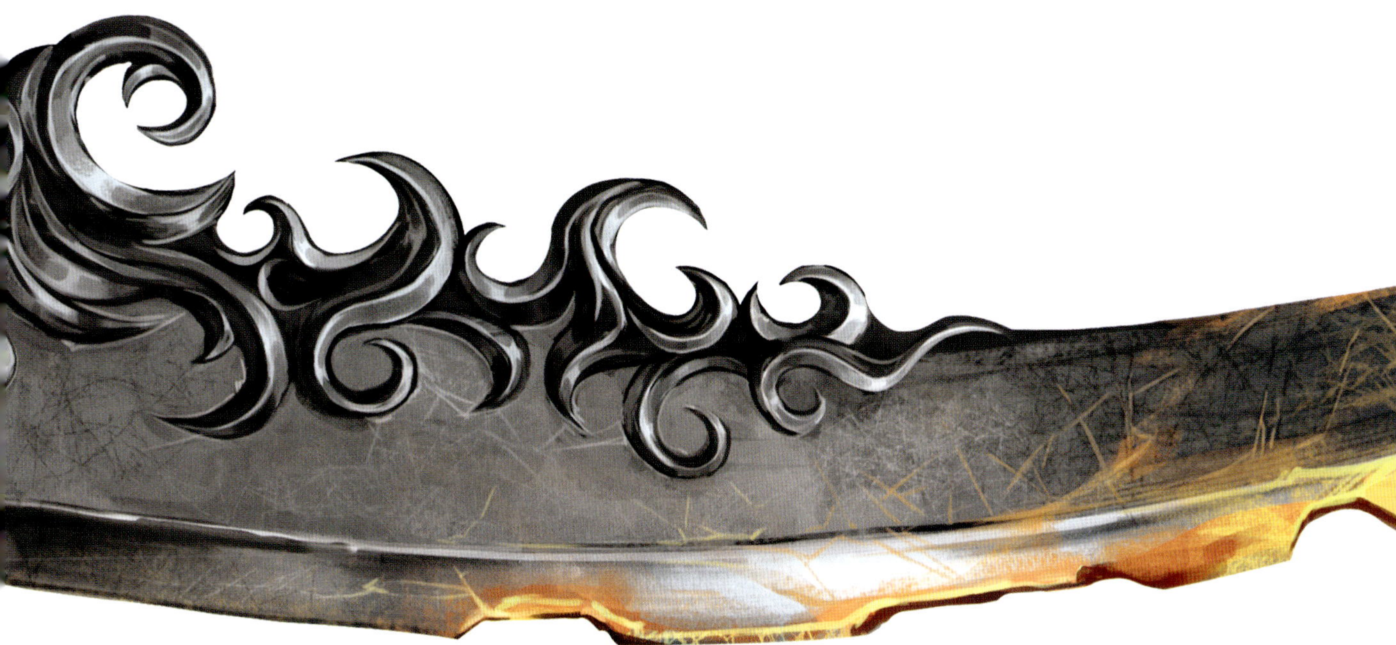

VEX'AHLIA

White Dragon Armor

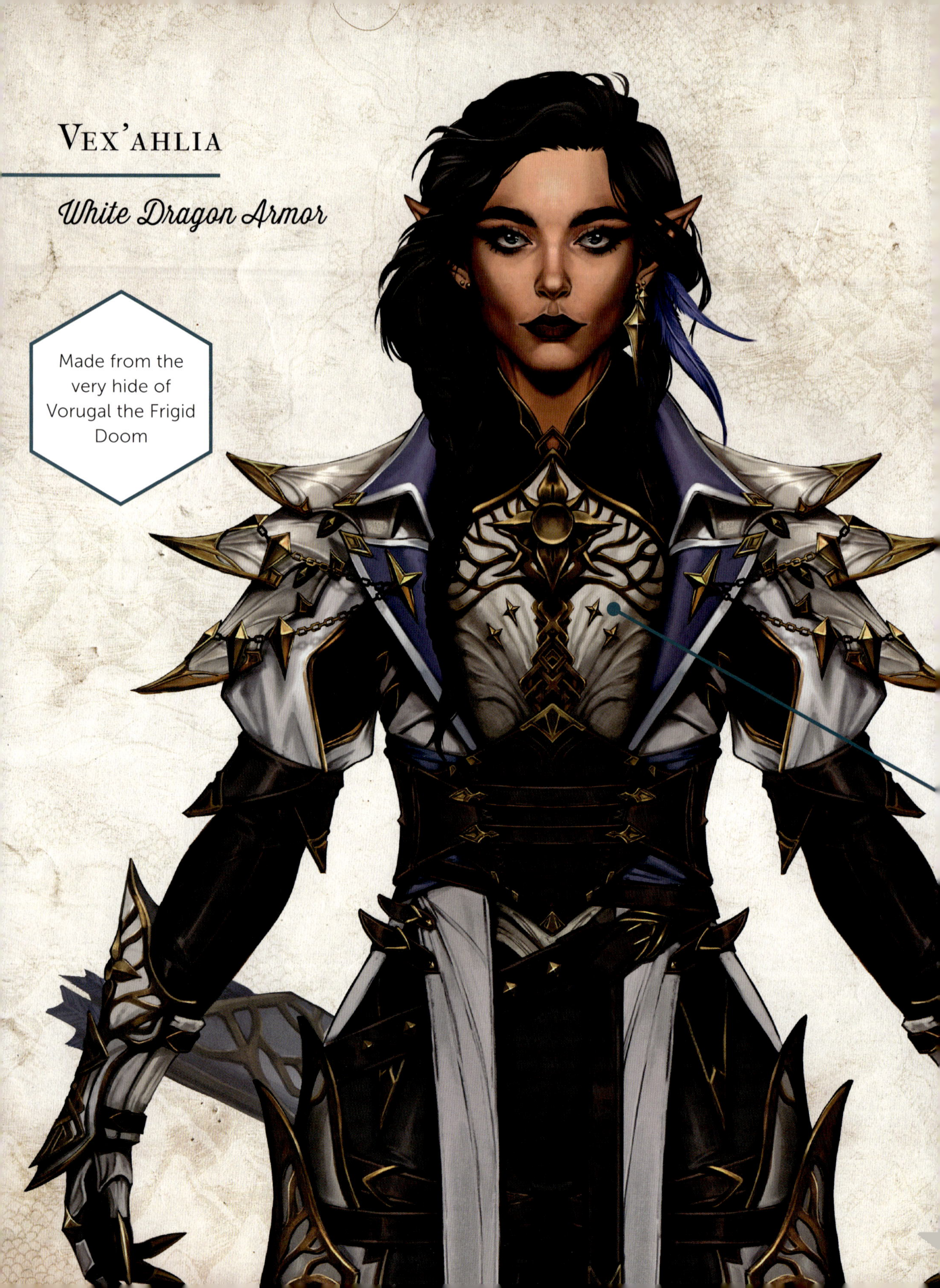

"There are many words that could apply to the Lady de Rolo, Vex'ahlia Vessar, of Whitestone: stylish, beautiful, cunning, elegant, saucy, intelligent, captivating, and yes, charming. But in my estimation, the one that works best is this: dangerous. The Mistress of the Grey Hunt is an excellent foil to her deceased brother, a light to his shadow, but much like him, she is quite formidable. Perhaps more so, if only because where her brother sought the darkness, Vex'ahlia, like any good predator, hides in plain sight. Make no mistake: there is a reason she wears the armor of the dragon she slew. When she enters a room in full battle gear, the brilliant ivory shine of Vorugal's scales is meant to dazzle the way a lanternfish lures its foes, or a peacock stands out. She is both seen and unseen. She declares her presence just as smoothly as she disguises it. She need not draw her knives, or bow, or sharp tongue until you realize it is too late. I do not often use this word, but Vex'ahlia de Rolo née Vessar is breathtaking the way a dragon in flight takes your breath, right before its rapid descent directly toward you."

—Oren Keth'Kaylis, pulled from the files of the Tal'dorei Council

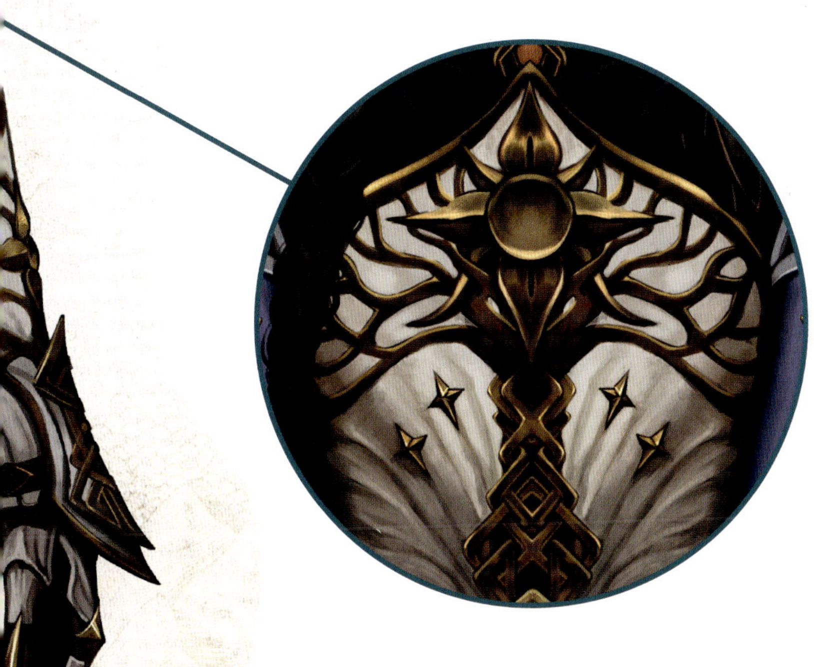

This beautiful, bright white armor was built for Vex'ahlia by adventuring companion and brilliant craftsman, Taryon Darrington, in the year of rest Vox Machina experienced between their defeat of the Chroma Conclave and the ascension of the Whispered One. Taken from the hide of Vorugal the Frigid Doom, this ancient white dragon member of the Chroma Conclave was felled by Vex's arrow. This armor utilizes the fearsome hunter's scales to become armor akin to thick plate while also keeping the dragon's innate resistance to the cold. Vex'ahlia wore this armor until the end of her adventures with Vox Machina.

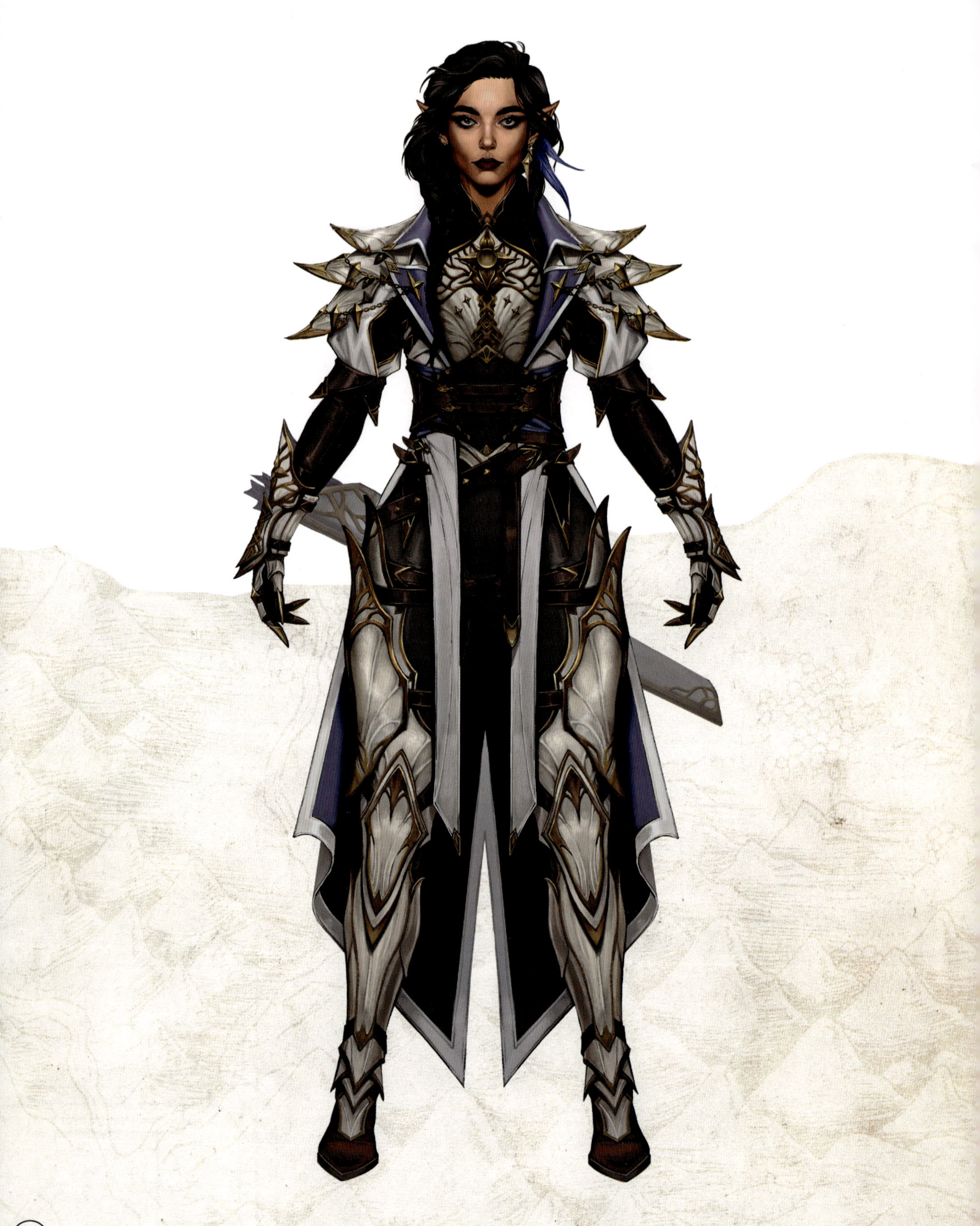

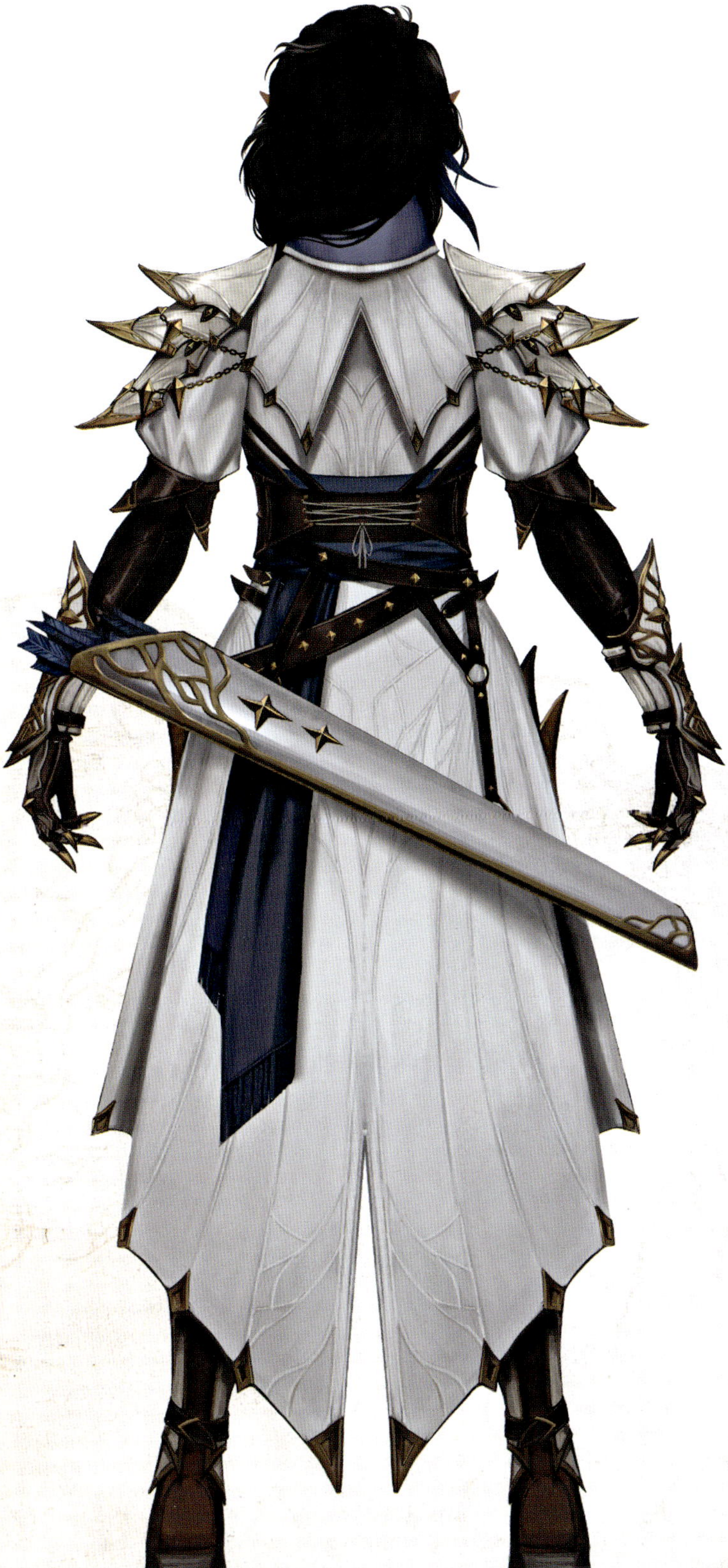

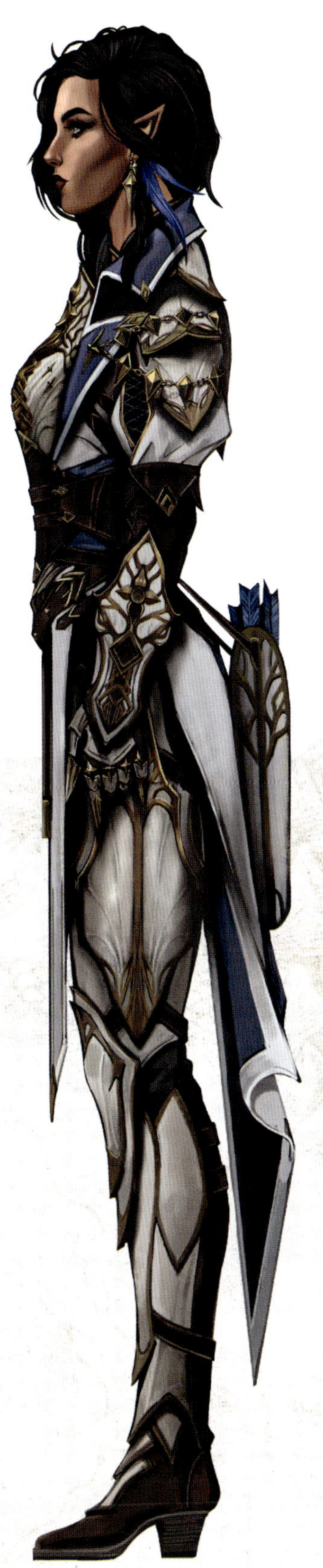

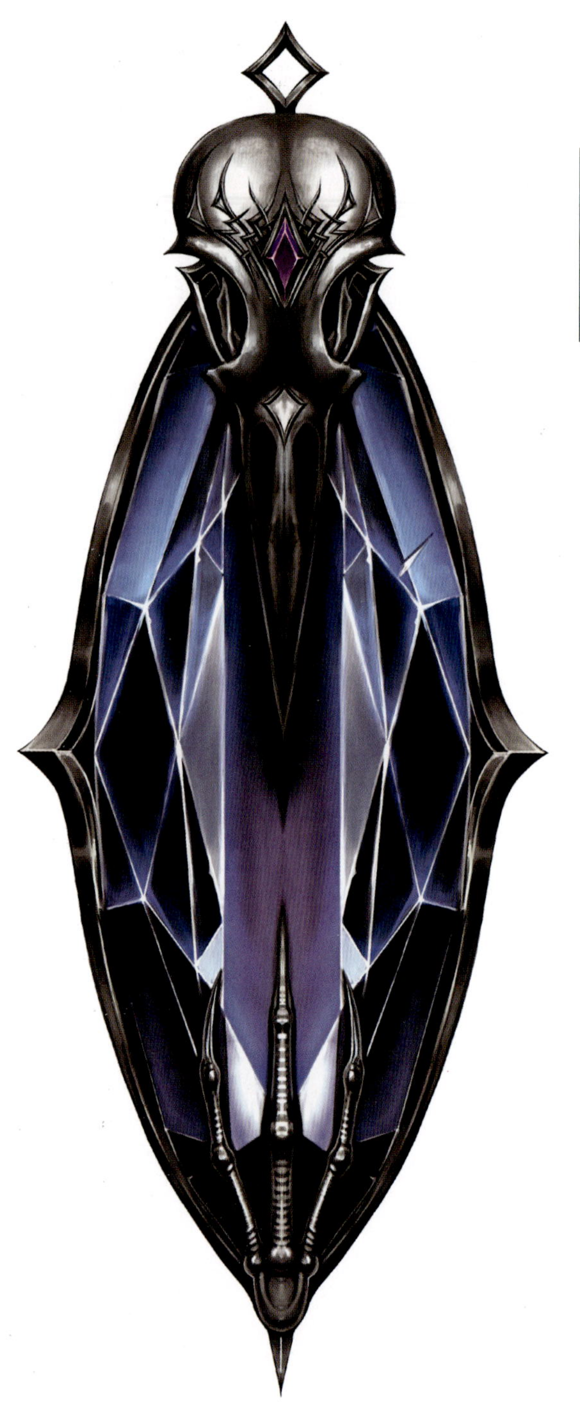

Formerly held by Purvan Suul, used to house his companion, the Wolf Galdric

Raven's Slumber

Found with the Deathwalker's Ward, this small black gem was used by the previous champion of the Matron of Ravens, Purvan Suul, to house his wolf companion, Galdric. When the gem was discovered by Vox Machina, Galdric was discovered to still reside within the gem's demiplane, a place where time pauses for whomever lives within. After Vox Machina freed him, Galdric gave his blessing and became guardian to the Parchwood around Whitestone. The amulet then passed to Vex'ahlia, who found the demiplane was the perfect place to house her beloved bear companion, Trinket, when combat proved too dangerous.

Within the gem lies a chilly, gray stone room with a simple stone throne and a window peering into the world outside. Members of Vox Machina have also benefitted from the demiplane, with both Grog and Vax'ildan placed inside to keep them safe during dangerous encounters.

Band of Shrouds

As the threat of the Whispered One's reemergence grew across Exandria, Vox Machina became a key asset in handling him and his growing force of undead, cultists, and more. At a meeting with the Dawn Marshalls of Vasselheim, Highbearer Vord of the Platinum Dragon recognized that the would-be god's prying eyes and powerful magic would make planning his downfall difficult.

Gifting the ring to Vex'ahlia, Highbearer Vord bought Vox Machina valuable time to disappear from the Whispered One's sight. They hid from him long enough to infiltrate the resurrected earth titan, which became the Whispered One's base of operations for his assault on the Dawn City. There, they positioned themselves for the ritual that would eventually banish him.

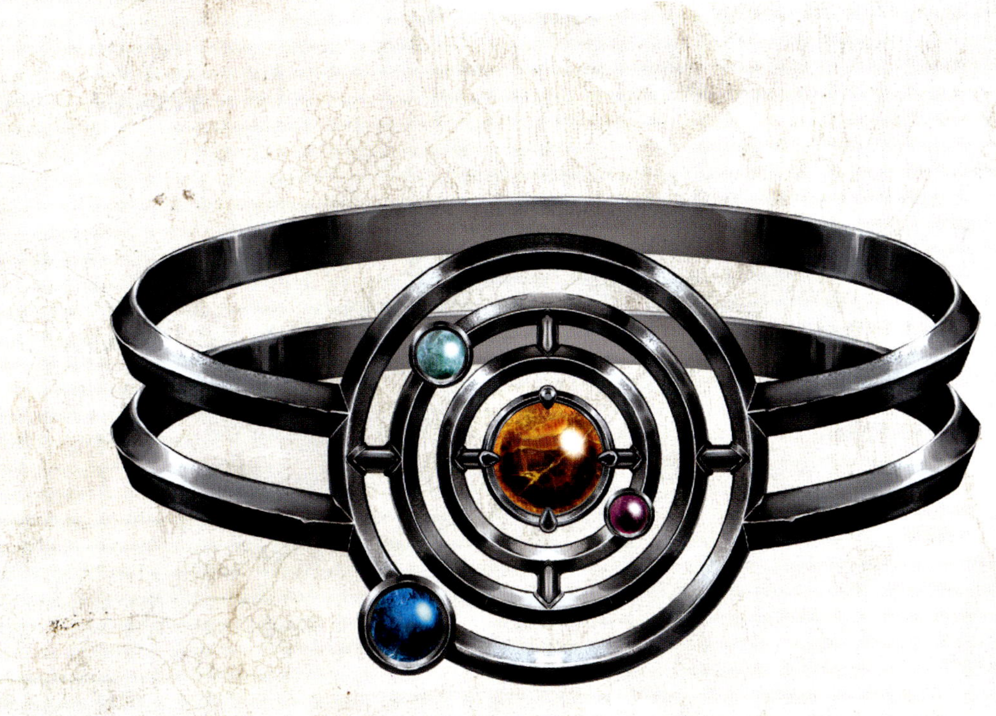

"By the blessing of the Platinum Dragon, keep this bearer safe from all unwelcome eyes."

—D'Rishk Dawnscale, reciting the draconic runes within the ring

Formerly wielded by Saundor, corrupted archfey

Fenthras

One of the legendary Vestiges of Divergence, the greatbow Fenthras found its way into the hands of an archfey named Saundor, a Warden of the Fey Realm from which he hailed. A bow of significant strength and magic, Fenthras channeled the power of the wild into each arrow fired from its vine-enwreathed recurve, infusing elemental power and brambles to ensnare its targets. After the defeat of a long-corrupted Saundor, Vex'ahlia made use of the Vestige. With expert skill and precise aim, she took down numerous foes and eventually unlocked the true power of the greatbow. It was thanks to her prowess and the ability to scry through Fenthras's arrows that the threat of the Whispered One made itself known to Vox Machina.

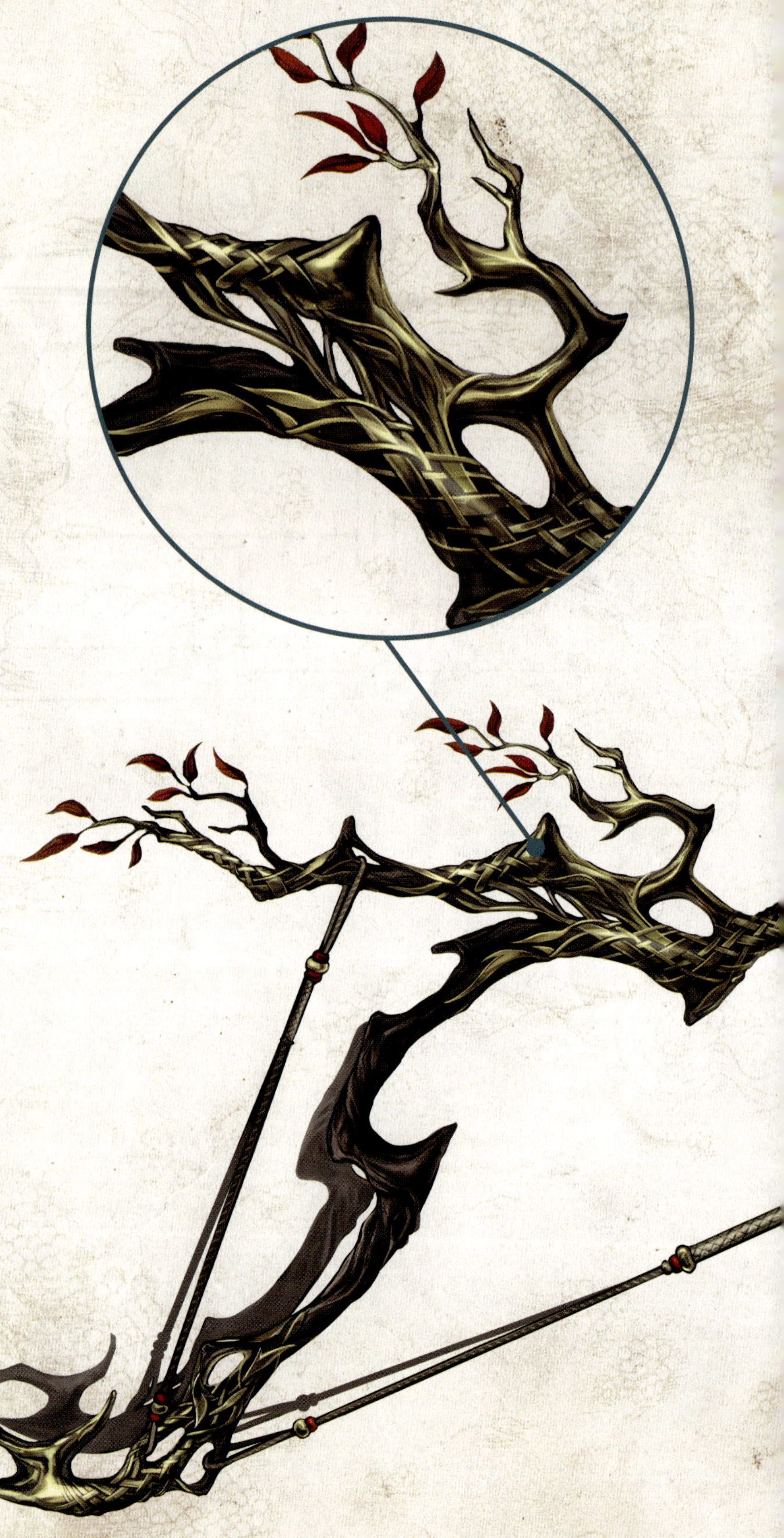

"Love betrayed forever burns
A white-hot flame that never dims
Look now, upon the broken man
Who even now
Weeps hatred, screams sorrow
The land of Fey reflects its keepers
Yea and now see, Saundor, Warden of the Wilds
Wrench all honor and love and joy
From within his heart

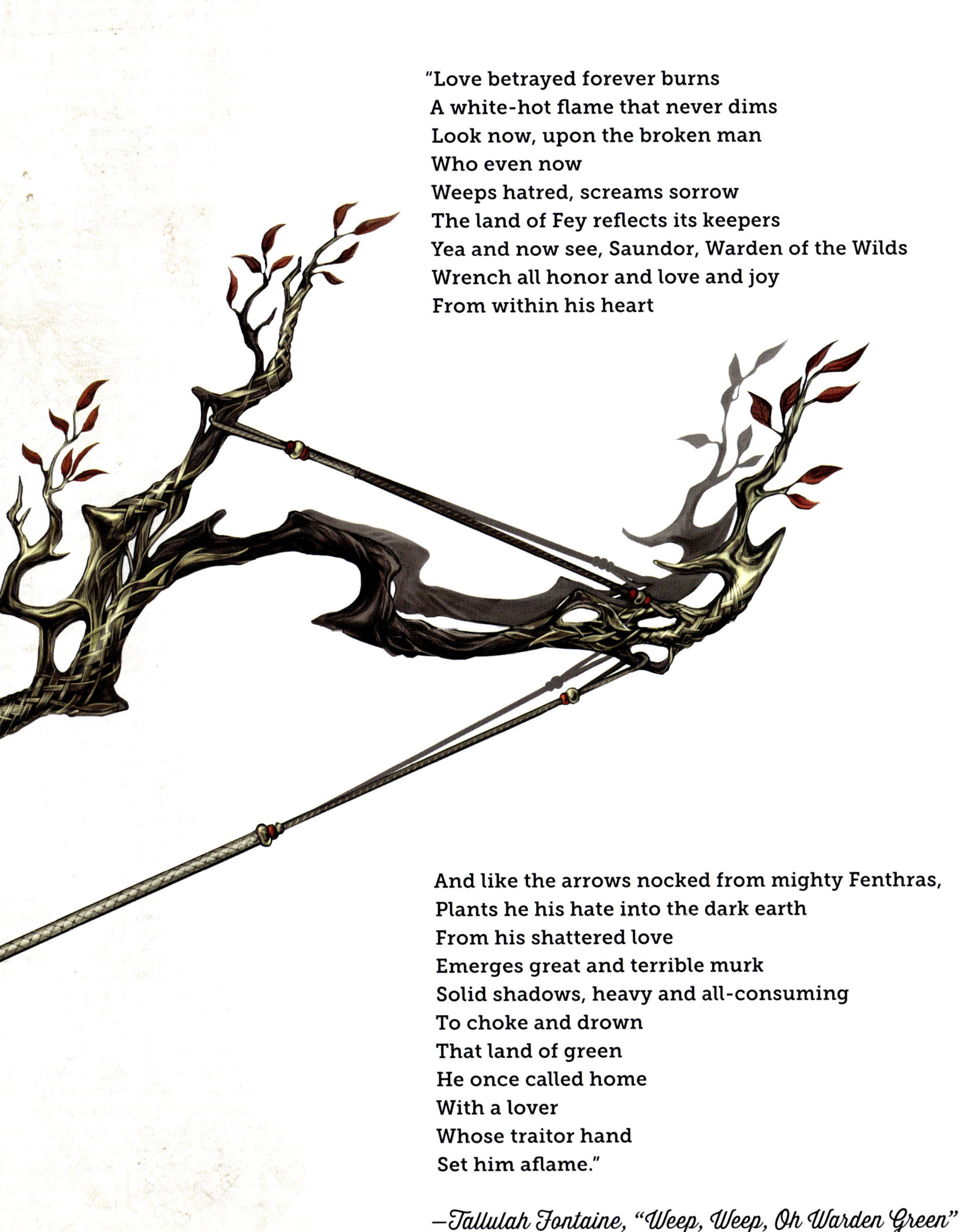

And like the arrows nocked from mighty Fenthras,
Plants he his hate into the dark earth
From his shattered love
Emerges great and terrible murk
Solid shadows, heavy and all-consuming
To choke and drown
That land of green
He once called home
With a lover
Whose traitor hand
Set him aflame."

—Tallulah Fontaine, "Weep, Weep, Oh Warden Green"

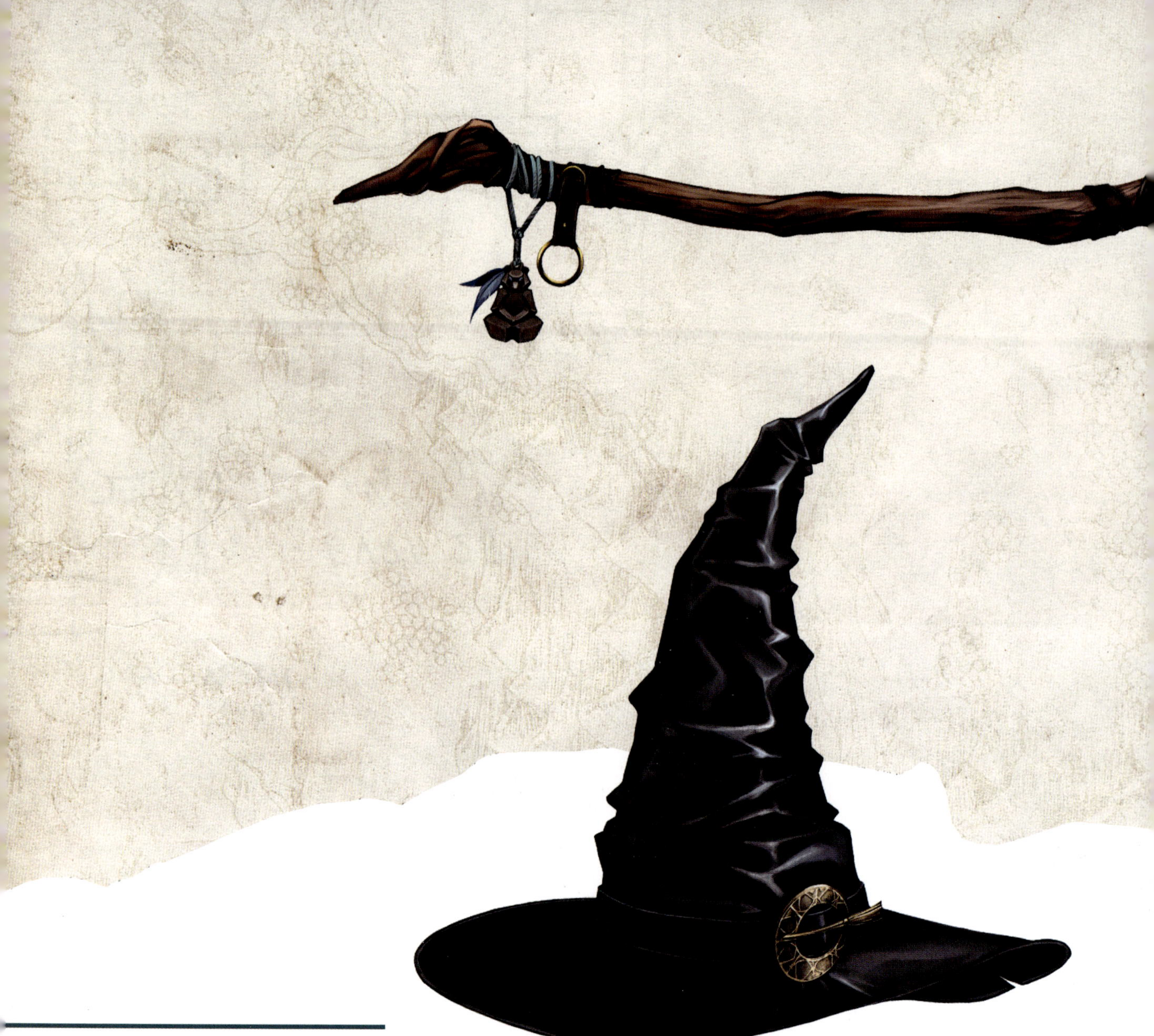

Broom Rider's Hat

Having Vex'ahlia owe you a favor is a precious thing indeed, not something easily secured from the guarded and sharp-eyed hunter. Especially when the favor you owe is to a one Scanlan Shorthalt, whose imagination is vast, unpredictable, and often outlandish. Yet, for teaching her how to ride the magical broom she came by, Vex put herself in the bard's debt, demanding to know what he wanted. He replied, "Not yet." It wasn't until after the battle with Kevdak and the Herd of Storms, when they survived an ambush by the demon Hotis, that Scanlan finally revealed the favor: that Vex had to wear a specific, wide-brimmed, conical hat every time she flew on the broom.

For once, she was more than happy to agree to Scanlan's wishes and her hat, very much shaped like that of a country witch, became iconic as she flew through the air, her striking silhouette lit by the sun, moons, and stars.

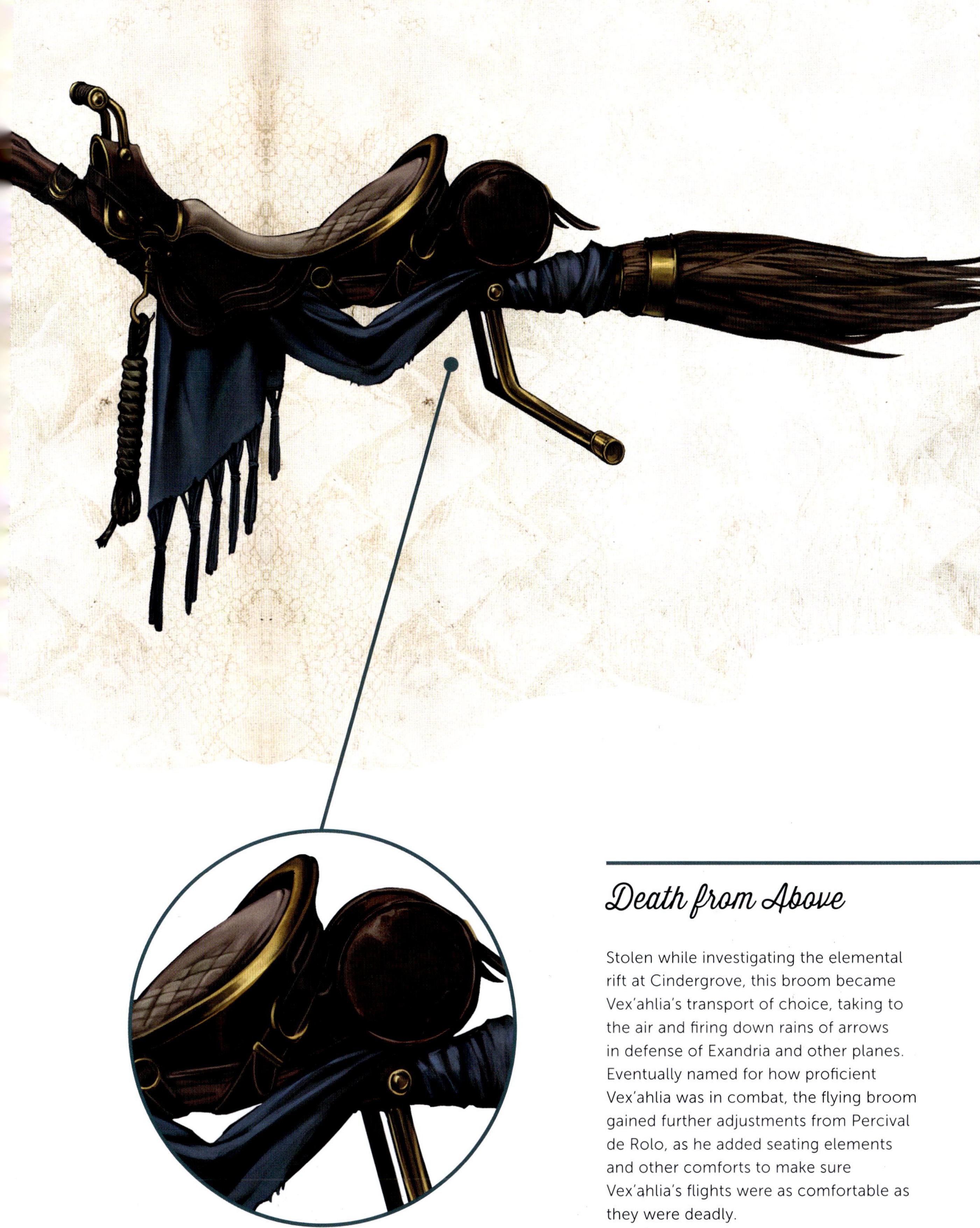

Death from Above

Stolen while investigating the elemental rift at Cindergrove, this broom became Vex'ahlia's transport of choice, taking to the air and firing down rains of arrows in defense of Exandria and other planes. Eventually named for how proficient Vex'ahlia was in combat, the flying broom gained further adjustments from Percival de Rolo, as he added seating elements and other comforts to make sure Vex'ahlia's flights were as comfortable as they were deadly.

Percival Fredrickstein von Musel Klossowski de Rolo III

Cabal's Ruin

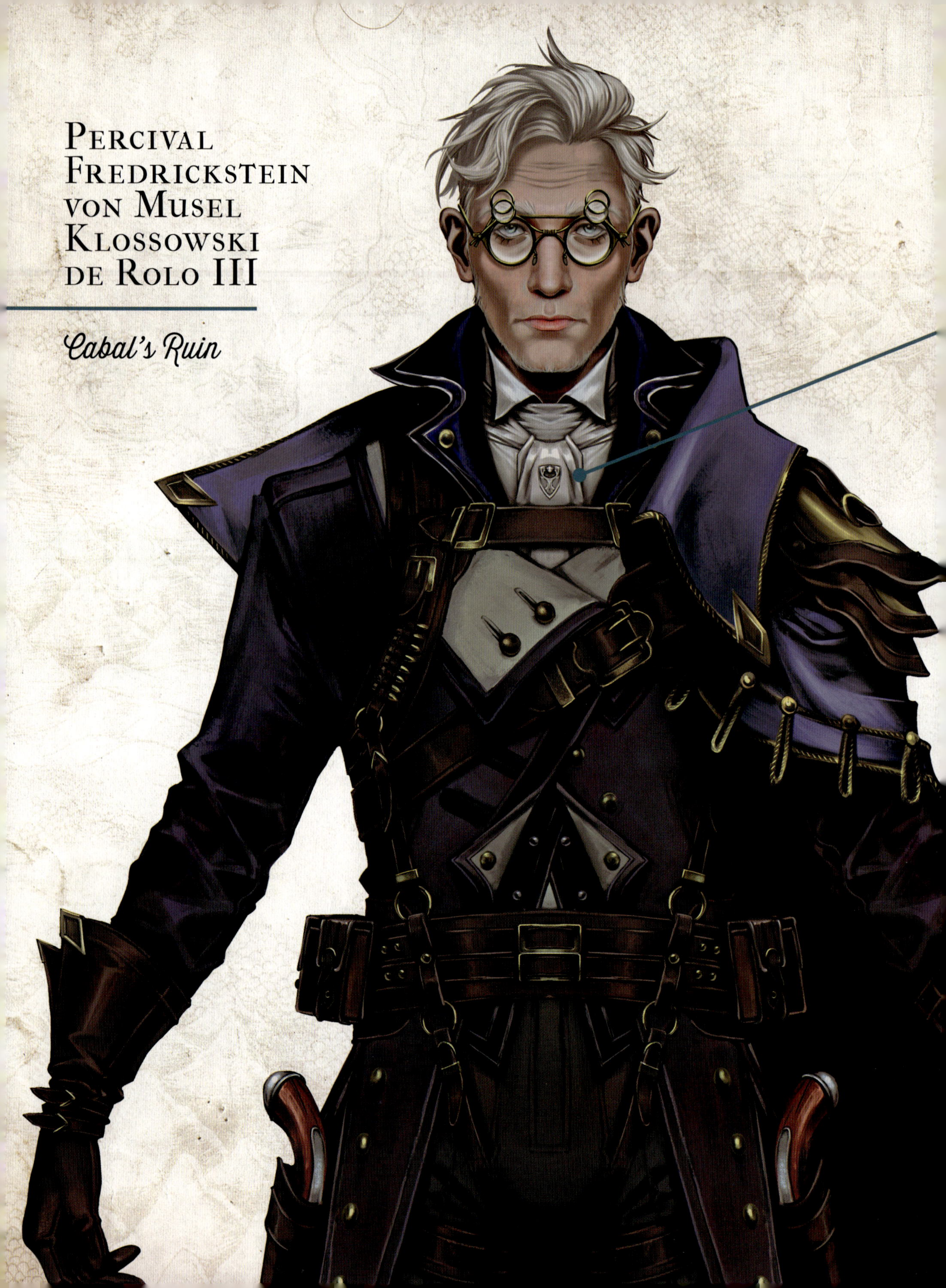

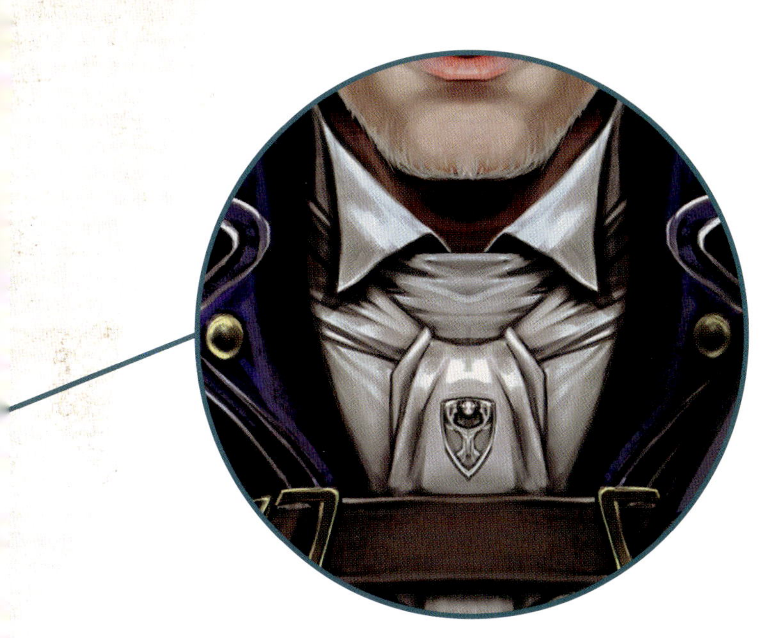

"Cabal's Ruin, also known as the Cloak of Endless Appetite, was infamous for its use in the destruction of the Den of Druja, whose sorceries disappeared into the dark of the Vestige. A powerful item that has found its way across the breadth of Exandria, it would be an asset for any who wished to protect themselves from the highest order of magics. My operative in Whitestone confirms it hangs in the bowels of the castle, no doubt protected by wards we cannot even imagine. Maybe even more so than the crime family whom the cloak ended, Lord de Rolo can be paranoid, especially about the power of a Vestige landing in the wrong hands. Luxon knows how he already feels about his inventions ending up in the hands of hundreds worldwide."

—*Oren Keth'Kaylis*

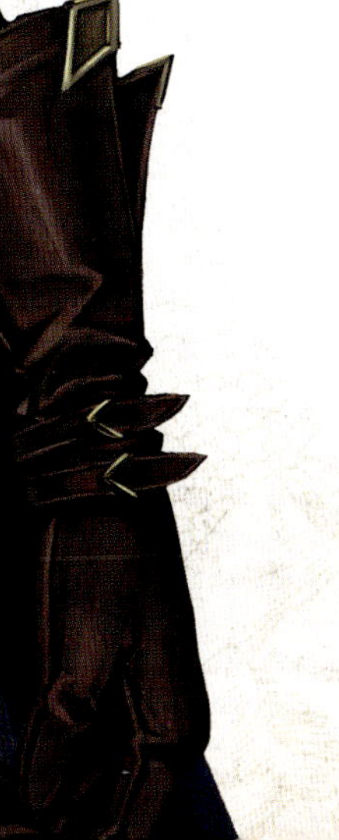

This blue-and-gold cloak, designed to protect its wearer from the arcane, was taken off the murdered merchant-warrior of Ank'Harel, Mistress Asharru, by scientist Dr. Anna Ripley in her gambit to acquire hidden Vestiges of Divergence ahead of Vox Machina. Once she was dead, it passed into the hands of the resurrected Percival de Rolo, who used its power to not just safeguard himself from the magics of dragons, djinn, and undead, but also to empower his already fierce modern firearms, each bullet now a blazing comet of magic and lead both. It came into its exalted state when it swallowed and absorbed a terrible spell during a battle with the duplicitous dragon, Raishan the Diseased Deceiver.

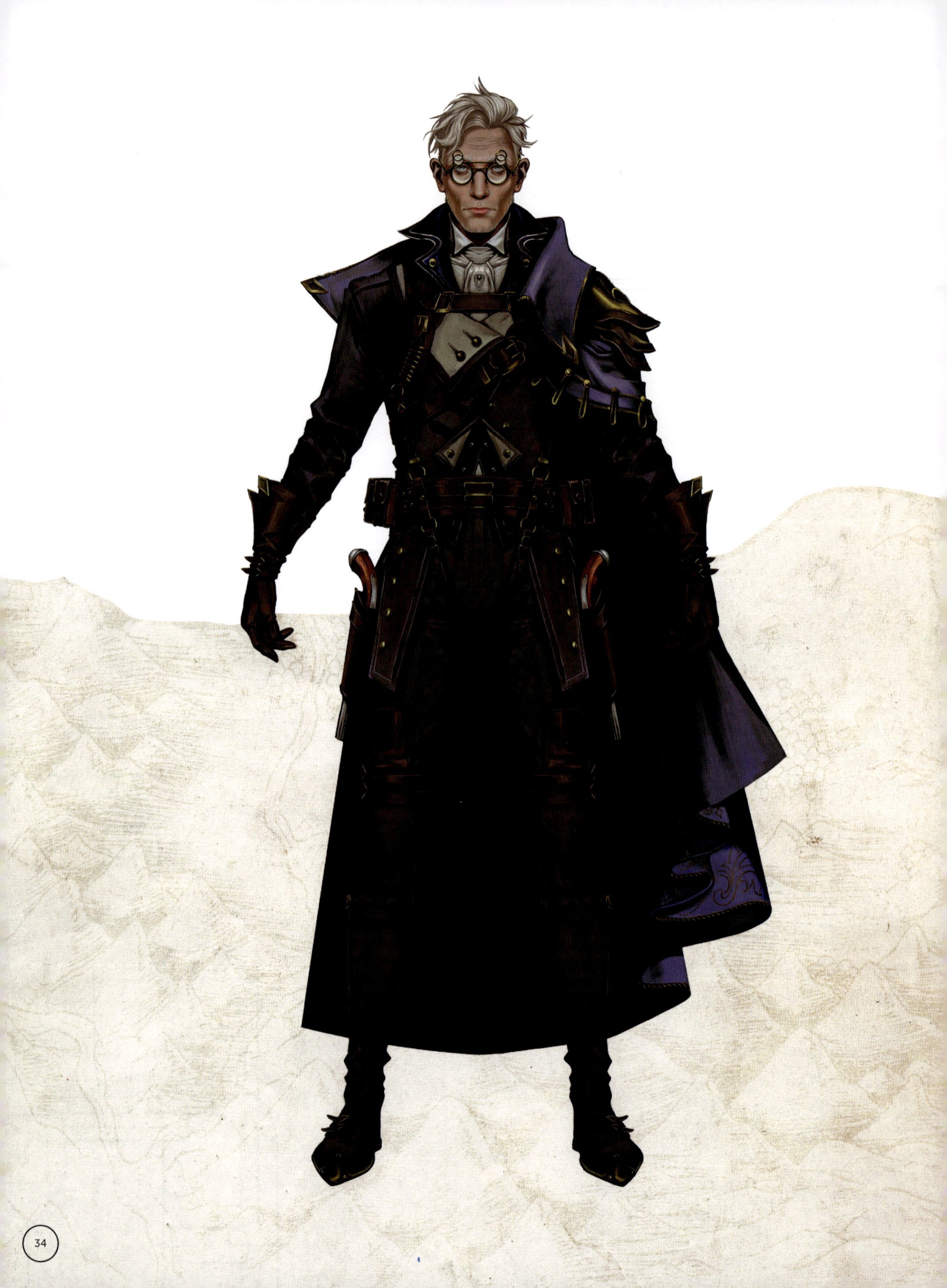

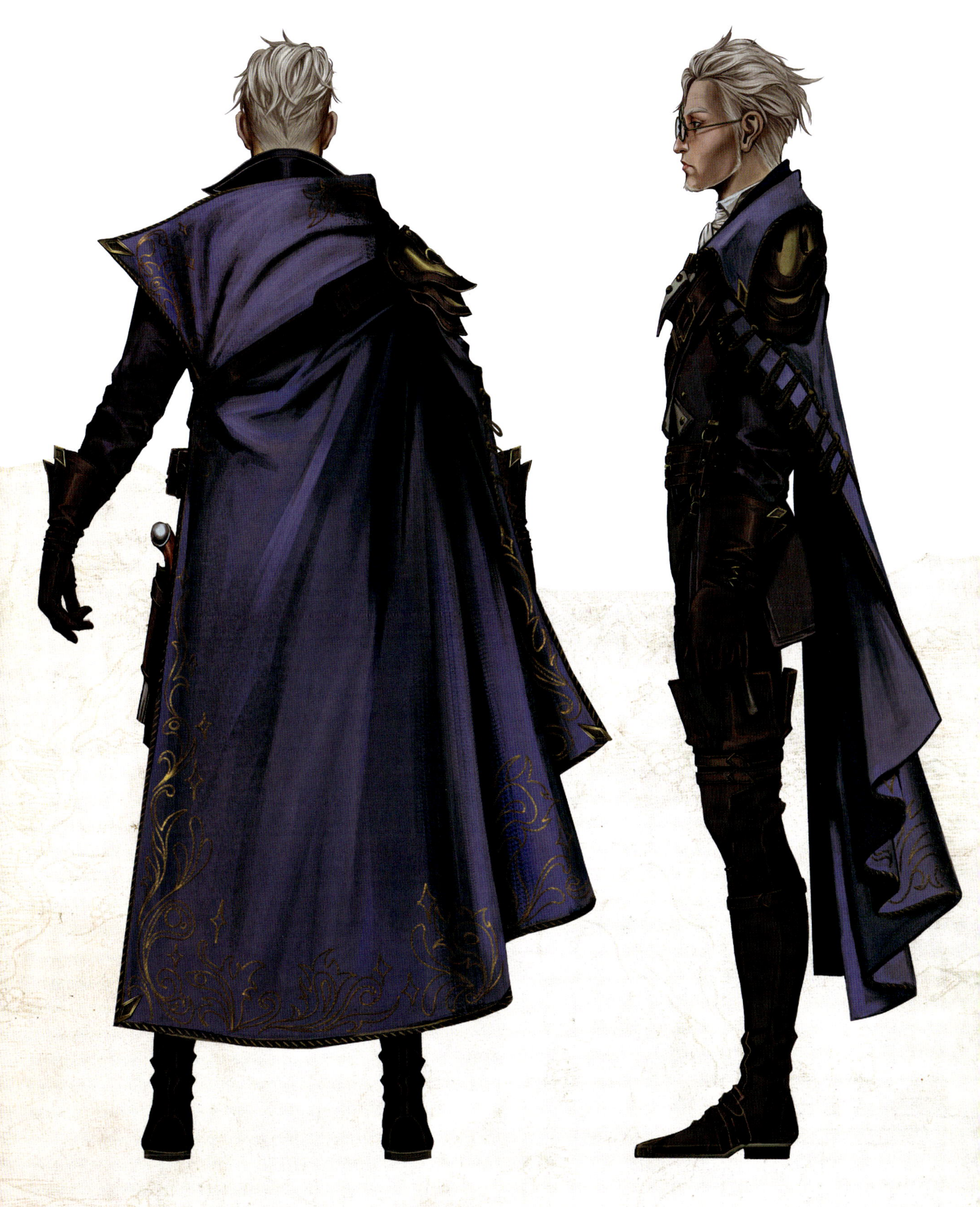

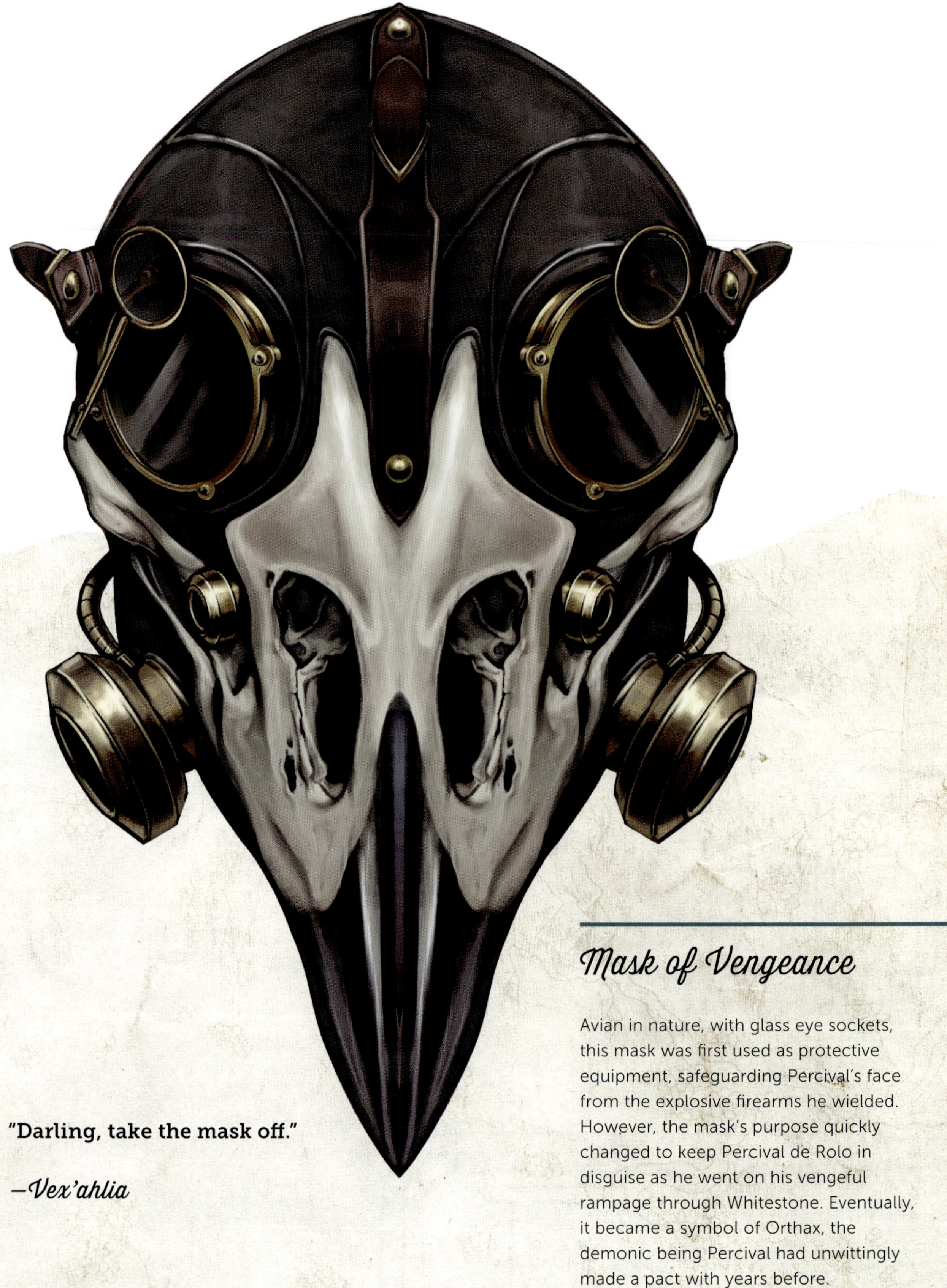

"Darling, take the mask off."

—*Vex'ahlia*

Mask of Vengeance

Avian in nature, with glass eye sockets, this mask was first used as protective equipment, safeguarding Percival's face from the explosive firearms he wielded. However, the mask's purpose quickly changed to keep Percival de Rolo in disguise as he went on his vengeful rampage through Whitestone. Eventually, it became a symbol of Orthax, the demonic being Percival had unwittingly made a pact with years before.

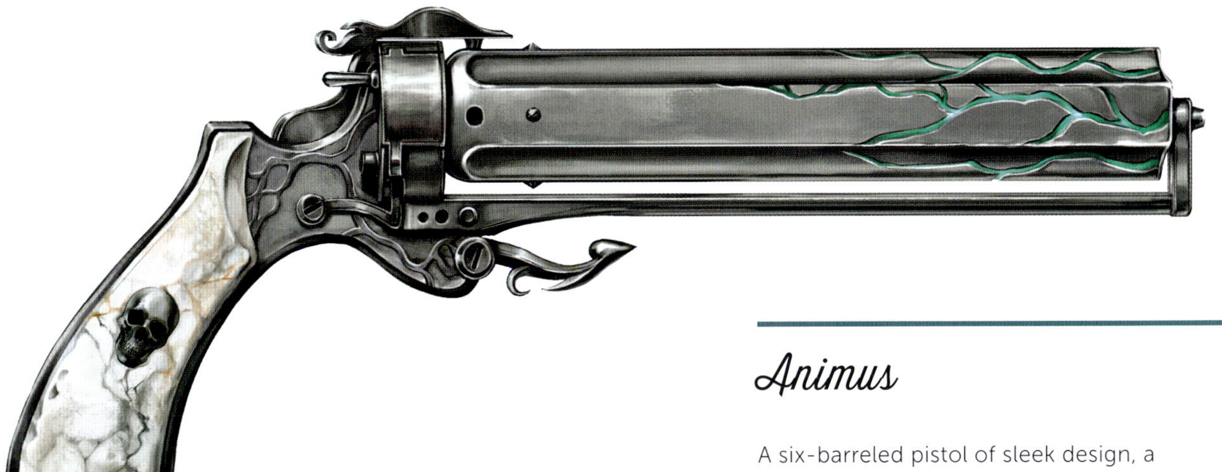

Animus

A six-barreled pistol of sleek design, a more refined version of Percival's original Orthax-fueled invention, Animus was the signature weapon of Dr. Anna Ripley in her time between fleeing Whitestone after the fall of the Briarwoods and her reemergence on the island of Glintshore where she was killed by Vox Machina. There, it was revealed that the demon Orthax had bound itself to Dr. Ripley, the two of them uniting under a common hatred of Percival de Rolo. And though Dr. Ripley killed Lord de Rolo in the fray, it wasn't long before she met her end at the hands of the remaining team of adventurers. Upon Percival's revival, he took up her pistol, its demonic influence and list of names on its barrels vanishing upon her death.

Percival wielded this weapon in battle for the rest of his time with Vox Machina, experiencing flashes of psychic pain whenever it broke, a final morsel of agony from one of his longtime nemeses.

"Our plant within the Augen Trust was able to uncover fragmented notes on various dissidents within the Empire; it never hurts to have such information in one's back pocket. Among those recovered and dictated were notes on one Dr. Anna Ripley, a thorn in the paw of both King Dwendal and Vox Machina that drew blood several times before being plucked and tossed to the Hells. An opportunist, a brilliant engineer, a manipulative sociopath, and above all, proud, Ripley would take any opportunity to survive, even falling in with the Briarwoods (see case file "Undead Love" for a full breakdown on Sylas and Delilah re: Dwendalian Empire).

As we can see in her second invention, refined and streamlined, with two additional chambers, she took every chance to blend the power of her newly forged pact within it. As such, the weapon engages in psychic warfare as well as lead. And though Percival de Rolo and his companions rid the world of her, I'm sure every time he feels a spike in his skull from Animus's feedback, he thinks of her."

—Oren Keth'Kaylis

Bad News

The first of its kind, though not the last, Bad News became Lord Percival's signature long-distance weapon. With special lenses atop the barrel to increase clarity and range, and armed with distinctive black powder and lead balls, Bad News became a crucial weapon when encounters called for support at a distance and was often utilized prior to Lord Percival's proper melee entrance into combat.

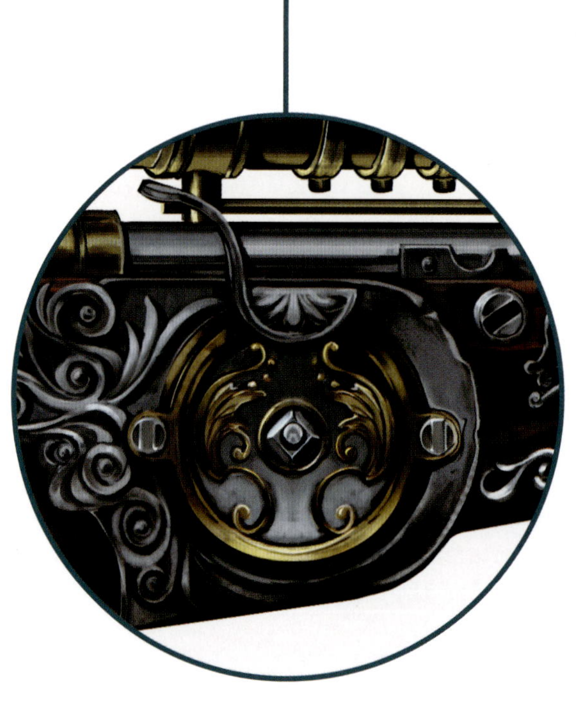

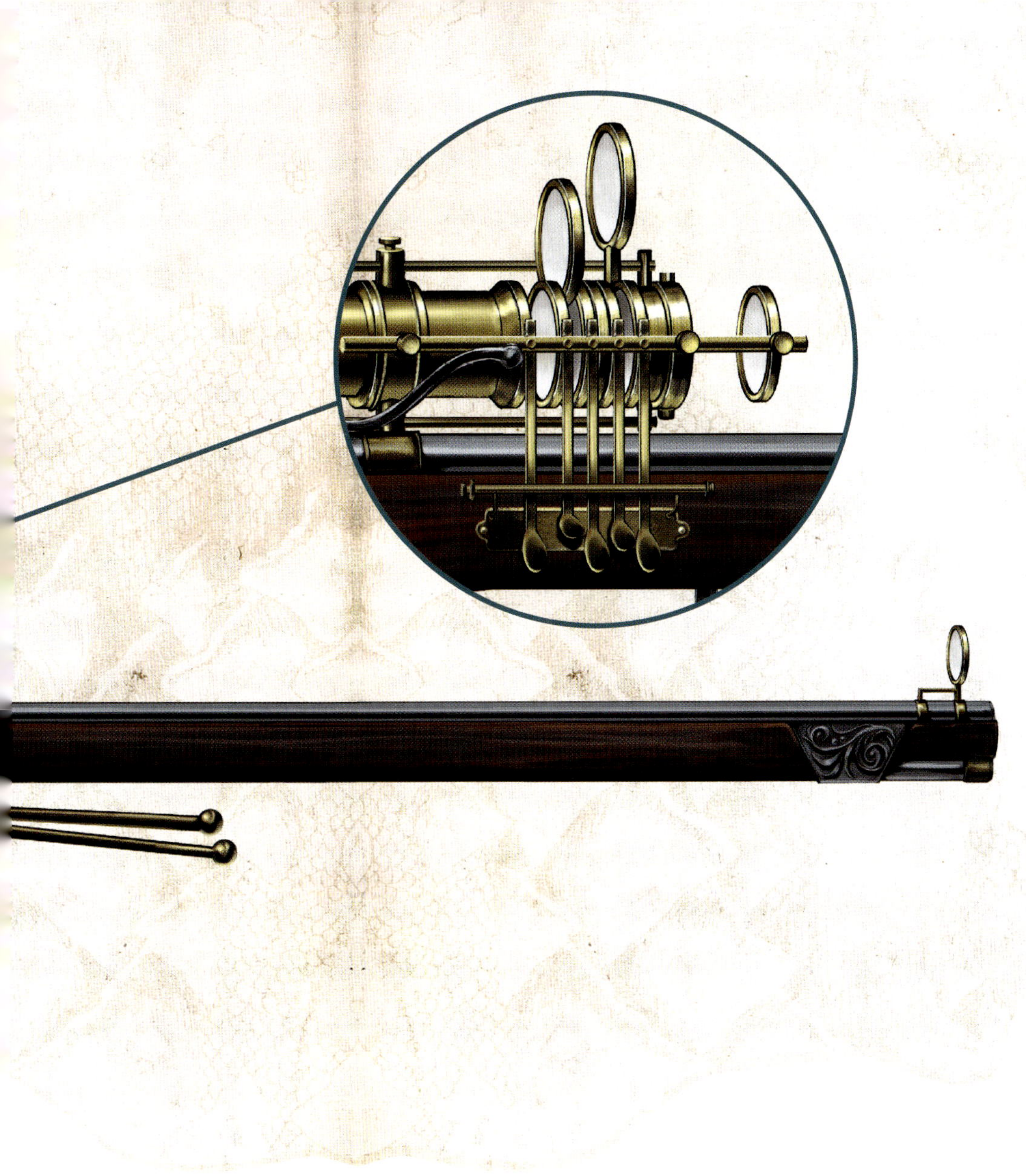

"It was terrible, terrible, I tell you! I was hunkered down with my wife, hiding from those half-giants running the town to ruin, when these colorful adventurers arrived. And they started fighting them! My wife and I, we made a break for it, when we saw someone's head just explode from nothing. Nothing! One second there, the next, poof! Like a snuffed candle, if candlelight was bloody red, by the gods. Never knew a magic could do that, but somehow a madman in a clocktower did just that!"

—Eyewitness account of the encounter with the Herd of Storms in Westruun, D'Rishk Dawnscale

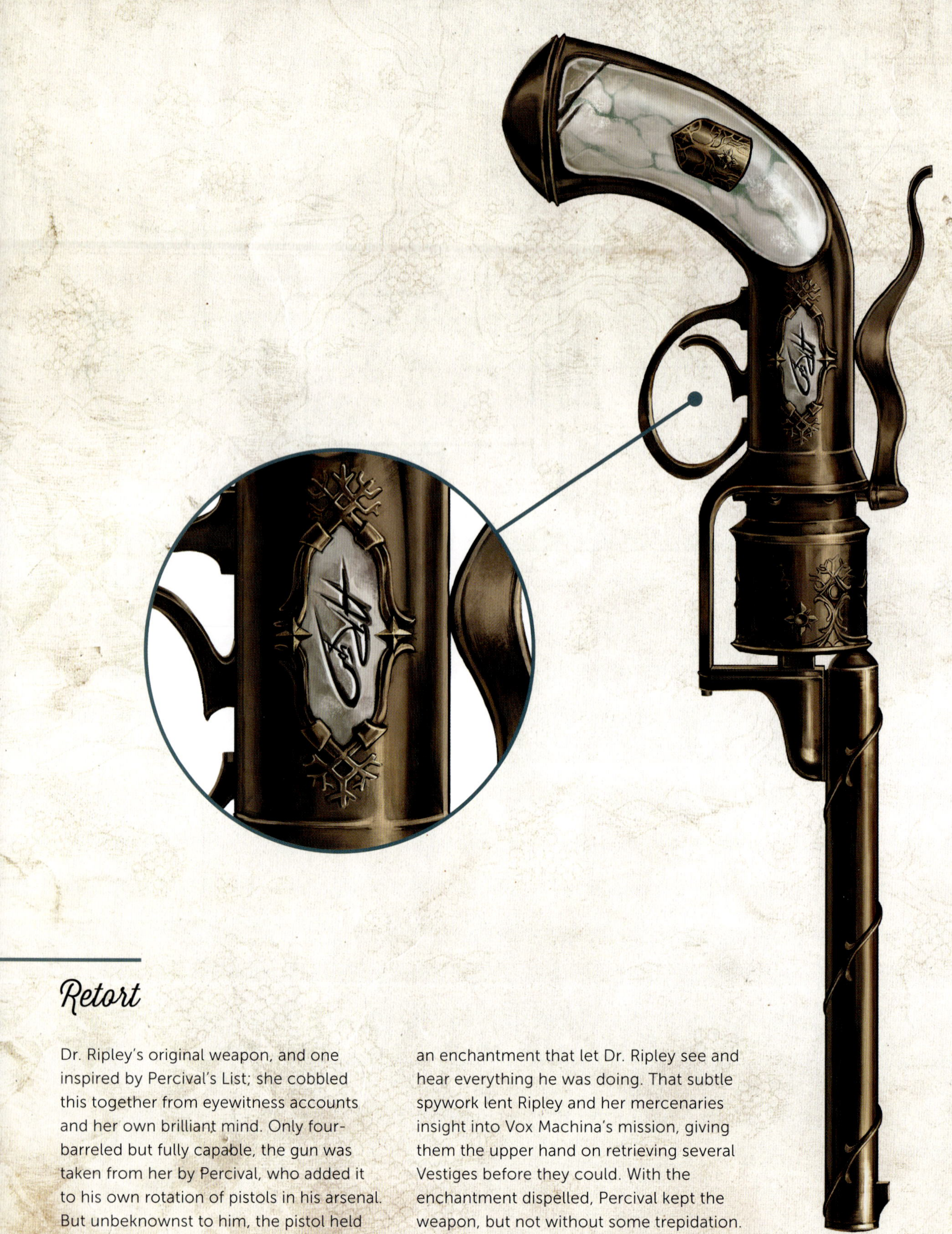

Retort

Dr. Ripley's original weapon, and one inspired by Percival's List; she cobbled this together from eyewitness accounts and her own brilliant mind. Only four-barreled but fully capable, the gun was taken from her by Percival, who added it to his own rotation of pistols in his arsenal. But unbeknownst to him, the pistol held an enchantment that let Dr. Ripley see and hear everything he was doing. That subtle spywork lent Ripley and her mercenaries insight into Vox Machina's mission, giving them the upper hand on retrieving several Vestiges before they could. With the enchantment dispelled, Percival kept the weapon, but not without some trepidation.

Diplomacy

In preparation for Percival's confrontation with the Briarwoods, he put his intellect to work and constructed a mechanical gauntlet to wear on his hand, should he find himself in melee with the ferocious Sylas Briarwood or any of the undead under Delilah Briarwood's command. Diplomacy, so named because of the handshake needed to activate its electrical charge, became a staple of Percival's arsenal. He most often used Retort in melee combat when he needed to buy himself respite and breathing room.

In the time between the fall of the Chroma Conclave and the rise of the Whispered One, Percival worked with fellow science lover and engineer, Taryon Darrington, to enchant it with a spell of silence, rendering the area around Percival mute for a time, aiding a new layer of stealth to his combat.

"You think the Lord of Whitestone is terrifying at a distance? Brother, piss him off enough to get him to come in close. They say Percival de Rolo shakes the hands of friends with his right and the hands of foes with his left. And in combat? De Rolo is only left-handed, I promise you that."

—Tallulah Fontaine, overheard at a bar in Whitestone

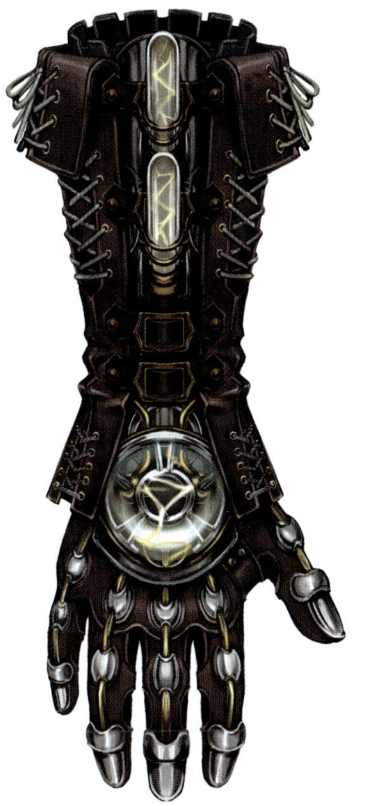

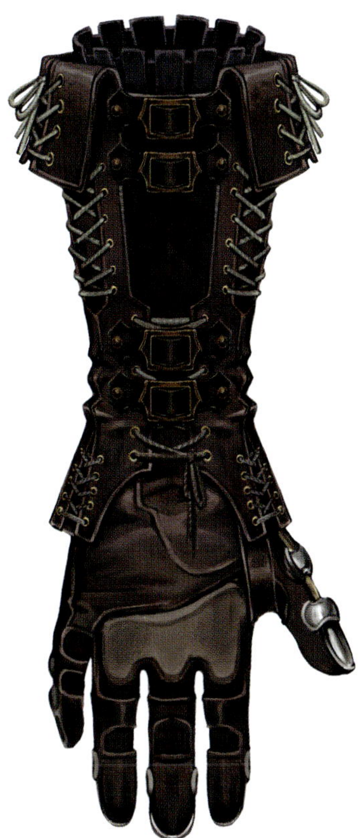

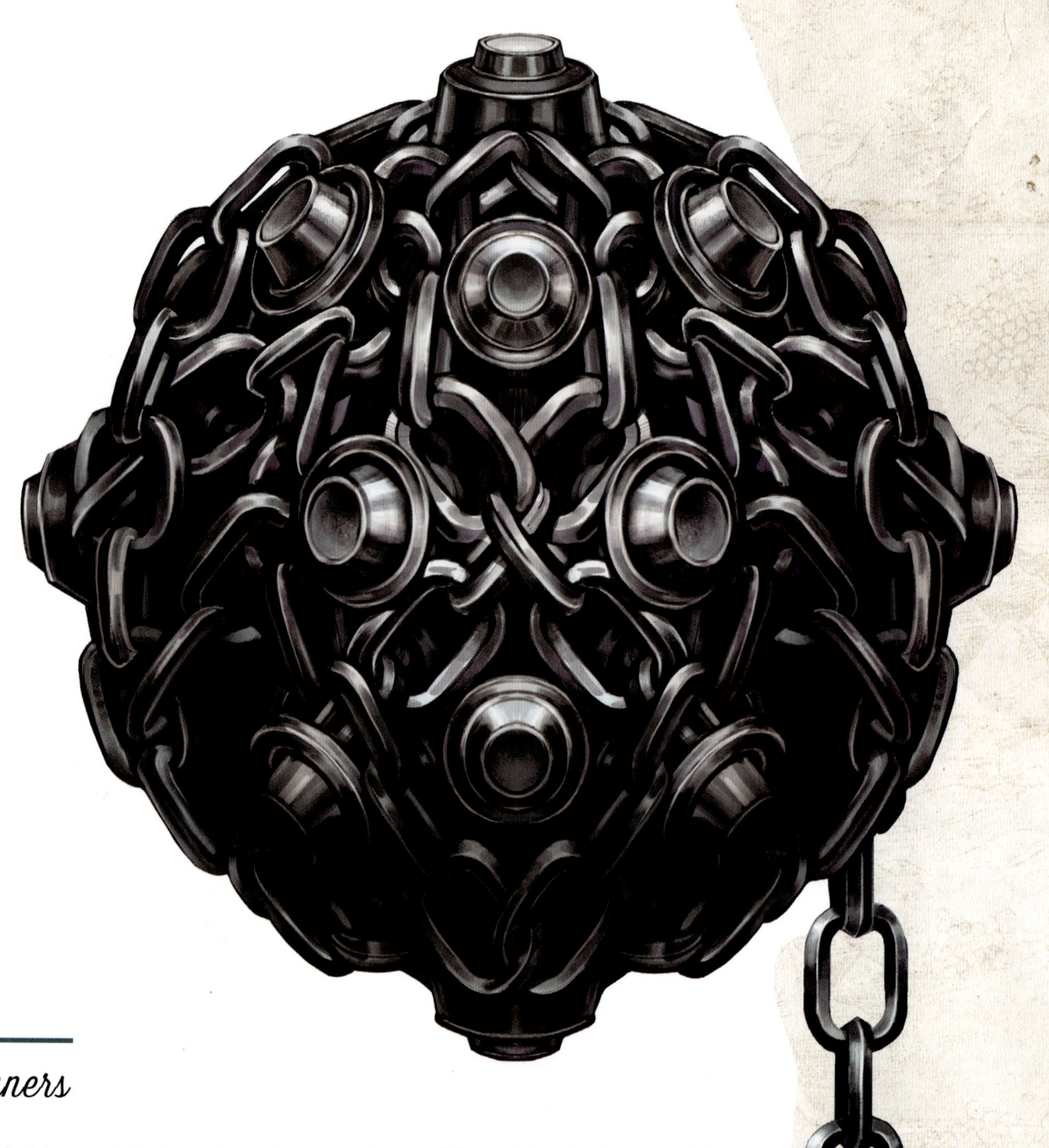

Manners

As Vox Machina made their way toward their second confrontation with Delilah Briarwood at the ziggurat in Marquet, they discovered this iron ball–like contraption, and Percival quickly realized how useful this device could be for ensnaring enemies. It also became quite handy at fending off allies as well, encasing a magically besotted Scanlan (courtesy of a love potion in the hands of Vax and Grog), who was held at bay long enough for said potion to wear off.

Manners would join his growing arsenal of weapons and gadgets, continuing to make him one of the most terrifying opponents on the battlefield, for, at the height of his prodigious career, no one could truly know what Percival might take from his belt to make your life a living hell.

The List

The List is a weapon that came to Percival in a night of terrible invention, the very first firearm he would create with vengeance burning in his heart; unbeknownst to him, it was the item upon which his pact with the shadow demon Orthax was sworn. It gained its name for the list of five names etched into the barrel, people whom Percival swore to murder in his quest for vengeance. One by one, under the thrall of Orthax and consumed with his own revenge, Percival ended their lives, each death erasing their name from the barrel. As Percival ran down his list, losing more and more of his soul, he had a sinking feeling that his list would never truly end.

Even with Orthax defeated, the weapon's existence would always tether Percival to the demon. The quick action of clever bard companion Scanlan Shorthalt saw the weapon tossed into a vat of acid that destroyed not just the weapon, but the final tether on Percival's soul as well.

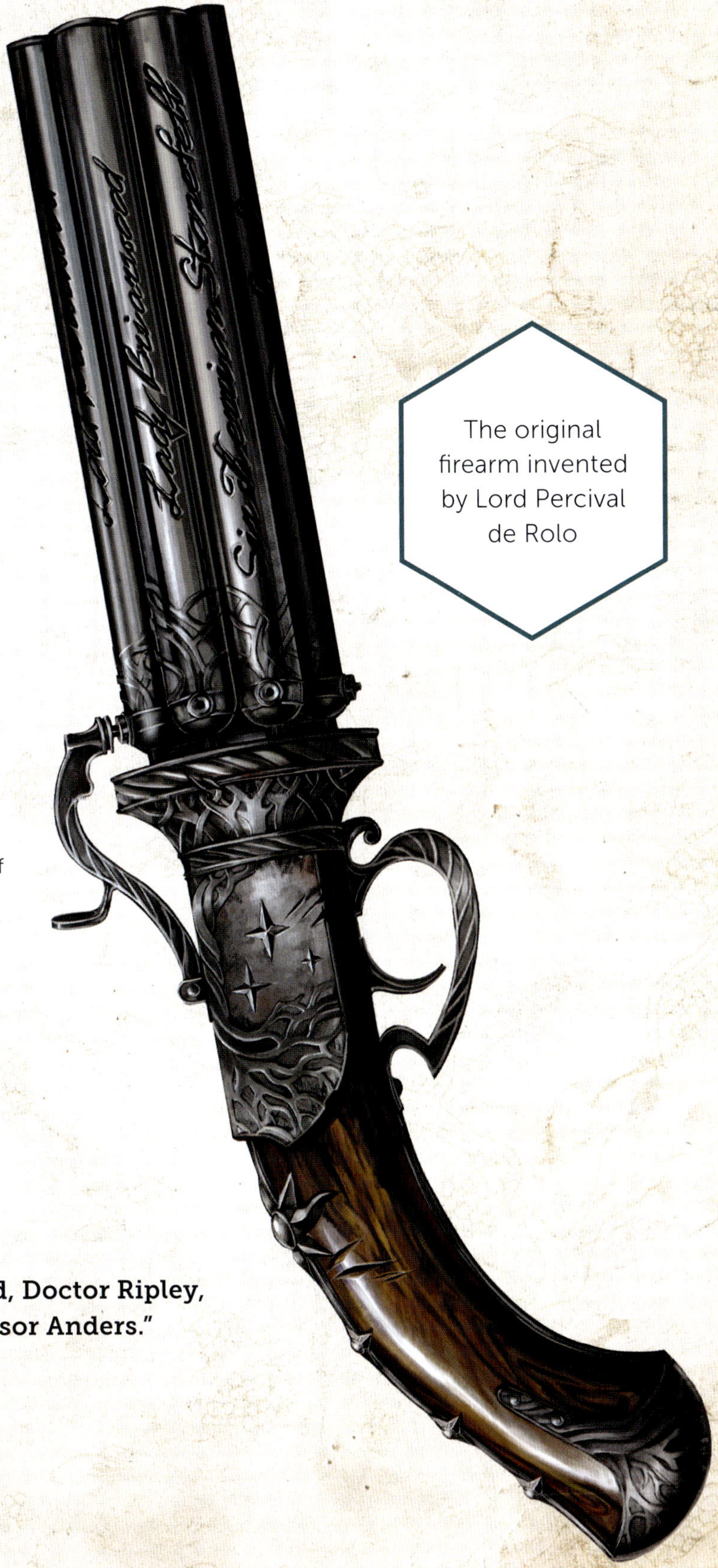

The original firearm invented by Lord Percival de Rolo

"Lord Briarwood, Lady Briarwood, Doctor Ripley, Sir Kerrion Stonefell, and Professor Anders."

–The names engraved on five of the six barrels of The List

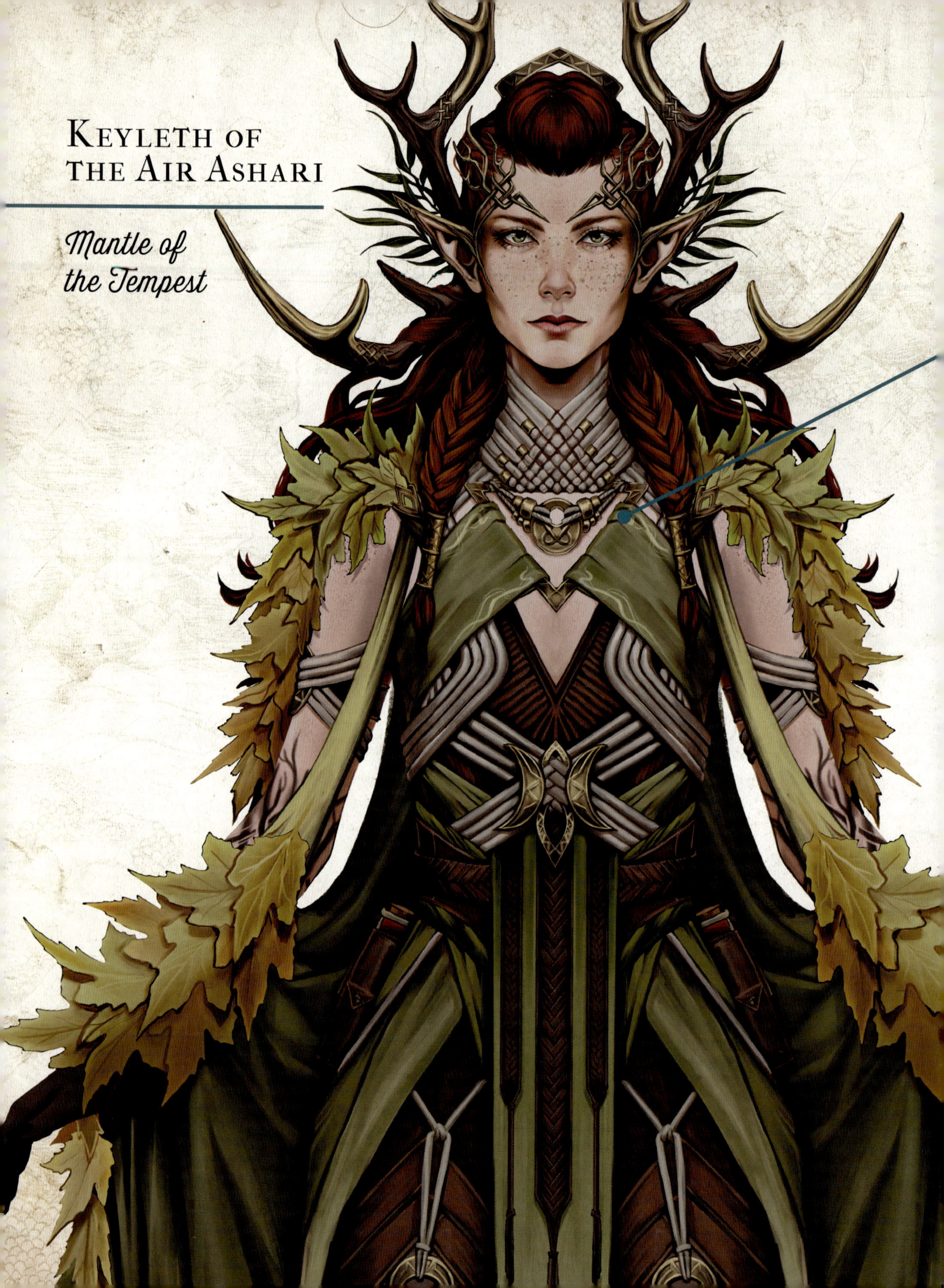
KEYLETH OF
THE AIR ASHARI
Mantle of
the Tempest

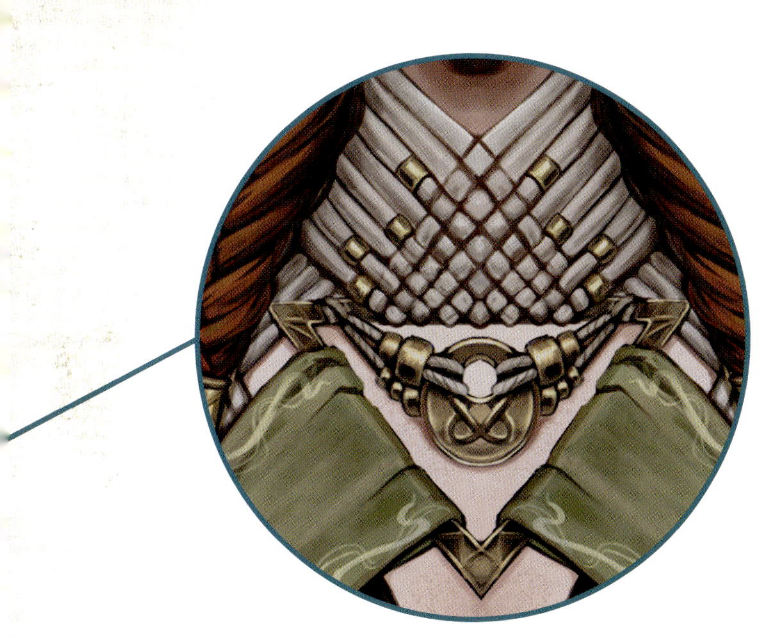

"Oh, my heart, crow-stolen and dark
How I cannot bear that we're now apart
You've taken wing into darkest night
How I wish to join your flight
But to the land, I remain and stand
Ever watchful for your pale hand
Look for me in autumn leaves,
Clad aflame in nature's weeping
For autumn is that sweet time of death
And isn't that what you're seeking?"

—Tallulah Fontaine, "The Raven and His Tempest, The Tempest and Her Sorrow"

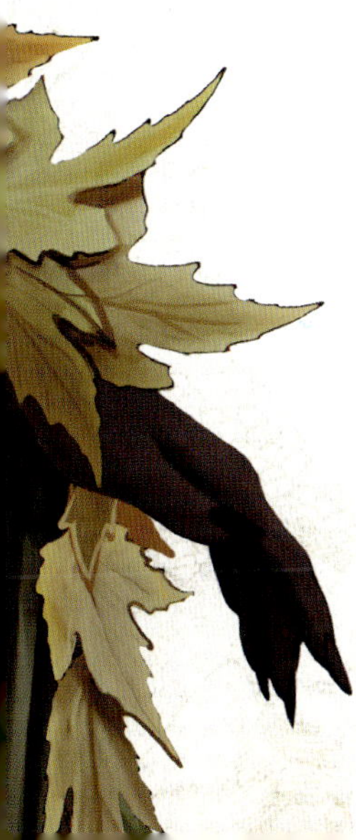

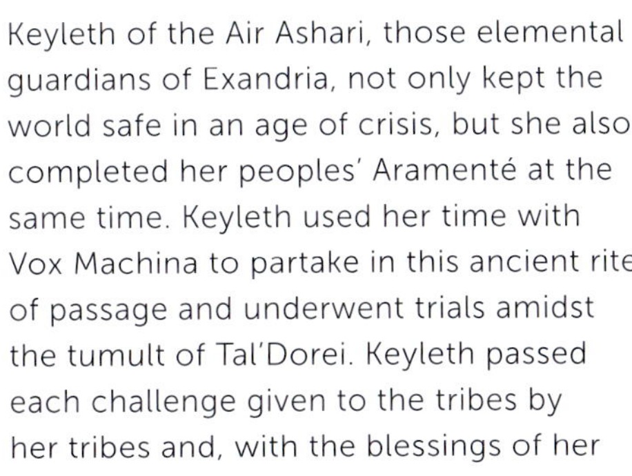

Keyleth of the Air Ashari, those elemental guardians of Exandria, not only kept the world safe in an age of crisis, but she also completed her peoples' Aramenté at the same time. Keyleth used her time with Vox Machina to partake in this ancient rite of passage and underwent trials amidst the tumult of Tal'Dorei. Keyleth passed each challenge given to the tribes by her tribes and, with the blessings of her fellow leaders, returned home to take up leadership of the Air Ashari as Voice of the Tempest.

As part of her new station, Keyleth was gifted a symbol of her wisdom, growth, and status: a cloak woven together with hundreds of leaves in autumnal ombre. This raiment represented the souls and earth she was responsible for from that day forward and to this day still.

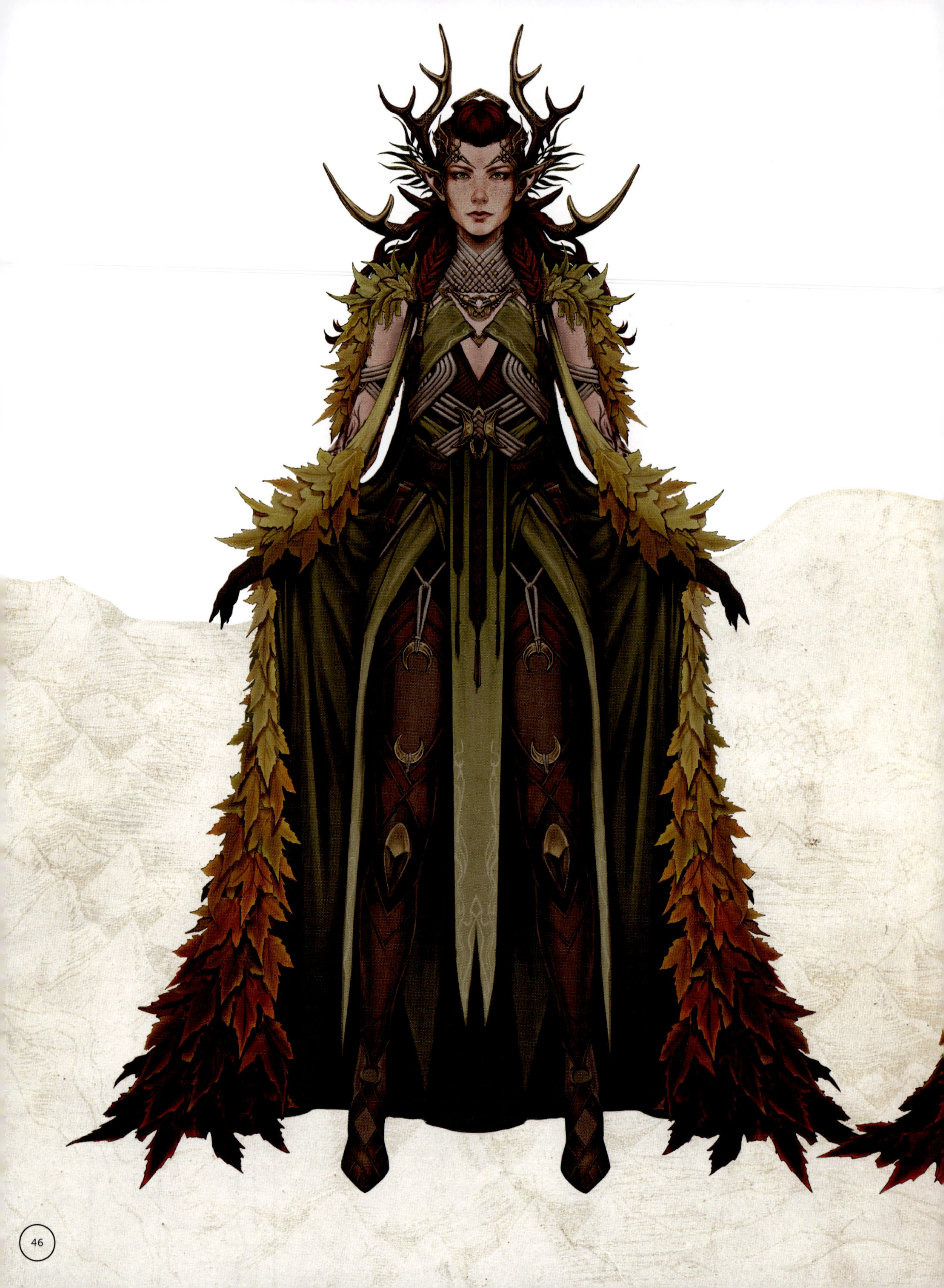

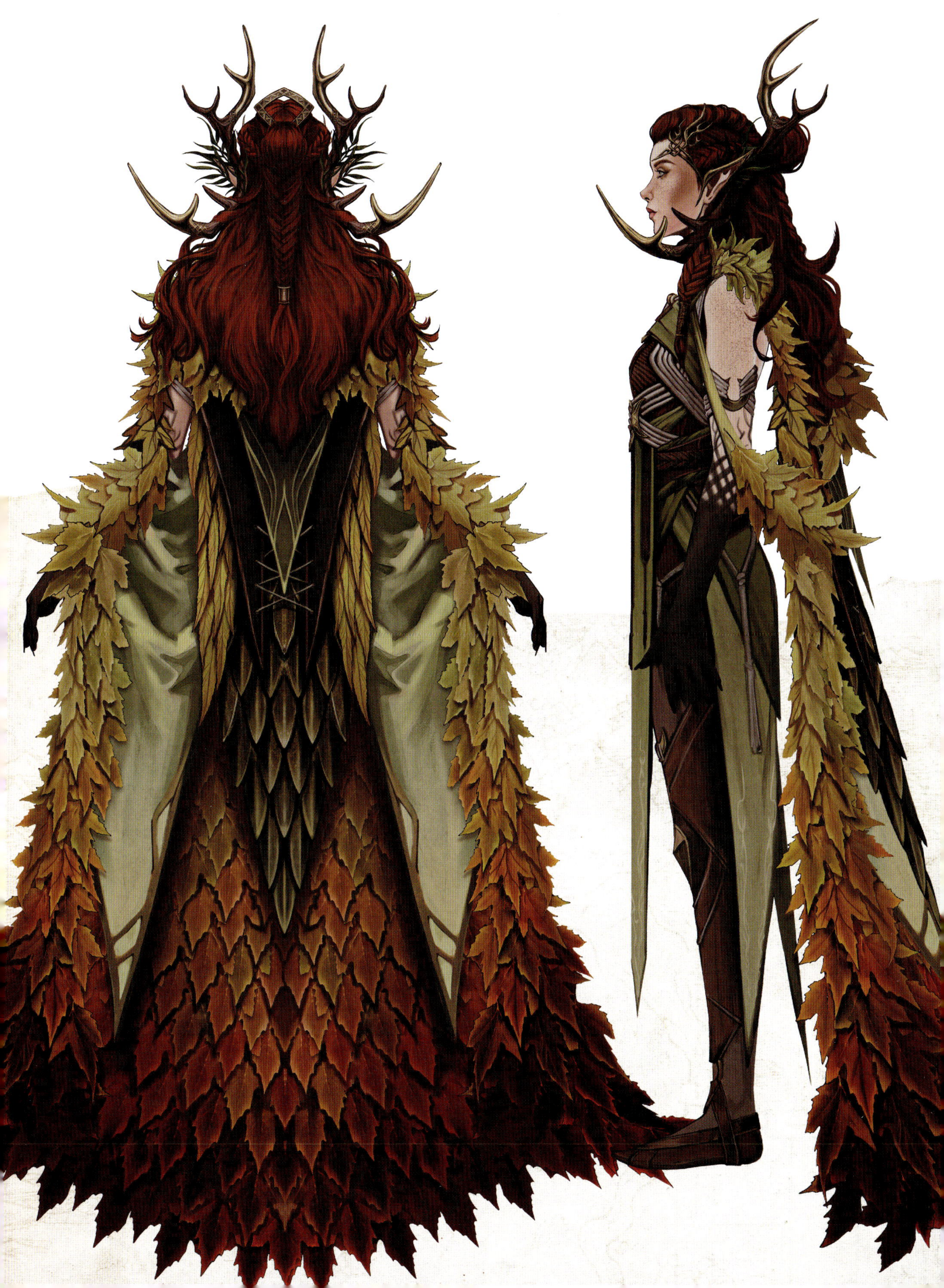

Keyleth's Antlers

This circlet was one of the few things to leave with Keyleth as she began her Aramenté, the trial of leadership that would see her visit the other tribes of the Ashari peoples, earn their blessing, and come home to Zephrah as its new leader. However, Keyleth left in the shadow of her mother's disappearance, herself and her fate lost to the Aramenté, a journey upon which not everyone is guaranteed to return.

On the eve of her departure, her father, Korrin, gifted her this beautiful circlet adorned with antlers, an old magic item of her mother, Vilya. What he said, we cannot know, but we can imagine it did Keyleth's young, anxious heart good to walk out into the future wearing such an important piece of her past.

She would carry that legacy with her from her early days with the group that would become Vox Machina, and to this day, she wears her antler-adorned crown, using the wisdom and charm it grants her to guide and safeguard her people as the Voice of the Tempest.

"Like breath of sky and spark of flame
Our children carry on our name
Like roots of green and blue of sea
Our children grow in boundless glee."

—Ancient Ashari proverb, recovered from a piece of barkpaper

Sphere of Sight

A cloudy glass ball, this enchanted item was found on the dead body of an assassin sent by a devil trying to get his vengeance on Vox Machina. It became instrumental in the hands of Keyleth, who used its scrying potential to track and hunt down various enemies in their time together, such as Dr. Anna Ripley, the Green Dragon Raishan, and the legendary Blade of Undeath's Traitor, which was significant in the final fight against the Whispered One.

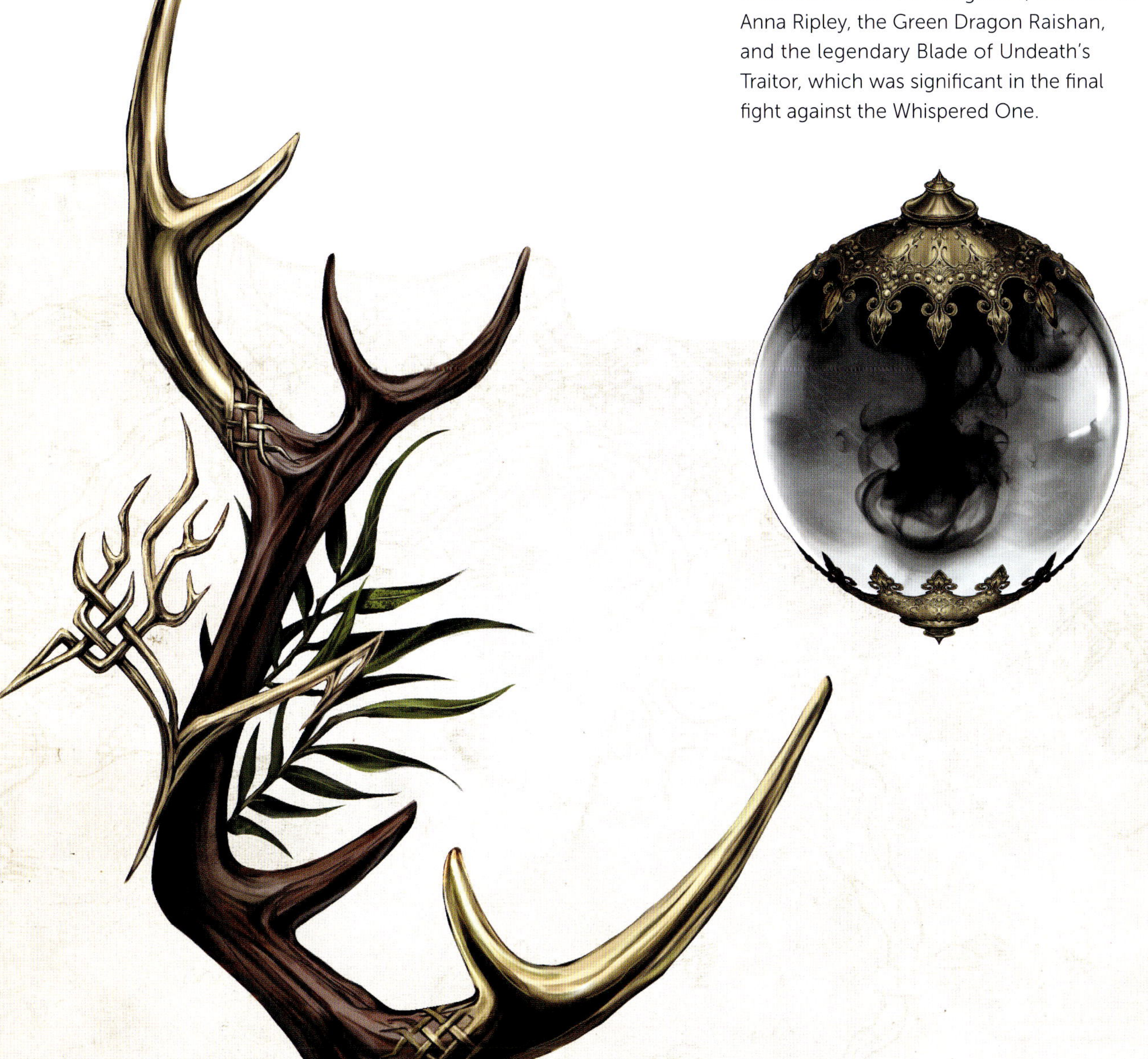

"A powerful Vestige, this. Often, it was said, the creation of numerous Vestiges appeared in sparks of divine inspiration, clerics of forge and flame, followers of ingenuity and passion taking the divine gifts given and crafting wonders imbued with their gods' power. But the Spire of Conflux was not forged but transformed from the very breath of the Wildmother, who loves the very world itself, and in her breath, made a weapon to safeguard it. Scholars have theorized that its name comes from the location of its creation; in other papers, you will see hypotheses that illustrate how the Spire of Conflux came to being at one of the few locations in Exandria where all leylines meet, converging into one focal point of power.

But I would argue that the conflux in its name doesn't speak to its power, but its purpose. For in the hands of the Wildmother's followers, it is people who will come together. And in all of Exandria's history, there is not a more powerful force than peoples united."

—D'Rishk Dawnscale

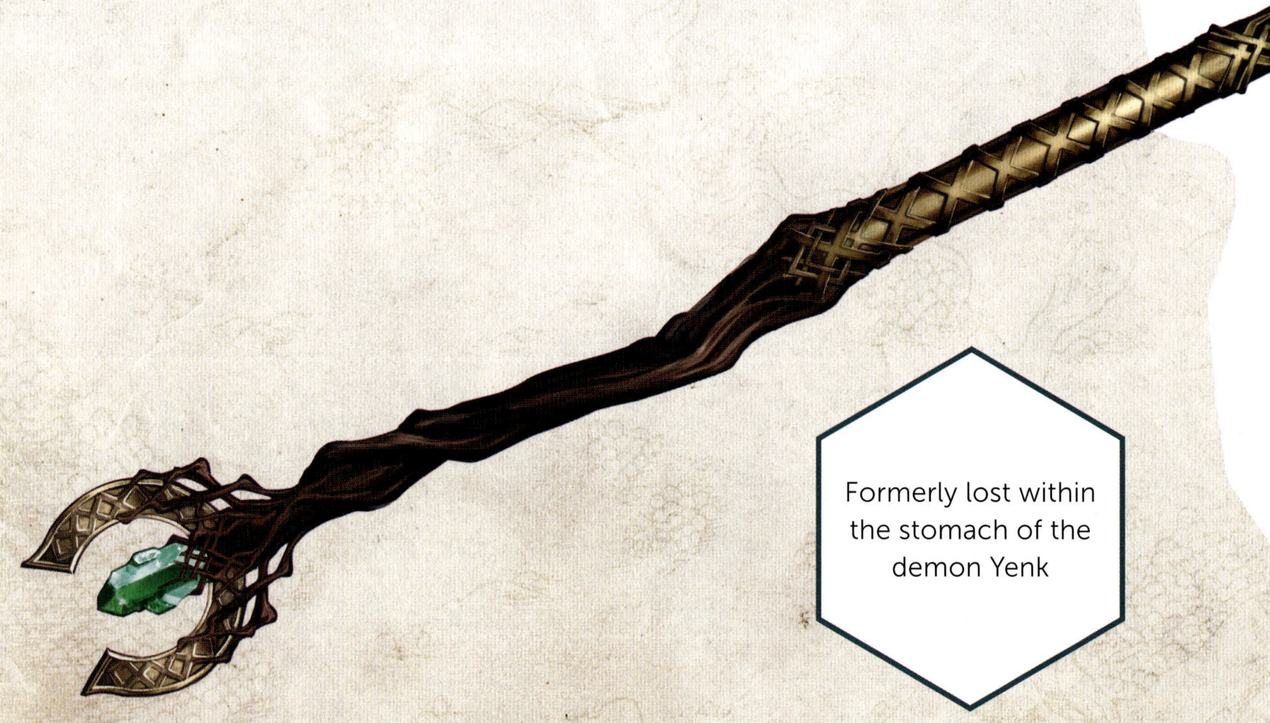

Formerly lost within the stomach of the demon Yenk

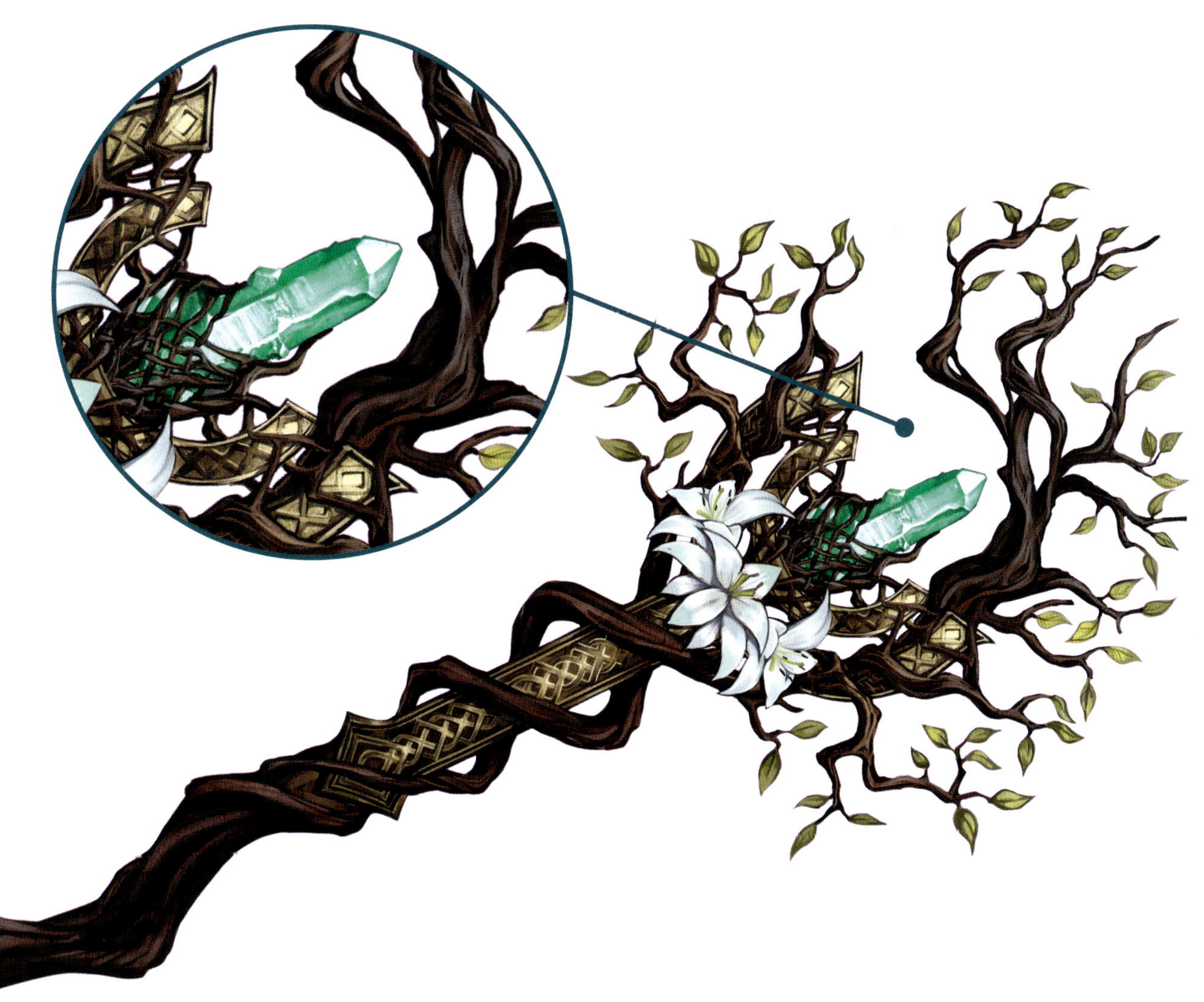

Spire of Conflux

A wooden staff with vines and flowers intertwined and ending in a hook, the Spire of Conflux was a Vestige destined for that of Keyleth of the Air Ashari. As Vox Machina sought Vestiges across Exandria to defeat the members of the Chroma Conclave, they realized the Spire wasn't on Exandria. Rather, it was in the stomach of a demon wandering an endless maze of madness. But here, Vox Machina killed two birds with one stone.

Calling upon that very demon, they tricked it into fighting Vorugal the Frigid Doom, an ancient white dragon of the Conclave. As they battled, Vox Machina came between them and killed both. Upon Yenk's death, Keyleth found the Spire of Conflux within its belly. This powerful staff enhanced Keyleth's elemental abilities and spells and greatly increased her standing as a leader of the Ashari. To this day, she still wields it in all its power and has promised it back to the followers of the Wildmother when her use for it has passed. That she seemingly will live for centuries does not seem to have bothered the followers of the Wildmother, for there is nothing more patient than the earth.

Scanlan Shorthalt

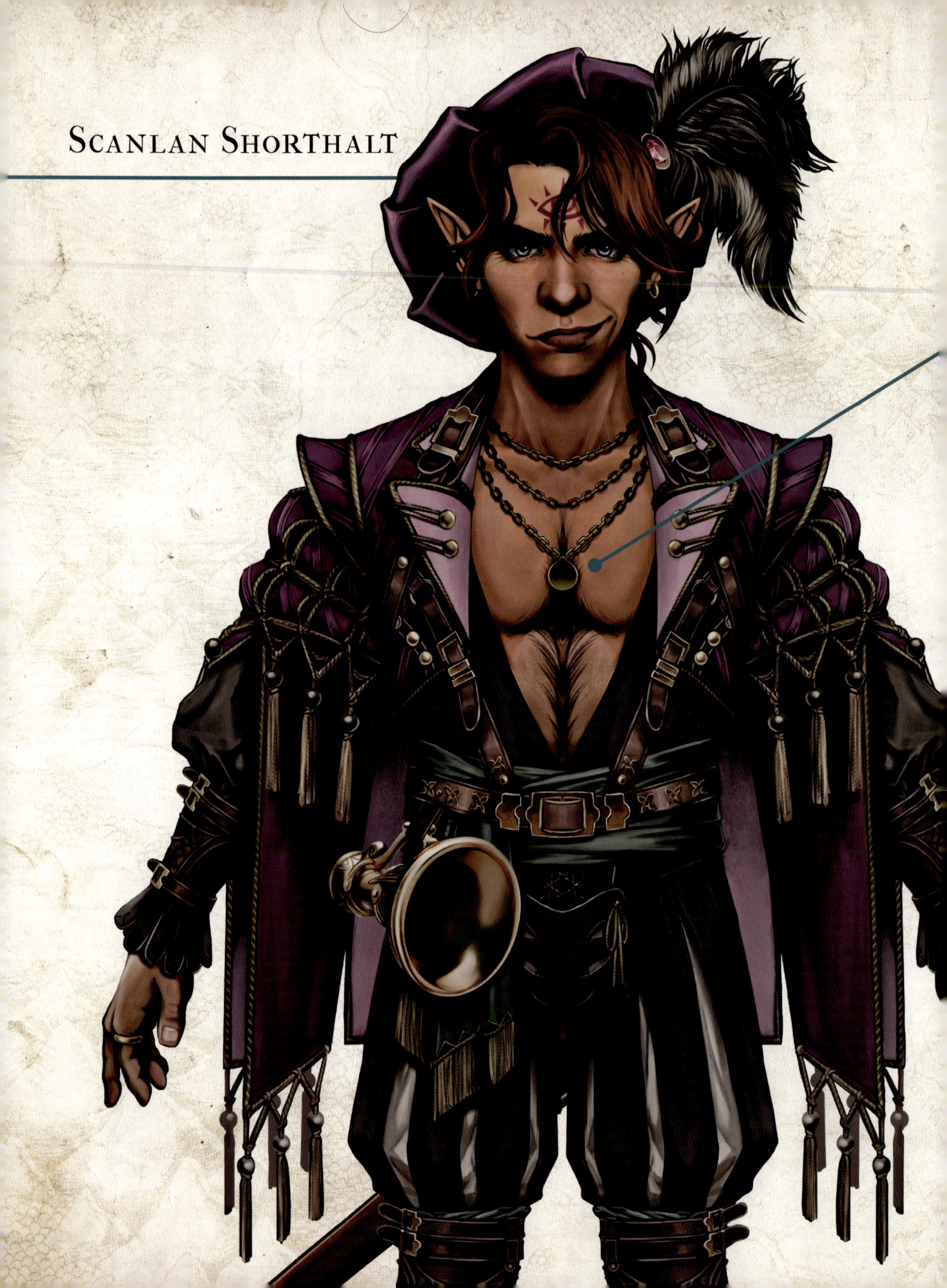

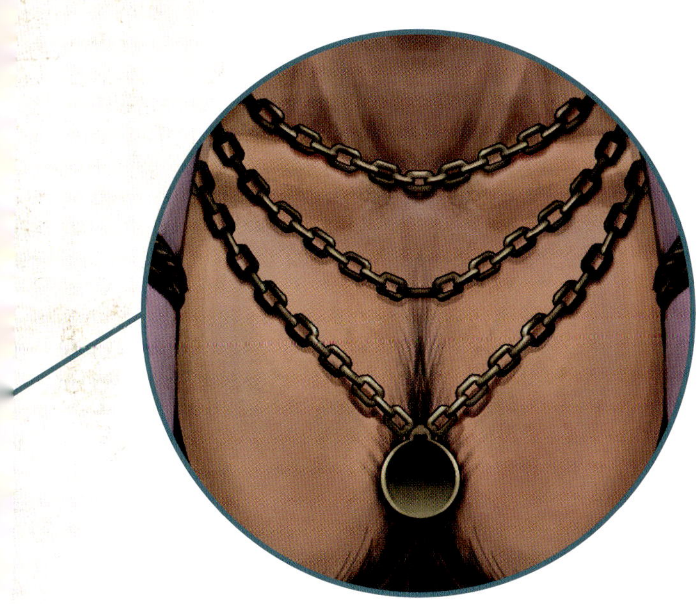

"What can be said about Scanlan Shorthalt that has not been said by the man himself? In fact, all that may be left to say is that which is unsaid. That which even the master bard himself would hesitate to speak of, let alone admit. His own attire was often flamboyant, bright, shades of purple, little armor to speak of save that which he spoke into existence, and whatever he wore was often off his body as fast as it was put on (at least in his younger days).

But to learn the truth of the man, you must get beneath the armor of stories he has made for himself. You must pry it apart to get at the core of him. And according to his friends, his chosen family, his enemies, and his daughter, Scanlan Shorthalt is this: a lecherous leech. A bona fide swindler. A rapacious negotiator and a very bad card shark. Quick with a joke, quicker with an insult, quickest with a song. And he is brave. Courageous, if anxious. Worried of living up to his own myth. Worried to let down those he loves.

But when it is time, there is no worry that can overcome his instinct to protect those who need it. Especially the little guy. Because like any good joke, Scanlan Shorthalt only punches up. Literally and metaphorically. May we all have such courage when faced with overwhelming odds. May we all learn to dress in colors other than purple."

—Tallulah Fontaine, back corner of an afterparty in Marquet, four cups in

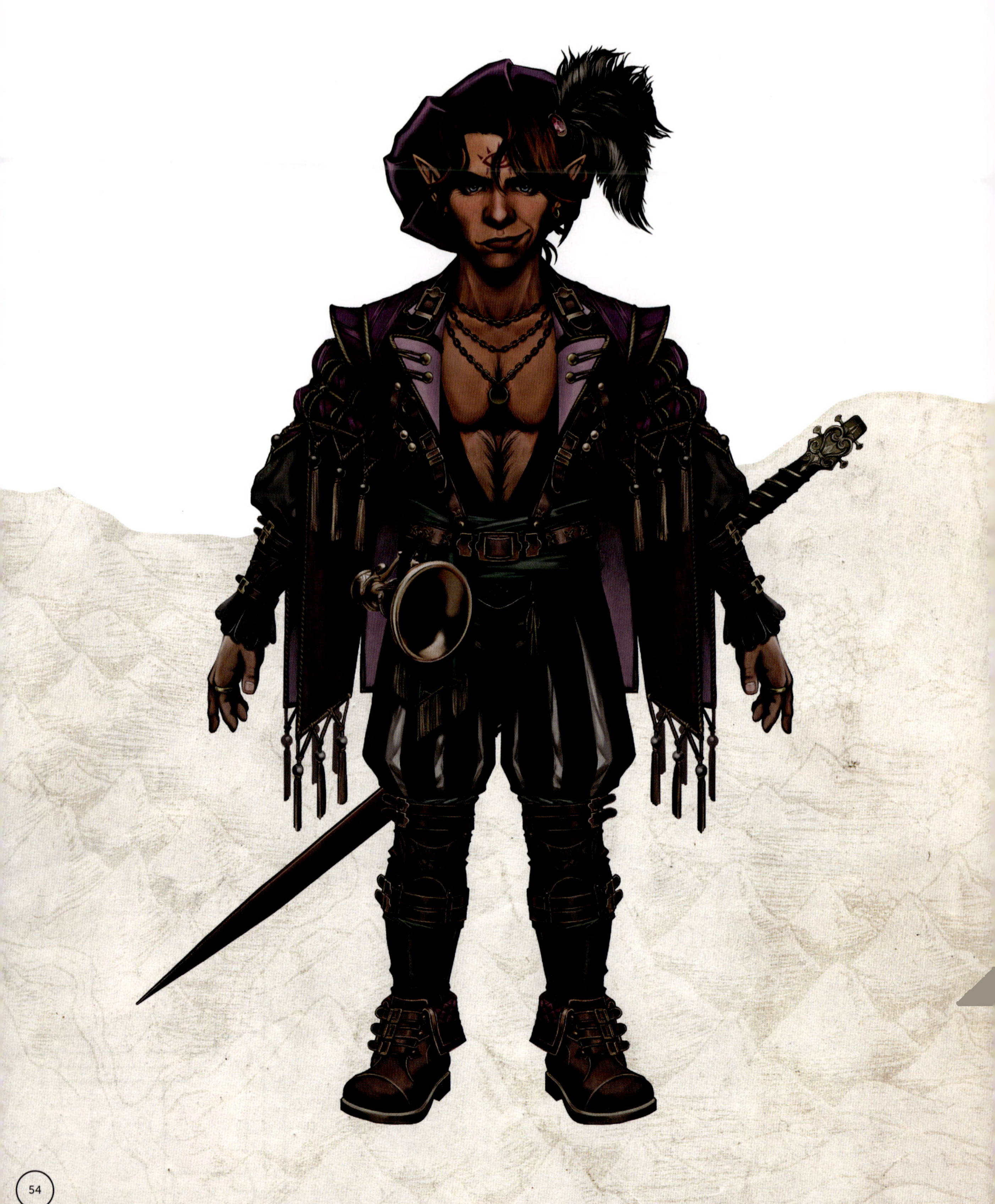

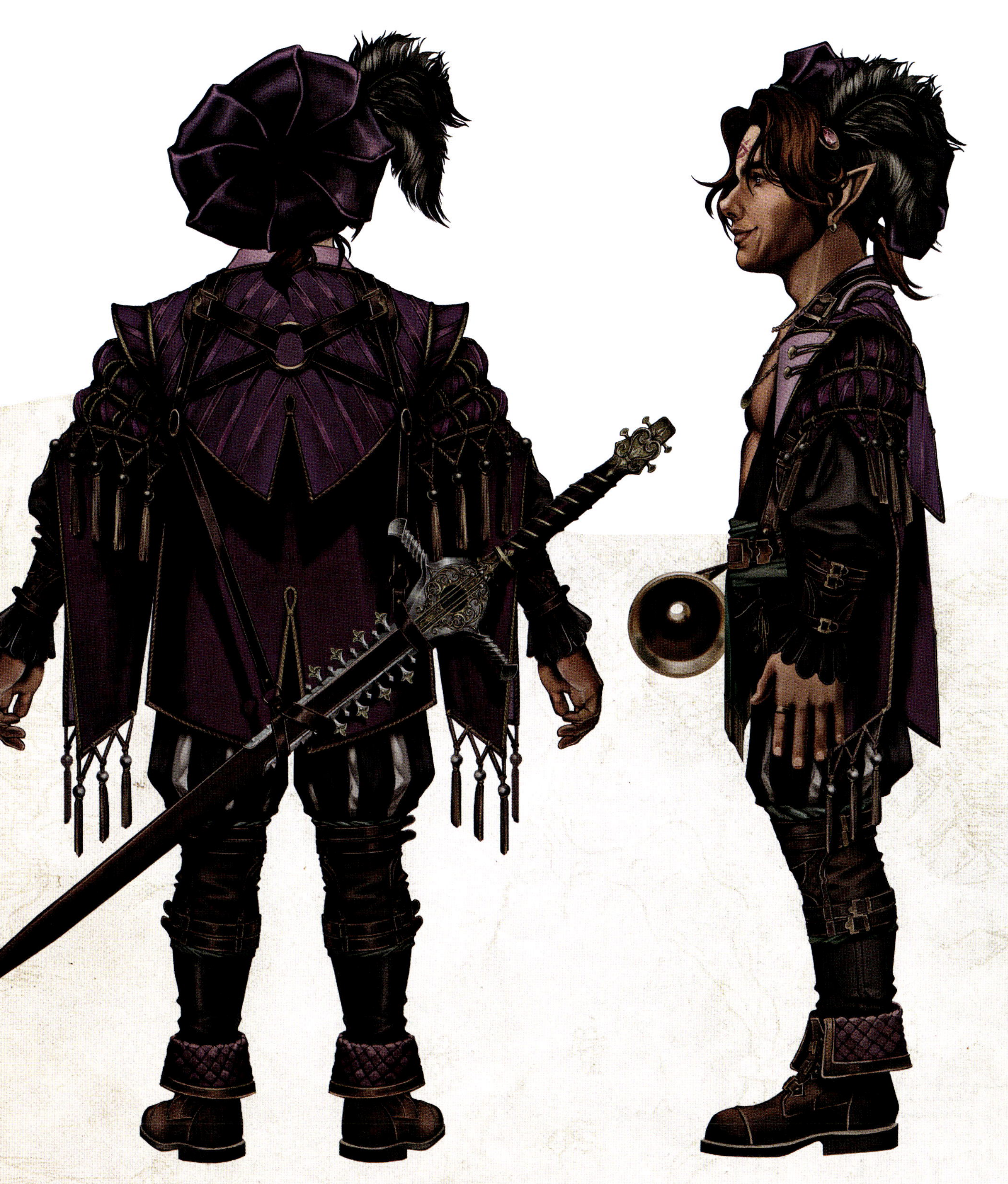

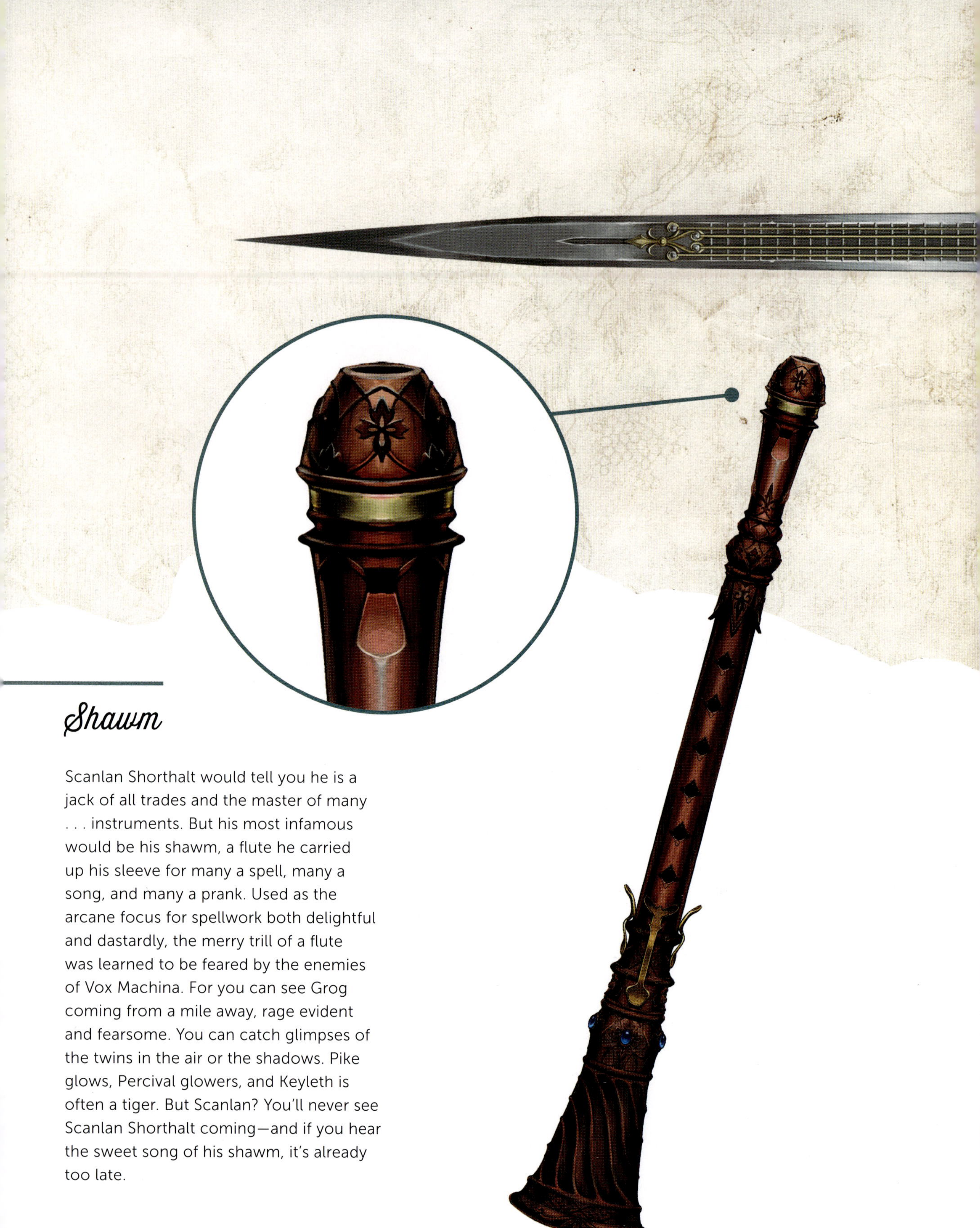

Shawm

Scanlan Shorthalt would tell you he is a jack of all trades and the master of many . . . instruments. But his most infamous would be his shawm, a flute he carried up his sleeve for many a spell, many a song, and many a prank. Used as the arcane focus for spellwork both delightful and dastardly, the merry trill of a flute was learned to be feared by the enemies of Vox Machina. For you can see Grog coming from a mile away, rage evident and fearsome. You can catch glimpses of the twins in the air or the shadows. Pike glows, Percival glowers, and Keyleth is often a tiger. But Scanlan? You'll never see Scanlan Shorthalt coming—and if you hear the sweet song of his shawm, it's already too late.

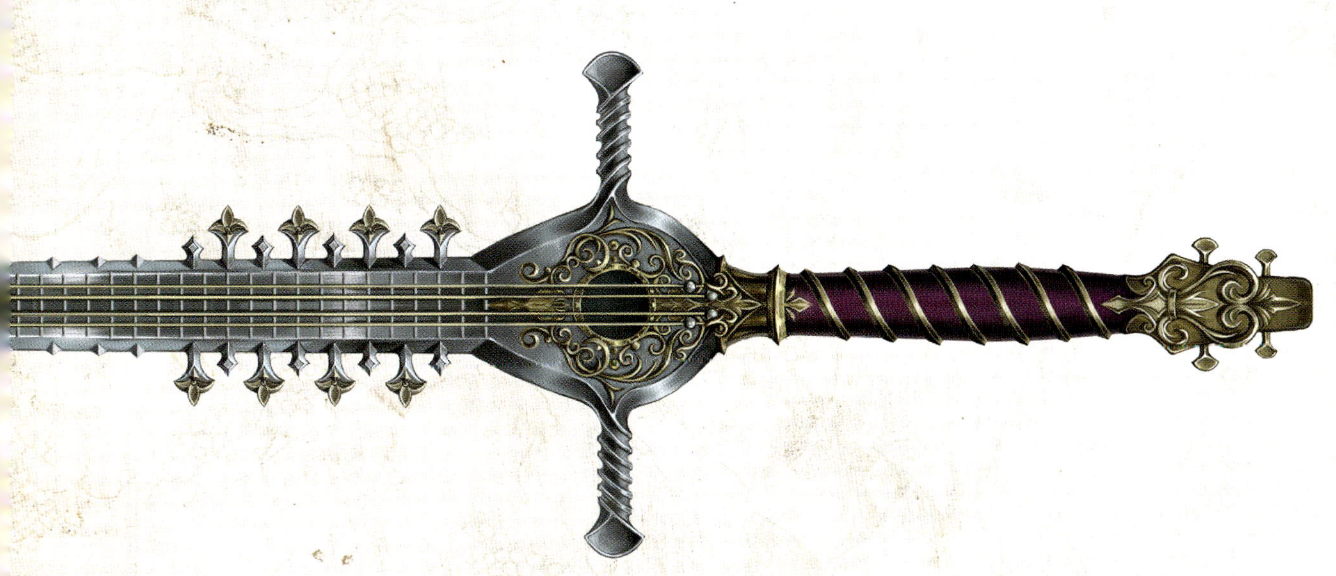

"Of all the Vestiges I'm familiar with, I'm often most moved by the stories of Mythcarver, that infamous blade of battle bards. Its most famous wielder, of course, is the White Duke themself, but I find myself more interested in those bardic warriors who did not seek the life such a blade would gift them. Those who, by necessity, embraced the legendary weapon. To protect themselves or others from harm. To stand before chaos and bring harmony with this shining, singing steel. Those who found themselves suddenly a part of the grand, cosmic tale of Exandria, and do or die, decided to defend it with their life, regardless of their personal story.

—Oren Keth'Kaylis

Mythcarver

Entrusted to the sphinx guardian, Kamaljiori

A Vestige forged in the harmony of music and magic, Mythcarver began its life wielded by names lost to time, until passing into the hands of the founder of the Golden Grin, the White Duke themself. Gifted to the androsphinx Kamaljiori before his death, Mythcarver eventually found its way to the one and only Scanlan Shorthalt, a master bard in his own right. Not known for being a ferocious melee fighter, Scanlan found sporadic use with Mythcarver as a blade, but it truly came alive in Vox Machina's time in the Plane of Fire. There, the party hunted a pit fiend named Ghurrix, enacting the vengeance of a fire giantess within the city in order to gain a different Vestige.

With the tide thoroughly turned against them, it fell to Scanlan to slay the pit fiend. Even as he doubted himself, he remembered the promise he made to a daughter newly discovered, Kaylie: that he would try his hardest to live. In doing so, he caused Mythcarver to become Exalted.

Channeling the power of the bards who came before him, he laid into the pit fiend, ending its life and saving his friends. Through his own growth as a warrior and individual, Scanlan was able to unlock the mythic resonances lying within the blade, using it henceforth in his duets of heroism and heart. We can only hope he still has it, or at least has entrusted it to someone of some kind of honor.

Hand Cone of Clarity

An ostentatious cone that amplified the voice of Scanlan and thus increased the potency of his various bits of bardic spellwork. As it had been crafted by an old friend for him, Scanlan always kept the Hand Cone of Clarity on him, utilizing it in times of crisis and also whenever he felt like it. This dutiful little arcane amplifier helped Scanlan through many pickles and with it at his side, increasing his sheer magical potency, he has bested dragons, demons, the undead, and many more, leading Vox Machina's charge with a song none could fail to hear.

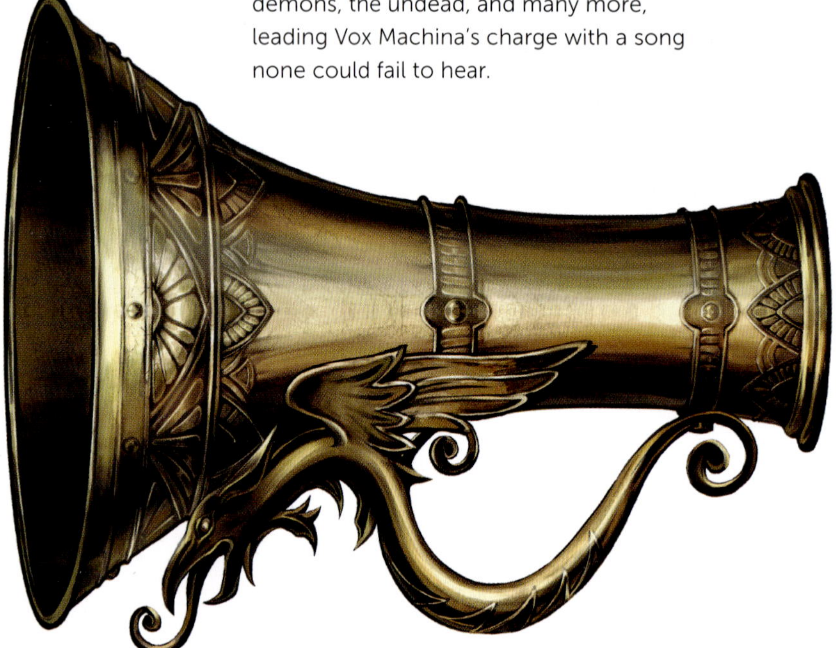

"There is no finer example of the perfect marriage to be found when a magical item's goal and a warrior's soul entwine, creating the finest example of each. For Scanlan Shorthalt, in this item (which cannot be found anywhere else in Exandria, to the chagrin of many a bard), the hand cone gave what every bard could ever wish for: the ability to be heard. And looking at the path he forged for himself through the tomes of Tal'Dorei's history, we can rest assured: Scanlan Shorthalt was most certainly heard."

—D'Rishk Dawnscale

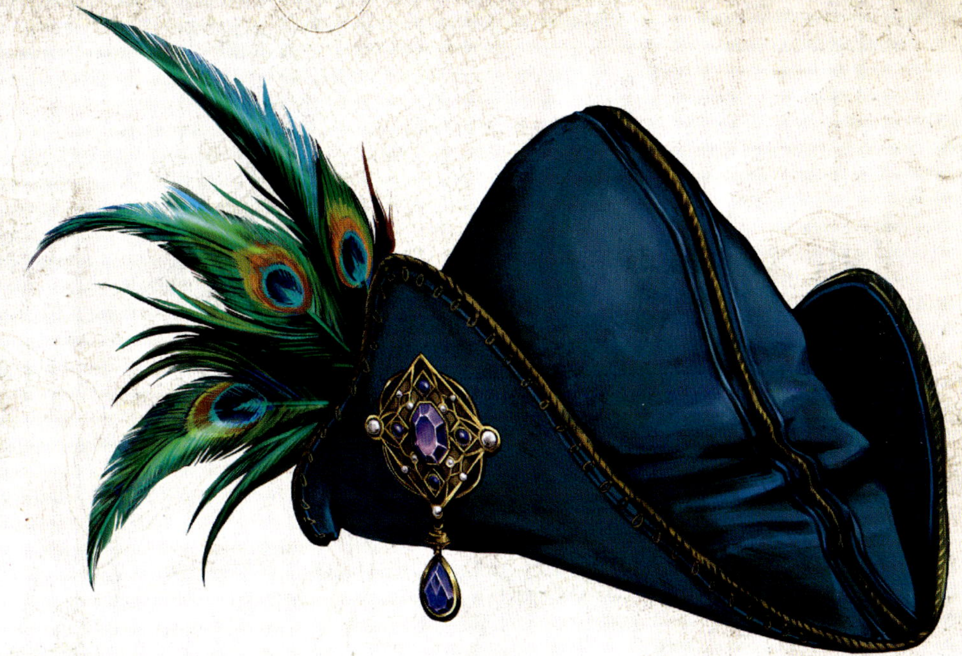

"I swear, he's out there! A huge shadow in the night, he stalks the streets of Ank'Harel. The Hands of Ord are useless against him! Every time they seem to corner him, the man vanishes. He can't be found; he can only be discovered once he's right on top of you! A fearsome foe, a brilliant tactician, with a sense of style and a mind for business that's downright terrifying. Oh, you watch, friends, you just watch! The Meat Man is coming for you. Don't be surprised when he appears right under your very nose."

—Tallulah Fontaine, overheard at Drake's Splendor, a bar in Ank'Harel

Helm of the Mirage

Scanlan has always enjoyed a good disguise. Often using magic and illusions to add different facial hair styles, change his voice, tweak his height, and more, Scanlan has often used his high charisma and natural magic of storytelling to tell the world a different tale than what they see or hear. It got a lot easier after acquiring the Helm of the Mirage, a magic item found in a dragon's lair in their early days of adventuring. After the helm passed hands from Percival to Vax and finally to Scanlan, his first use of this beautiful beret was to turn into a persona he called the Meat Man, which he used to vandalize and terrorize the offices of the Luck's Run casino, after he was cheated over "spice" in Ank'Harel. Later, he would use the disguise of the Meat Man in conjunction with his daughter, Kaylie, to start a business in Ank'Harel with the Meat Man as their front.

After using the hat to disguise himself in front of Vox Machina, Vex saw right through the illusion, and Scanlan came back to the group to assist in stopping the Whispered One's ascension. He has since given the hat to his daughter, Kaylie, who, much like her father, continues to use the hat to do business as the Magnificent and Menacing Meat Man of Marquet.

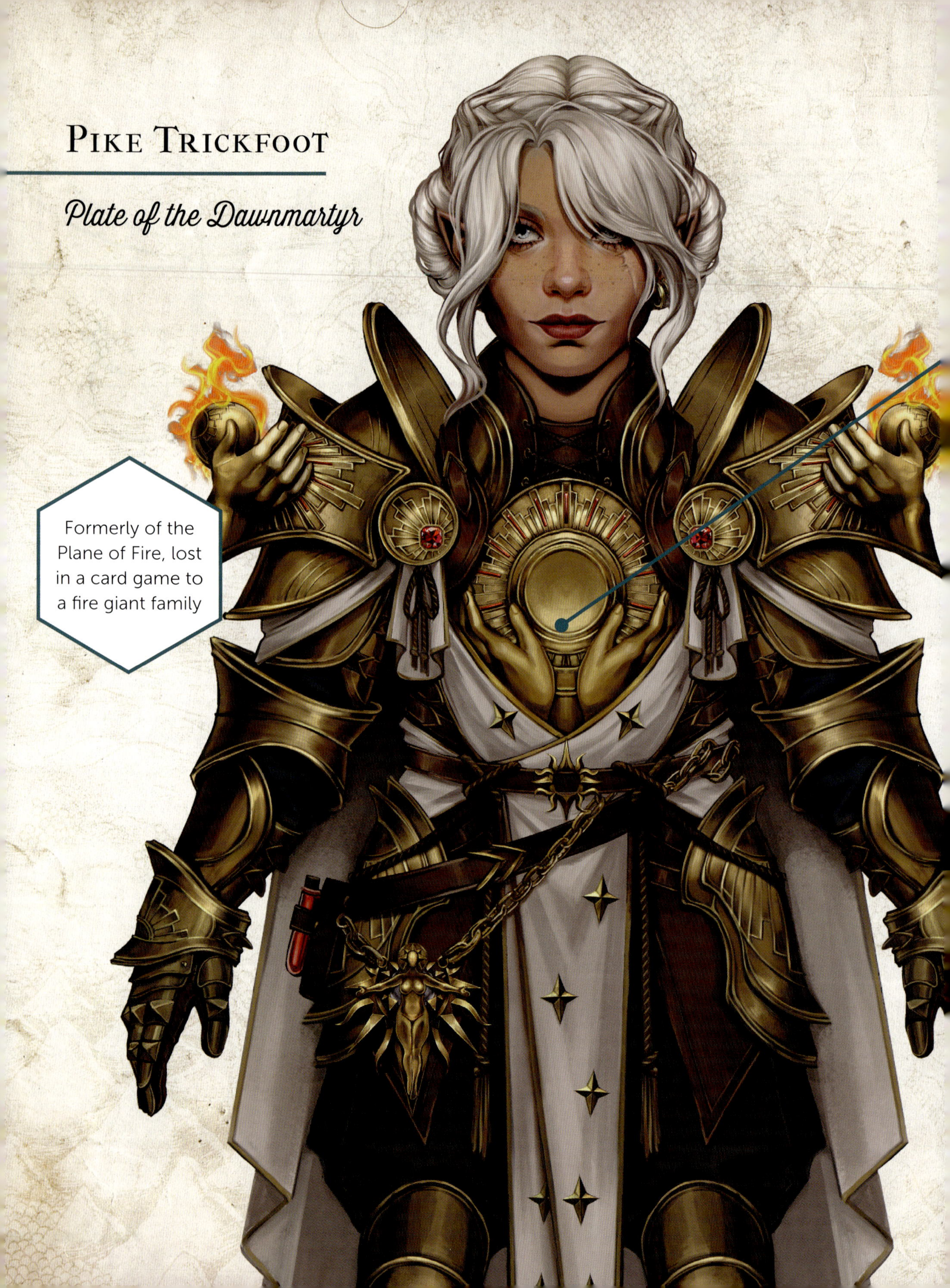
Pike Trickfoot
Plate of the Dawnmartyr
Formerly of the Plane of Fire, lost in a card game to a fire giant family

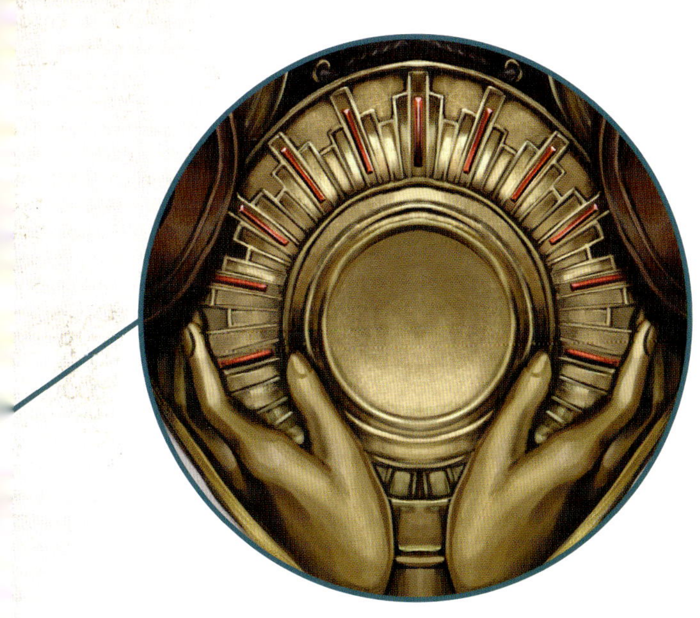

"Aye, friends! Hear me, and fear not. For though we march into darkness, we will not march alone! Already, the sky brightens with His gaze, those molten eyes that burn the wicked, even as they warm the faithful! Ahead, Ghor Dranas, yes. Ahead, shadow and blood. Ahead, torment and yes, death. But behind us, He shines. He shines, friends! We do not march alone, but with the Dawnfather at our back. Let us bring His burning judgment to those Betrayers, who even now recoil at the brightening gold of morning. We are His morning, friends! And if we do our jobs today, we will become a force just as bright and beautiful as His star! The Lord of the Hells may have gathered his shadows to him, but even the deepest shadow knows to fear the glorious sun! Forward! To Ghor Dranas!"

—D'Rishk Dawnscale, reciting from the last known speech by High Priestess Duana, Final Lightbearer of the Calamity

A mighty set of brass and gold plate armor studded with rubies and silver script, also known as the Beacon of Protection by the faithful of the Dawnfather, for whom this armor was first crafted. Worn by a high priest of the mighty sun god, this armor was thought lost in the heart of Ghor Dranas where she died, at the very center of the Betrayer Gods' land during the Calamity. However, when the armor resurfaced, it was hanging on the wall in the City of Brass, owned by a fire giant who had won it from the family who uncovered it.

Vox Machina gained the armor by slaying a pit fiend in vengeance for the fire giant, who had lost a lover to his devilish predations. Pike donned the armor, already Exalted, and it turned the healer from a bright light on the battlefield to a true and burning sun, punishing attackers with flame and brilliance. In addition, the powerful magic of the Dawnfather could stave off death once a day. She wore the armor through legendary battles with the Chroma Conclave and the Whispered One. With the power of the Dawnfather's plate and the Everlight's blessing, Pike Trickfoot was, for a very short time, one of the most powerful divine priestesses on Exandria.

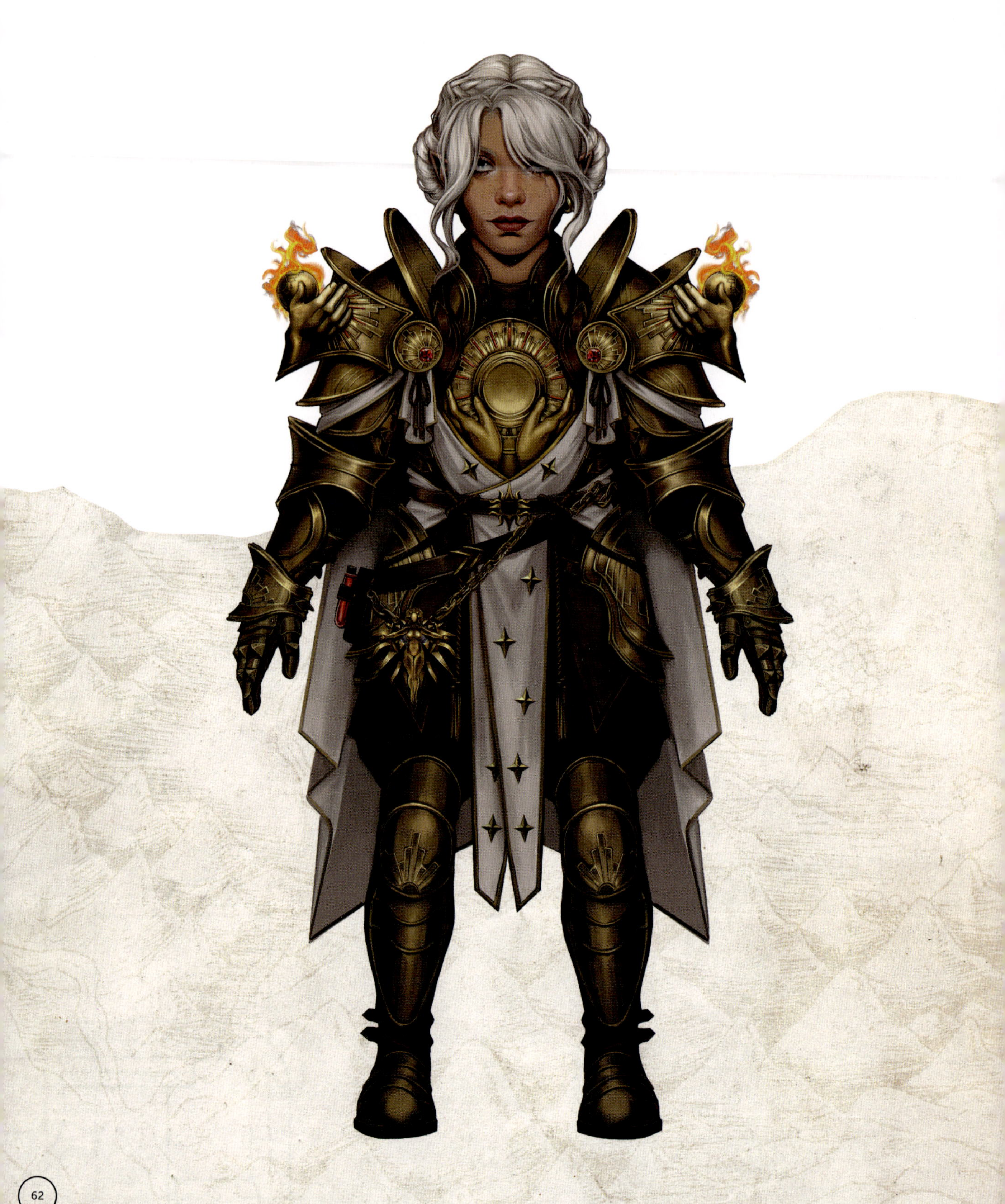

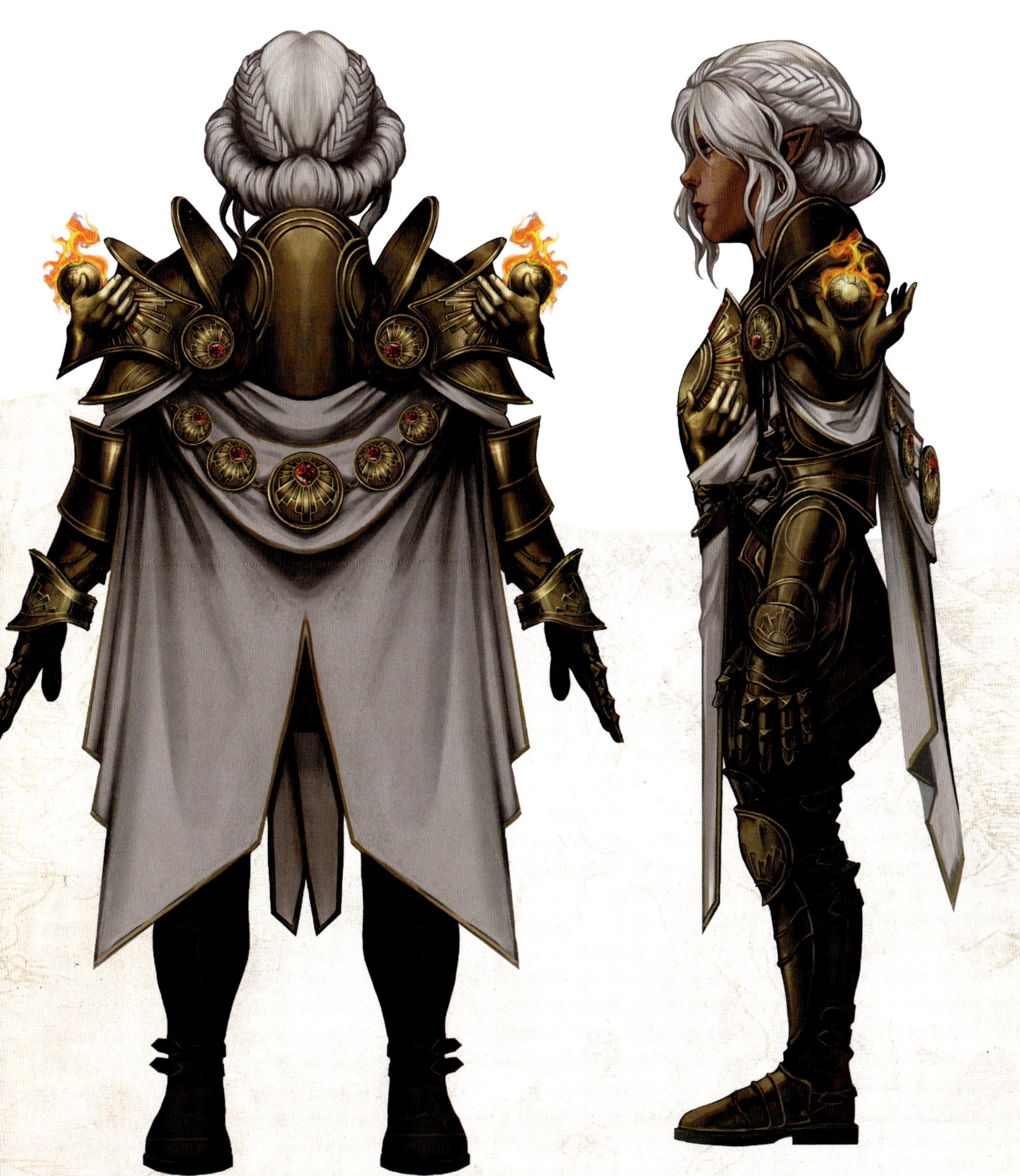

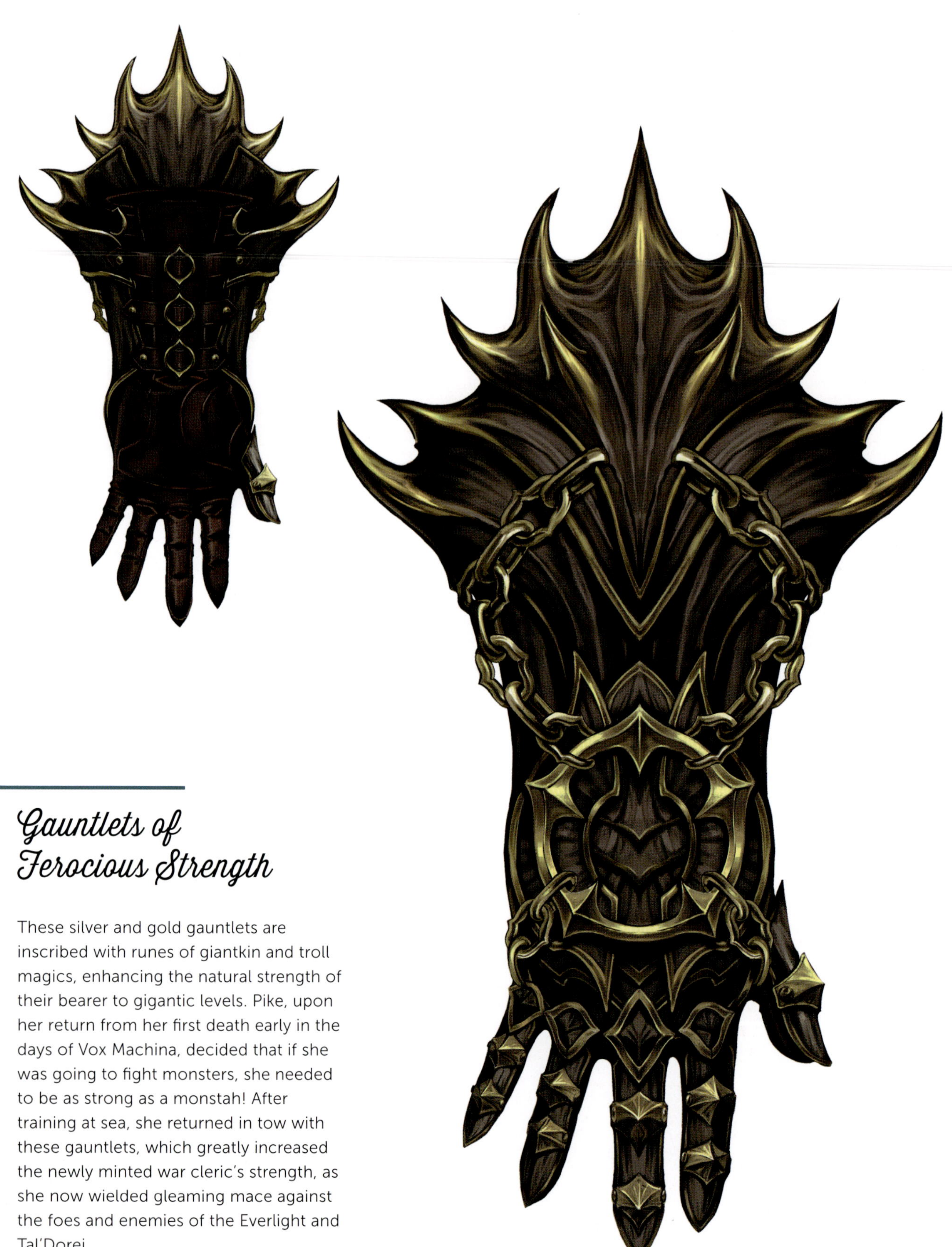

Gauntlets of Ferocious Strength

These silver and gold gauntlets are inscribed with runes of giantkin and troll magics, enhancing the natural strength of their bearer to gigantic levels. Pike, upon her return from her first death early in the days of Vox Machina, decided that if she was going to fight monsters, she needed to be as strong as a monstah! After training at sea, she returned in tow with these gauntlets, which greatly increased the newly minted war cleric's strength, as she now wielded gleaming mace against the foes and enemies of the Everlight and Tal'Dorei.

Holy Symbol of the Everlight

This holy symbol is shaped as a beautiful golden emblem of a woman with her arms outstretched, her hair a mane of fire. It was passed down to Pike by her great-great-grandfather, Wilhand, who had become a devout follower when Pike was young and went to live with him. This holy symbol became the foundational fount from which her own faith sprang, igniting in her a passion to tend to the poor and helpless and use her power and the faith of the Everlight to protect those in need.

The Everlight was there for Pike every hour, dire and joyful, even as Pike renewed herself as a battle priest following her death at the hands of a demon. But every god needs a warrior, and Pike threw herself into battle as a shining beacon, the symbol of the Everlight always with her, igniting faith in the goddess's waning light, for many had forgotten about the Lady of Redemption. From granting powerful resurrection magics to bring her friends back from death to powerful healing in the midst of battle, the Everlight has even manifested for her dear cleric, striking down monstrous and wicked foes from dragons to gods and more.

She even invited Pike and Vox Machina into her celestial realm, granting them a divine audience to give her blessing. And though Pike has retired from adventuring, baking in Whitestone, she still wears her symbol to this day.

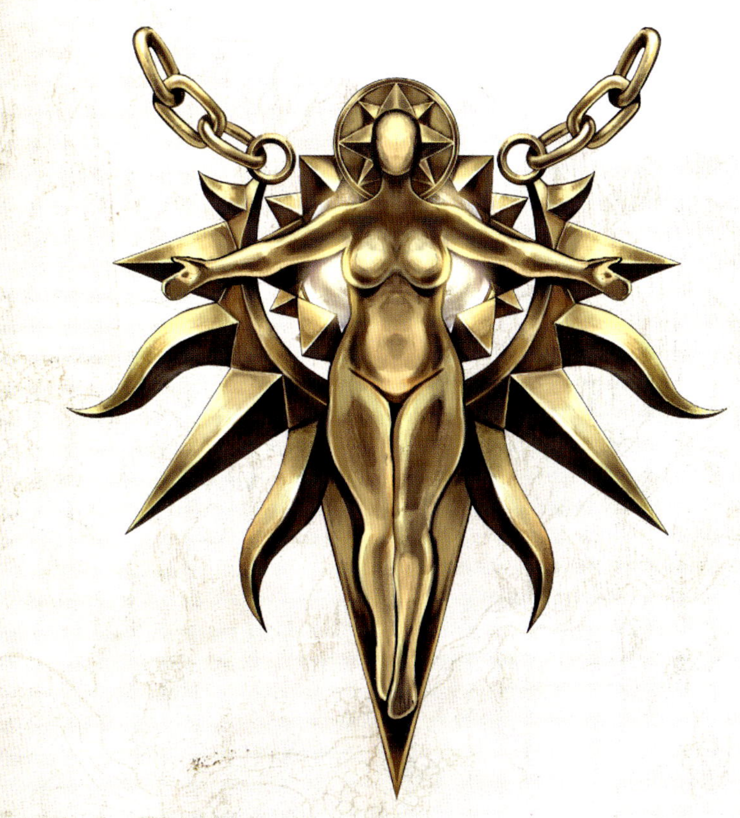

"Of course, she is the goddess that all the Betrayers fear most. What traitor wants redemption to exist in the world? Why do you think they wish to eradicate her image from Exandria? Because any world in which her light shines is a world in which they could be wrong for what they did, and worse, be forgiven."

—D'Rishk Dawnscale, reading from "Whom Did We Betray? A Spoken Treatise of the Final Days of Calamity"

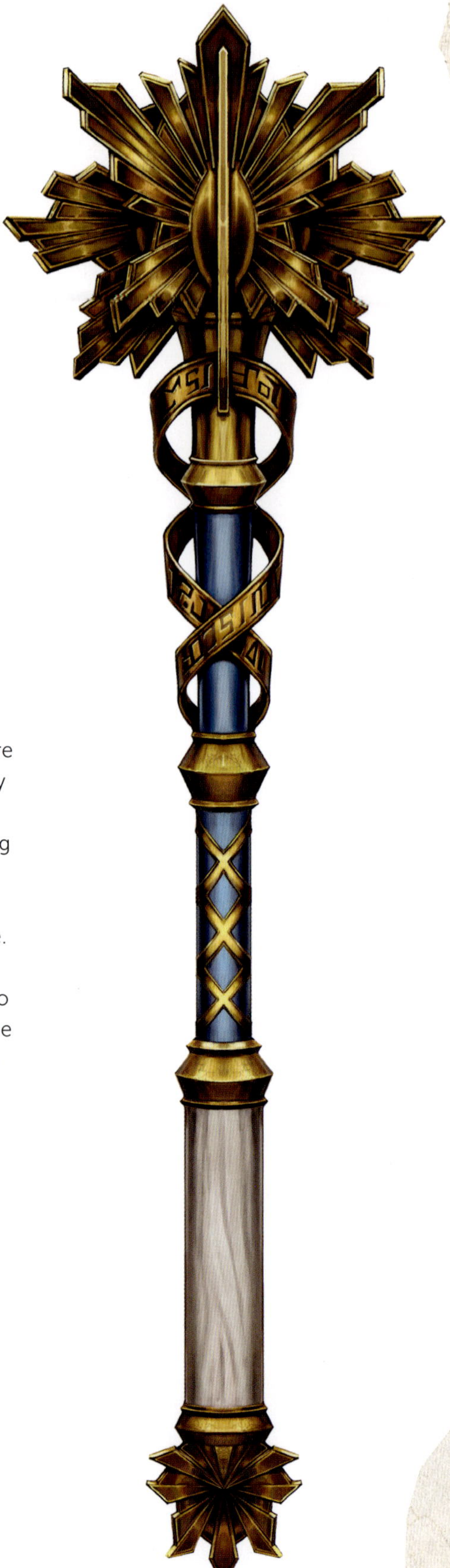

Mace of Brilliance

A shining, heavy mace of silver steel that glows golden in the embrace of a holy wielder, this weapon became the signature melee choice for Pike Trickfoot, especially after her return from training at sea. With the Gauntlets of Ferocious Strength gifting her tremendous power, it was no hard task to lift this mighty mace and swing it with the power of her goddess at her side. Although Pike healed and safeguarded those around her, she was always eager to throw herself into battle, often side by side with her best-buddy-in-arms and chosen brother, Grog Strongjaw.

"Size and speed ain't nothing to factor when face-to-face with the true meat and heat of combat. If your heart be good and your arm be strong and you really fucking care, you'll be there, no matter what. And if someone discounts you for being small, you take an extra second to smash 'em in the lower bits so hard they see all the stars of Exandria, and you tells 'em Grenk sent you!"

—Tallulah Fontaine, quoting infamous kobold brawler Grenk the Tiny Terror

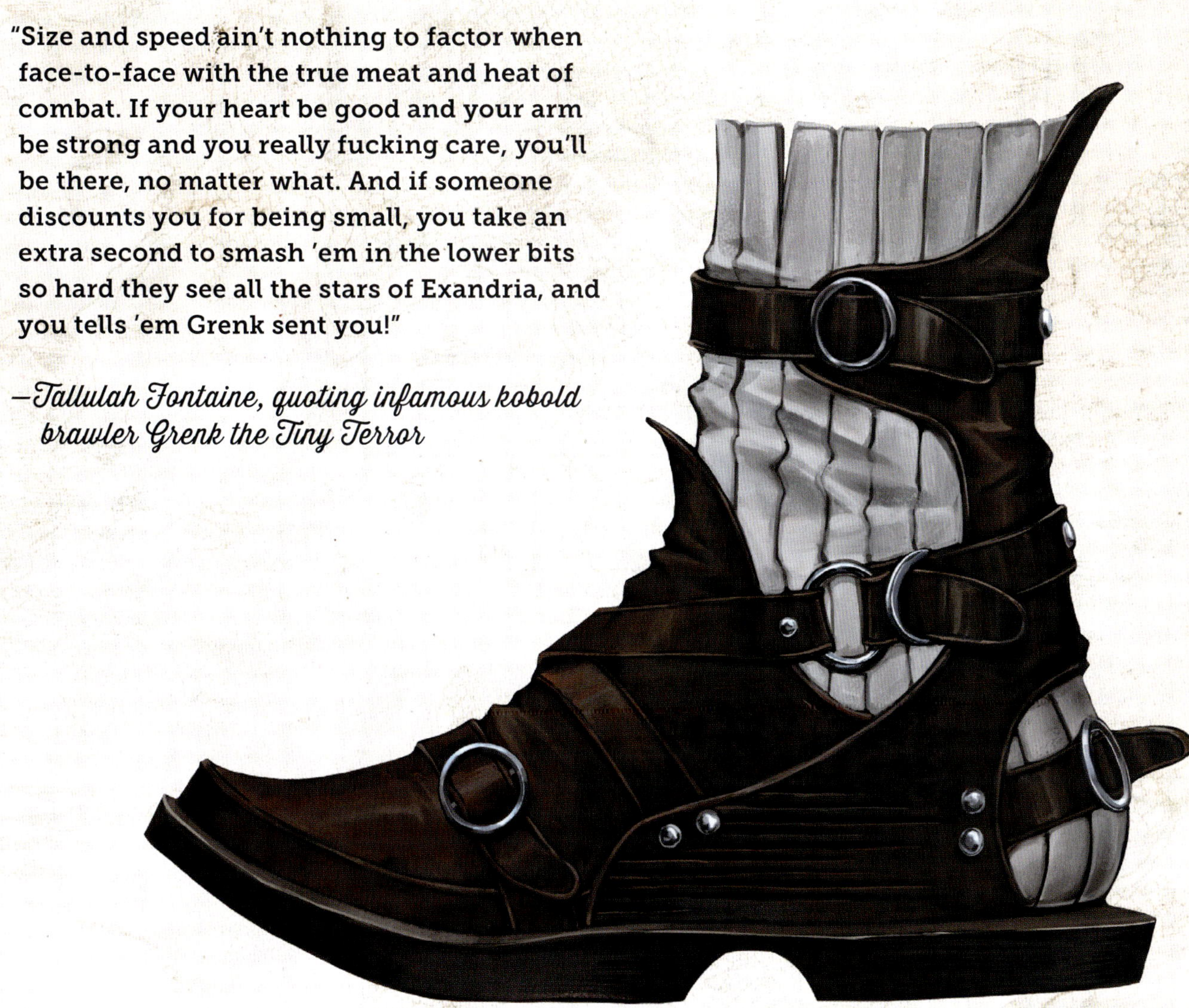

Sprinter's Boots

Pike has never been fast. Her heart has always been true and her arm always strong, but there were many times throughout her adventuring that Pike didn't just need to move, she needed to move *fast*—for felling foes on the battlefield, but also for providing a strong amount of healing to her allies. But between her gnomish stature and her protective plate, she'd need help. Enter the Sprinter's Boots. Pike picked these up just after her time at sea, training in her newly learned ways of war. They were the final ingredient in Pike's rejuvenation as a cleric, gifting her short but powerful bursts of speed in the middle of combat.

They didn't last forever, but when it counted (and it counted many times), all Pike had to do was click her heels and make for a friend in need.

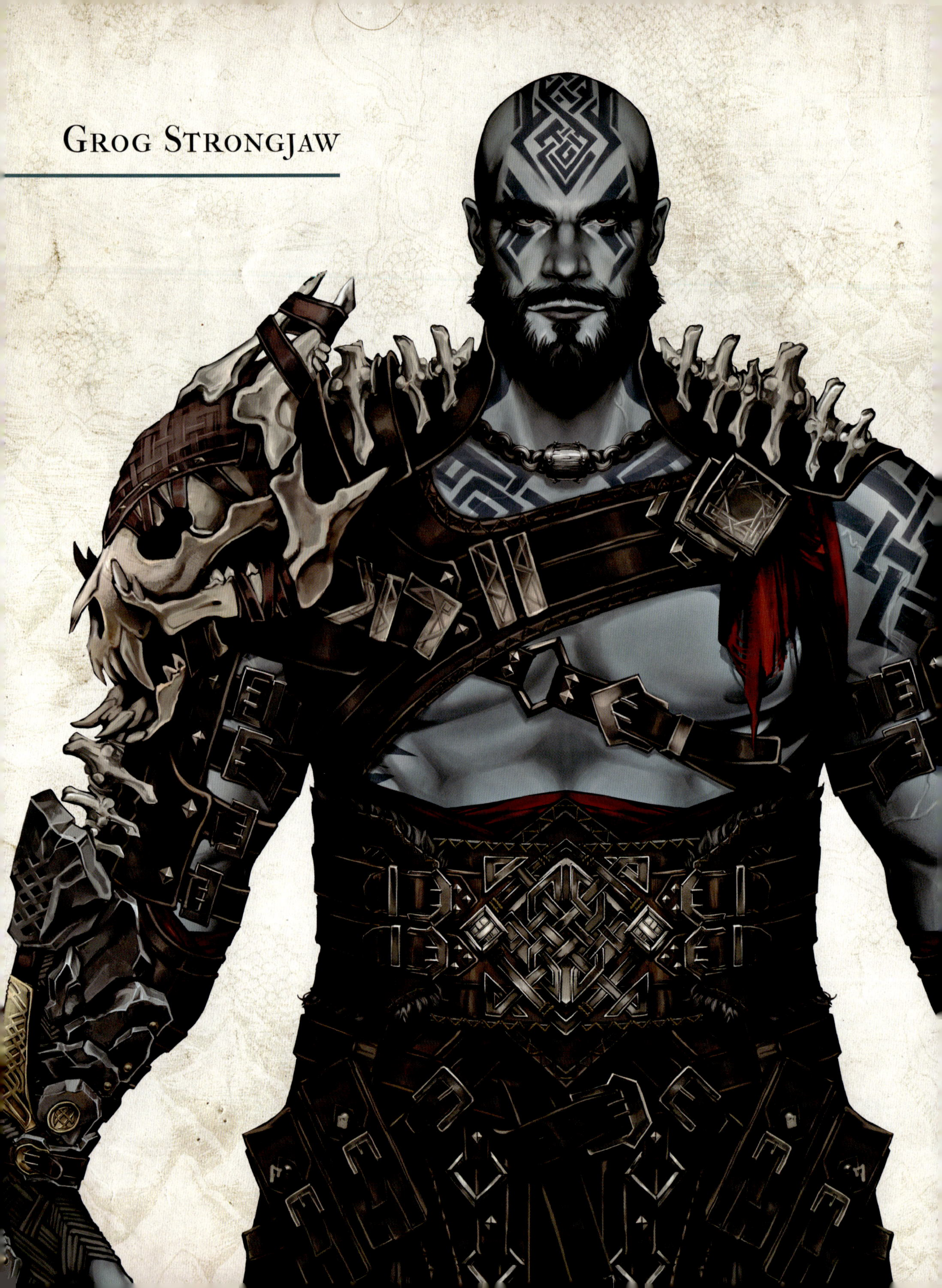
GROG STRONGJAW

"I know he is of the giantkin, and thus more robust than I and certainly heartier than I, but how Grog Strongjaw traipsed about Exandria in little more than a huge belt and ill-fitting pants is truly beyond me. When asked at one time, he responded by saying, 'My weapons keep me warm!' and then he growled, as though that was a suitable answer, and it was the questioner who was rude. And maybe they were."

—D'Rishk Dawnscale

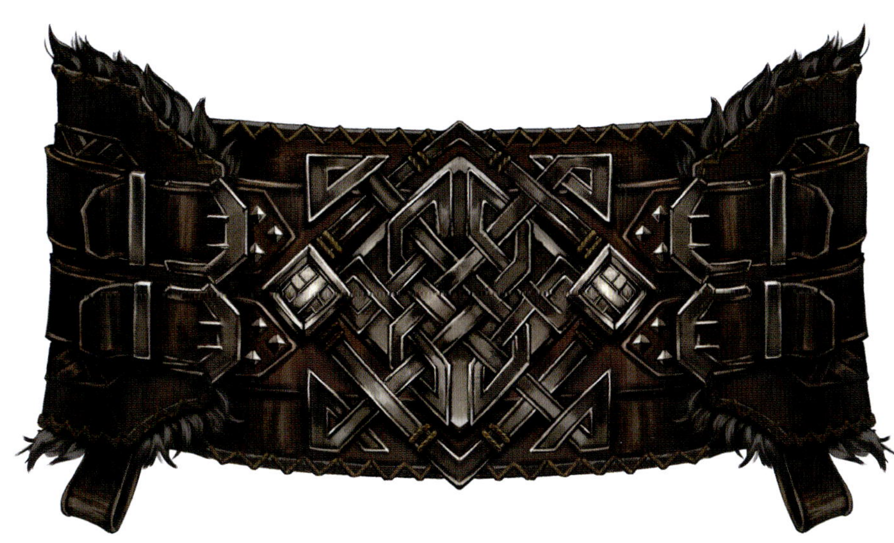

Belt of Dwarvenkind

Often, magic items across Exandria and the myriad planes help dreams come true—power given to the powerless, natural abilities enhanced to mystical levels, and other such wonders. And for Grog Strongjaw, with the Belt of Dwarvenkind he purchased from dear friend Shaun Gilmore of Gilmore's Glorious Goods, he achieved his dream of growing a beard. Along with his follicular fantasy, this belt enhanced his already powerful constitution and gifted him numerous dwarven capabilities. He wore it for the rest of his days as he tapped into new might and new facial hair.

However, along with all the benefits of this ancient dwarven relic, it gave him a new problem: a target for many of Vax'ildan's pranks against the towering half-giant. With a deft and steady hand, Grog once awoke to find half his newly acquired beard shaven away and the half-elf pain in the ass far from sight. It was at these times, it was said, his rage was greatest.

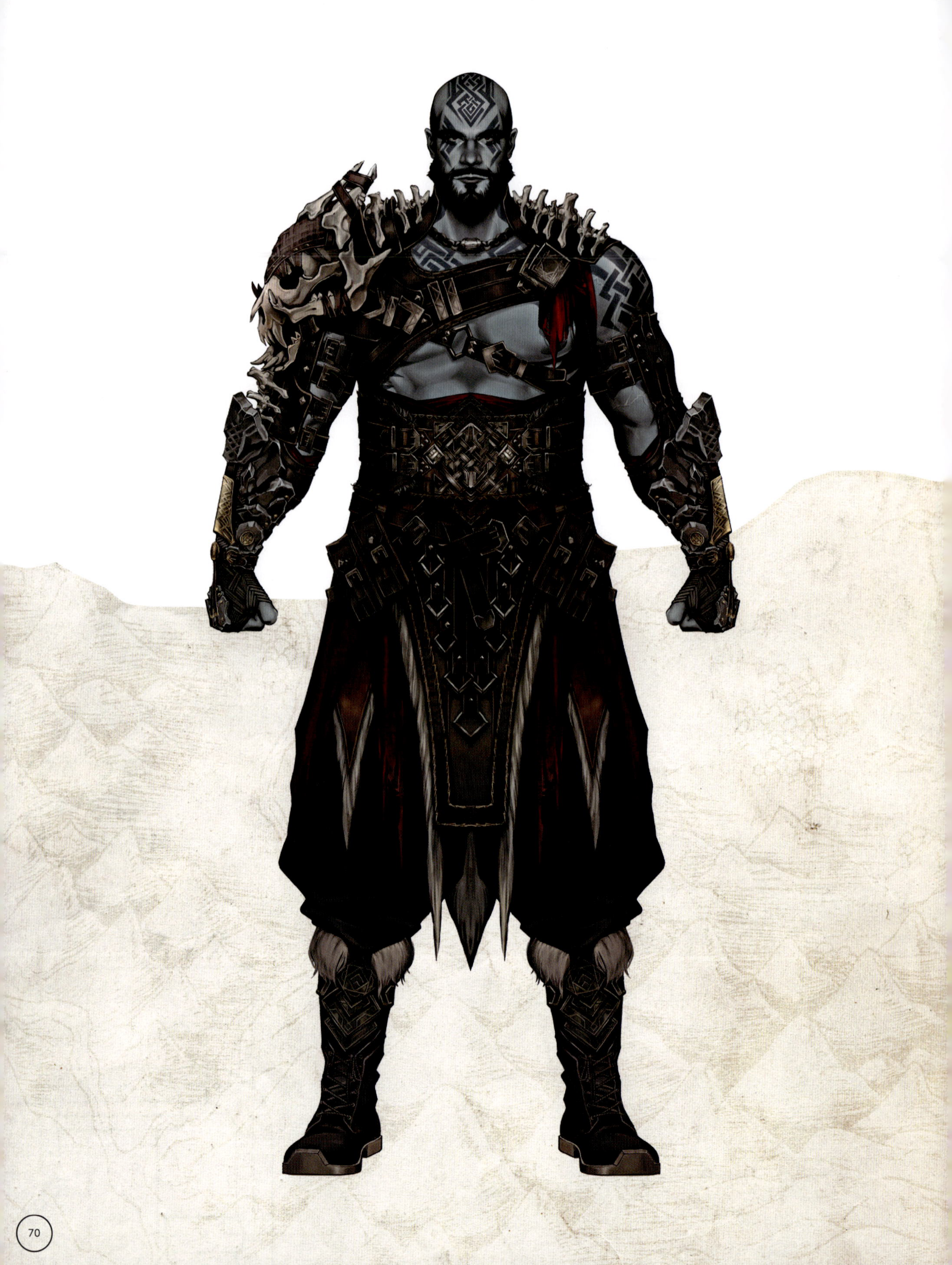

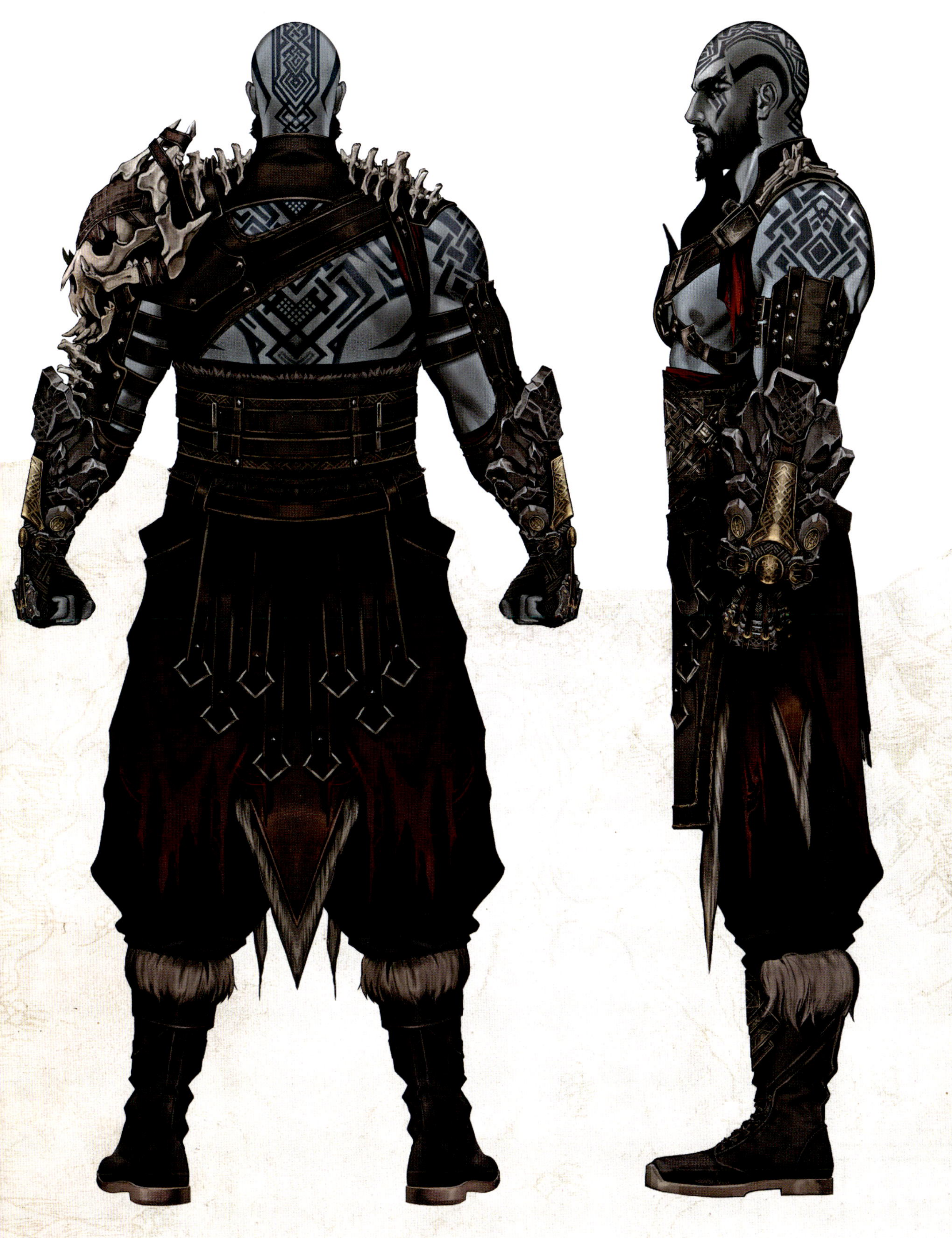

Bloodaxe

Once wielded by Grog's terrible and bloodthirsty uncle Kevdak, former leader of the Herd of Storms, this dark metal axe passed into Grog's hands when he defeated his uncle in one-on-one combat, with Vox Machina at his back. With some necrotic magic within the steel and crimson-edged axe, Grog was bolstered by this weapon's enchantment, dealing death in more ways than one, gaining vitality for each enemy struck down. But unlike some of his other weapons, the Bloodaxe had no mind of its own and thus Grog was kept safe.

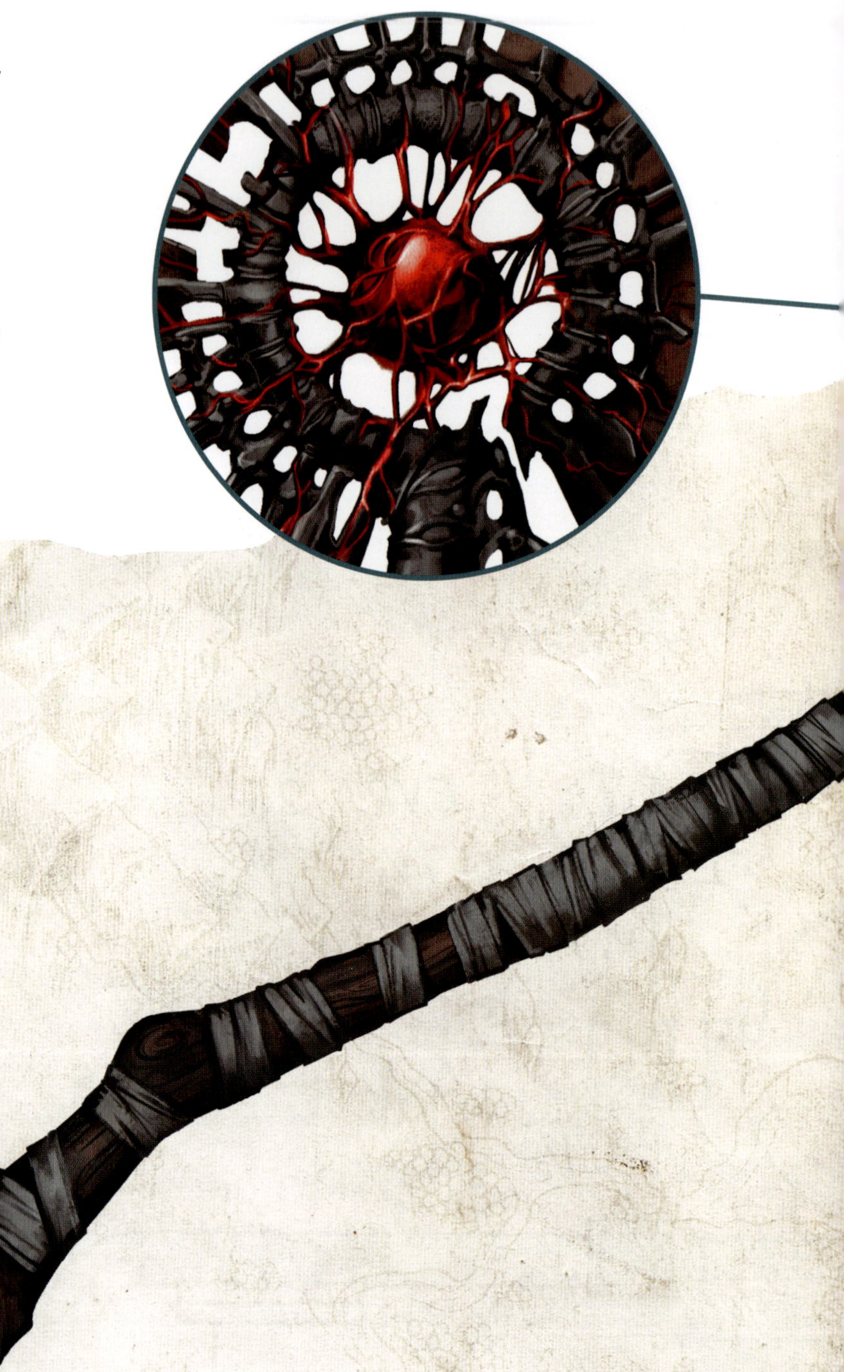

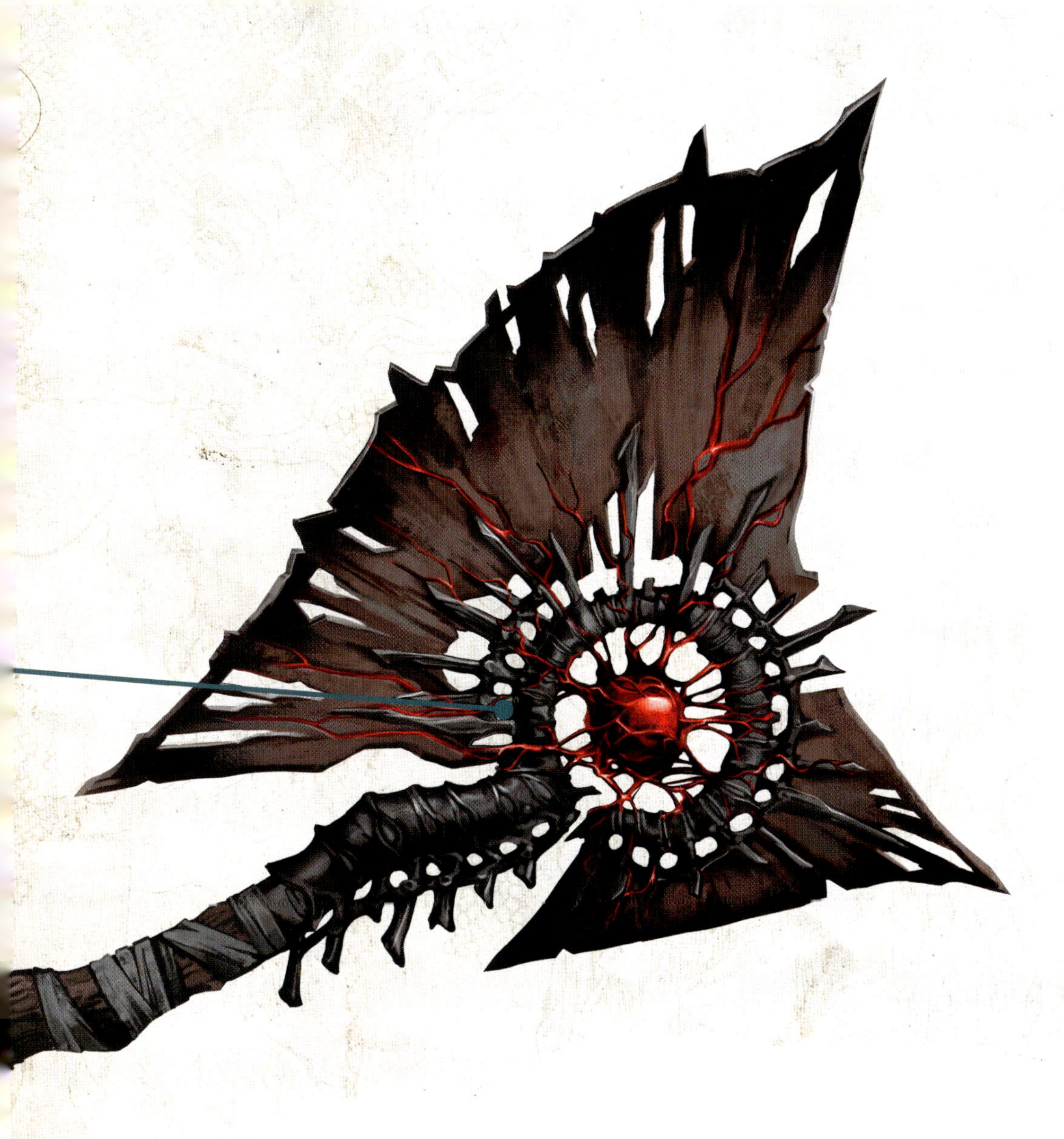

"Blood is the basis for many primordial magics, and it is from such foundational arcanics that some of the deadliest weapons have arisen. And though the art of hemoforging was abandoned early on in the Age of Arcanum, its arts were never erased, only purposefully forgotten and hidden away."

—Oren Kath'Kaylis, pulled from the file of Roots of Arcanum, Vol. III

Craven Edge

A signature weapon of one of Vox Machina's greatest enemies, Craven Edge is a sentient greatsword that was once wielded by Sylas Briarwood, vampiric husband to the powerful necromancer, Delilah Briarwood. It was not just the weapon's mind that grew the more it fed on the blood of its enemies—its curse did as well. This curse hardly affected a being of malice such as Sylas, but it preyed on Grog Strongjaw's simple mind as he sought to do good with this evil blade. Recovered after the first death of the undead Sylas, Craven Edge and its insidious magic became one of Grog's main weapons, used in combat following their time freeing Whitestone from the grip of the Briarwoods.

As Grog used the greatsword, it made bloodshed addictive, draining the strength of those it killed. Grog grew enamored, refusing to sleep so he could maintain the weapon's horrible strength. But Grog soon realized the error of giving himself fully to Craven Edge's dark hunger. After nearly losing his best buddy, Pike, from the blade's influence, Grog tried to get rid of it. Craven Edge then took Grog's life.

Once Grog's soul was recovered through Pike's light and love, Keyleth teleported the cursed weapon into an empty pocket plane so no other could find it, use it, and be used by it. It waits there still, ever hungry.

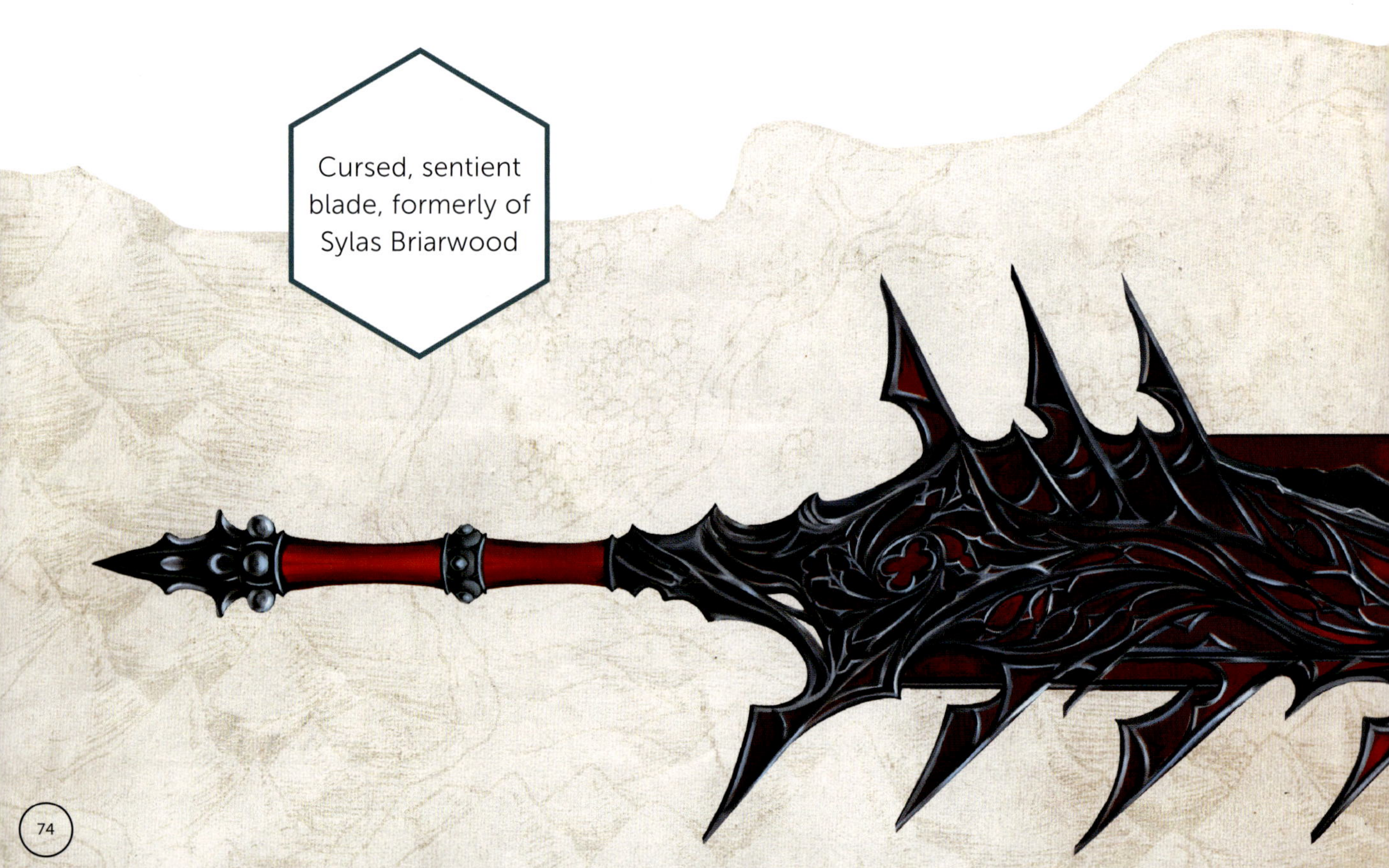

Cursed, sentient blade, formerly of Sylas Briarwood

"Sentient weapons in Exandria and across the myriad planes are rare but not unheard of, and most of them, like Craven Edge, are born of malevolence and cruelty. That cruelty is often intentional, punishing or delighting in a mind ripped from its body and placed into a vessel undying, though some fell servants would gleefully serve within a weapon (see Xartaza re: Mace of the Black Crown). The man that would become Craven Edge had his name scorched from history, the endless hunger of his curse all that remained. A terrible curse, this. For nothing matters, not even to a fiend, when all that drives you is appetite.

Do not pity Craven Edge, or the man who became it, but even I pause, thinking of the torment it feels still, ravenous at the edge of the world, and unable to do more than rage at the unending pit of its heart."

—D'Rishk Dawnscale

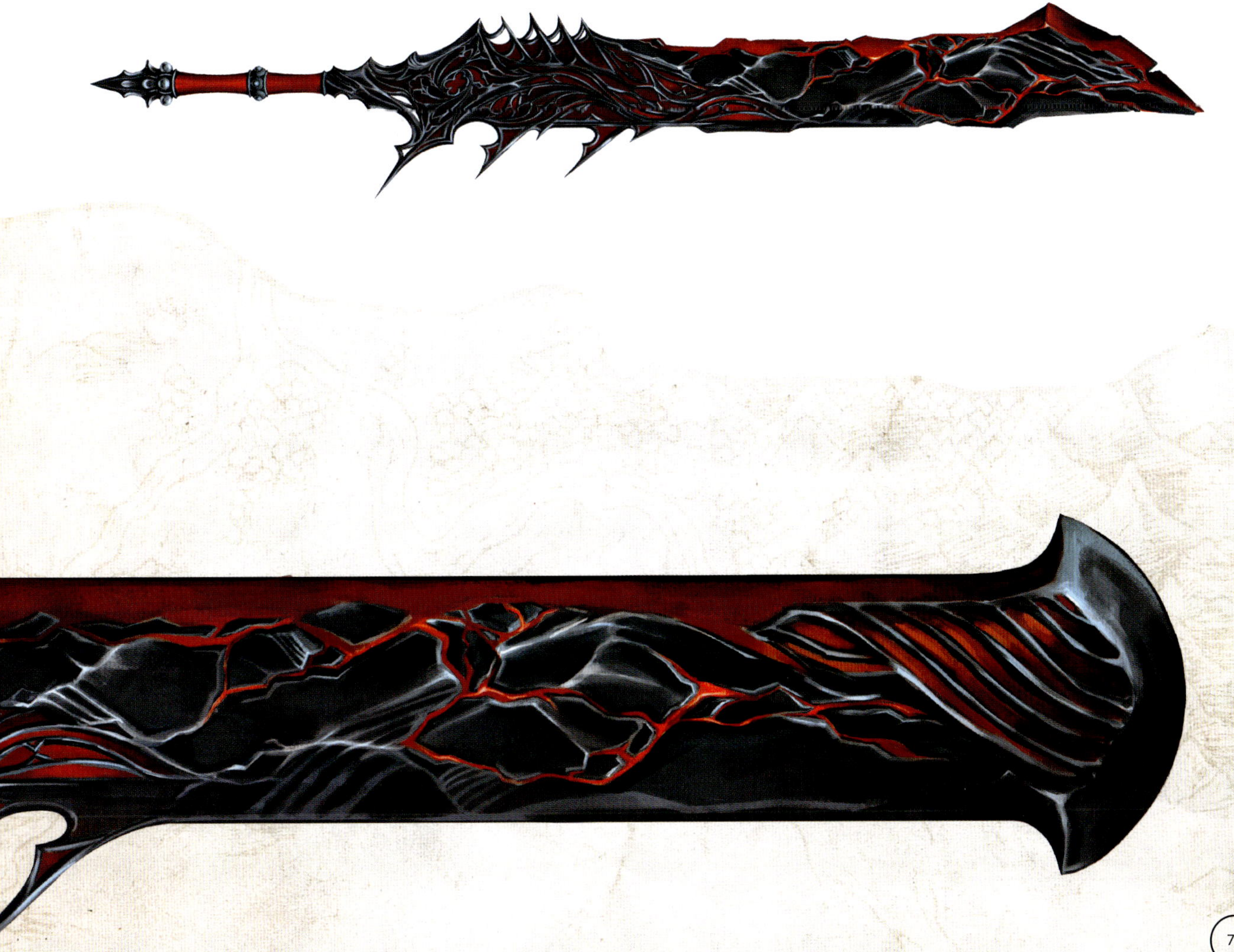

Vestige carved from the heart of an earth titan, formerly of Kevdak of the Herd of Storms

Titanstone Knuckles

These beautiful stone gauntlets were carved from the very heart of an earth titan felled during the Calamity, its heart taken and chiseled into the form of these knuckles, hundreds of intricate runes tapping into the titan's natural power. Lost to legend, they were recovered and placed on the bloody hands of Kevdak, Grog's uncle. The warlord then used the power of the gauntlets to rule with ferocity and fear, crushing opposition and punishing weakness. Such weakness as a young Grog saving Pike's grandfather from the Herd of Storms, for which Kevdak beat his nephew nearly to death.

After Kevdak's defeat and death at the hands of Grog and Vox Machina, the Knuckles passed on to Grog, who wore them with pride, unknowing of the enchantments yet to be unlocked. It wasn't until Grog was tested by Earthbreaker Groon, the master hand-to-hand combatant and spiritual leader of the Stormlord, that he learned the gauntlets did more than make him stronger. The Titanstone Knuckles reached their full potential when Grog finally realized the source of his true strength: the love of his chosen family, Vox Machina.

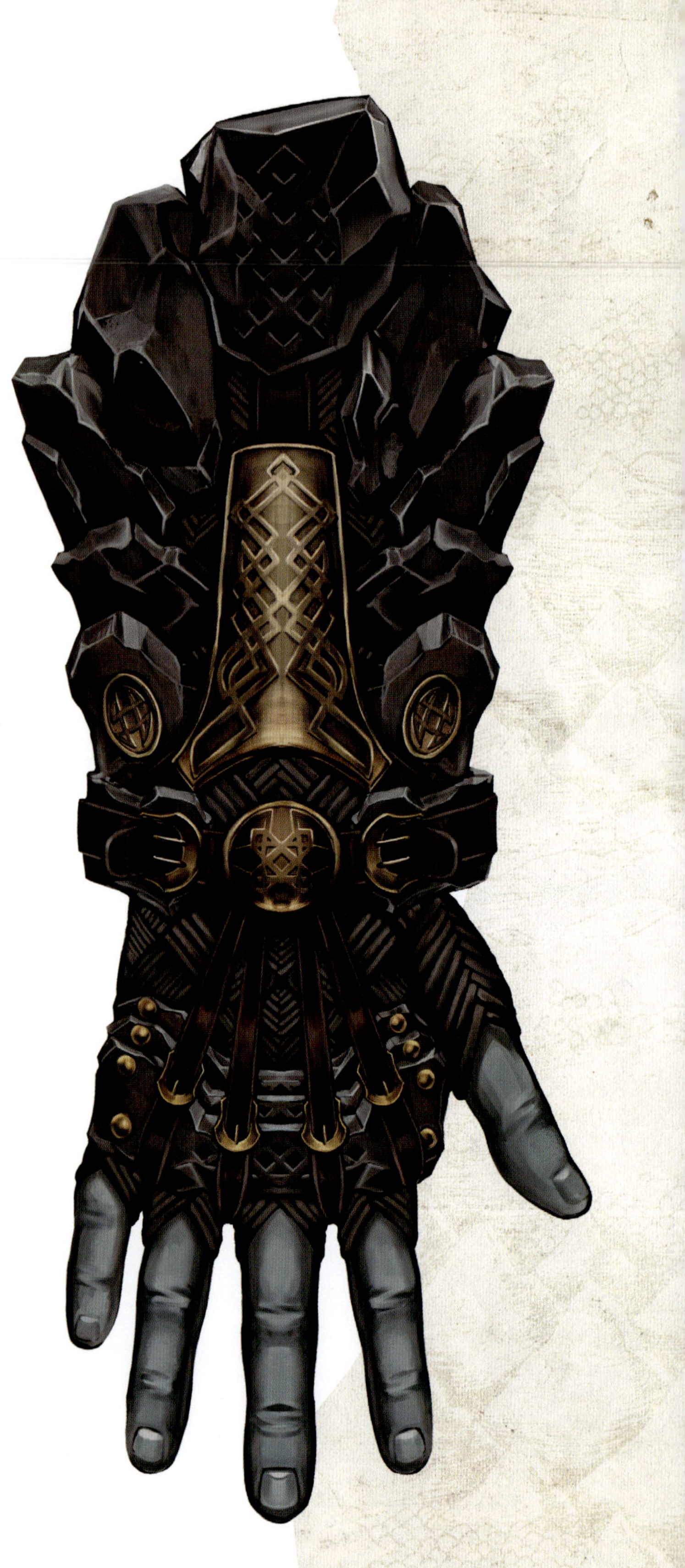

"Time touches not the beauteous stone of earth, nor the raiment jewel of gems within, scattered like stars from velvet night. Flame nor cold nor storm does the rock respect, and the holy light of radiant scions mean nothing. Even death commands little fear, for what fear does the earth have of unending slumber? Nay, the stone only respects the strength to split stone, the hand that holds titanic hammer high and brings it sweetly to the earth. Only titans such as these do titans fear."

—Tallulah Fontaine, quoting from the poem, "Primordial Hearts, Titanic Tears"

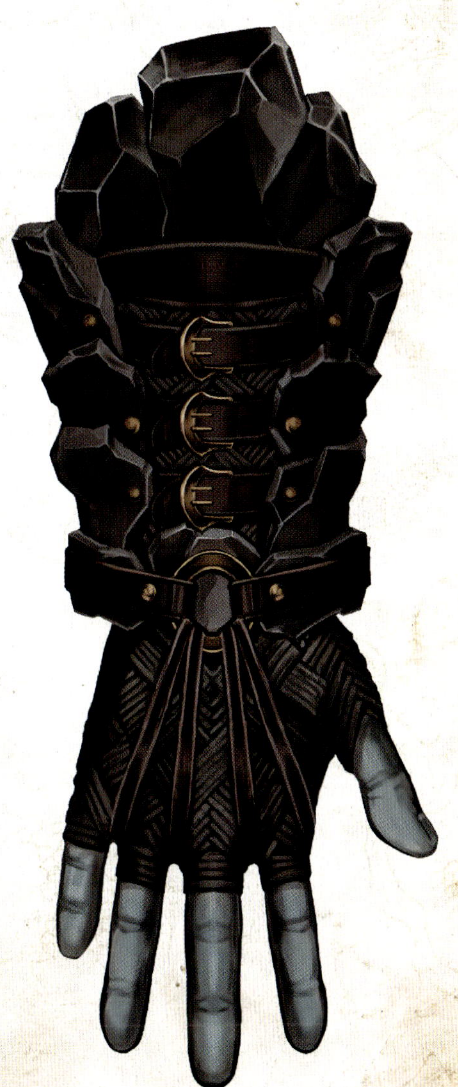

When the gloves entered their exalted state, Grog could grow to titan-like proportions and weather the elements. In one of his final adventures with Vox Machina, the Knuckles met the very titan they had been carved from. As Vox Machina made their way through the undead primordial that the Whispered One raised to assault Vasselheim, Grog felt the Knuckles vibrating, as though sensing something familiar. Grog couldn't help but feel guided by the former heart of the earth titan he now wore on his hands, taking them to the very top where the Whispered One awaited.

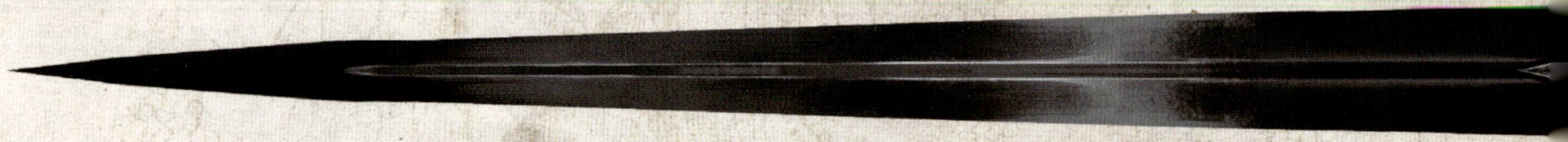

Amulet of the Drunkard

A tarnished silver chain with a stylized barrel, smelling of ale-soaked bar wood, this was a gift given to Grog from Scanlan's daughter, Kaylie, in exchange for keeping her father safe. Grog, a heavy imbiber already, took to this like a duck to water, and throughout the rest of their adventures, he found good use in turning ale into health.

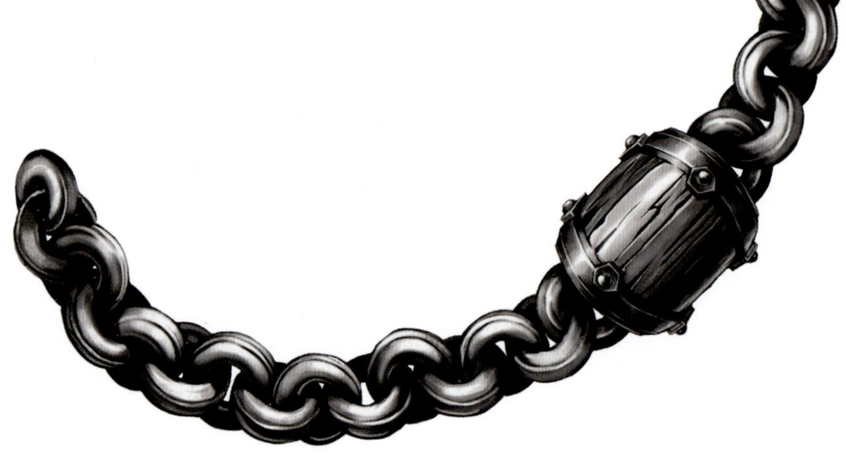

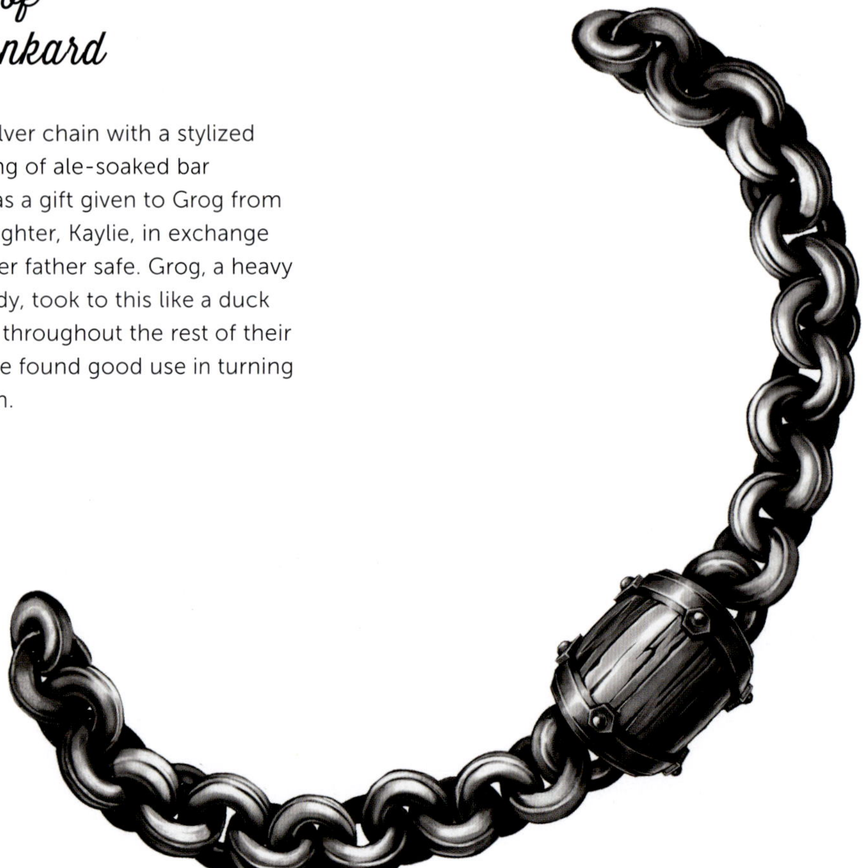

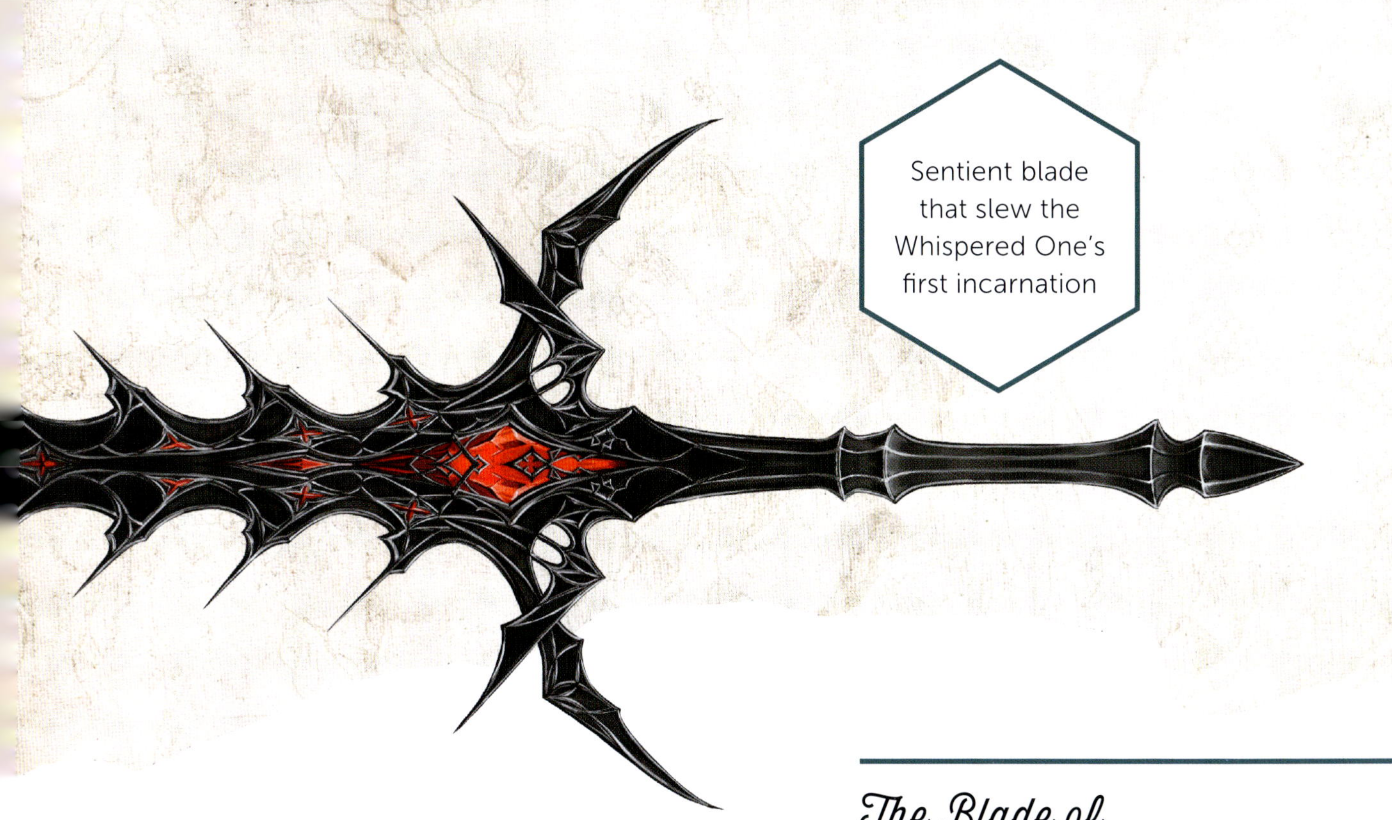

Sentient blade that slew the Whispered One's first incarnation

The Blade of Undeath's Traitor

To Groq's credit, he wasn't looking for another sentient sword to wield, especially not during the fraught time of the Whispered One's ascension into godhood. But as the infamous mage returned to Exandria, his undead follower had a role to play once more. With their will and hatred now embedded in their former blade, this traitor's only purpose was to slay the Whispered One. Buried deep within the undead earth titan, Vox Machina found the blade at dire cost, having to flee away lest they risk capture.

Sequestered in the Fey Realm and having struck a bargain with the archfey Artagan, Vox Machina rested and returned with only an hour having passed, Grog attuned to the terrible blade. Using it in the defeat of the Whispered One, the traitor almost didn't let go of Grog's mind in the time after. But with one bad experience with a sentient blade under their belt, Vox Machina didn't have a difficult time freeing Grog from the blade's influence. After, they housed it with the keepers of the Platinum Dragon.

"Undead mages are creatures of arrogance; you have to be, if you'd stave off death itself, eh? And so, why would that Whispered One ever think to fear one of his red-handed right hands? Well, he should've! I hear that's how the old bones ate gravedirt in the first place. Some traitor to his undead cause. Some raging soul who realized that the undead are selfish and any who promise you eternal life are talking outta both sides of their gray mouth. If they got a name, this traitor, it's deader than they are. All I know is they foiled that first great plot of their Whispered One and plunged a black blade straight and true into the skeletal monster. And how's that for a last laugh, eh? That so great was their hate, some part of it stayed in the steel, ready to do it all over again. Funny that. Their old master was the one who sought immortality, but its Undeath's Traitor who lived forever."

—Tallulah Fontaine, quoting an ex-Remnant of the Whispered One, whispering in the dark

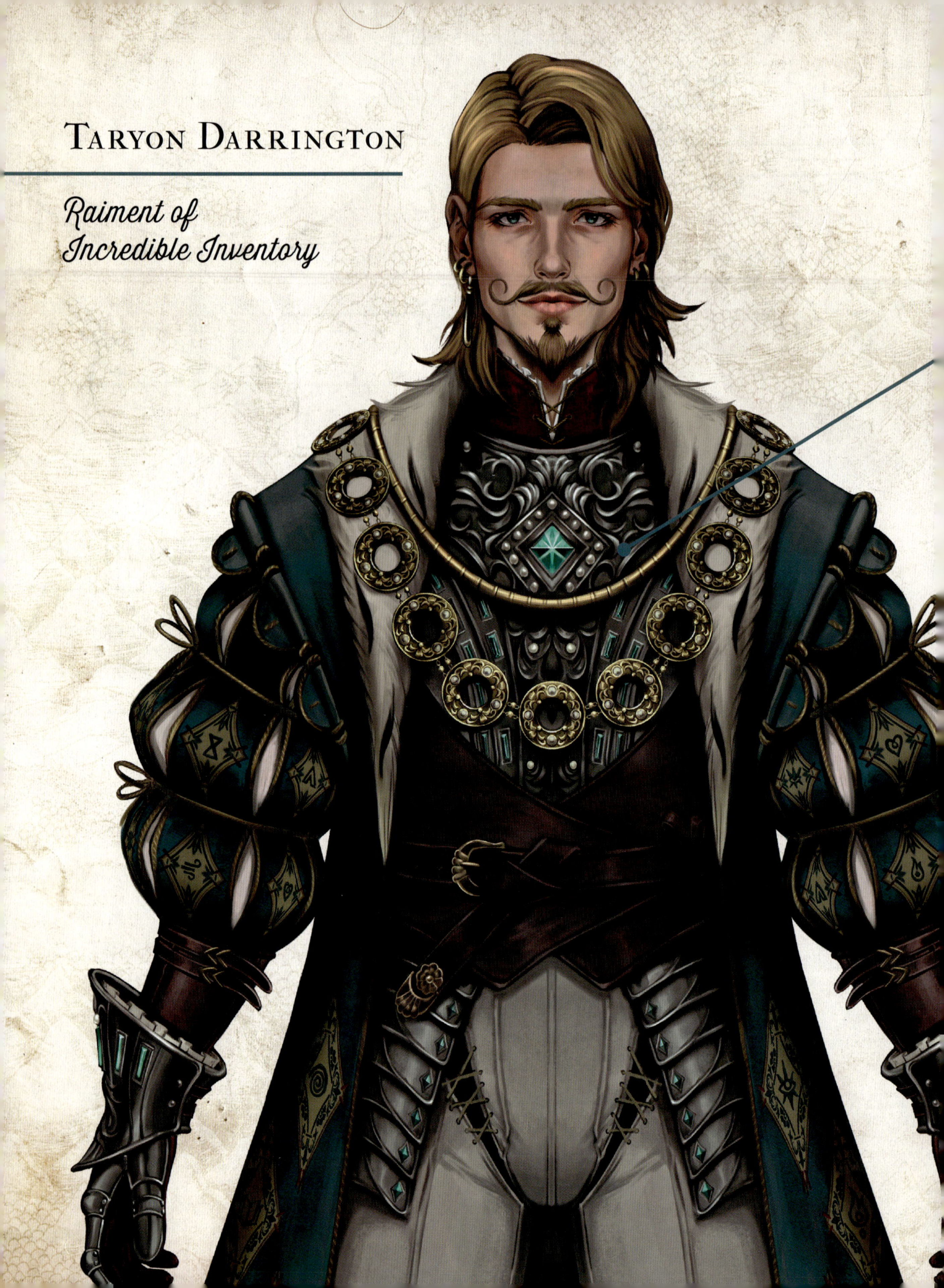
Taryon Darrington
Raiment of
Incredible Inventory

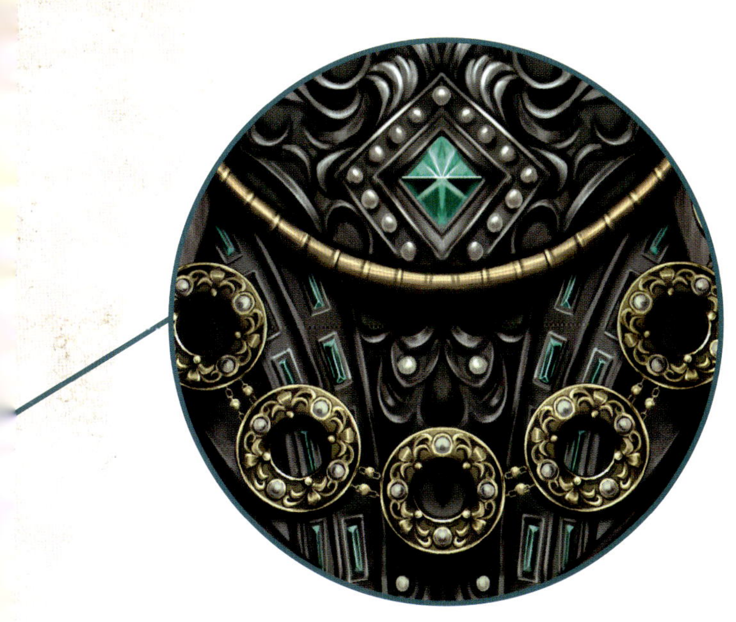

Something that "every adventurer needs to have in their pack," this ostentatious but practical robe was something Taryon Darrington utilized often. This outerwear, nestled amidst his brilliant gold and silver armor, had various tear-away patches of artificing engineering to help himself and Vox Machina during his time with the group. Such helpful instances were mostly found in the Hells, a place of much logic and little sense. Using patches to both attack various fiends and get Vox Machina into hard-to-reach places, it was one of the earliest moments where Vox Machina saw how their newest member's natural pomp and ego could greatly aid their adventures.

"Did I realize what sort of target I was painting on my back, dressing like that? Ha! Of course I didn't, not at the time. The bright colors, the countless gems and priceless weaponry and the forest green and mauve cravat and all that gold! Was it a little much? Maybe! But did it keep me alive? *Of course!* And remember, I was wearing that while facing down a kraken, too! Not that my foes appreciated it. 'Oh, is that the 810PD certified gold dragon ring out of Tal'Dorei?' it might ask as it swallowed me whole? Ha!

But the outfit wasn't *for* beasts and creatures. It was for me! I was Taryon Darrington! A brilliant young inventor. Son of a wealthy but cloistered house. I was striking out. I was going to make a name for myself. I was going to take the chip on my shoulder and make my father eat it, whether he was hungry for it or not. I had all these ideas about who I should be. I wanted my life to be like one of the stories I grew up on. And I wanted to appear just like that: like I had sprung from a story and become real. A real hero showing up for real people with real problems.

I wear *armor* now, to help with the whole 'painting a target on my back' part, but I still have the cravat. Just because you're being practical doesn't mean you can't have a little class, yes?"

—D'Rishk Dawnscale, quoting from The Daring Trials and Tribulations of Sir Taryon Darrington, page 23

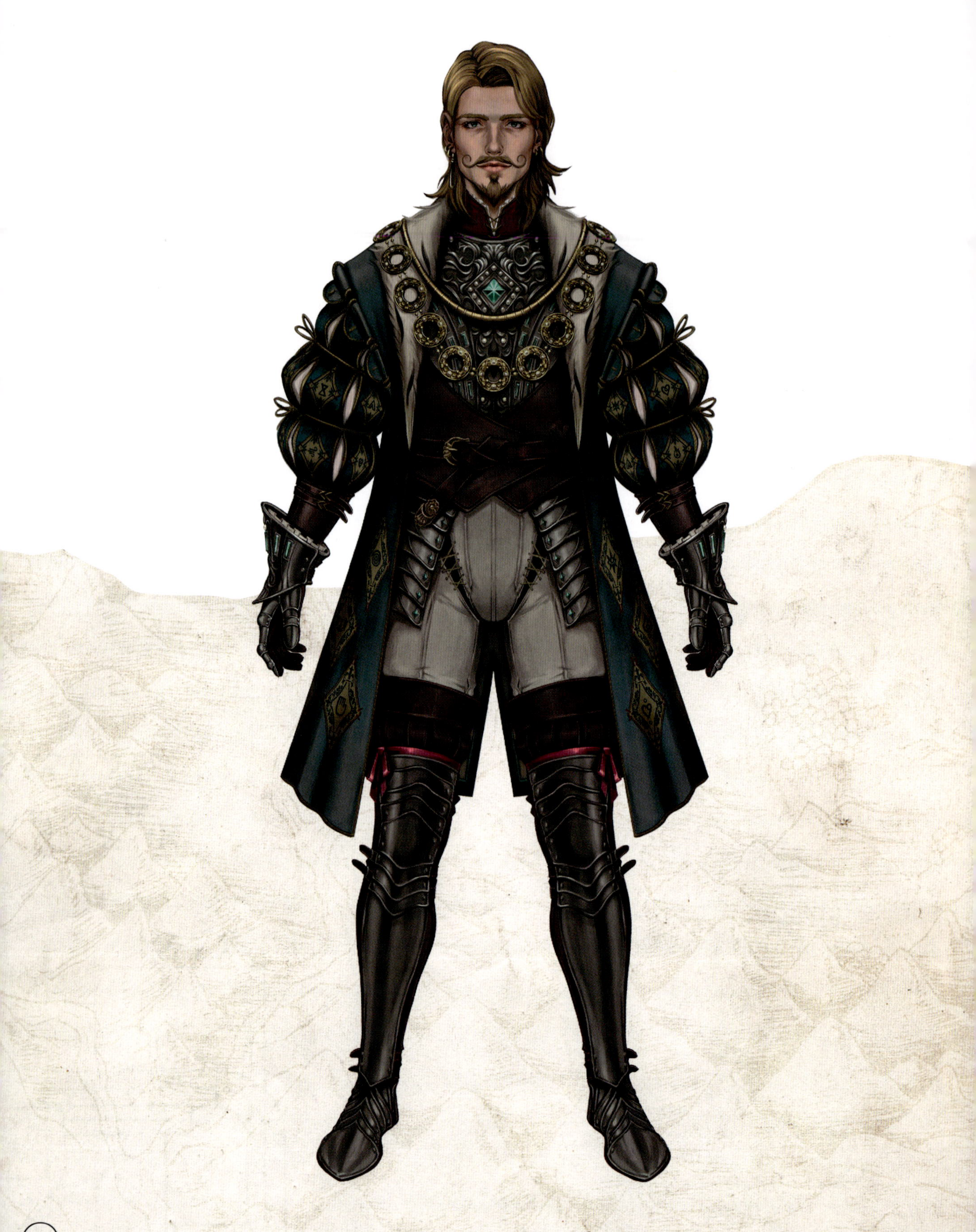

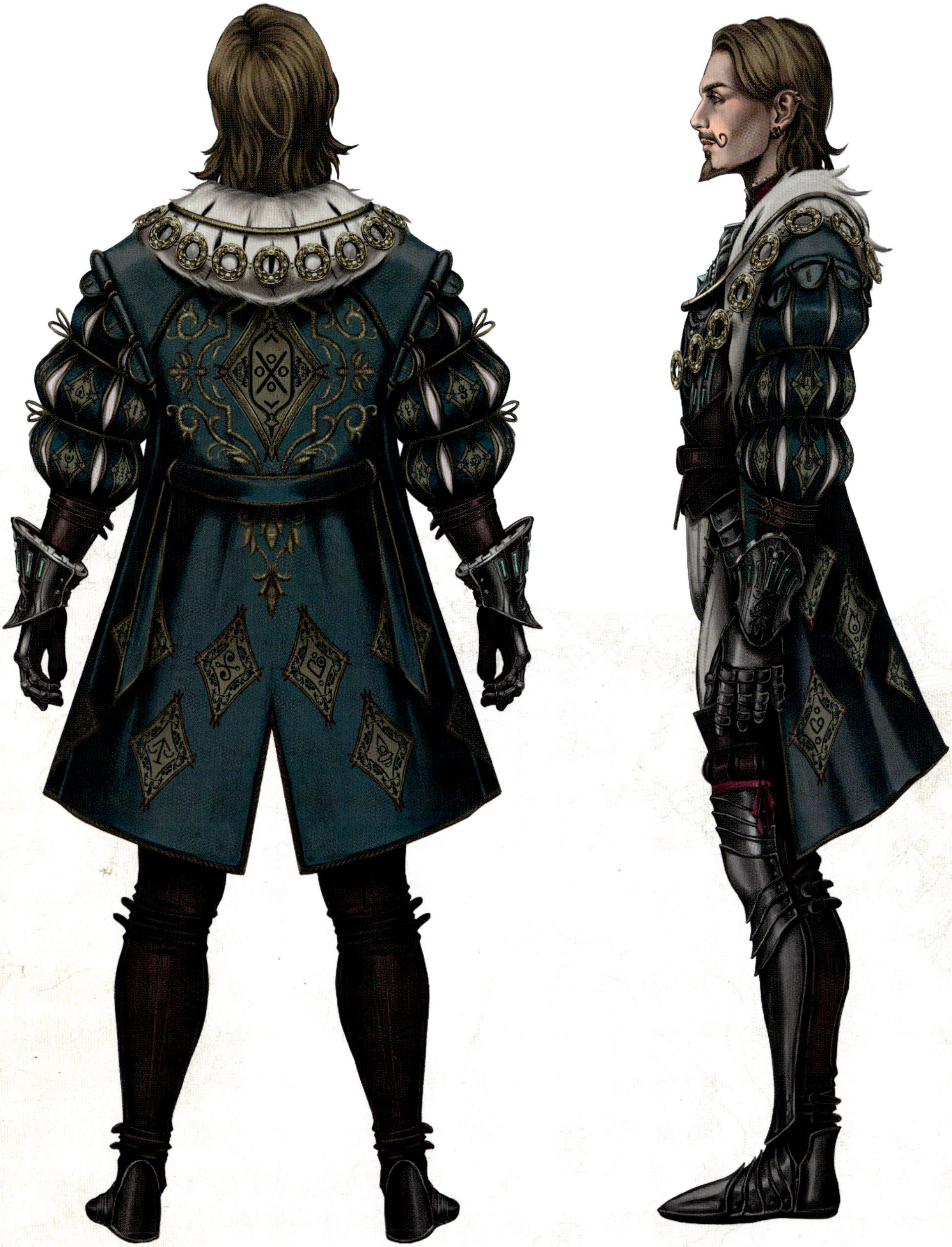

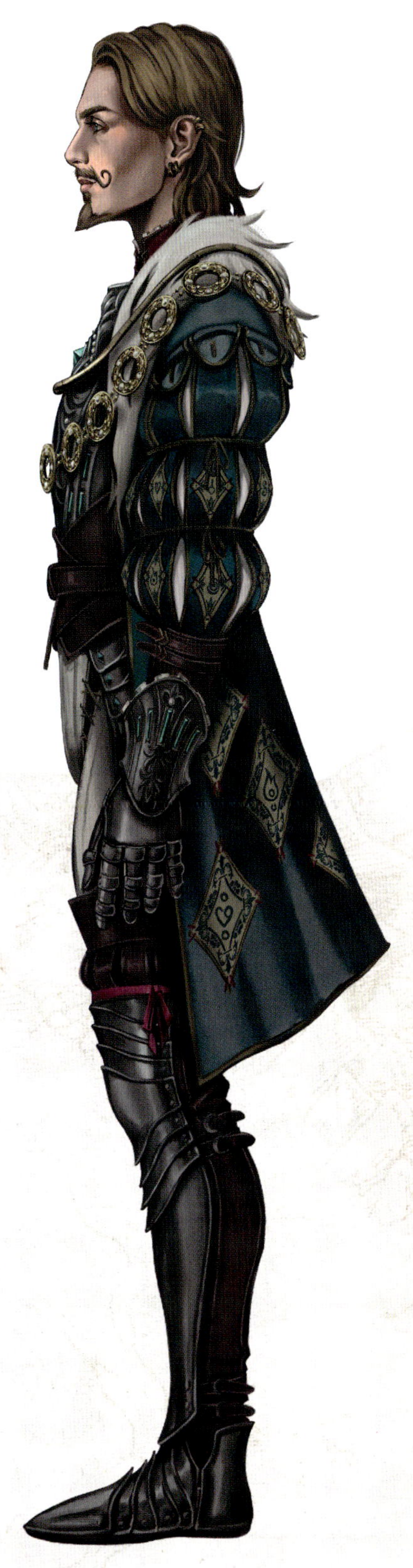

Gembearer's Helm

Yet another tool in the inventor's rather mighty and extensive tool kit, the Gembearer's Helm is quite the rare magical item. This glittering piece of headwear is studded with a plethora of diamonds, rubies, and other splendid, rare cuts of gems, each enchanted to cast powerful spells out of them. Taryon, of course, finds this massive assortment of wealth secondary to the magical prowess they gave him, as he utilized several battle spells in "training" with Vox Machina, where they tested him for his own value on the battlefield. But once Taryon was inducted into the group and aspects of his ego began to recede, others began to see through to the core of the engineer and his desire to help others.

Vox Machina began to experiment and tinker with Taryon's work and many artificing items, especially Percival, his fellow "science brother." Eventually, the two of them began to adapt the various gems on the Helm to different uses, such as light sources.

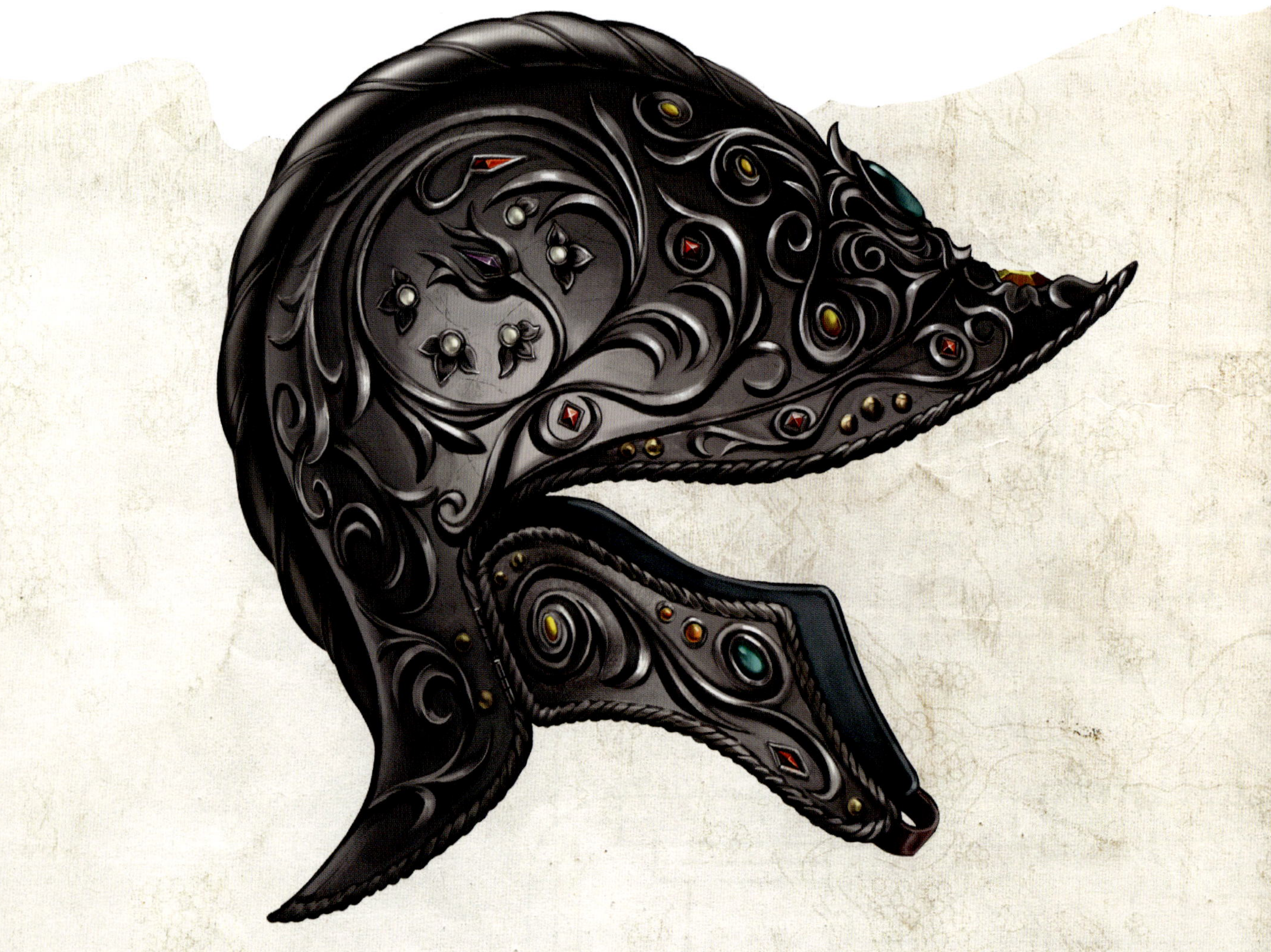

"You know, most, uh, adventurers end up returning these things. Not because they're faulty or broken, nothing like that. But because, to be frank, most of the swaggering, proud, vain creatures that buy these don't actually train with it. Don't learn to use it. And the first time they run across some kinda undead or something, they whip it out and end up stabbing themselves somewhere quite unpleasant. I tend not to have a return policy, but when I see the limp or the stitches, my heart goes soft. I thought the golden boy who bought one from me, that Darrington fellow, I for sure thought he was going to lose a limb. And he almost did. Came in the next day, brandishing it at me. But instead of demanding money back, he asked how to use it better. Kept coming back, day after day. I saw him sparring with that big metal friend of his.

And after a couple of weeks, he thanked me for my time, paid me way too much, and left. I really thought he'd give up or hurt himself, but turns out, he had a lot more heart and a lot more smarts than I think most give him credit for. Hope he turned out okay."

—Tallulah Fontaine, overheard at a tavern in Deastok

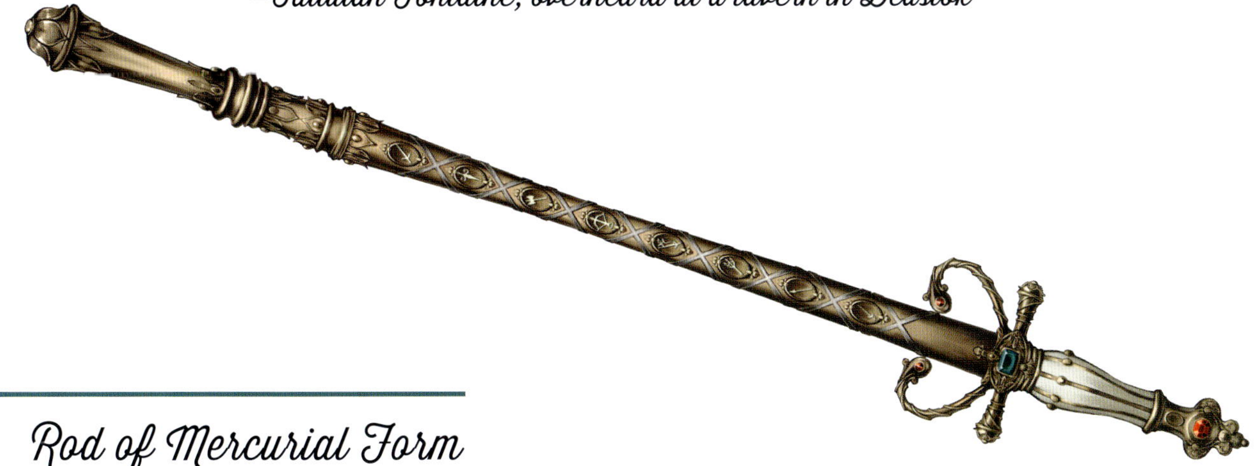

Rod of Mercurial Form

The primary melee weapon of Taryon Darrington, this quicksilver-colored, enchanted rod has the unique ability to morph into any weapon the bearer states, be it a sword, axe, dagger, spear, and more. Of course, Taryon being Taryon, he usually used this item's unique properties to impress others, especially Grog (some would argue the most impressionable member of Vox Machina). Though Taryon demonstrated the rod's shape-shifting abilities when they first met in Marquet, Vox Machina wondered if Taryon could even wield it properly or if he was just using it to show off. But in a surprising move from a surprising person, Taryon possessed the martial ability to use the rod in its many forms throughout his time with Vox Machina. To this day, he still wields it in his time with the Darrington Brigade and on his frequent nonprofit adventures.

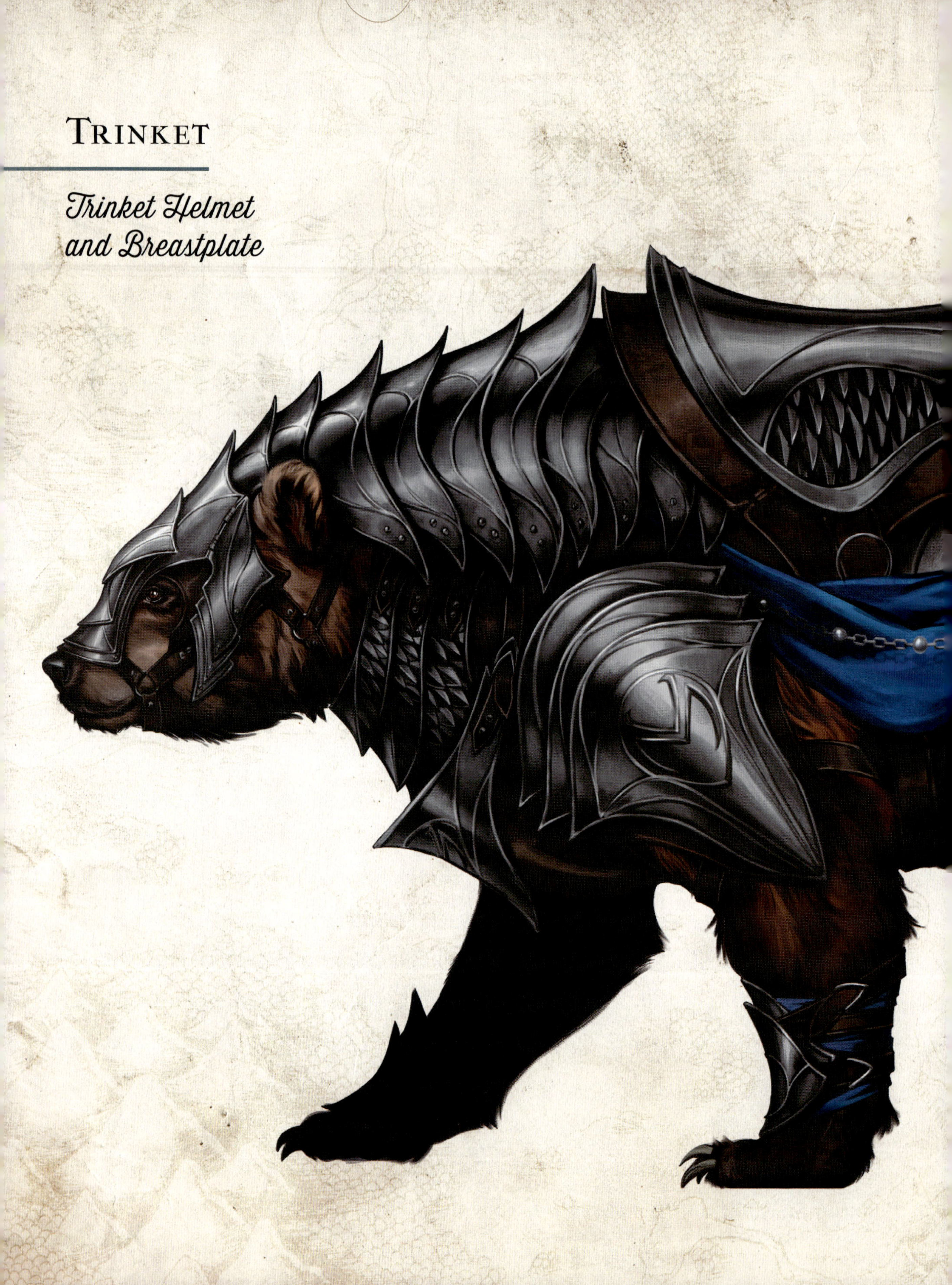

Trinket

Trinket Helmet and Breastplate

The ursine companion to Vex'ahlia and truly another member of the Vox Machina family, Trinket was a ferocious beast on the battlefield, baring his teeth and wielding his claws to protect Vex'ahlia ever since he was a cub. However, he was still flesh and blood, and often Vex'ahlia grew terrified something would happen to him. Harvesting the armored hide off a stone-digging beast, Grog was able to hand the material over to a blacksmith in Emon who forged a set of armor and a helmet for Trinket to wear into battle, increasing his natural resistance. And though he often spent time in the Raven's Slumber to keep him from harm, when he came into the battlefield, Trinket was never to be underestimated, especially when he showed up in his own set of custom armor.

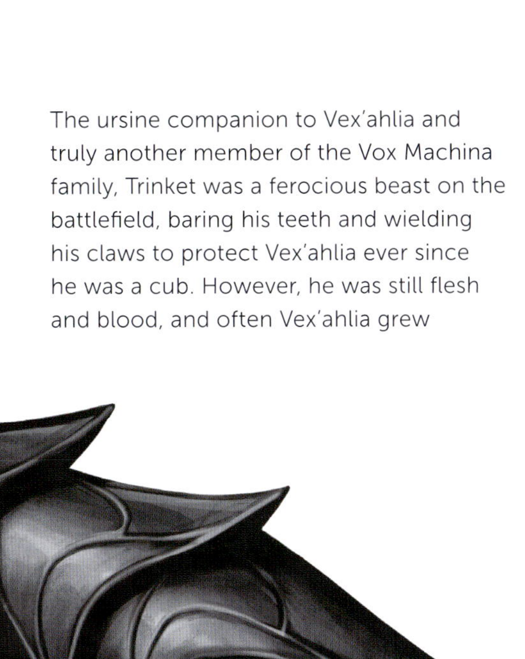

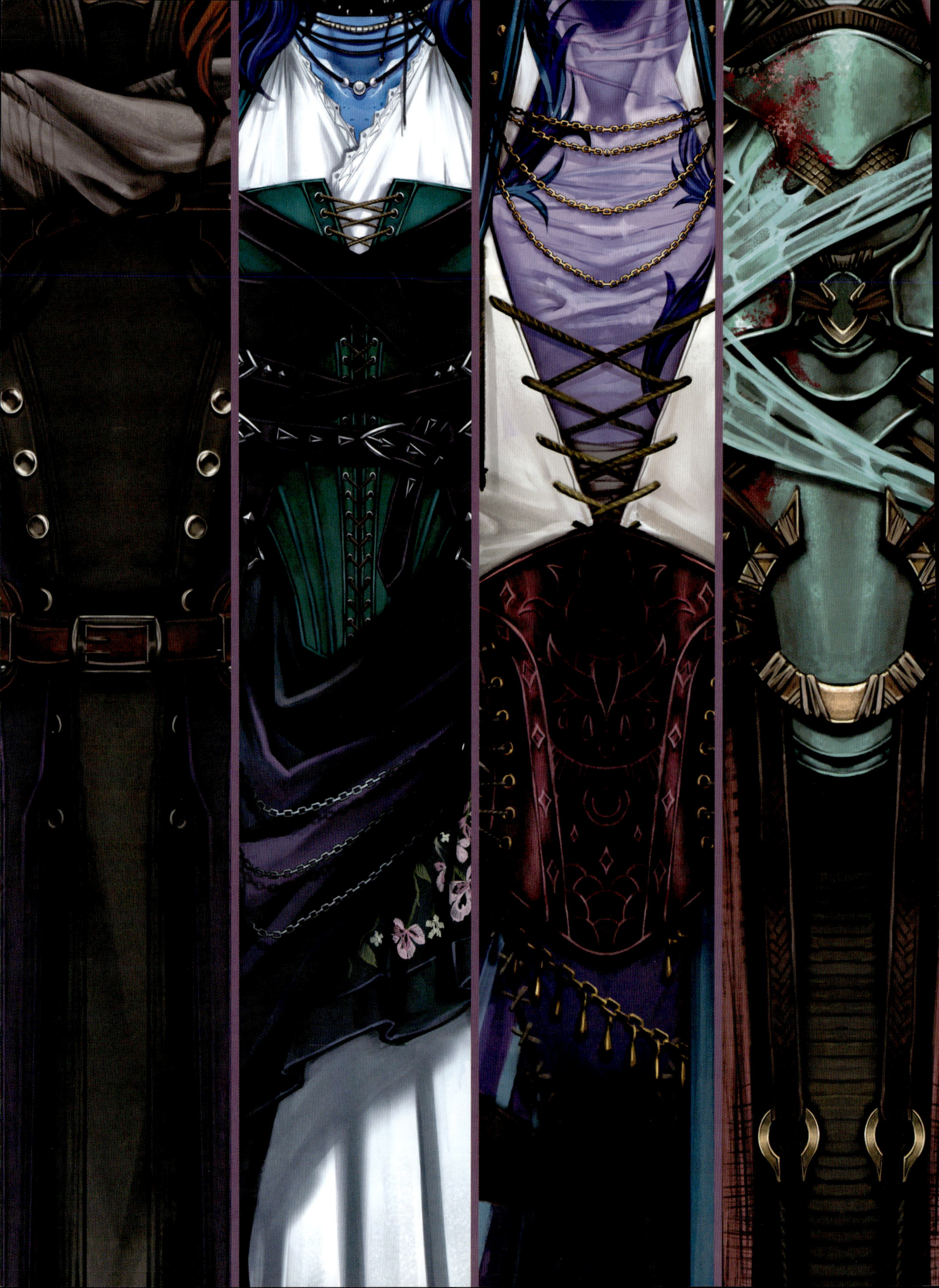

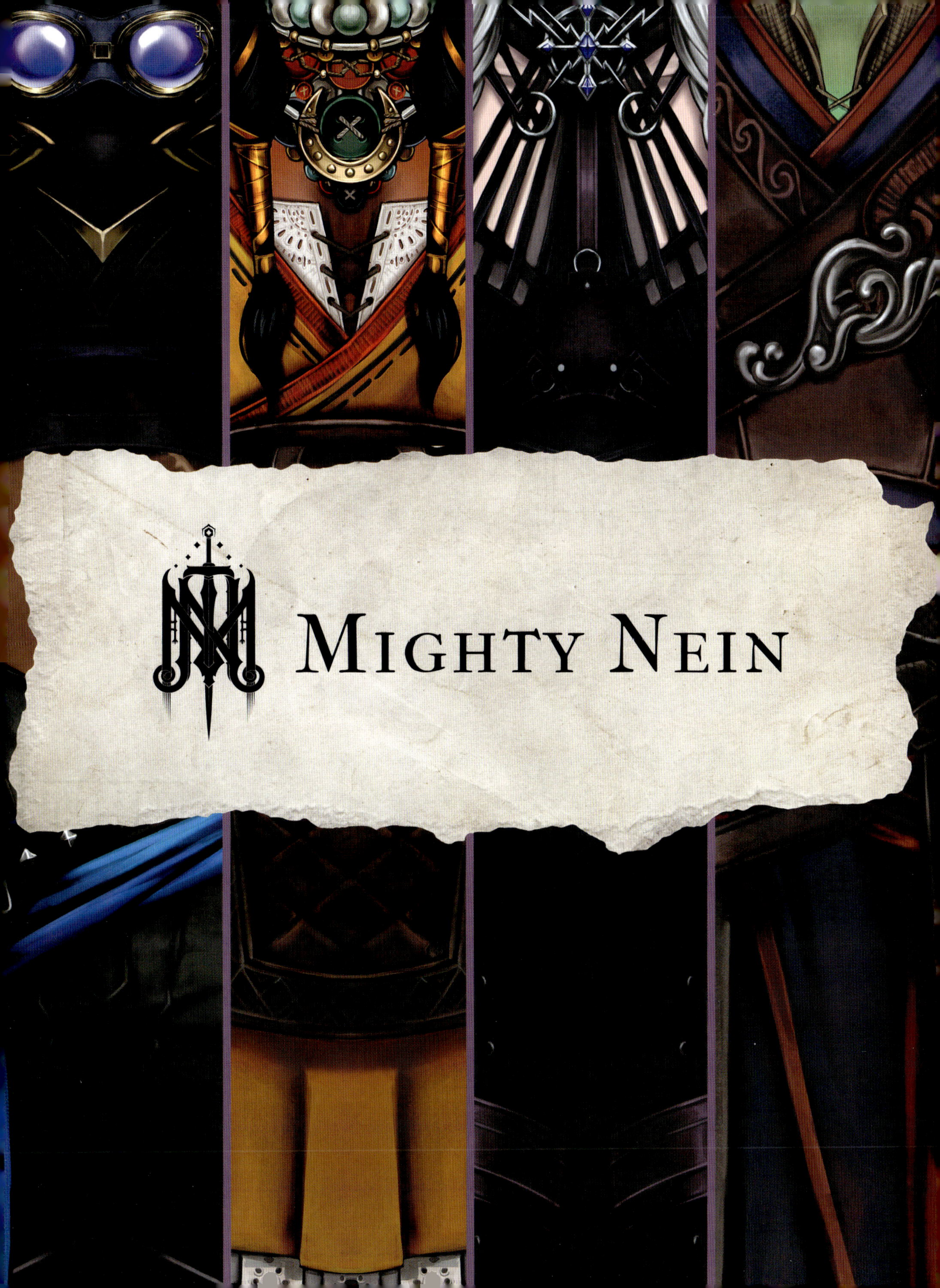
Mighty Nein

Mighty Nein

"For every hero, king, or god history remembers, there are hundreds who are forgotten. These people do not earn open praise, are not transposed into song or meter, and often don't wish for either. A good lesson, this: that were it not for the hard work of the many unsung heroes of Exandria, this world would have fallen to ruin some long time ago. And though history will not dedicate tomes to the deeds of Wildemount's Mighty Nein, we of Rosohna can and will. A group of wayward people seeking answers or adventure, each hoping to find that missing piece to make themselves whole; later, they'd see that it was each other they were truly seeking.

It was early days for these ragtag, wary new friends when they came across a precious Luxon beacon, one of the holy artifacts of our people. They were plunged into a world of politics and peril none of them desired, and yet, when faced with injustice, answered that call no matter how reluctant, even losing one of their own. Despite going to sea to skirt the war that had begun to boil at the fringes of the Empire, the Nein would be pulled into the conflict of their own volition. Returning our precious Beacon, they spent time in Xhorhas amongst the very folk the Empire had declared war upon. And as they grew closer, becoming family to one another, they found themselves at the crossroads of history time and again.

They battled fiends and the deathless chosen of the Betrayer Gods. They walked the halls of the demiplane known as the Archmage's Bane, confronting mages from the distant past. They faced ancient witches and eldritch patrons, breaking old curses and forging new oaths. By helping one another, the Nein's fate as a group became intertwined with that of the very continent. But their greatest challenge still lay ahead, as their slain comrade Mollymauk returned to life. Except it was not him but Lucien, the ambitious blood hunter whose first death created Molly to begin with. Dead set on resuming his holy mission with his blood hunter family, the Tombtakers, Lucien began his bloody work.

The Mighty Nein pursued him and his hunters to Eiselcross, into the ruins of ancient Aeor, and finally into the Astral Sea. There, Lucien's mission found him merging with the shattered minds of a living city, jettisoned across the planes during the Calamity, adrift and mad for centuries. The Nein stopped him and saved not just Exandria, but the very denizens of the planes themselves . . . and none of them will ever know of the Nein's heroic efforts. But here, in the shrouded halls of Rosohna, we will remember. And I promise, by the light of the Luxon, we will never forget those Mighty Nein, who stood against the horrors of the world time and time again and said, 'No.'"

—Oren Keth'Kaylis, Final Oral Recording into the Marble Tomes Conservatory, File Name: "The Mighty Nein of Exandria"

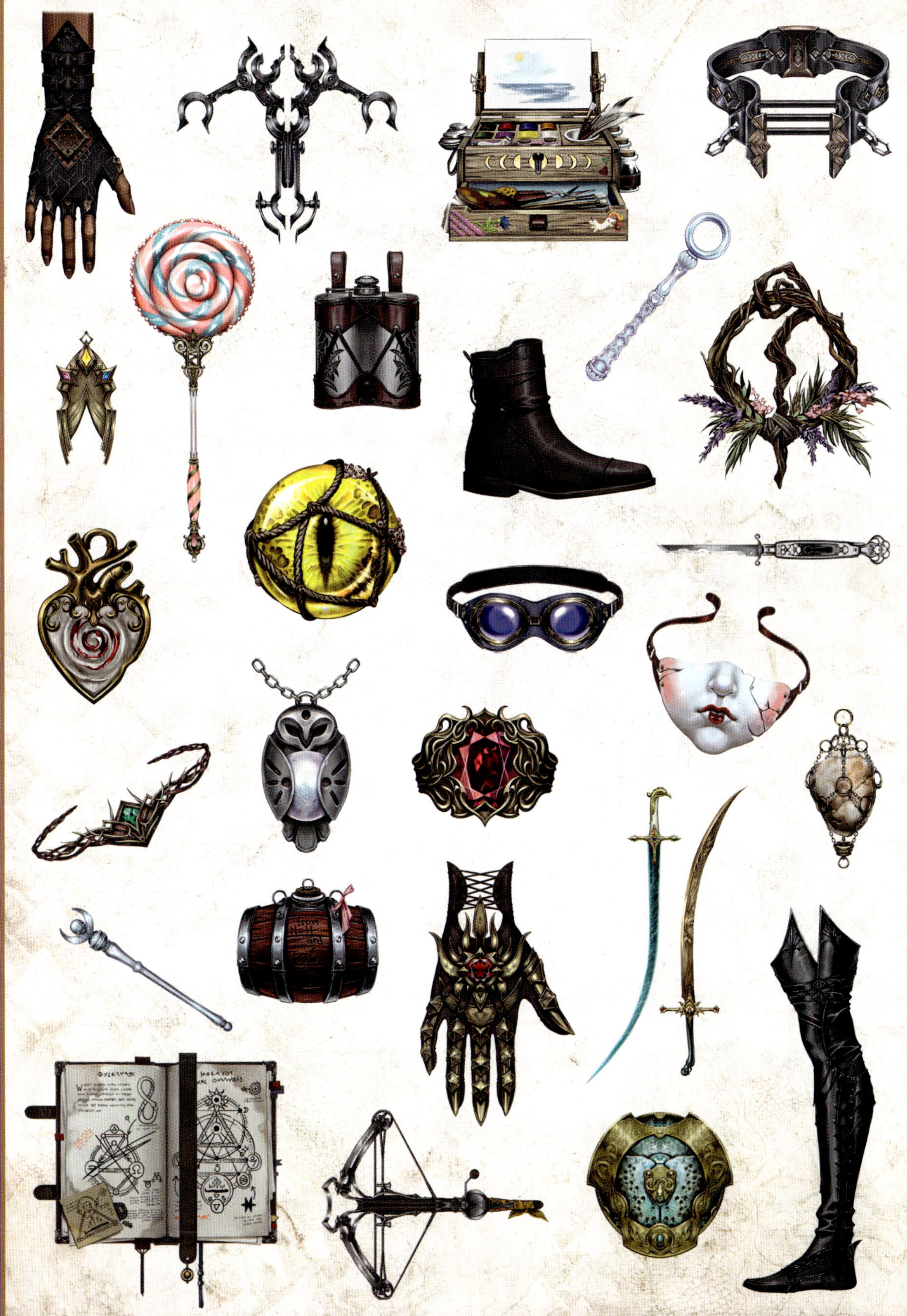

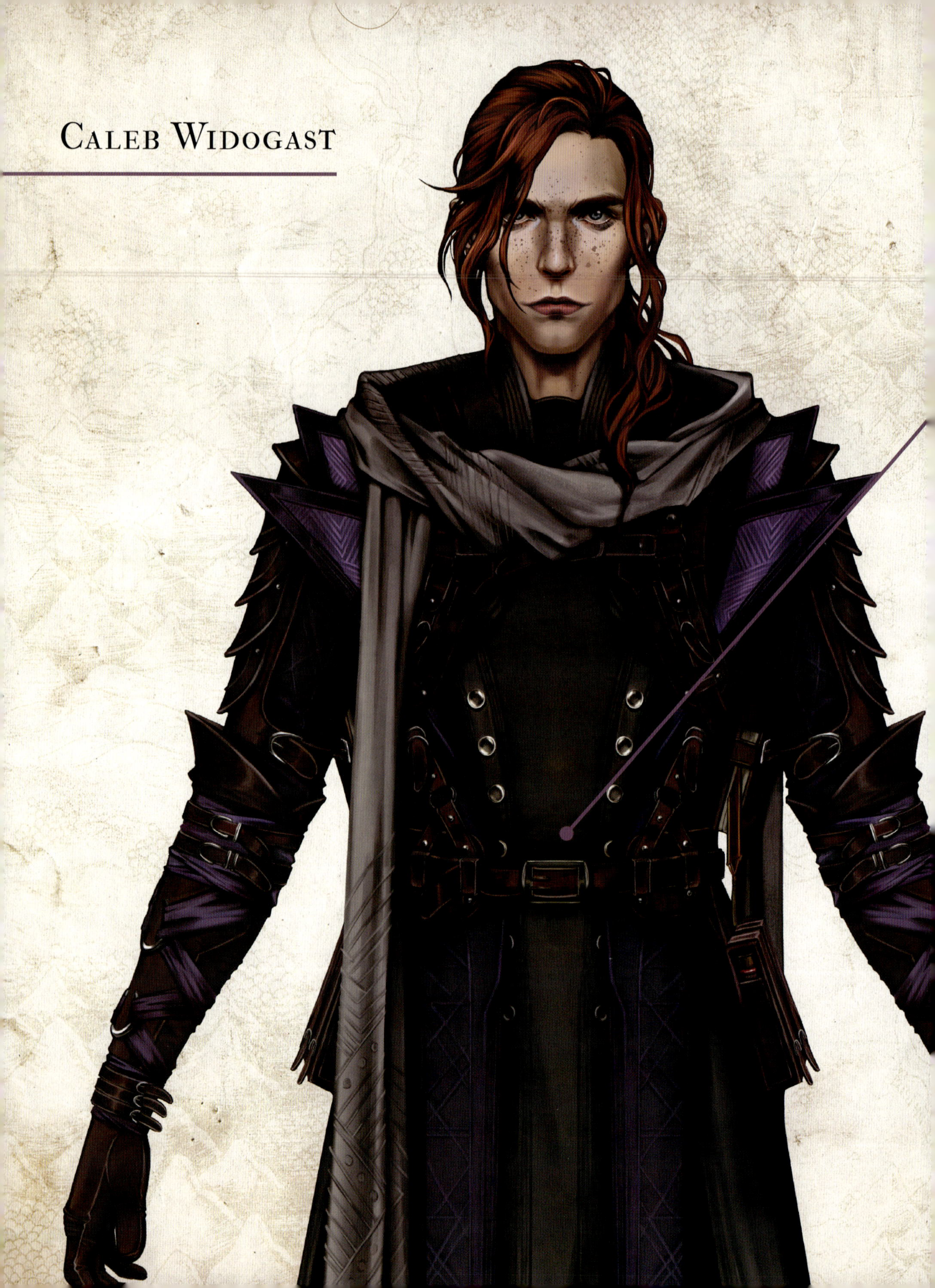

Caleb Widogast

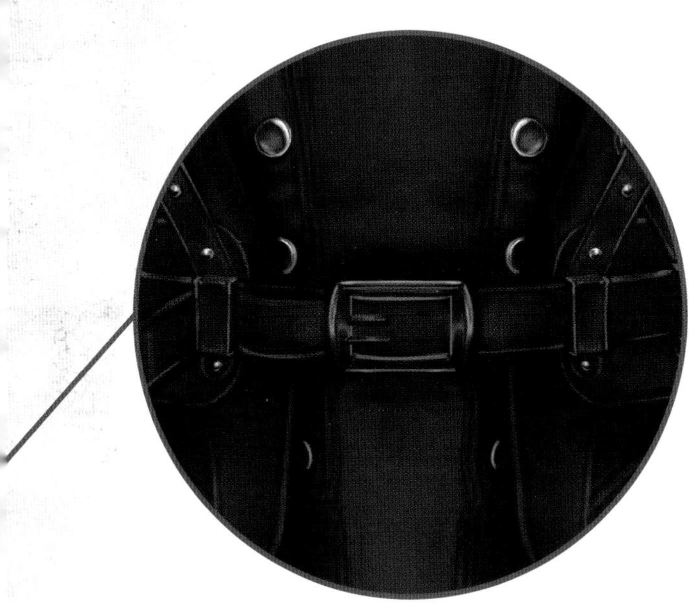

"From the Bright Queen's own assessment at the time of their first meeting: 'Dirty. Disheveled. Mud-caked. Faded. As though he might melt away into the background of any corner of Wildemount. As though any sturdy attention might make him wilt into nothing at all. And yet, in his eyes, a fire waited. Something burned in him, and when he held that Beacon before me, I saw as much as I heard the power within him. Diminished, but potent.'

Caleb Widogast remade everything about himself after his fleeing of the Vergessen Sanitorium, but he could not hide the spark of the arcane within him. Even the most humble of hedgemages possess it, and hiding it is akin to hiding one's very soul. And Widogast tried his best to remain hidden from the world and the archmages seeking him. He must be commended for the attempt. Just as he must be commended for when he stepped back into the light. For we met Widogast as he sat on the cusp of self-actualization. When he recognized that the time to hide was coming to an end, and he could embrace what came next, or limp toward the future.

And like any good wizard, Caleb Widogast sought control of his narrative and made it so. From his humble and dirty coat and shirt, the worn leather straps of his spellbook holster, he took on the raiment of the studied practitioner of the arcane. That is to say, regardless of what he wore, he finally began to stand with his head held high. He finally stopped hiding the fire inside him."

—Oren Keth'Kaylis

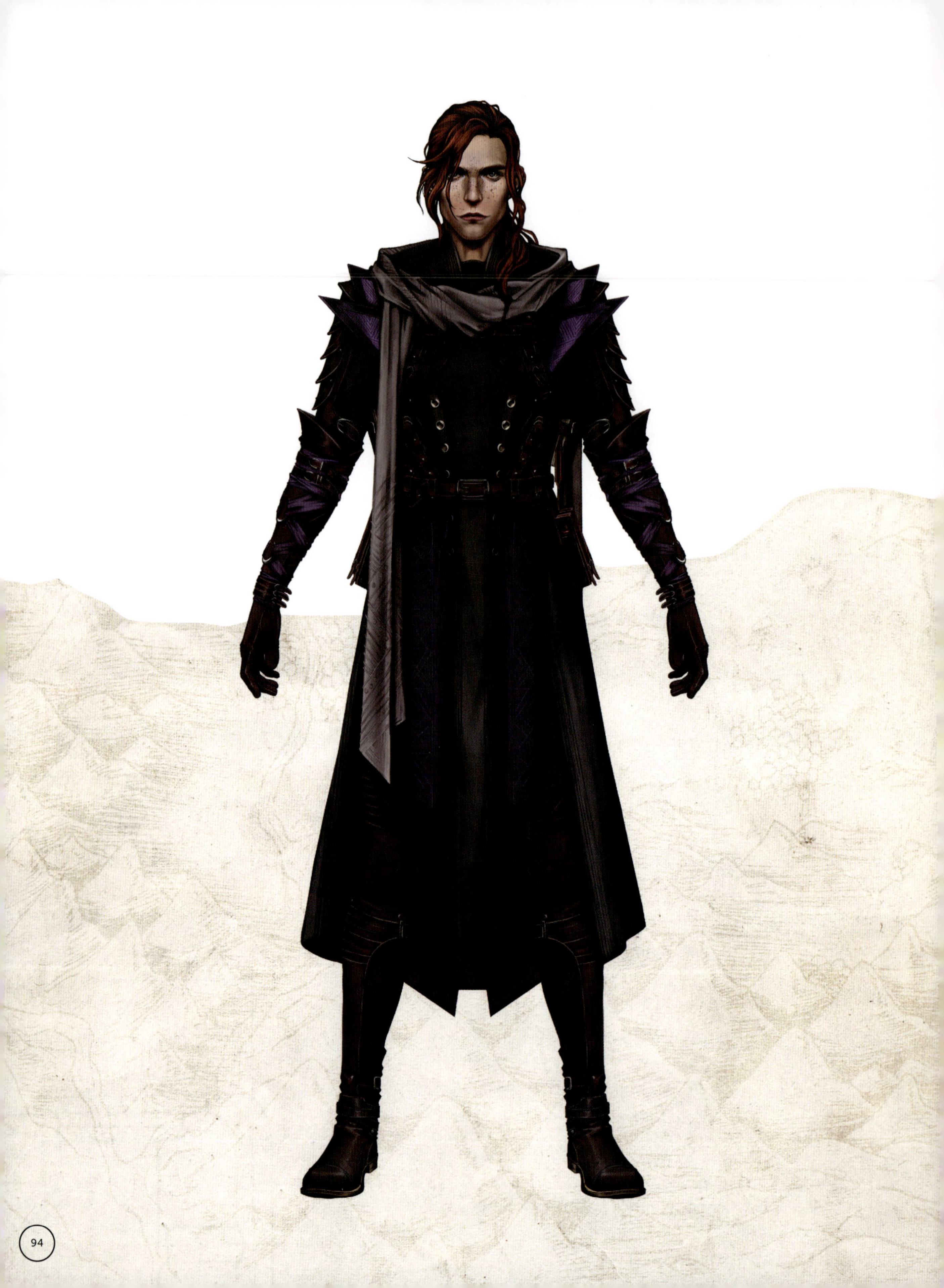

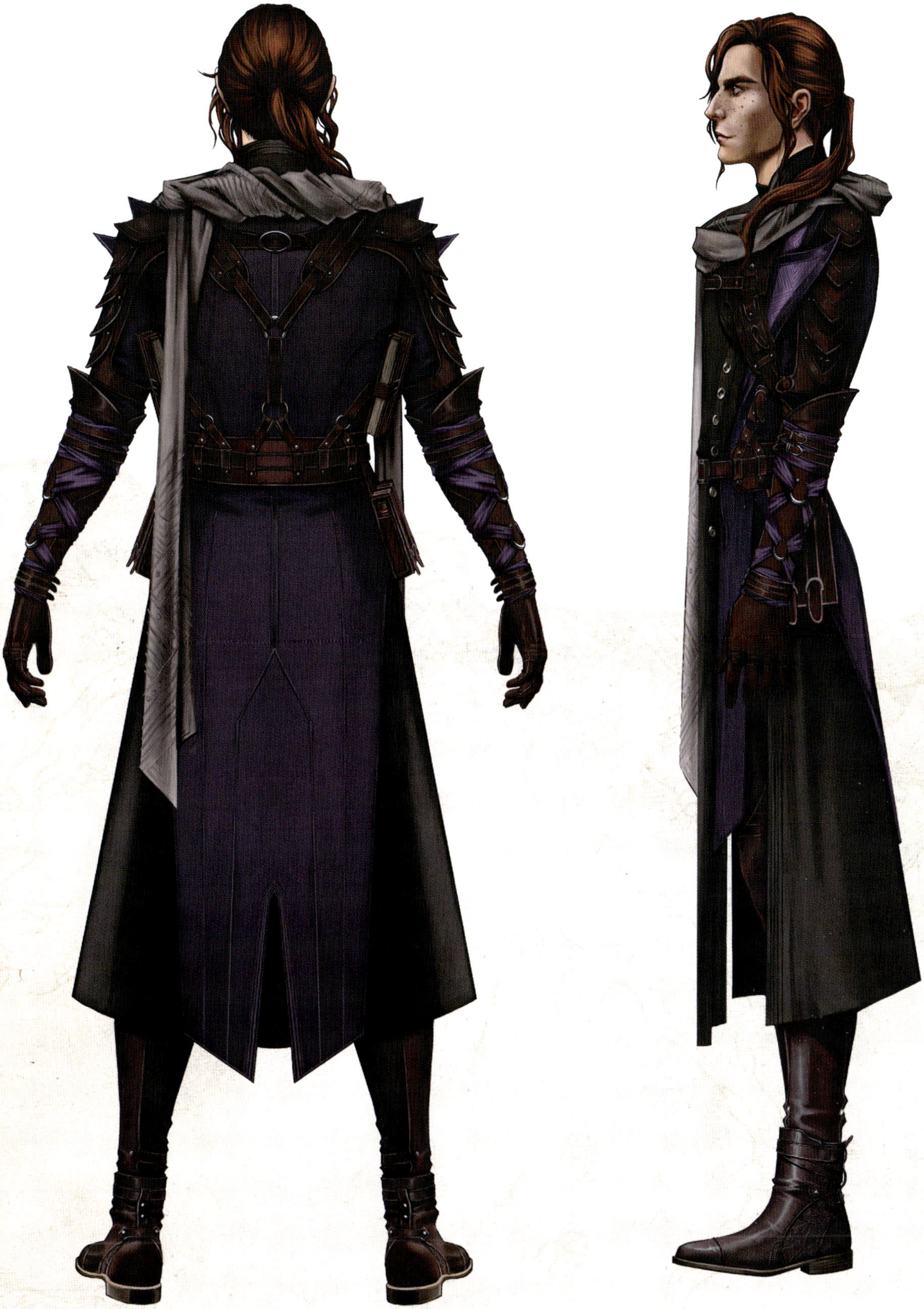

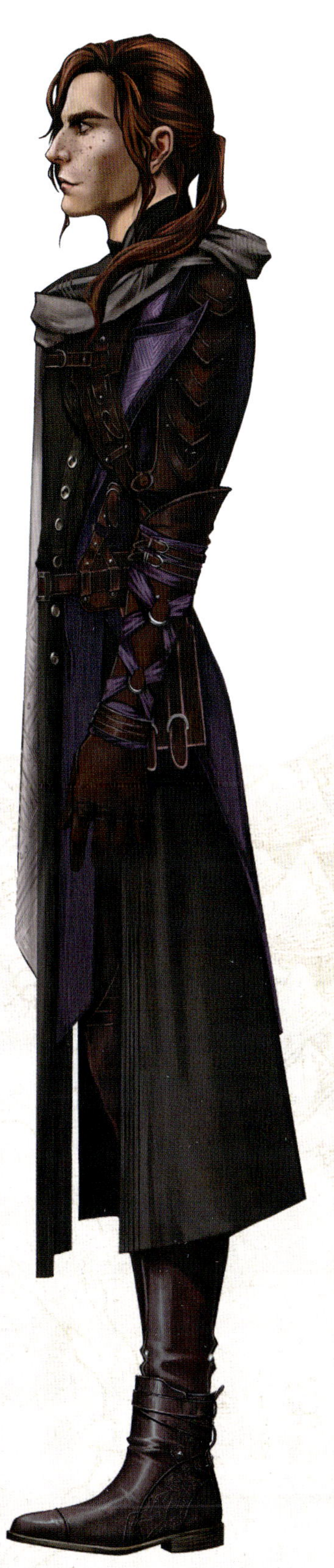

Widogast's Wizard's Spellbook

Caleb Widogast carried two tomes on him at all times: one of them was a book of letters he kept in honor of his deceased parents, filled with everything he wished he could tell them. The other was his arcane spellbook, which required enchanted paper and ink. Caleb began to cobble together his new spellbook, his old one presumably taken when he was admitted to the Vergesson Sanatorium. But within his new spellbook, Caleb wrote down what he remembered from his days as a young wizard in the Soltryce Academy. He brought forth the remnants of cantrips from memory, and some rudimentary spells of protection, alertness, and defense. And as his time with the Mighty Nein began, one thing became clear: Caleb was as hungry as the rest of them (though what he sought were spells).

Some were purchased from the shelf of Pumat Sol in the Invulnerable Vagrant, others found in the depths of shrouded tombs, demiplanes, and far-flung ruins, a few taught to him by arcane mentors and allies, and still some were born from the frenzied flame of Caleb's intellect and ambition. To this day, his spellbook remains in the holster at his side, packed to the brim with some of the most powerful arcane magics on Exandria. What happened to the other book is only for the dead to know.

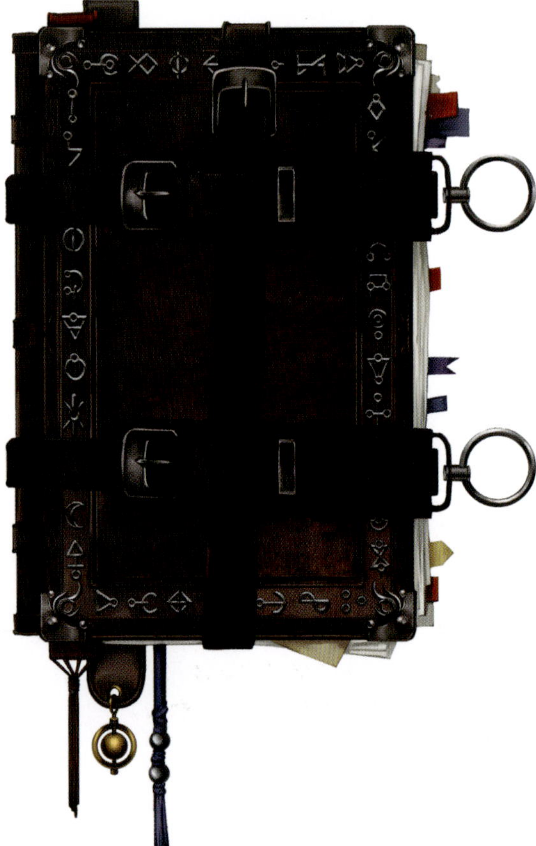

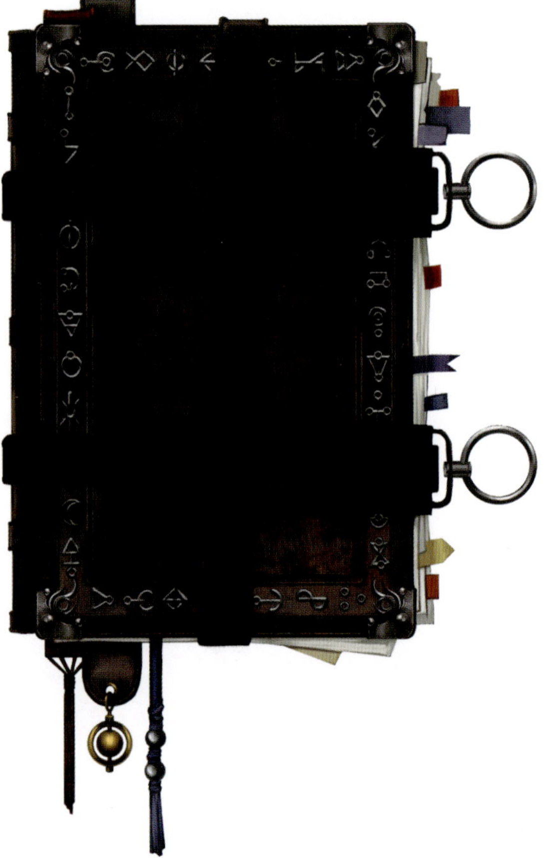

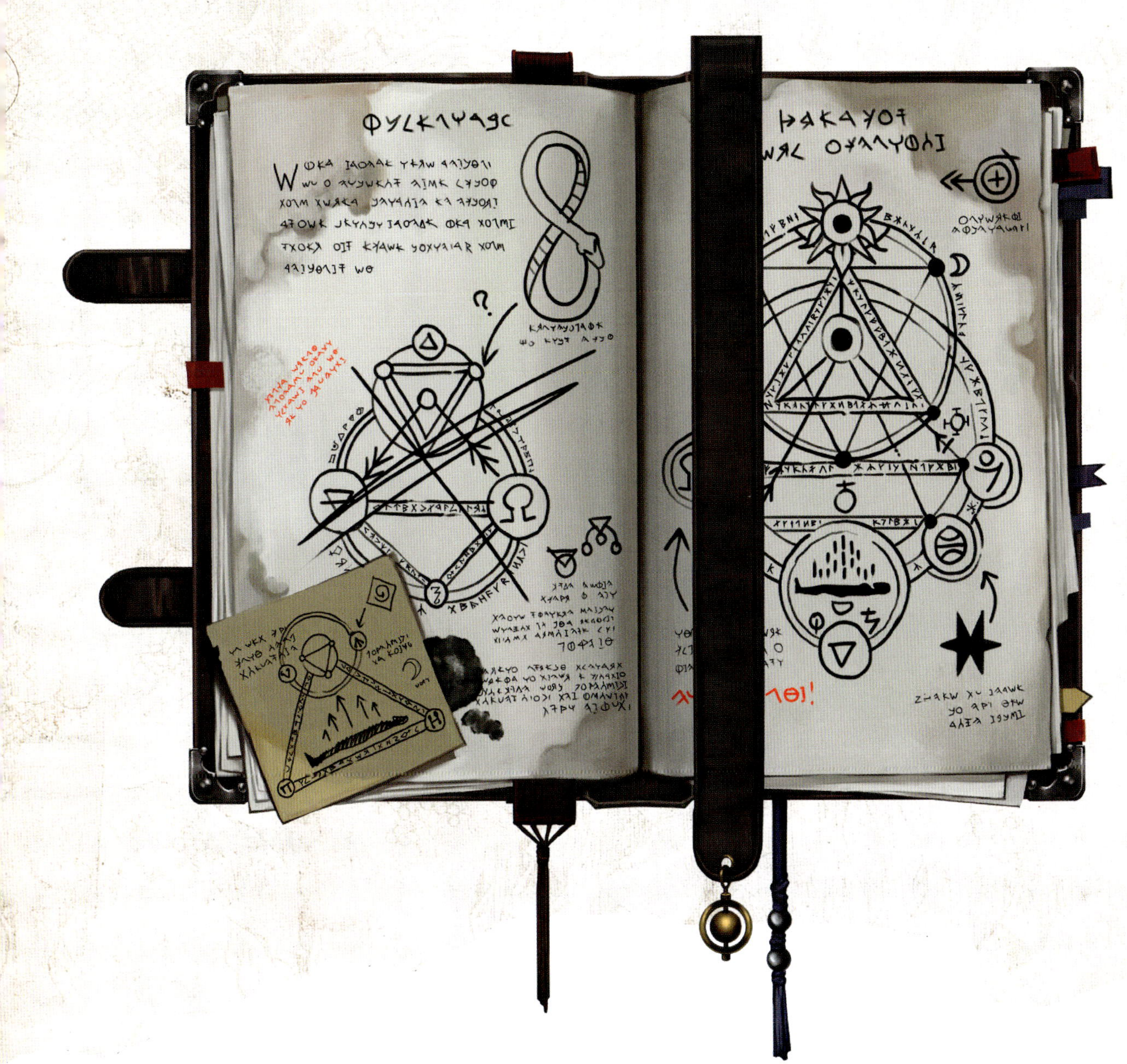

"As a practitioner of the arcane arts, I can assure you, an arcanist's spellbook is their soul on vellum. It is more than a priest's holy text, more than a dark magus's contract, more than a bard's songbook. An arcanist doesn't ask for magic or wake up to it or bargain for it. They learn it. They study. They research. Every spell in my book is more than ink. Each one acts as a marker on the long road of my life. When I turn to these pages and read these spells, I can taste the morning coffee the day I cracked a certain theorem. I can smell the tallow of a candle burnt low as I notated and translated dragonkin lexicons into a teleportation spell. I can see the joy on my face, the tears in my eyes, as the ink of a newly written spell glows cobalt and silver and I know I did it."

—Oren Keth'Kaylis

Stormrider Boots

These dark leather magical boots were found by the Mighty Nein in the lair of Vokodo, an extraplanar being who made a home for itself on the island of Rumblecusp, setting itself up as a god. In his hoard, these boots were found, as well as other magical items. Becoming a part of Caleb's arsenal, these magical boots gave the wizard a burst of sudden flight, using the power of storms to fire him into the air for a short time and powerful arcs of lightning to discourage attacks and pursuit. Used in the later days of their adventures, Caleb used this to escape danger across the ruins of Aeor and the Eiselcross ice fields, evading undead, dragons, and blood hunters.

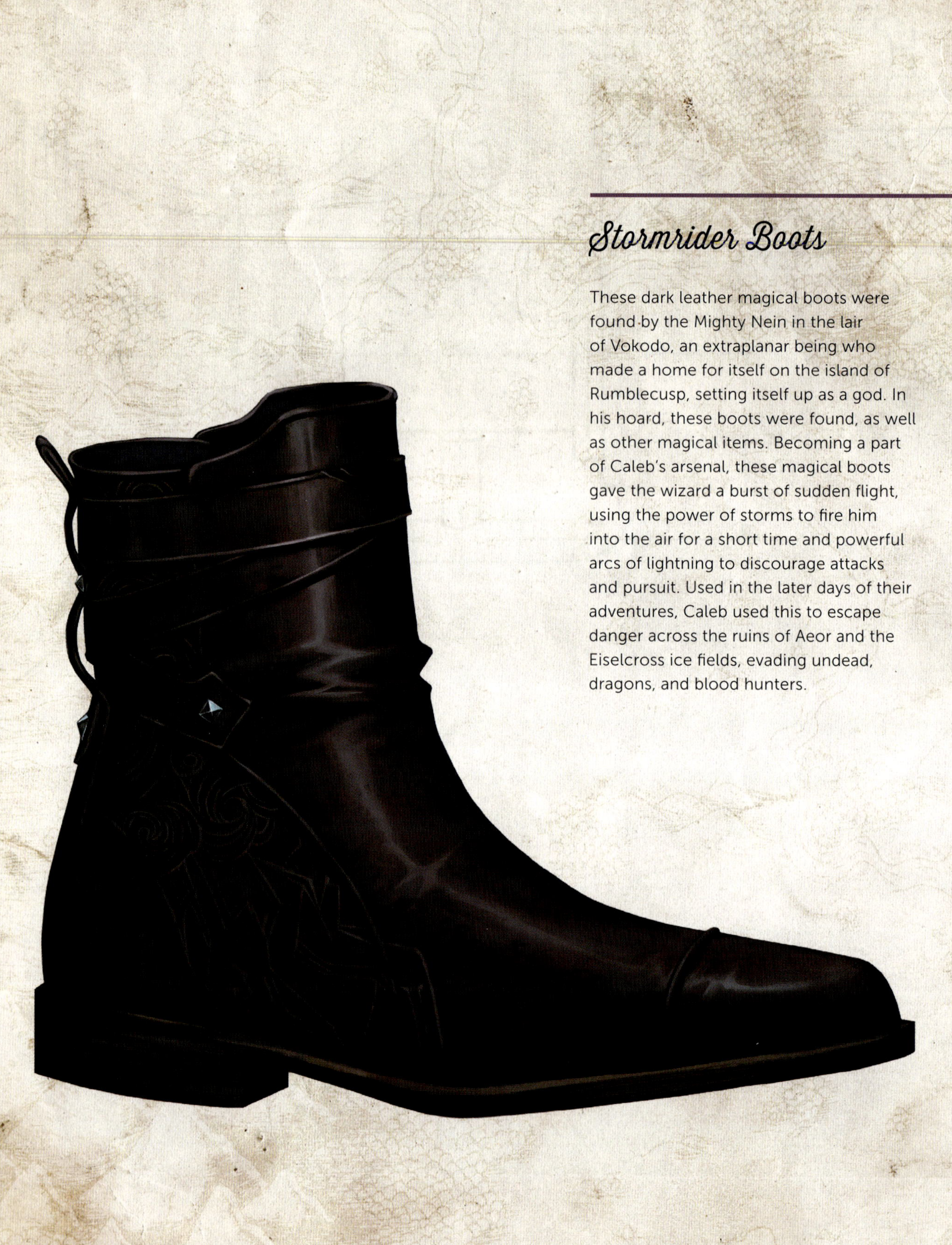

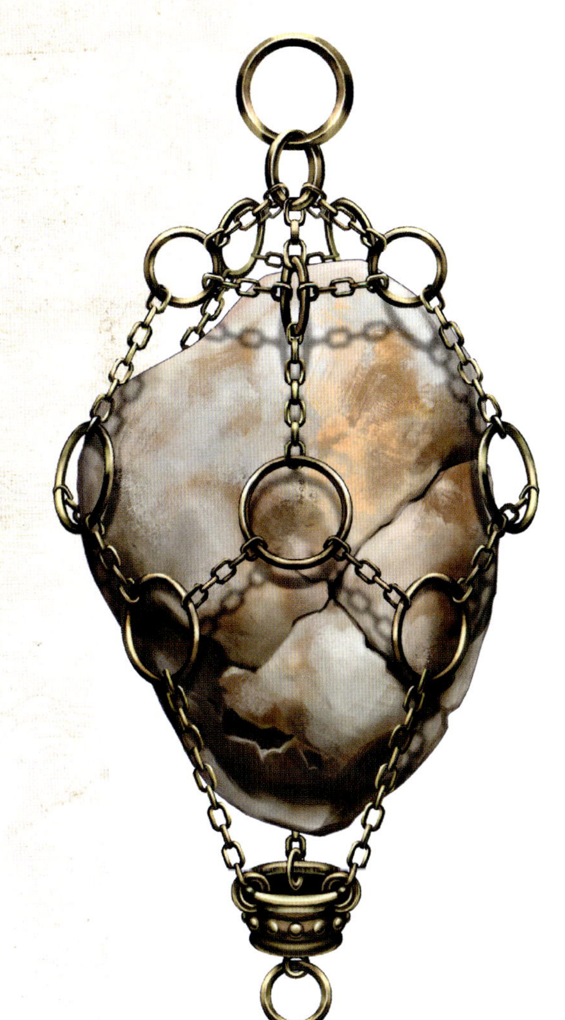

"The former Volstrucker, Bren Aldric Ermendrud, had an affinity for flame that his former teacher, Trent Ikithon, used to drive him to madness. When he escaped decades later from the Vergesson Sanatorium, he realized in the years to follow that he could outrun his past, but not his curiosity. In secret, the man now known as Caleb Widogast slowly returned to that which he loved most: magic. Those flames that once burned away his life could instead protect him and those he came to care for, forging him anew. Though I try my hardest to keep subjective statements from my intelligence reports, I must admit to a deep respect for this wizard of fire, who realized his chosen element could give life as much as it could destroy.

And so at his lowest, when one may give into the darkest part of their heart, he attempted to attain that which every person at their lowest wishes they could do: through the School of Transmutation, Caleb Widogast learned how to change."

—Oren Keth'Kaylis

Transmuter's Stone

After creating this smooth, polished stone that began its life in the Labenda Swamp, Caleb began to use it as a spellsink for his transmutative understandings, using latent spell energy within to slightly change his body to see in the dark, move faster, become hardier, or gain resistance to certain kinds of damage. Eventually, as Caleb neared the pinnacle of his arcane study, the stone's built-up spell energy could be released to cause acts of transmutation bordering on the miraculous. One such occurrence was the attempted resurrection of Mollymauk Tealeaf following the battle with the transformed Nonagon, destroying the original stone. To this day, Caleb keeps a new stone on him, ready to use its prodigious transmutative power to change the very fabric of the world, be it age, disease, or death itself.

"Very few mages ever manage to find, craft, and hang on to these rare arcane foci. Magical staffs such as these are not just useful for the casting of spells, nor for the temerity of that very magic, but often hold within them dozens and dozens of spells that have been painstakingly collected over the course of their arcane study. That Caleb Widogast was even allowed to hold Allura Vysoren's staff, let alone borrow it for an extended period, either speaks to her incredible generosity, or the true severity of the danger him and his cohort were walking toward."

—D'Rishk Dawnscale

Allura's Magical Staff

This beautiful ivory staff, the pinnacle of arcane achievement in the world of mages, was only in the hands of transmuter Caleb Widogast for a brief time. While in his hands, it was put to good use in the ruins of Aeor and the eventual confrontation with the noted blood hunter mercenary group, the Tombtakers. Their leader, Lucien, would go on to challenge the Somnovem, a mysterious faction of ancient Aeor, twisted and changed by their time in the Astral Sea following the overture of the Calamity. Lent to Caleb by powerful arcanist and ally to Vox Machina, Lady Allura Vysoren, this staff was used multiple times in the Mighty Nein's conflict with the Somnovem, its robust collection of spells providing Caleb and his companions with powerful elemental, defensive, and offensive magic before being returned to the generous Lady Allura.

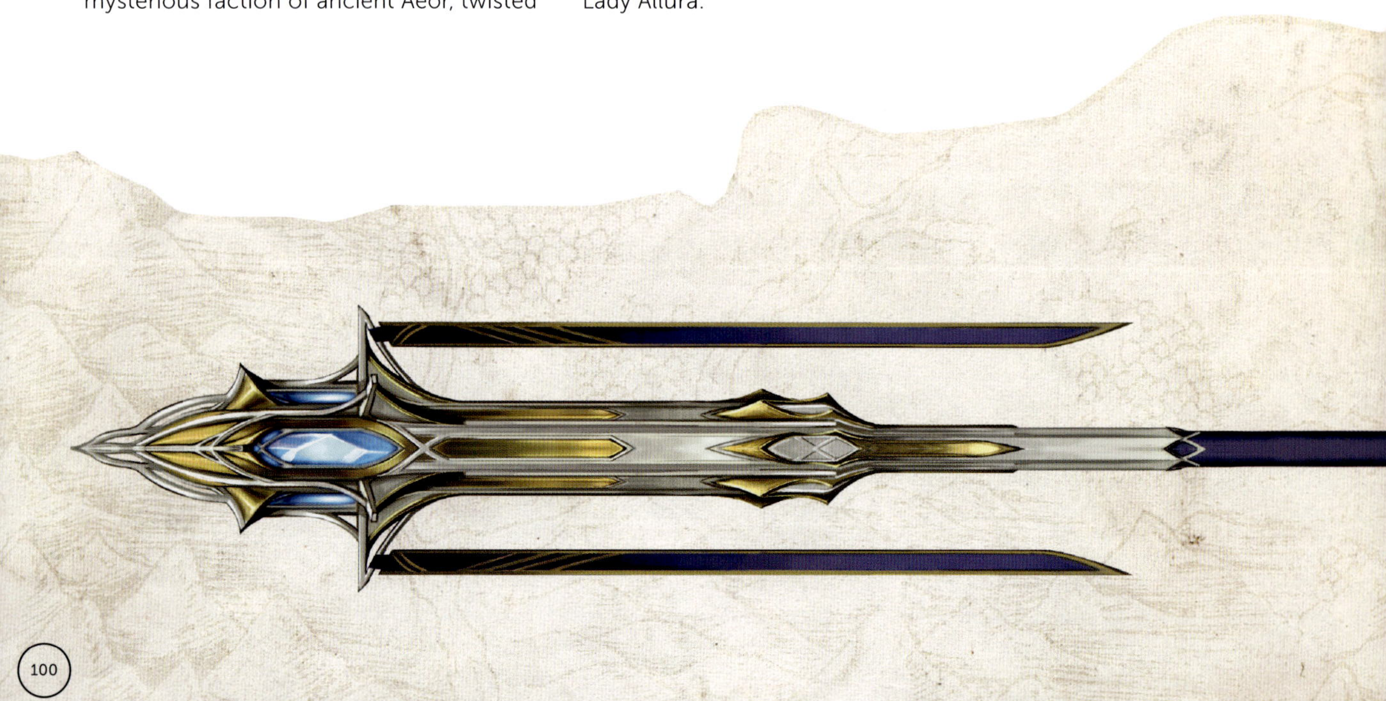

Veiler

A magic item taken by Caleb Widogast in his flight from the Vergesson Sanatorium, this amulet was ripped from the body of a dead Volstrucker sent to keep watch over him. Fearing for his life and the fury of his former master, Archmage Trent Ikithon, Widogast kept this amulet on him at all times while on the run, using its magic to block divination spells meant to discover his whereabouts. As the notoriety of the Mighty Nein grew and Caleb began to find himself in the orbits of both the Empire and the Cerberus Assembly, he struggled with whether to keep it. After offering it to Vokodo as something precious to him, he took it off, revealing his whereabouts. And though he got it back, it was soon passed to Fjord to keep him safe from the golden gaze of Uk'otoa.

In the end, the entirety of the Nein broke into that same Sanatorium so they could steal a wealth of these amulets, keeping them safe from the prying eyes of the Assembly and the Tombtakers as they worked to defeat the threat of Cognouza.

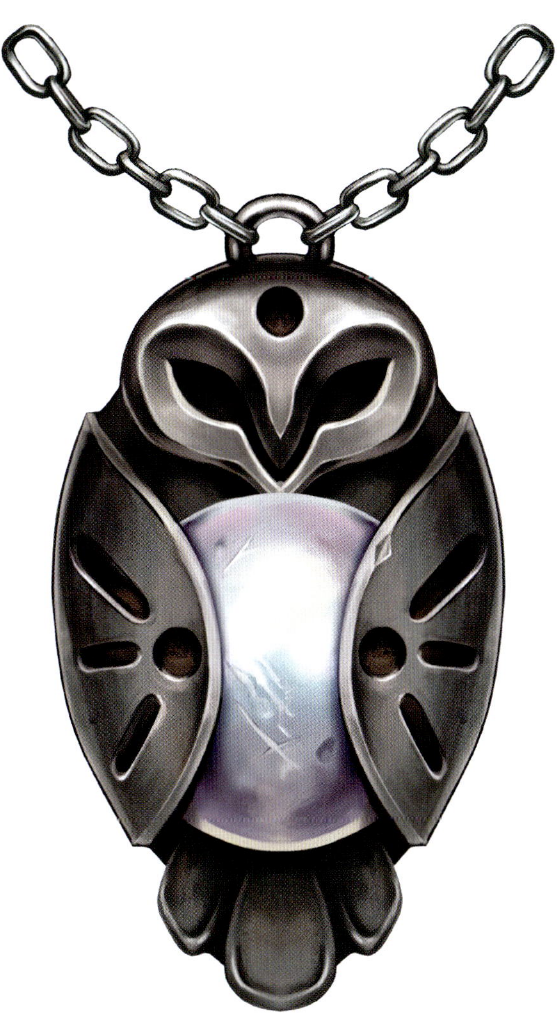

Collar of Silence

First forged in the Age of Arcanum, these silvered enchanted collars, each set with a ruby in the center, were used to silence, bind, and imprison experienced mages. These collars made vocal magic impossible, and with their hands bound and locked, rogue mages could do little to free themselves. Collars of Silence were first experienced by the Nein in the depths of the Halls of Halas, the Heirloom Sphere. The halls' Mage Hunter golems used them on the Nein's arcane ally, Yussa Errenis, and then Caleb Widogast, to shut off their respective spellcasting. Once taken off, Caleb kept his collar to use in battle against his former master and teacher, Trent Ikithon, where it stayed, rendering him silent until the rise of the Red Moon broke its enchantment, leading to Trent's escape.

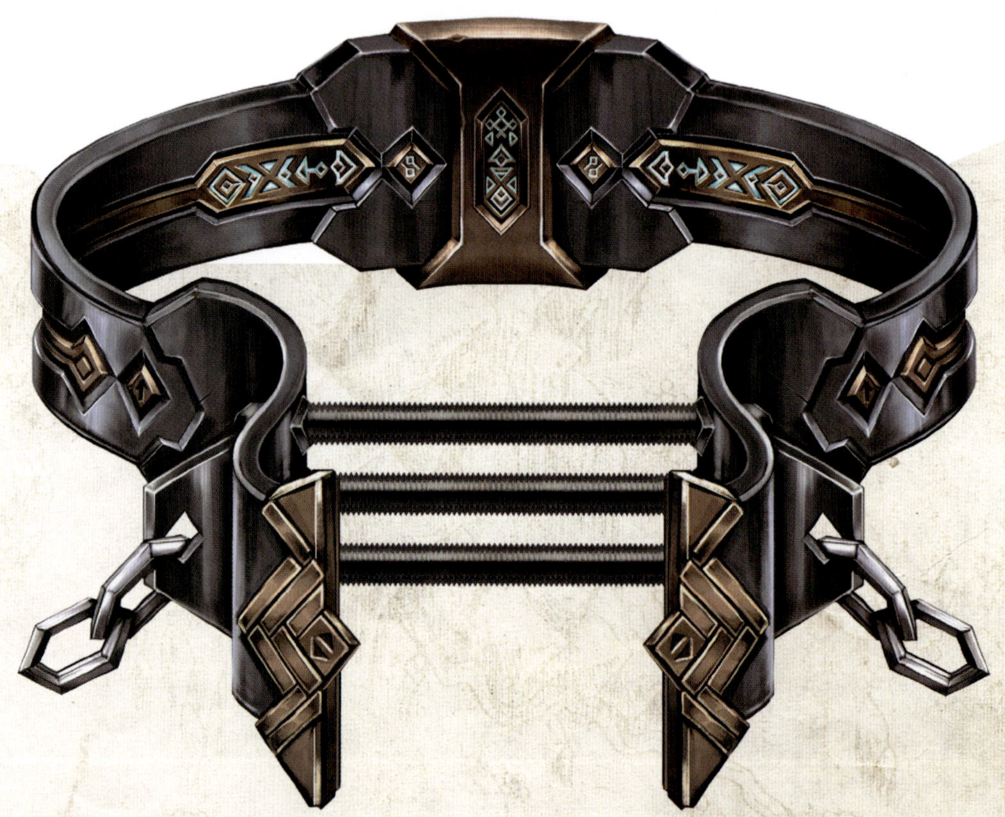

"The best sound in the world? A mage's vocal cords straining in effort as not a whisper emerges, nor a spark from their spasming fingers. Pure bliss."

—Oren Keth'Kaylis

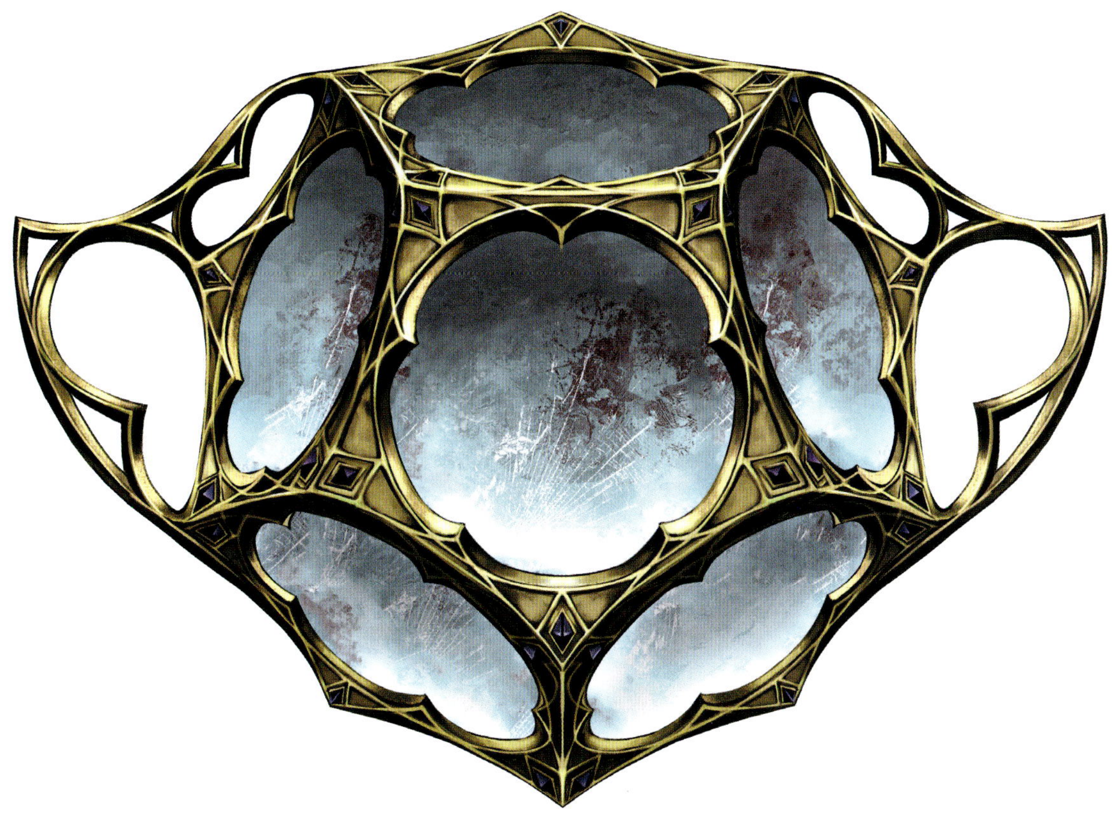

"Like many of my order, I've only ever read of this legendary artifact, its vast capabilities, and its religious significance to the Kryn Dynasty. I've seen sketches and illusions from secondhand witnesses, but all pale compared to the truth of it. A truth glimpsed by the few. I found a snippet of a Kryn prayer that illuminates its importance:

'From your brilliance, may we find continuance,
A path out of death's shadow, forever walking
Toward life's light
Gift us better tomorrows,
So we may redeem this world today.'

It tells us what we already know, but it is evidence that these Beacons are not simply sources of power for the Empire's use; they are gifts from a god older and stranger than any Exandria has known. If that doesn't garner respect, I don't know what will."

—D'Rishk Dawnscale

Luxon Beacon

A shining, twelve-sided artifact of glass, set with two golden handles on either side, the Luxon Beacon glows with a brilliant smoke and ivory light, holding vast arcane power in its core. The Mighty Nein found a Luxon Beacon early in their time together, rescued from a Kryn operative within Zadash. The Nein then kept and protected this Beacon from both Empire and Dynasty agents, uncovering its use in the powering of dunamantic spellwork, its heart of potentiality, and ultimately learning of its significance and role within Kryn society. Their Beacon was gifted back to the Bright Queen, Leylas Kryn, winning her admiration and saving the group from imminent imprisonment.

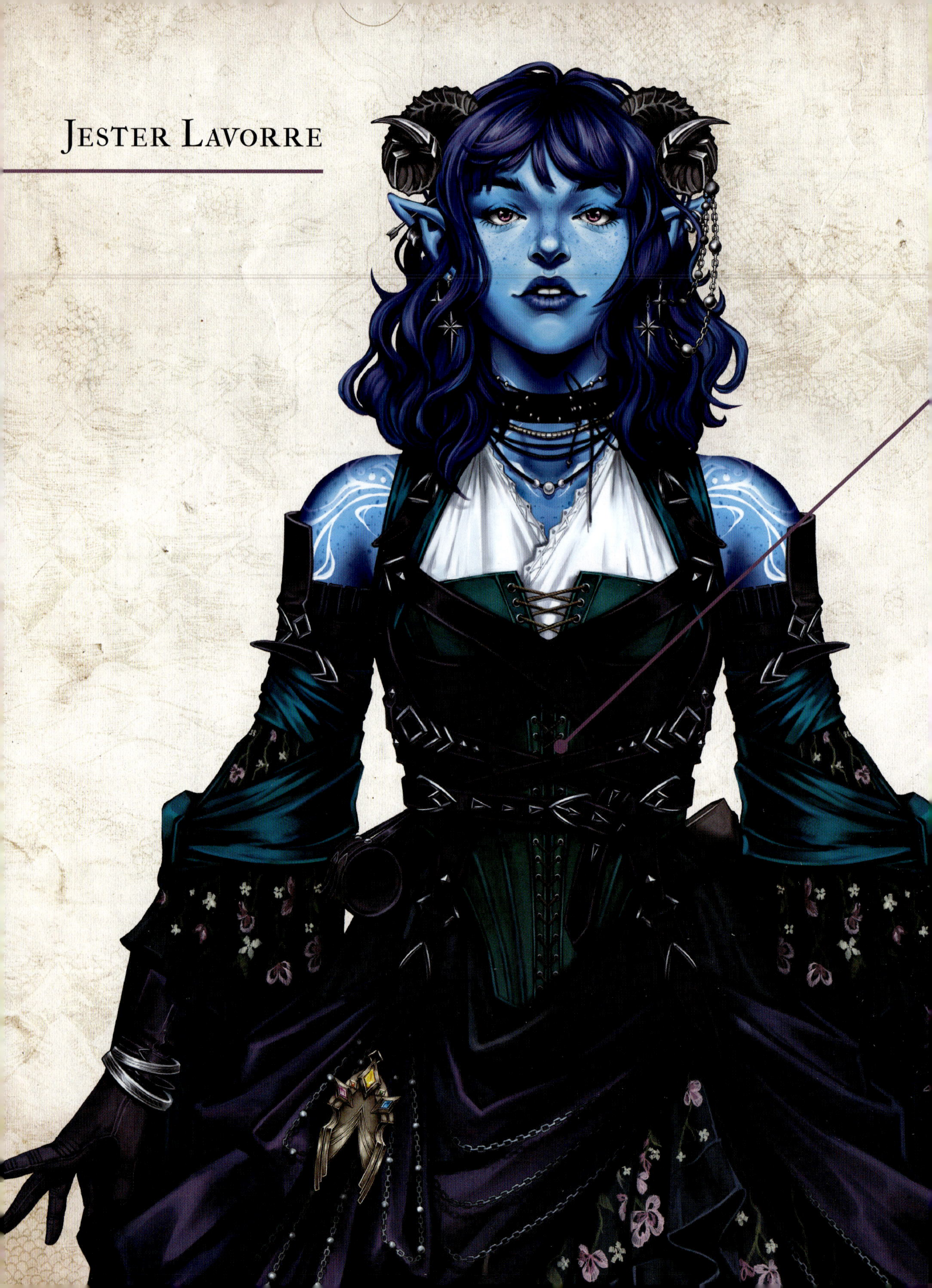
Jester Lavorre

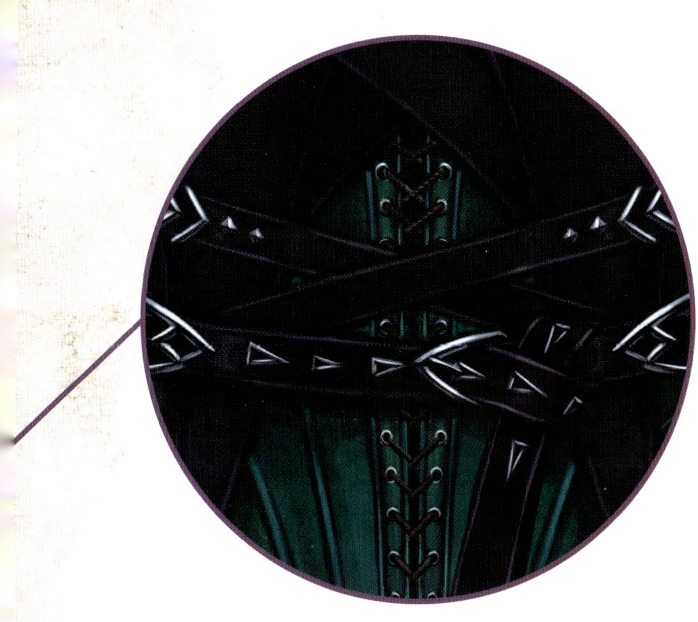

"Jester Lavorre, of all the people to make me consider religion, is the only one who actually made me think about it for more than a few moments. No, not because of the Traveler, whoever the Hells that is; no, it was because of her. Her sheer joy to be out in the world. Her huge smile, present for any who needed one. I don't know if you know anything about Darktow, but, uh, smiles are not very forthcoming. Not here at the heart of the Lucidian Ocean's, ahem, maritime profiteering ring.

Anyway, she came in here one evening and was the only one of her crew with anything close to happiness. She drank. She swore. Preached at a couple of people. Danced a waltz with some awkward red-headed stiff. And then that's when she pounced on me. Asked me with a heavy Nicodranian accent if I'd heard of the Traveler. And when I said, 'No, piss off,' she immediately countered that if she pissed off, I'd have to piss on, to balance it all out. First time I've laughed all week!

I don't think I'll ever encounter a cheerier, more brightly-dressed, youthful spirit again, at least not on Darktow. But I'll always remember Ms. Lavorre, the first ray of light Darktow has seen in many a year."

—Tallulah Fontaine, interviewing anonymous "profiteer" at The Misty Mooring in Darktow

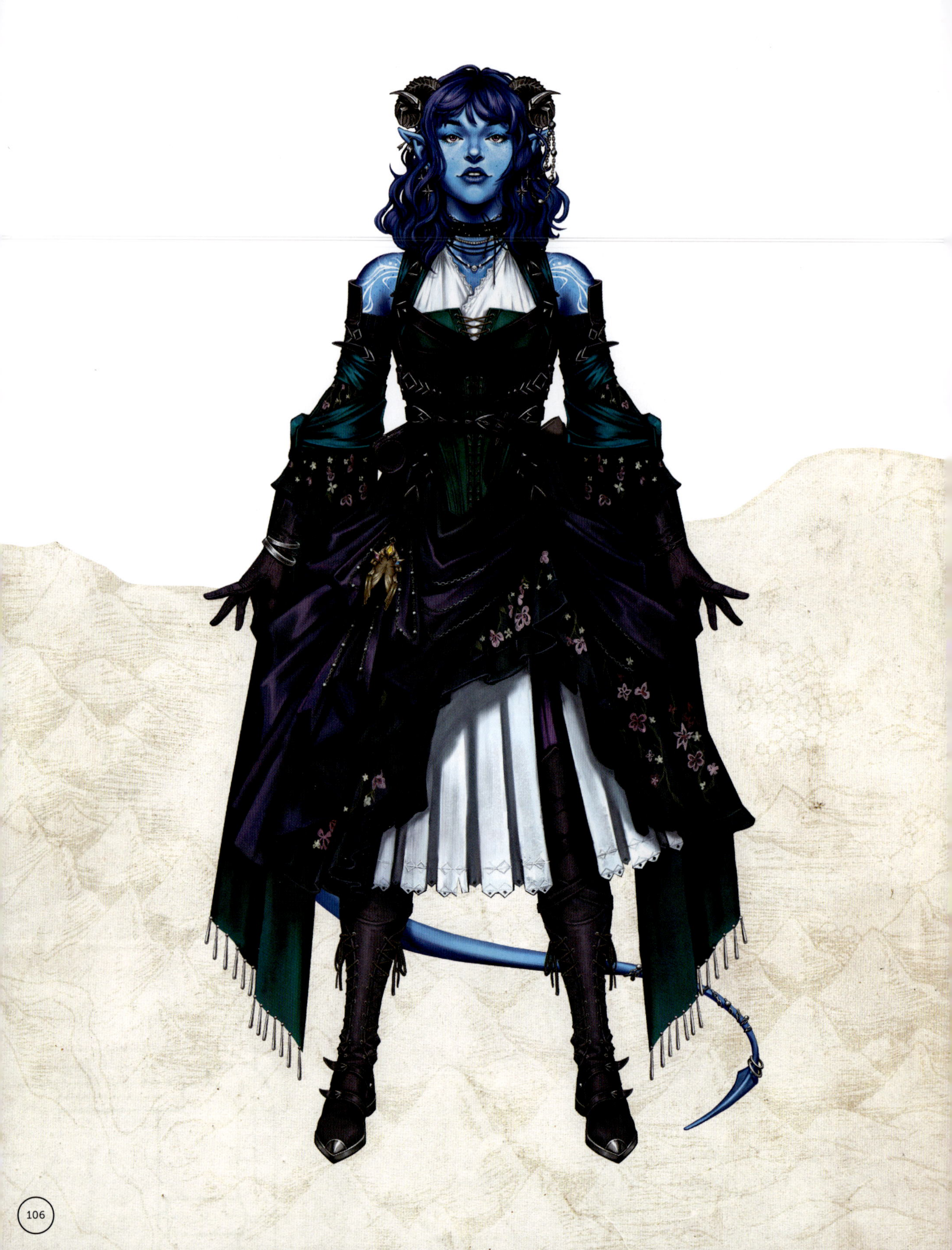

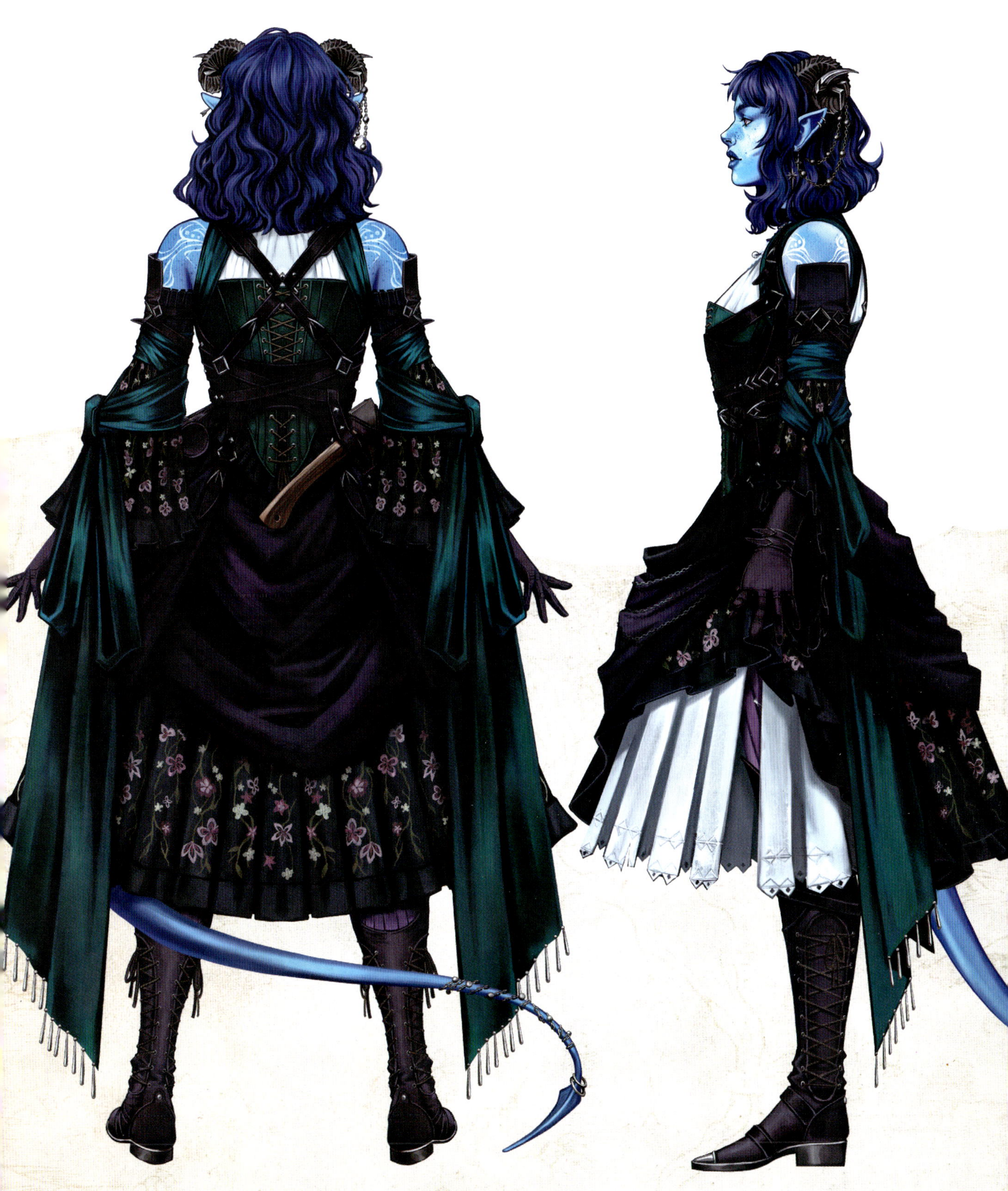

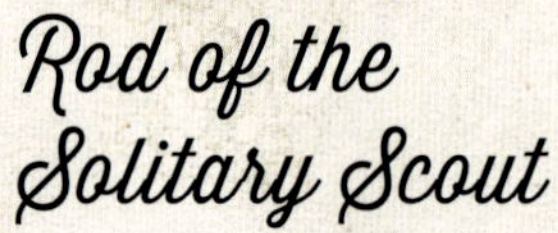

Rod of the Solitary Scout

Found within the Folding Halls of Halas, deep in his Arcane Armory, this very magical item found its way to Jester. The mischievous healer not only benefited from its potency, as it empowered her divine spellwork, but also its inherent spells, which created grease, increased one's speed, and allowed her to leave messages for others. This absolutely delighted the impish and beloved priestess of the Traveler. Though she didn't use it often, when she did, it was with glee that she engaged in that domain which she was master of: trickery (though Jester preferred to call it chaos).

Celebone

A little twist of a magic item, this small trinket can be cracked in half to emit light within twenty feet for an hour. And from the moment the Nein encountered them at the magic shop of Dimble Thaydeen in Rexxentrum, they bought as many as they could and used them as often as possible, none more so than Jester.

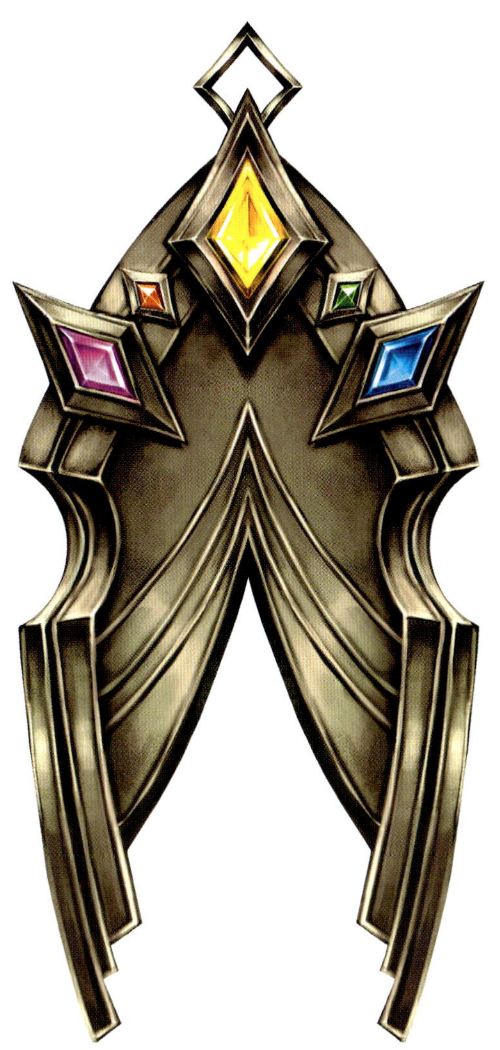

"Oh, the Traveler loves to travel,
It's why he chose his name
Moving all around the world
And even across the planes
He empowers mischief
And gifts his faithful power
He leaves his friends with smiles
And leaves his enemies dour
By the light of Fey-bright suns
By moon of deepest night
The Traveler loves to travel
Won't you join his flight?"

—Tallulah Fontaine, "Oh, Precocious Traveler," Verse I of IIIIV

Holy Symbol of the Traveler

A holy symbol designed for the divine power of the Traveler to flow through, his icon is depicted as a sinuous roadway framed by two stones to either side to form a doorway. An archfey both famous and infamous, Artagan has long been a being to eschew the two Courts of the Fey Realm, preferring chaos to control. After an encounter with Vox Machina in their fight with the Whispered One, he extracted a favor from them in exchange for a place to rest and his protection: They would create a permanent doorway for him from the Fey Realm into Exandria, a whole planet on which to cause mayhem. It wouldn't be long before his antics started to attract the attention of worshippers seeking divine intervention from a being outside the current pantheons. And though many would go on to some notoriety, there was none more infamous than a lonely, little blue tiefling girl in Nicodranas, who so desperately desired a friend. And where she found a friend in the Traveler, she found a god, too.

Spiritual Lollipop of Pain

Jester Lavorre never settled for something simple when something silly would do better in its place. Her divine magic took forms others might deem cute or nonsensical, but many underestimated those sparkles, colors, and sheer inanity to their detriment. Chief amongst them was pure divinity made physical in the form of a massive, glowing pink lollipop, conjured from the Traveler's will and Jester's imagination. Any who doubted its power or Jester's strength soon learned otherwise, as she often used it to bludgeon enemies into submission. And as Jester's wisdom and faith in the Traveler grew, so too did her sugary spiritual lollipop, appearing with serrated edges, larger and deadlier than ever.

It is said that on the seas of the Lucidian Ocean, pirates of the Revelry know to fear two things: the name Tusktooth, and a massive, glowing pink lollipop bobbing menacingly in the distance.

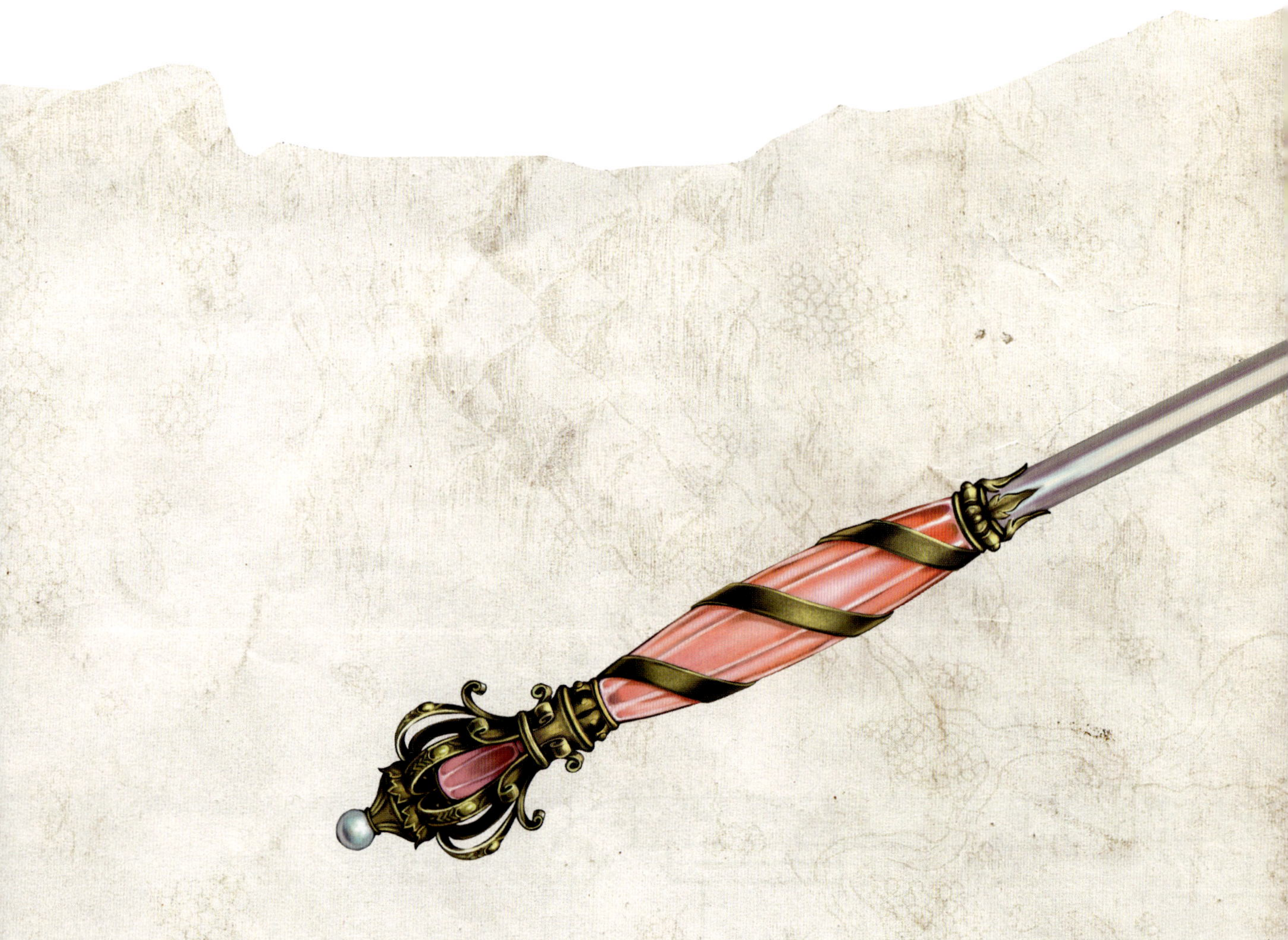

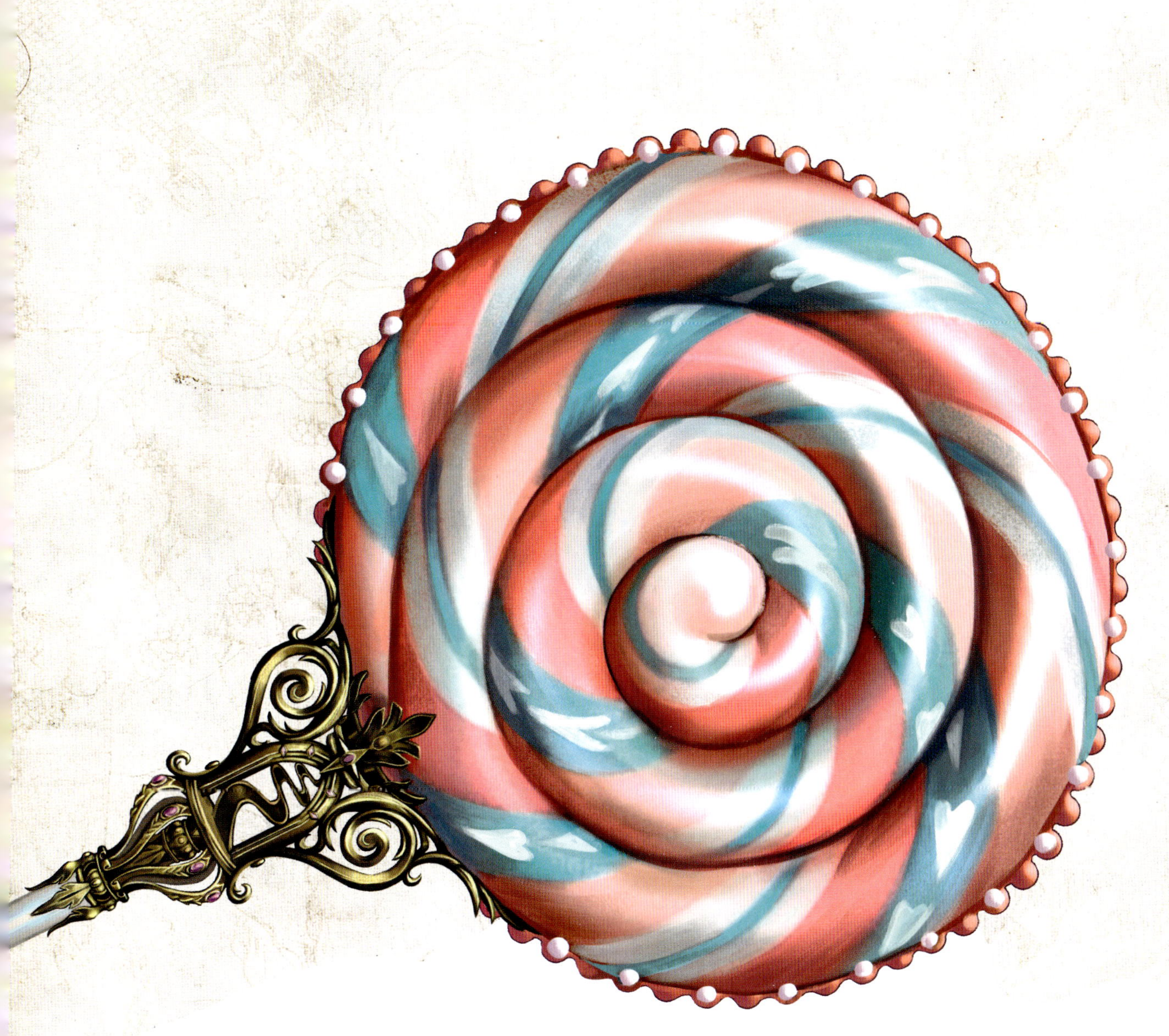

"Oh, Jester, high priestess of the Traveler,
Lend me your sweetness,
A sweetness so powerful, so sharp
It may knock nonsense into my enemies
And destroy evil as much as it destroys logic.
By the words and deeds of the Traveler,
Let your radiant lollipop smite my foes,
In colors bright and saccharine."

—"Prayer for a Joyful Priestess," overheard by Tallulah Fontaine outside a candy shop in Rexxentrum

Jester's Pack of Perplexing Paints

Jester Lavorre was always an artist at heart, drawing on the walls of the Lavish Chateau where she was raised mostly in solitude. And in that solitude, she turned to two things: first, a being who called himself the Traveler and became her best friend and personal god; and second, art. Throughout her time with the Nein, Jester painted and drew frequently, often crude, humorous depictions of anatomy, which brought her and the Traveler nothing but delight. However, after stumbling upon these paints, under guard from the Clovis Concord of the Menagerie Coast, Jester found all her dreams coming true. For with these paints, anything she drew became real.

Statues of the Traveler, phallic tokens, and many painted doorways, gates, holes, and more—Jester painted it all. The many gateways let Jester, the Traveler, and the Nein into nearly any and every room they wanted. The full list of items Jester has created is extensive and mostly dick-shaped, but when she could, she helped her friends with passages, parasols, and yes, penises.

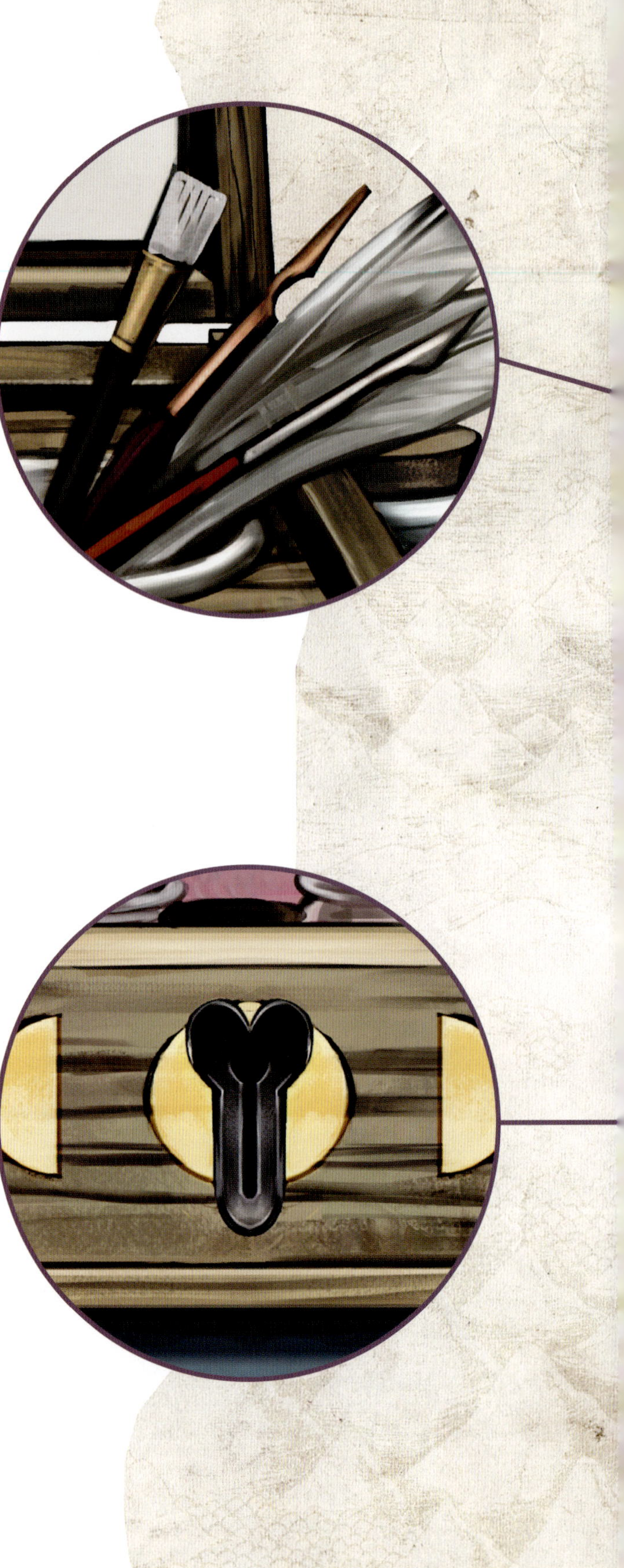

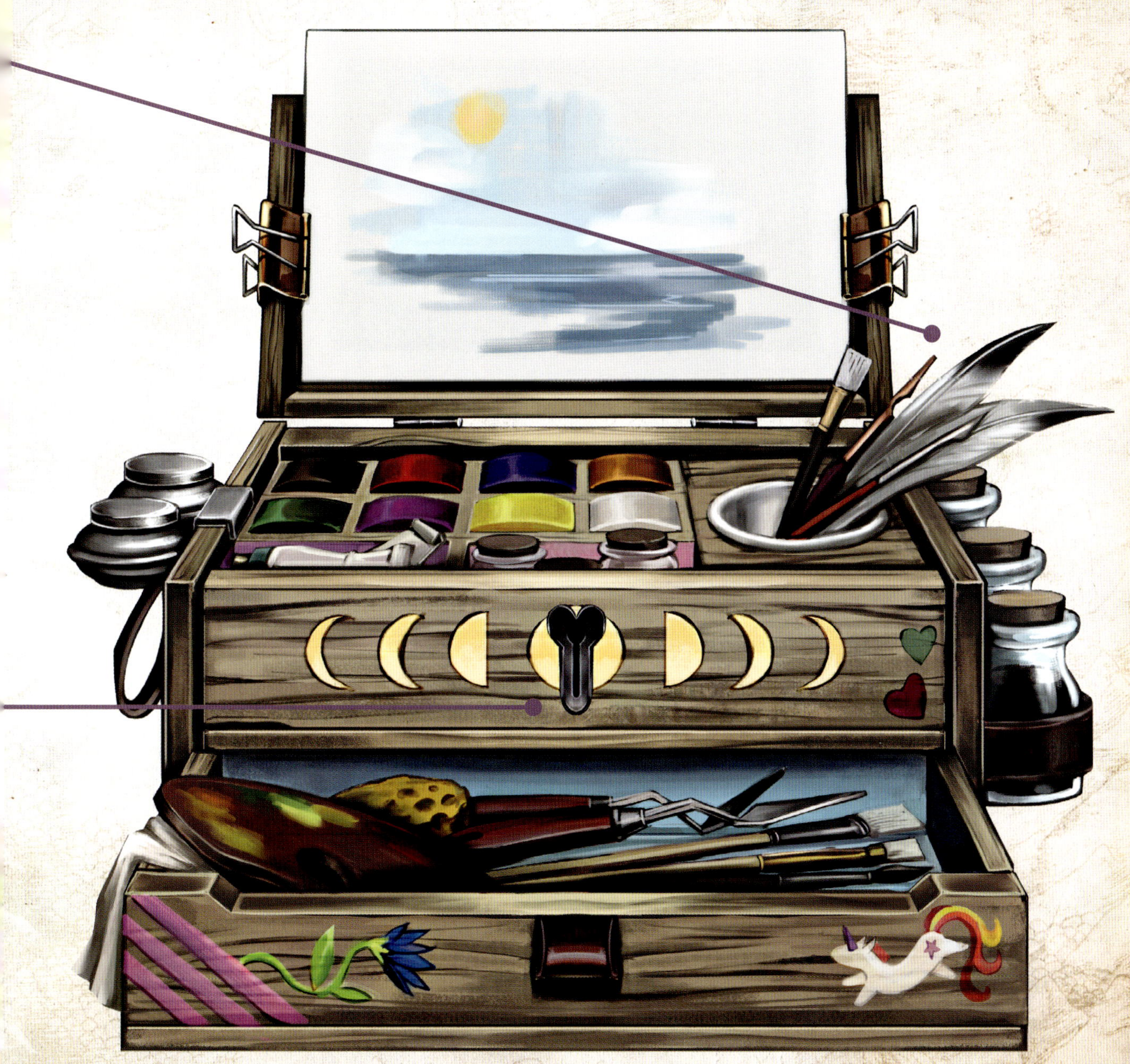

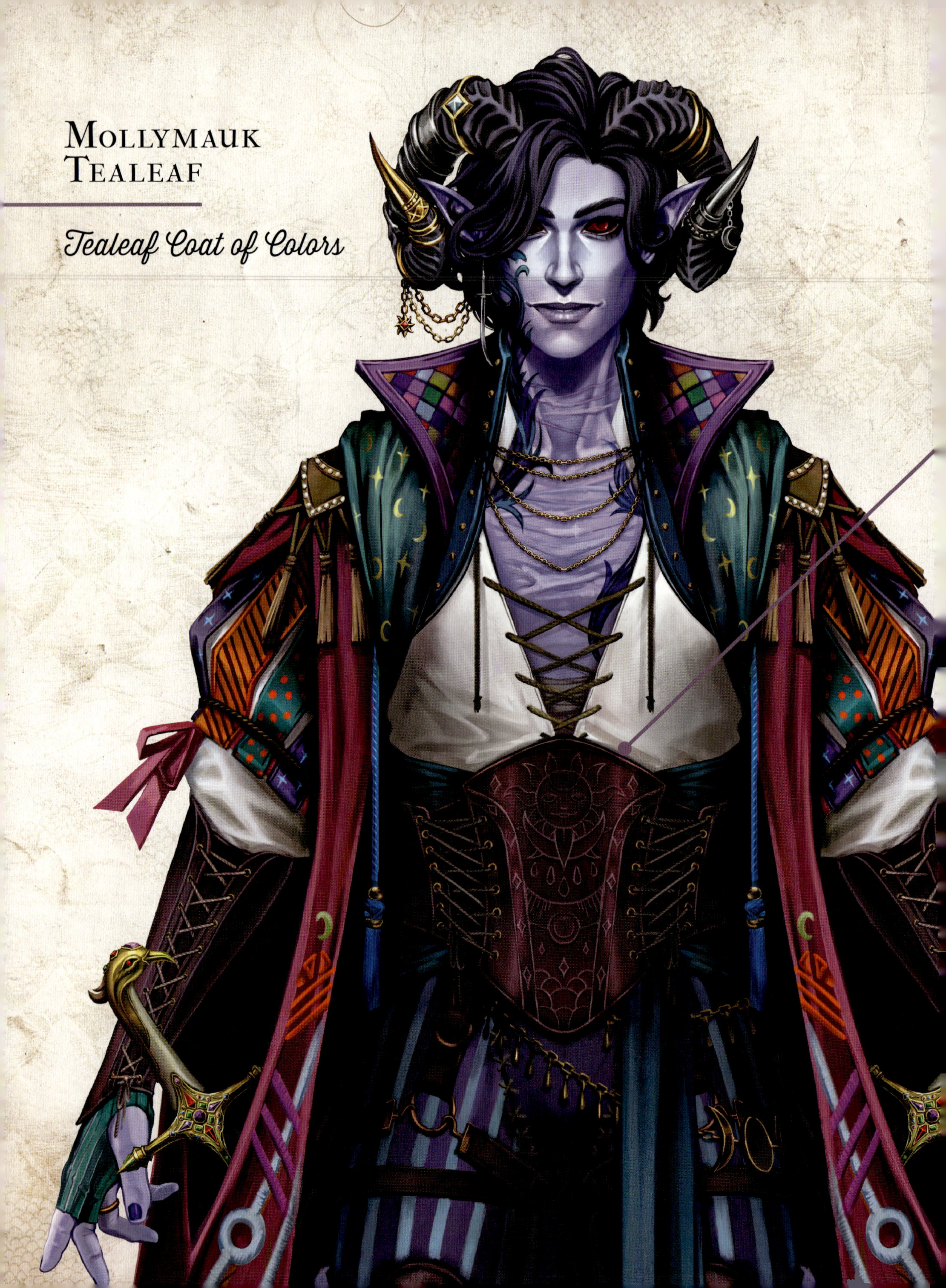

Mollymauk Tealeaf

Tealeaf Coat of Colors

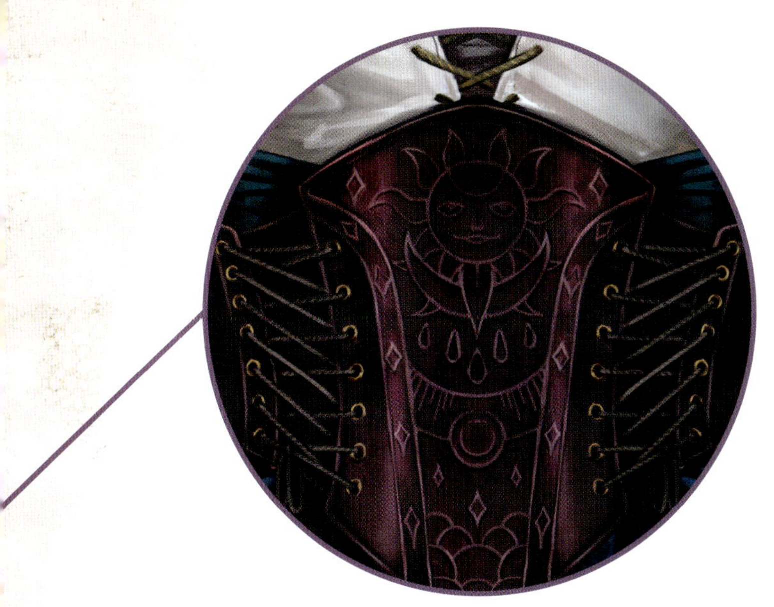

A beautiful and sumptuous robe of red riddled with iconography found in various religious practices, holy symbols of gods, and tarot-like symbols of importance, this coat came to Mollymauk as he was getting his bearings following the ritual that wiped his memory. As he found himself amongst the many wonders of the Carnival of Curiosities, so too did he find a family. And as he became Mollymauk Tealeaf, this ostentatious, peacock-like coat adorned him, cementing him as both a figure dramatic and suave, perfect for his new life.

"Cheeky bastard didn't take my question seriously at first. Just laughed and downed a swig of their ale.

But I asked again and didn't let up. I was going to make them answer, and I finally annoyed them enough to make them wheel on me, lip in a little snarl. 'The fuck do you think so, Gustav? Look at me! Purple skin, red eyes, curling horns, I'm covered in tattoos and marks and scars that I couldn't tell you where the fucking fuck they came from because I don't even know where I came from! People are going to look anyway, because people are awful and curious little birds. Might as well give them something to look at, if that's going to be how it is.' And then they said I was paying and stormed out.

I knew I'd struck a nerve, but as ringmaster it was my job. To know the how and the why; if I did, I could use it. Alchemize it, onstage and off. But after that day, I didn't speak of their coat, their blades, their tattoos, none of it. Just let Mollymauk do whatever it is they felt called to do. Enough people were looking, like they said. Didn't feel right to call more attention to them."

—Tallulah Fontaine, interviewing Gustav Fletching, tracked down in Rexxentrum

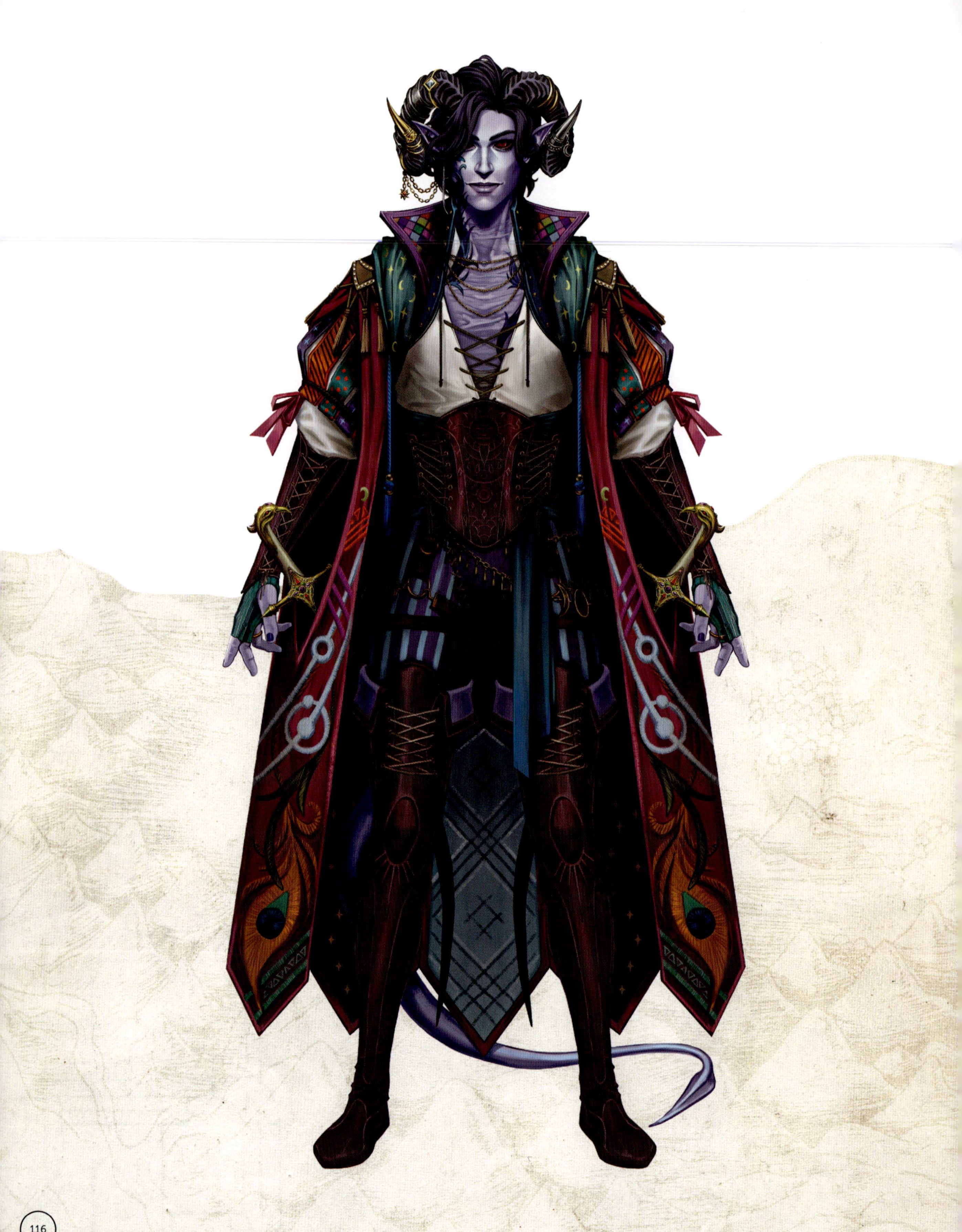

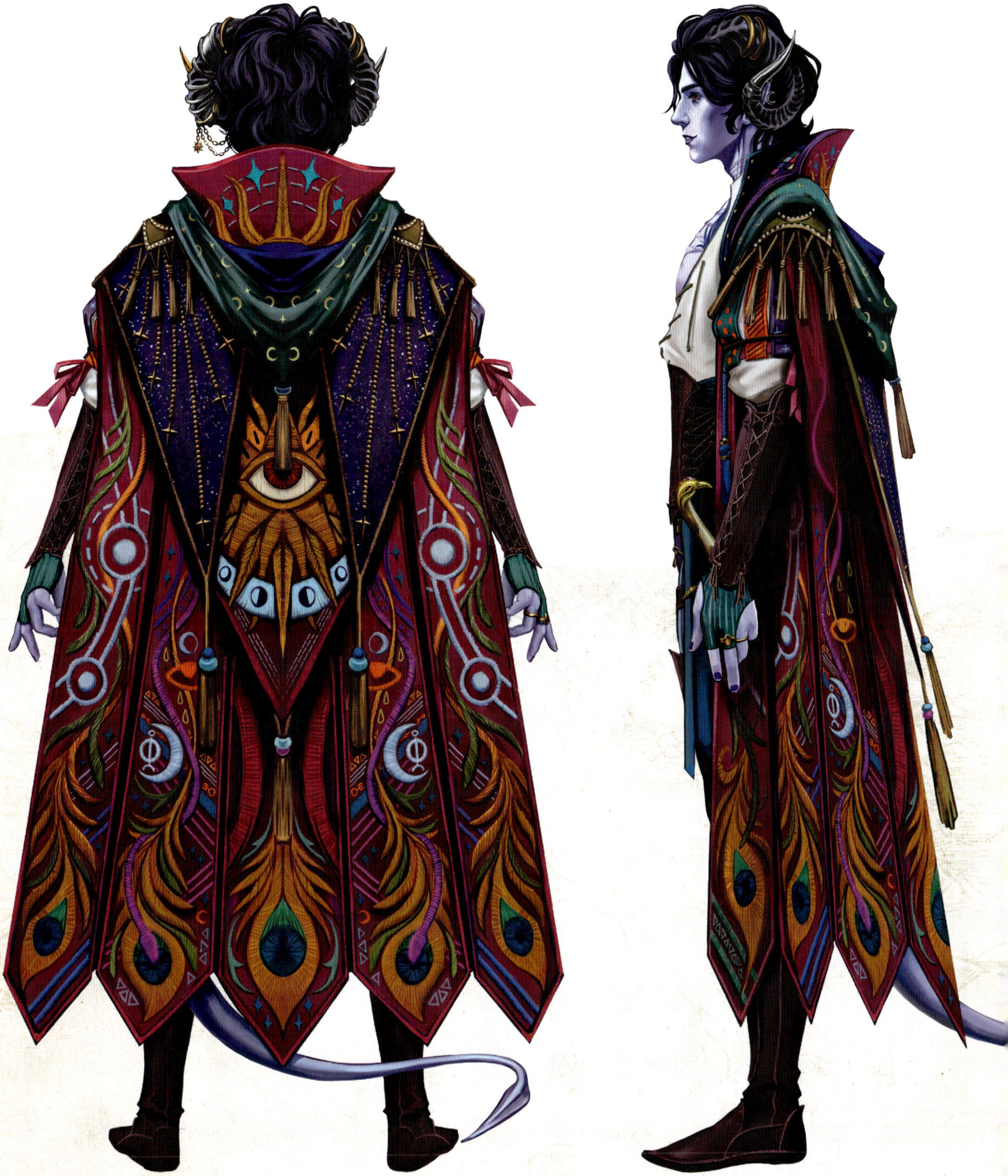

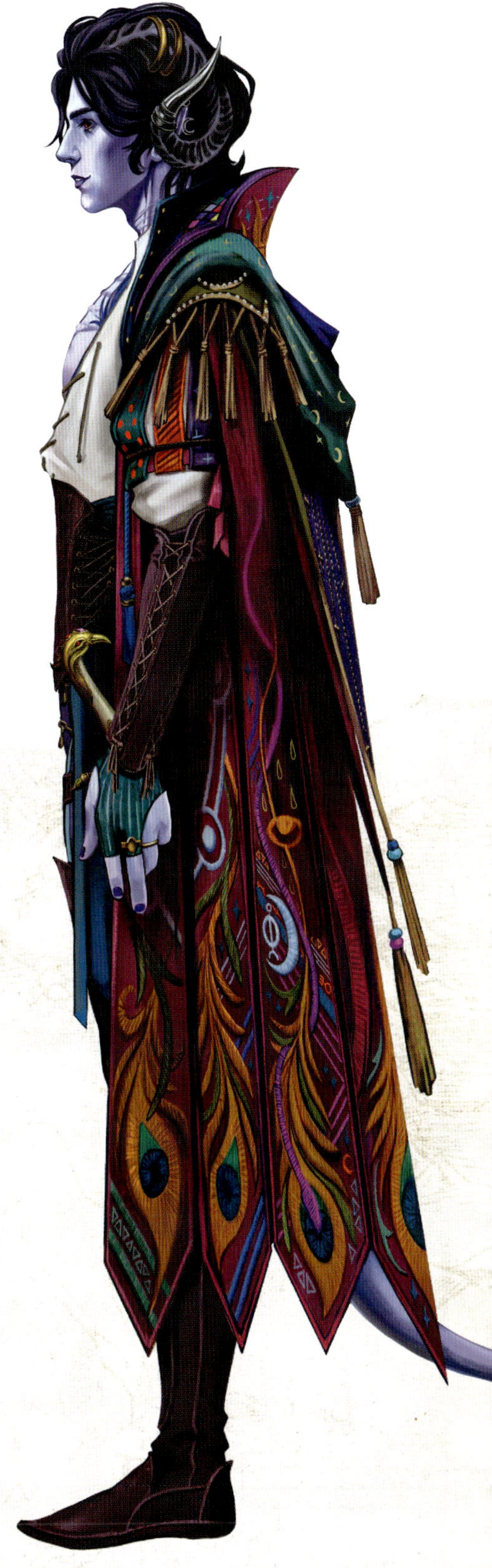

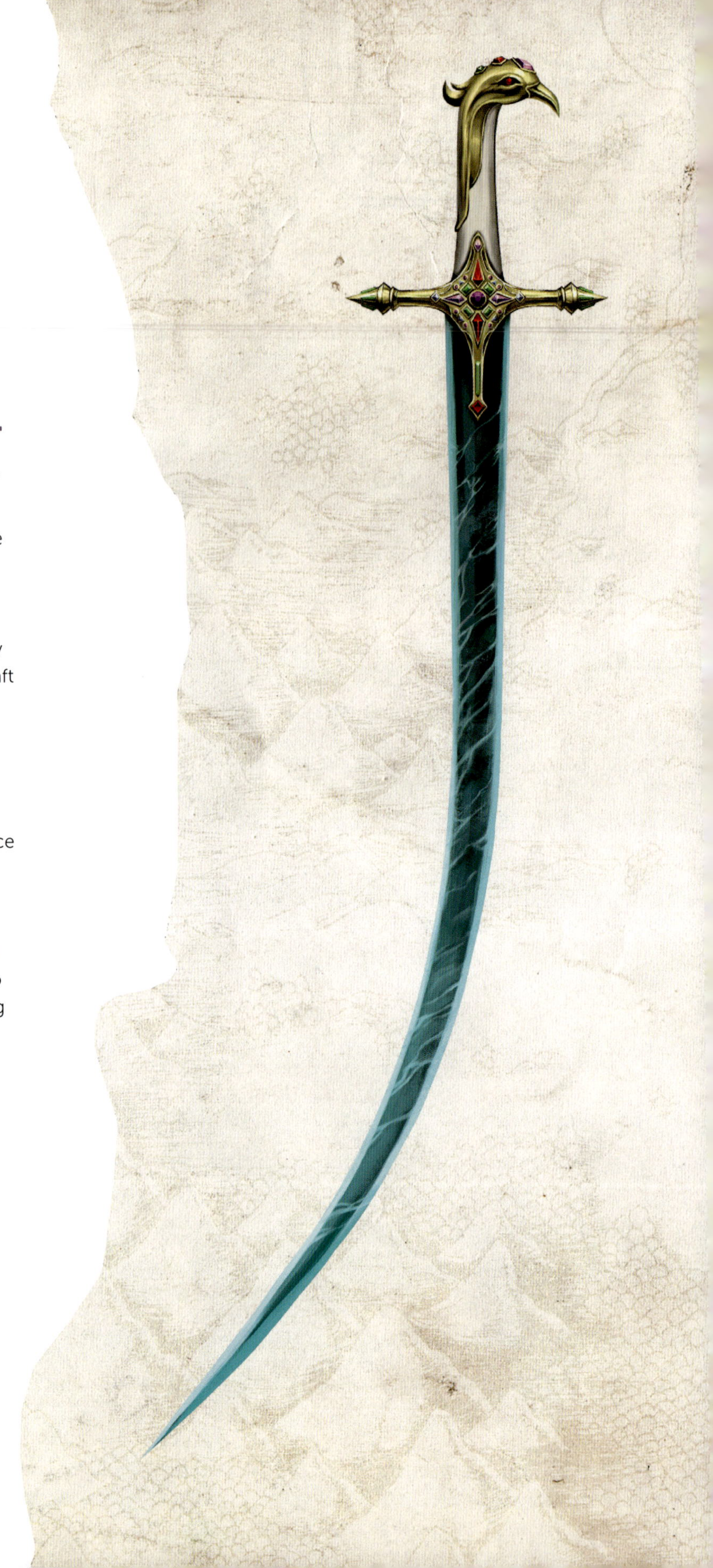

Carnival Glass Scimitars

When Mollymauk Tealeaf began his new life at the Fletching and Moondrop Traveling Carnival of Curiosities, deprived of the memories that made him who he was, he found a new life with the performers led by Gustav Fletching. Discovering the hemocraft that ran through his veins, a blood magic he couldn't recall acquiring, but one he began to unearth, he started training with these glass scimitars, lightweight and sharp, to draw blood in his growing life of performance. This earned him the name "Ice Spinner," due to the ice magic that coated the blades.

When Mollymauk joined the Nein from their initial meeting in Trostenwald, he used these twin scimitars, slicing himself open to draw on the cold magic in his blood, turning their now frozen edges on his opponents. Though his time with the Nein was short-lived, he never ceased to use these blades from the start of his second life.

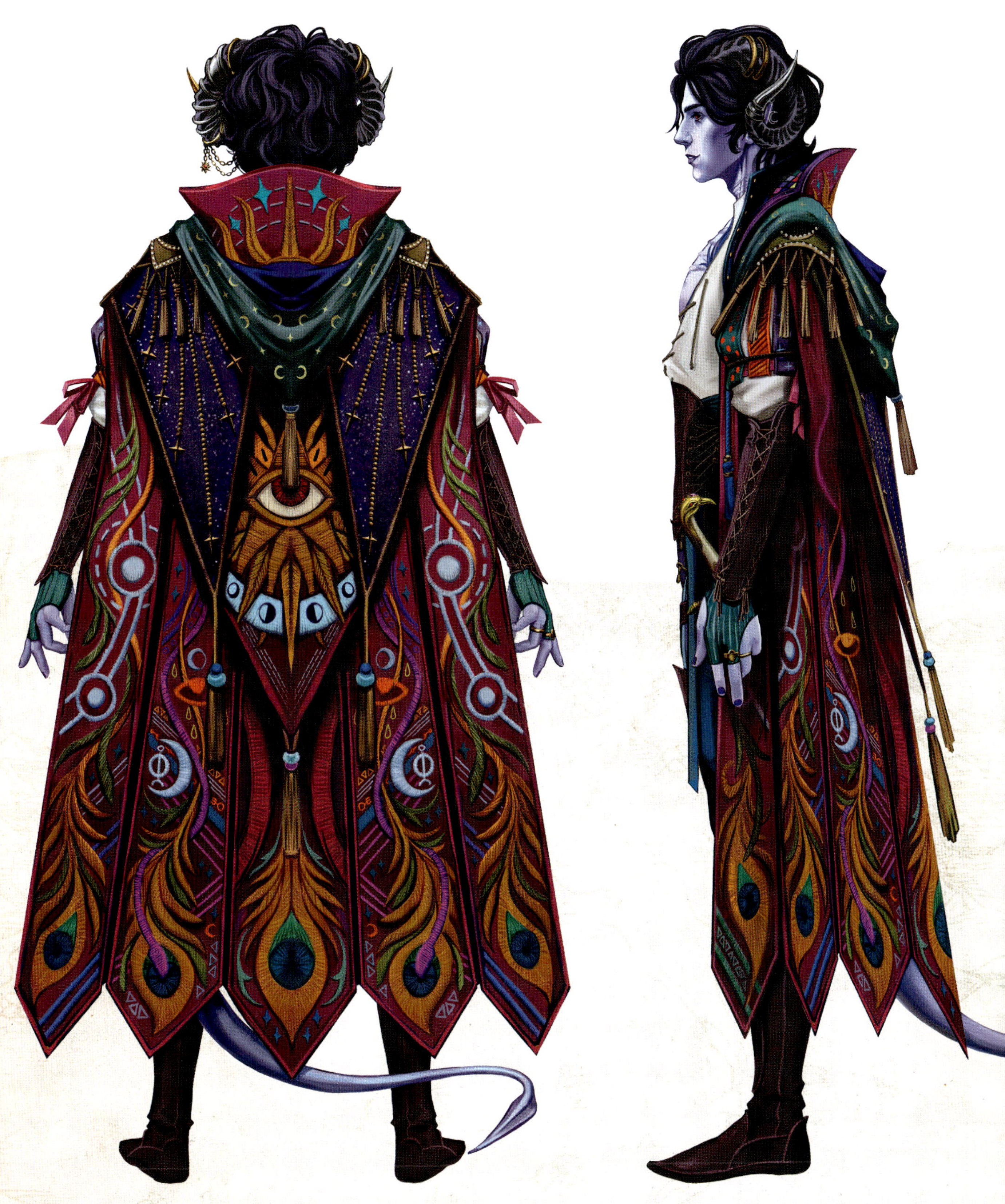

Carnival Glass Scimitars

When Mollymauk Tealeaf began his new life at the Fletching and Moondrop Traveling Carnival of Curiosities, deprived of the memories that made him who he was, he found a new life with the performers led by Gustav Fletching. Discovering the hemocraft that ran through his veins, a blood magic he couldn't recall acquiring, but one he began to unearth, he started training with these glass scimitars, lightweight and sharp, to draw blood in his growing life of performance. This earned him the name "Ice Spinner," due to the ice magic that coated the blades.

When Mollymauk joined the Nein from their initial meeting in Trostenwald, he used these twin scimitars, slicing himself open to draw on the cold magic in his blood, turning their now frozen edges on his opponents. Though his time with the Nein was short-lived, he never ceased to use these blades from the start of his second life.

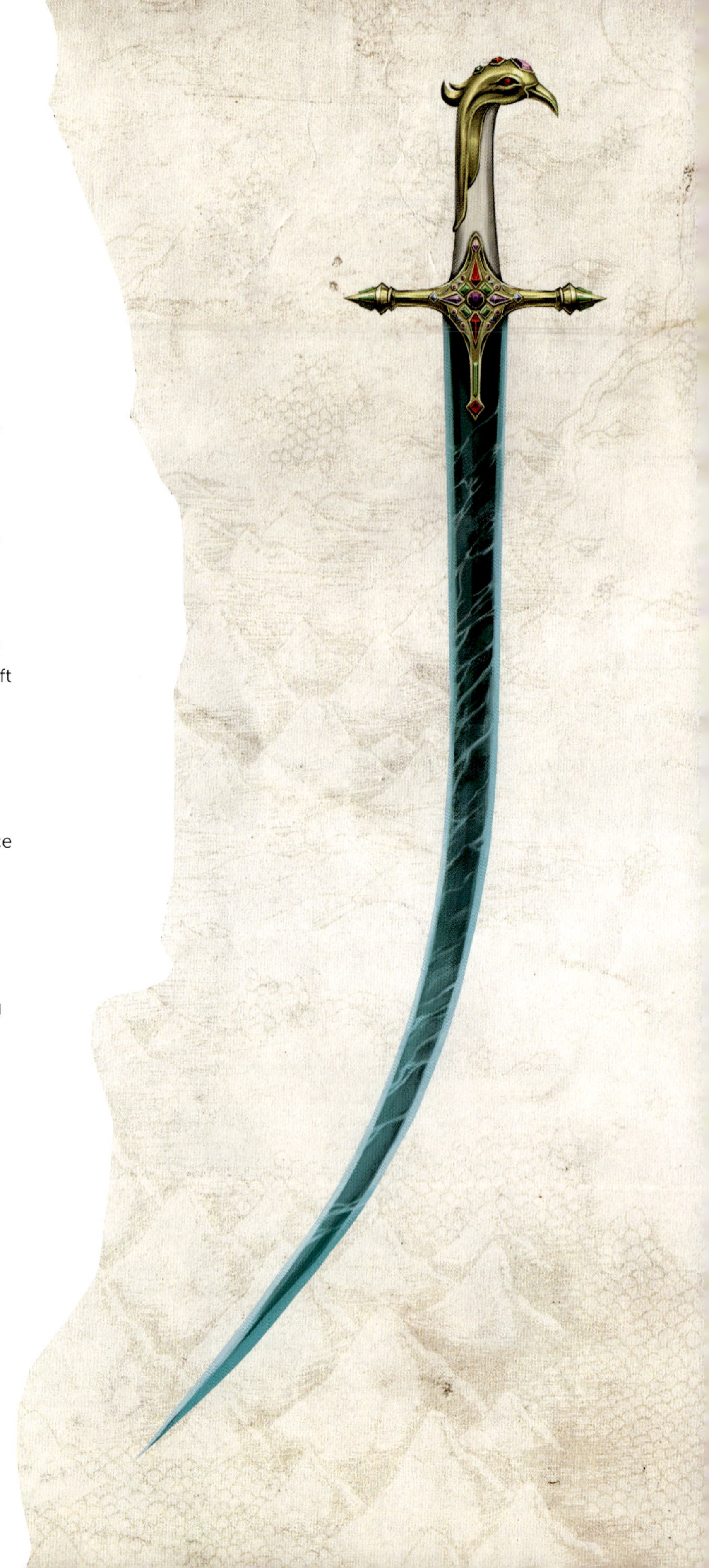

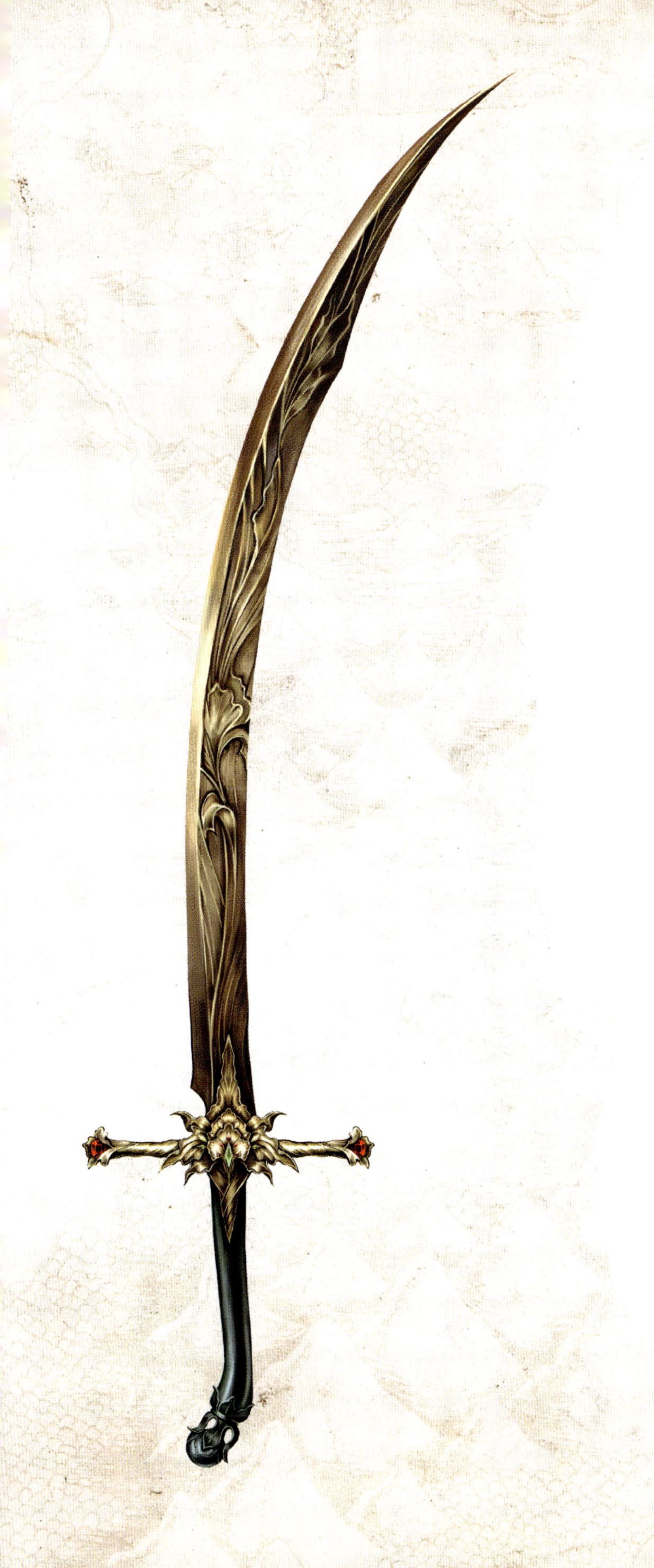

Summer's Dance

A beautiful, golden magical scimitar found in the Labenda Swamp in the early days of the Mighty Nein, this blade was taken by Mollymauk Tealeaf, who replaced one of his carnival glass blades with this magic one. Carrying a minor enchantment of teleportation within it, Summer's Dance served Tealeaf faithfully until his death at the hands of the Iron Shepherds. While mourning the loss of Mollymauk, Fjord fused the power of Summer's Dance into his own pact weapon, the Sword of Fathoms. Using the consumptive power of Uk'otoa, Summer's Dance faded into nothingness, and its power was joined to Fjord's weapon, where it served him for a time.

Kingsley Tealeaf

Fang of the Spire King

A beautiful, black steel rapier adorned with many different snake motifs, this rapier was gifted to the Nein, and specifically Kingsley, by the Betrayer God known as the Cloaked Serpent. Though he rankled at helping the Nein, Betrayer that he is, the Cloaked Serpent also understood he could do very little from outside the Divine Gate to tame his ambitious offspring. The Cloaked Serpent called on his dark power and gifted the group this legendary blade, imbued with all the force and rage of the dark god whom Uk'otoa would usurp. Kingsley, ever eager to prove himself, took it into battle against the Leviathan, recently freed from within the Lucidian Ocean's depths.

Kingsley used its power to vanquish and seal Uk'otoa once more; it is unknown if Kingsley still has possession of the blade or if he found some way to return it to the dark god of lies.

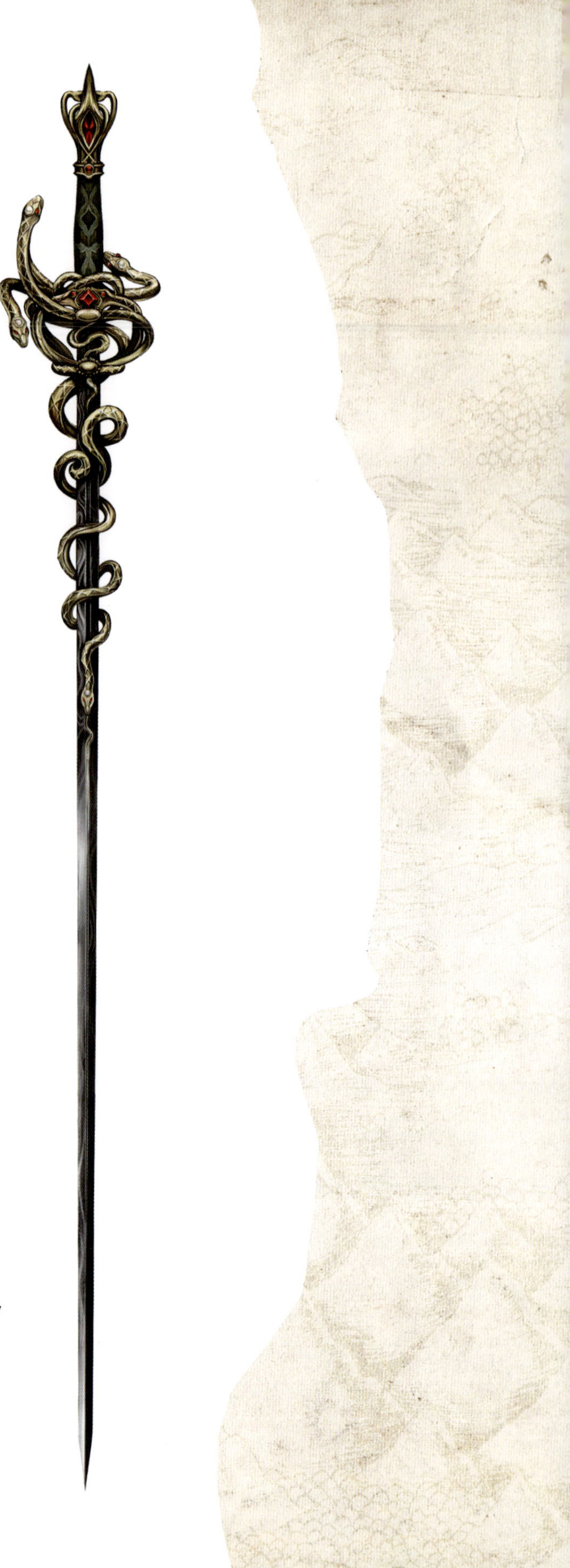

"Do not come to the serpent with expectation of comfort. The Cloaked Serpent delivers only thus unto faithful hearts: love. His terrible, jealous love. It is an awful, wracking poison. Agonizes the blood, addles the mind, burns the soul. It is glorious, that pain. Tender, that love. Let Him bite and rend and swallow you whole. Let Him love you. I swear, it may hurt. But so does love."

—Testimony recorded within the Bazzoxan gaol from a captured acolyte staring at the Betrayers' Rise

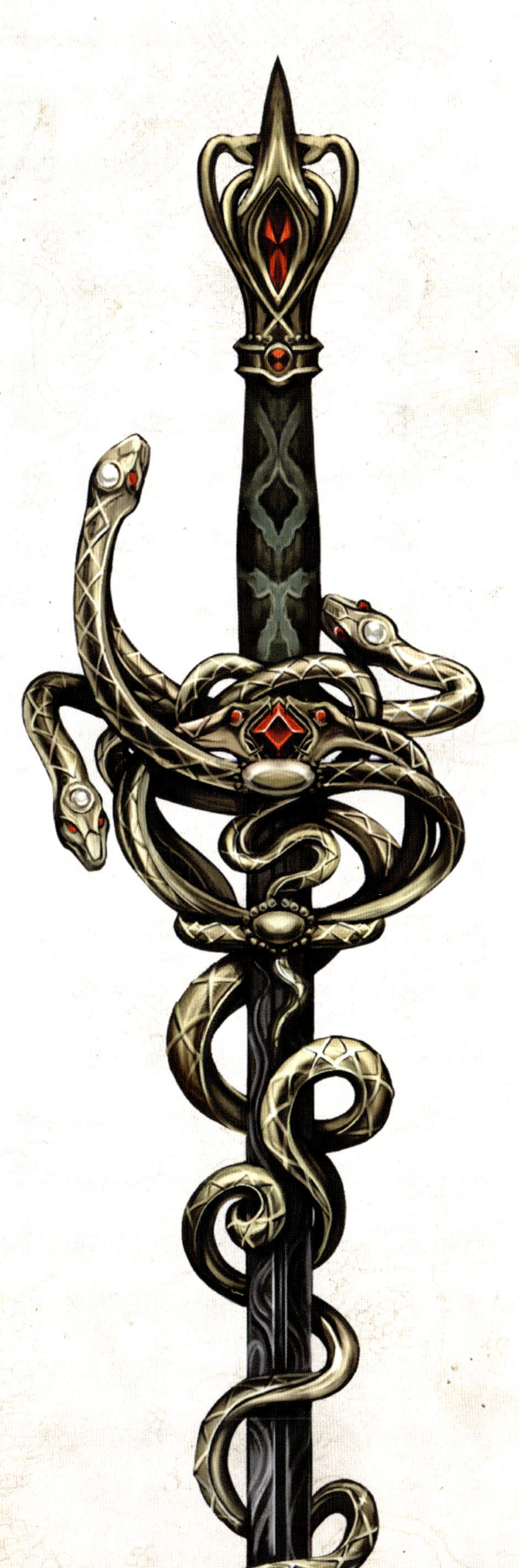

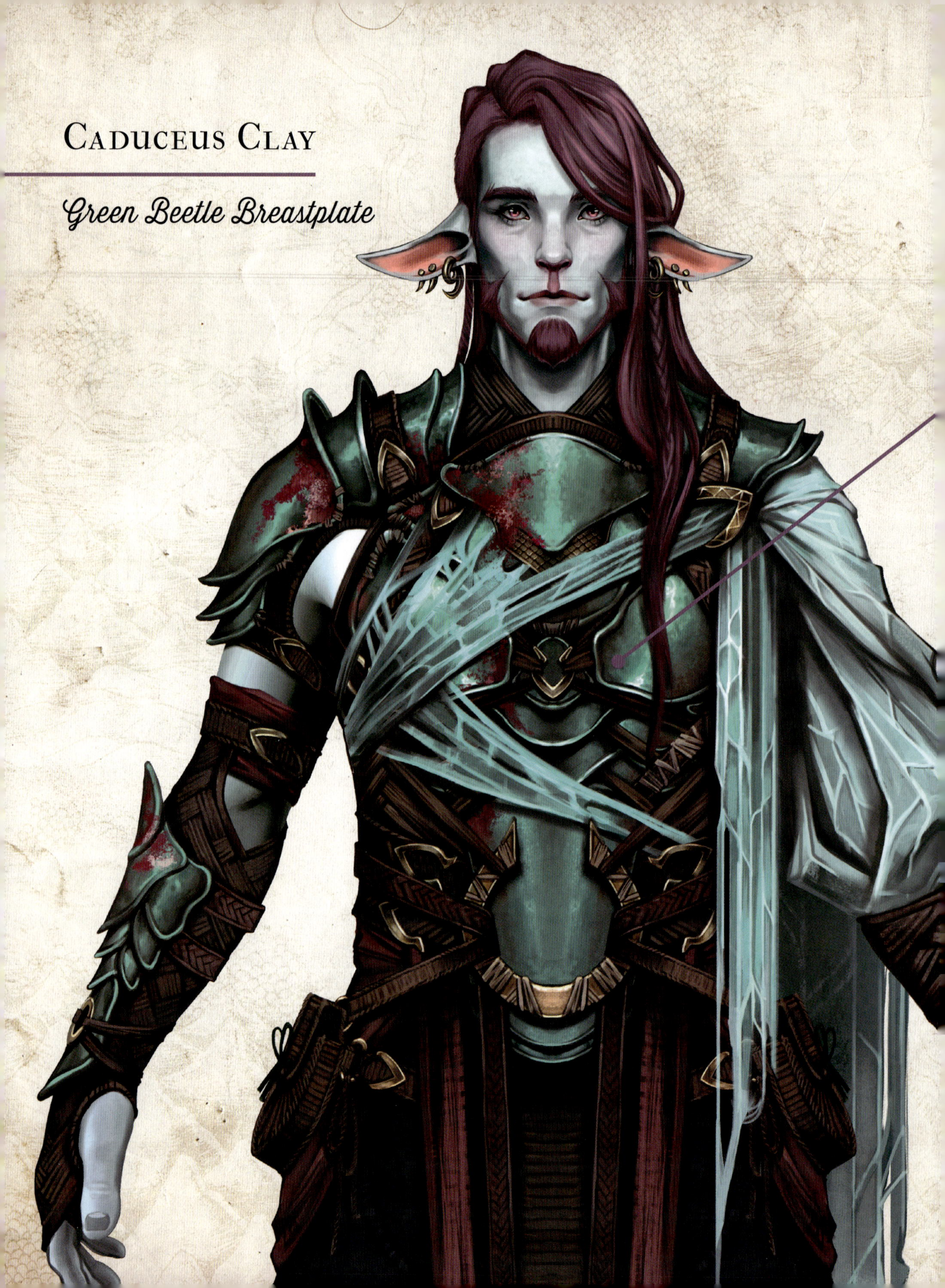
Caduceus Clay
Green Beetle Breastplate

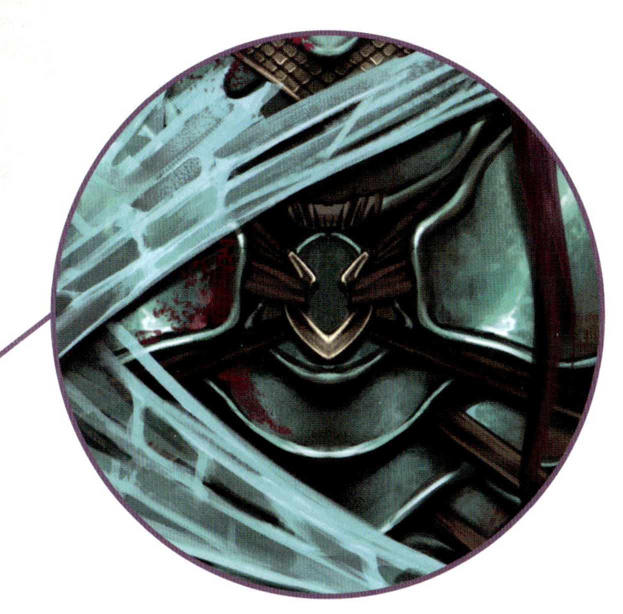

Designed and created by Caduceus's sister, Calliope, this breastplate is a cherished family piece, given to him in his youth, and a symbol of the Clay family; as his family left to investigate the mystery of the fading Blooming Grove, they left Caduceus behind. When eventually, he was moved by divine vision and the Mighty Nein's appeal for help with the Iron Shepherds, he brought that piece of home with him, using his family's legacy to help keep him safe on his journey across Wildemount.

"I find it difficult to speak on divinity and those who follow them. Not because I lack faith, or because I do not believe, but because my chosen goddess is she of knowledge. And one of her first tenets is thus: to know there is always more to know, to make peace with that which cannot bc known.

And so the Clay family, in my research, falls into both categories. The divine mission that the Wildmother tasked each of them with, calling them one by one from the Blooming Grove of Shadycreek Run . . . it is not lost on me that had any of them succeeded on the other side of Wildemount entirely, then young Caduceus might never have chosen to leave with the Mighty Nein to seek them. He might have been content to stay with the quiet dead of the north forever.

And so, this the peace I must make: if not for the failure of each family member, Caduceus does not go and find them. If not for the dedication to the Wildmother, Caduceus does not have the faith to go in search of answers. With no knowledge and nothing but faith, Caduceus Clay lives more by my tenets than I: he knew he did not know and had already made peace with the unknown. Such is the wisdom of divine healers, and I can only hope I practice such prudence when I need it most."

—D'Rishk Dawnscale

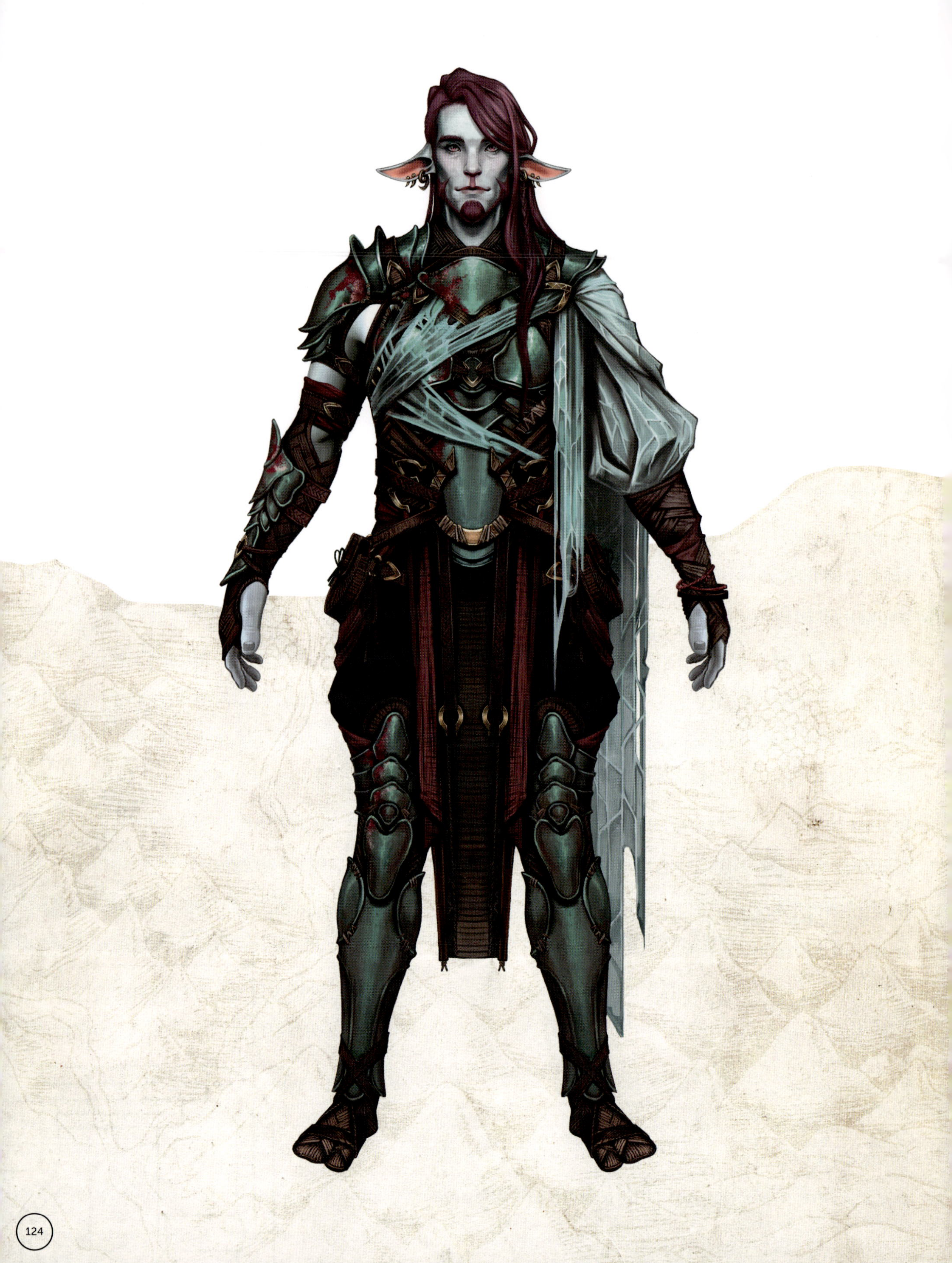

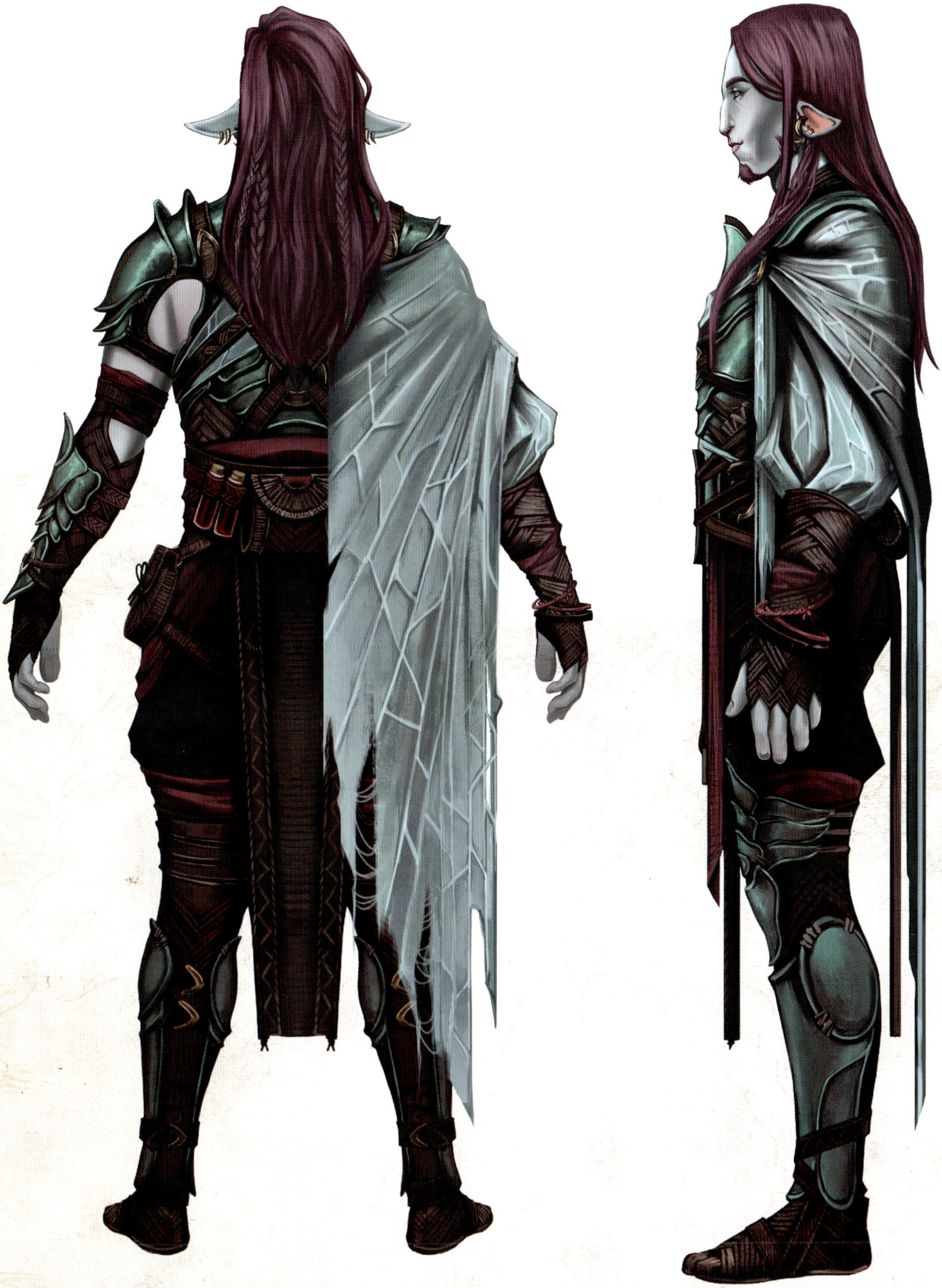

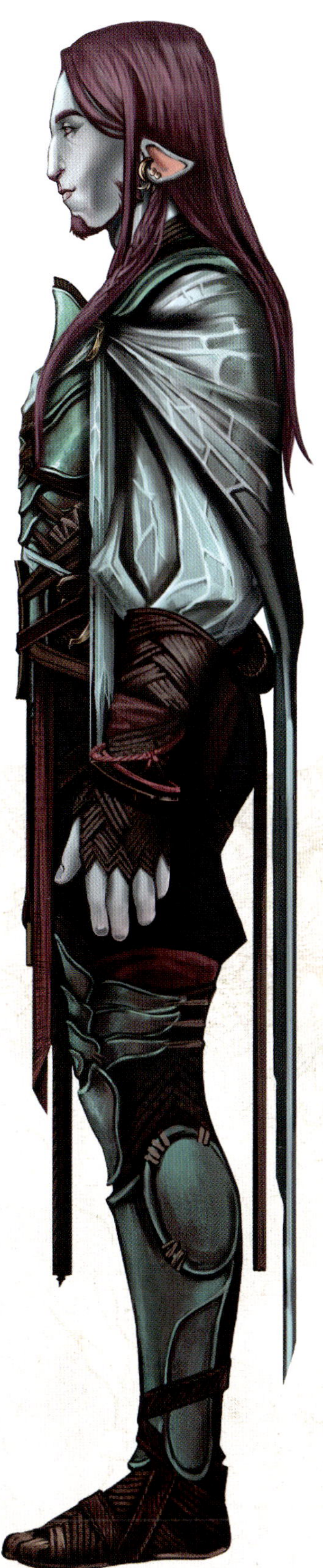

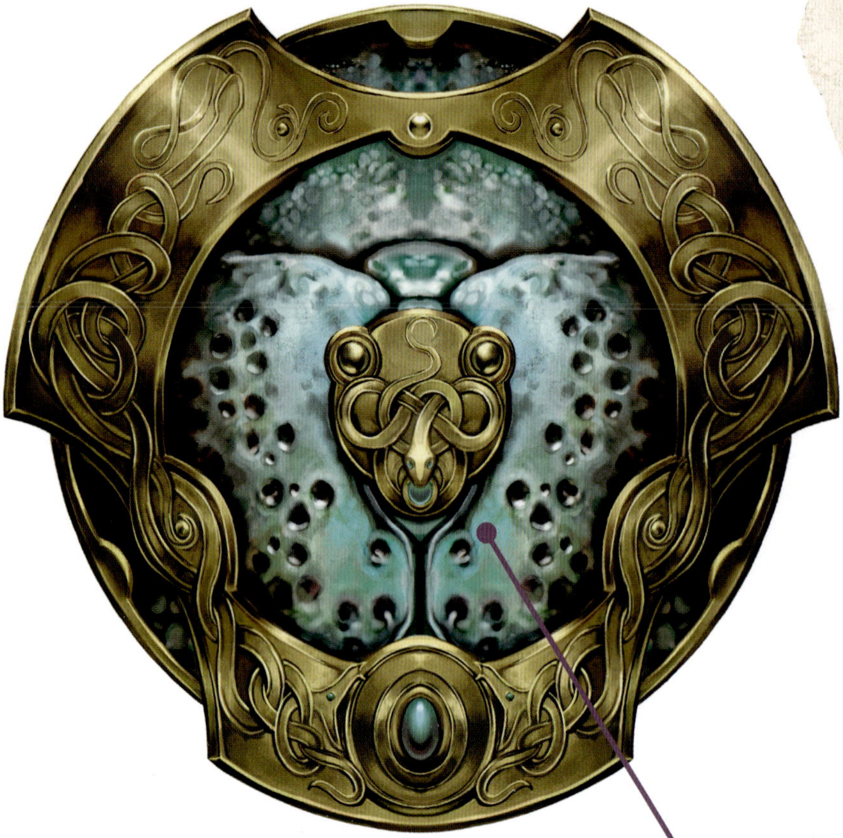

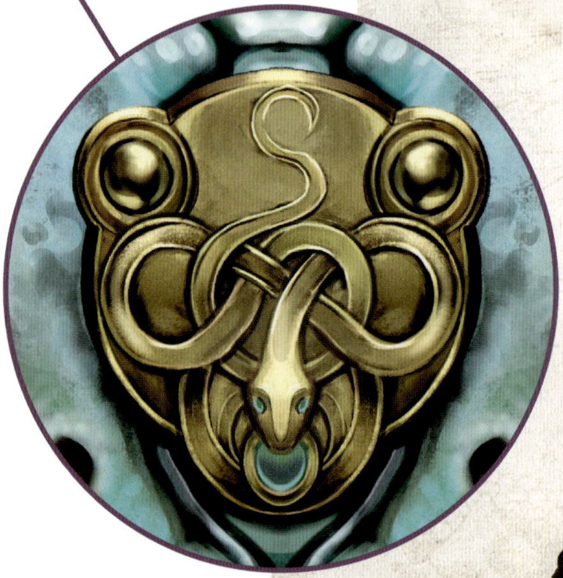

Shield of Retribution

A powerful shield found on the corpse of an abomination, deep in the heart of the Temple of the False Serpent on the island of Urukayxl in the Lucidian Ocean, this gold and marble shield is hefty, adding even more protection to the wielder. And even though it did its original owner little good, Caduceus got very good use out of it, adding it to his armor and invoking its enchantment to cause a retributive burst of energy against attackers, pushing them back twenty feet and giving the forest giant healer some breathing room. Later, as he picked up other protective items, he passed off the Shield of Retribution to Jester, who added it to her own repertoire.

Blightstaff

A reminder of home and a connection to the world of the Wildmother itself, this staff came with Caduceus from the minute he left the Blooming Grove with the Mighty Nein. Carrying a very light enchantment, the Blightstaff houses a colony of beetles within its wooden and crystal length, ready to emerge at the call of Caduceus and harry those who would harm the bearer of the staff. Though the beetles were called on from time to time, Caduceus often used the spells of his divine goddess in service to the Nein and found the staff as an item of home to lean on, both physically and emotionally, as he went in search of the rest of the Clay family.

"Blight makes right! "

—Caduceus Clay, constructing a prayer

"You can't spell blight without light, and like the sun above, may you find yourself warm as you fall to eternal rest"

—Caduceus Clay, constructing a prayer

"You know, wordplay is not a family strength. Forgive us for putting words to the nameless nature that is yours to command.
Gift us your touch and may all we encounter wither or bloom by your divine mission."

—Caduceus Clay, constructing a prayer

Aeorian Protective Chestplate

Found within the Genesis Ward of the devastated ruins of Aeor, deep in the northern wastes of Eiselcross, this dark metal chestplate is inscribed with dozens and dozens of incredibly small and intricate runes, not just granting a bolstered defense, but also imbuing the wearer with the effects of a heroic spell meant to transfer some vitality back in the middle of pitched combat. Caduceus found that the chestplate worked best for him and his attire, and so attuned it, bringing it with him for the remainder of their time hunting the Tombtakers and ending the threat of the Somnovem and Lucien.

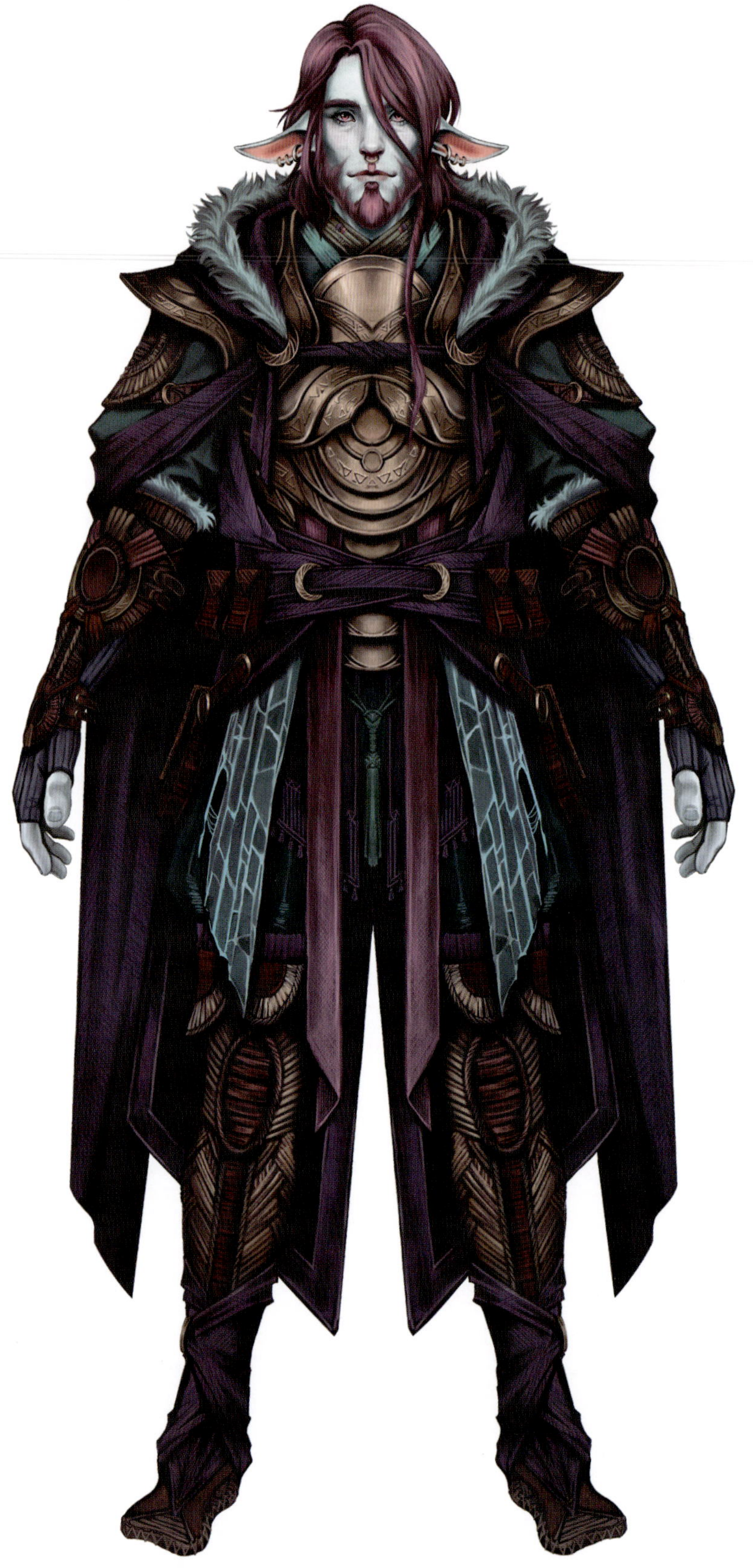

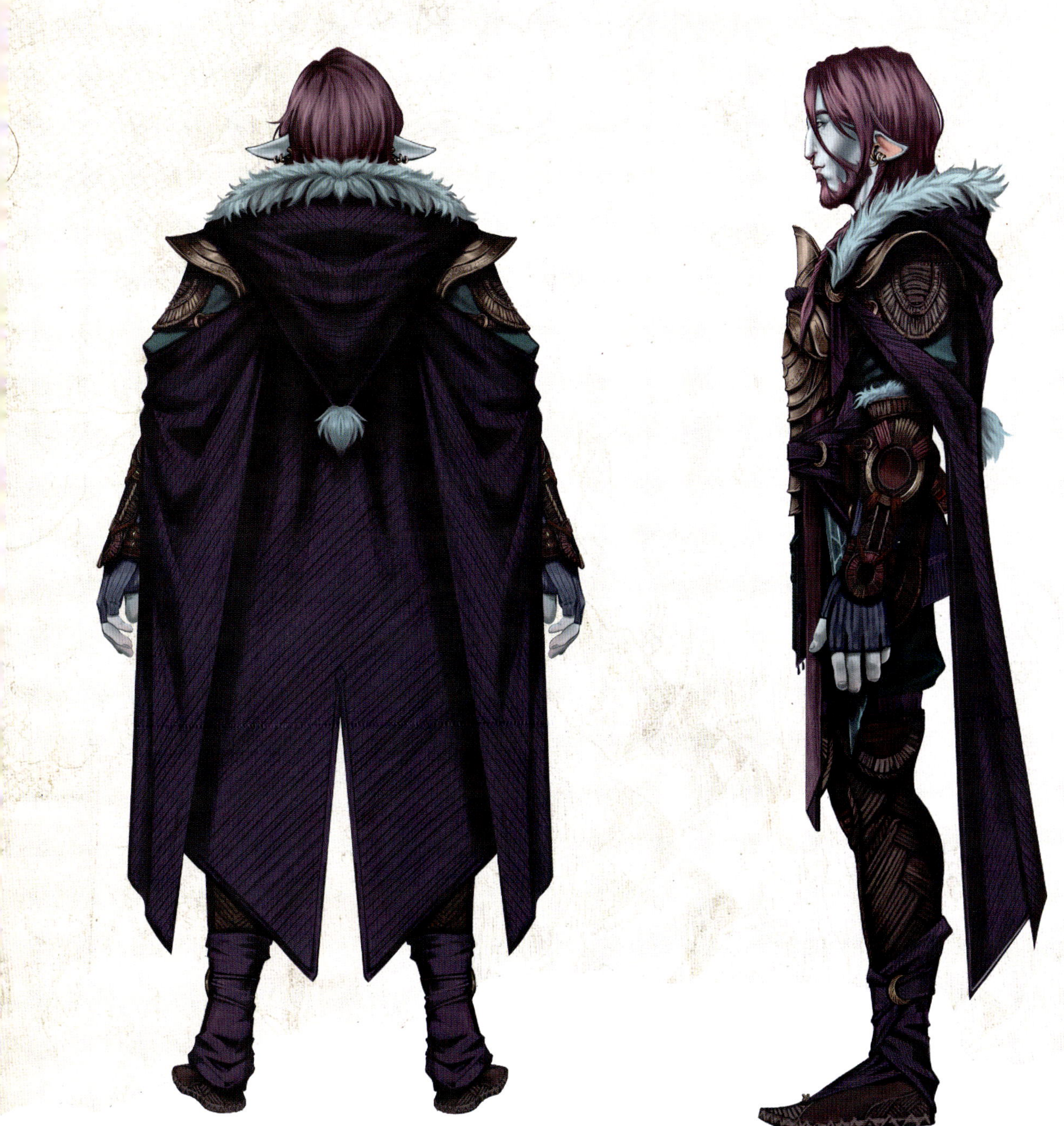

"That the mage engineers of Aeor found the time and funds to engrave a spell of vitality into the armor of thousands of soldiers but did not in fact deem it necessary to create failsafe mechanisms for the citizens of their floating city should tell you everything you need to know about this supposed arcane paradise."

—*Oren Keth'Kaylis*

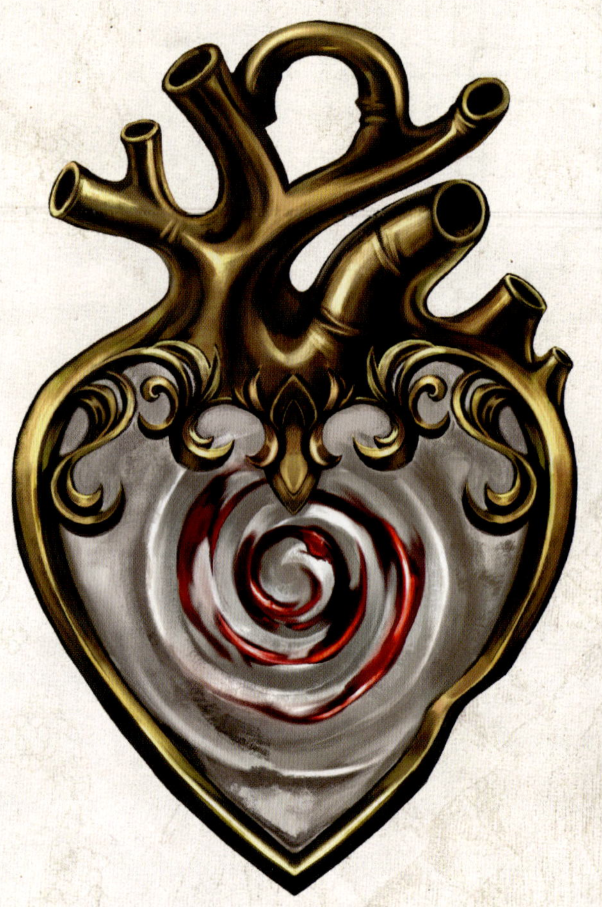

Periapt of Wound Closure

This item changed hands among the Nein several times before it ended up adorning Caduceus's armor. Originally purchased by Mollymauk Tealeaf in Zadash from Pumat Sol of the Invulnerable Vagrant, this item's restorative properties were not strong enough to halt Mollymauk's brutal murder at the hands of the ghoulish Lorenzo. The periapt went to Caleb Widogast, who made use of it to keep his fragile wizard's frame safe in several bouts of combat before it was finally offered to Caduceus. The healer, newly emerged from the Savalirwood that borders Shady Creek Run, was not used to a life of adventure, and he benefited greatly in combat with this handy item, safeguarding his life long enough for him to gain some experience out in the world. It has stayed with him since.

"This enchanter would encourage you simply not to pass out from extreme blood loss in the first place, nor put your fragile body in situations in which this could occur. However, barring that, kindly wait up to six seconds for this handy amulet to go ahead and stabilize you, and try to do better next time, adventurer!"

—Shopkeeper's note left on the item, signed Pumat Sol Prime

"The Betrayer Gods and their followers often underestimate the Wildmother, a goddess of tremendous strength and ferocity, and her acolytes; something tells me they find that just fine. The rose does not want you to remember its thorns. The ocean does not wish you to recall its crushing depths. The sky wants you to love its calm and clarity, not its crashing storms. The tiger desires you see its stripes, not its teeth. For many, the Wildmother is a deity of peace and growth, beauty and life. But the rose, the sea, the sky, the beast—there are wells of strength, fury, power, and sheer wildness waiting just out of sight for those who would set fire to the world she has loved and protected all her life. Underestimate the goddess of nature at your own peril, for blood can nourish roots as surely as water."

—D'Rishk Dawnscale

Holy Symbol of the Wildmother

The Wildmother's symbol is a wreath of leaves, berries, and flowers, broken down the center with a shepherd's crook of wood. And though the Clay family all worshiped her in their own way, it was Caduceus, the last left home in the Blooming Grove, who went on to have a deep and meaningful connection with the goddess of the wild and the earth, the harvest and the sea. As he grew in experience, his faith grew alongside him, and he became battle-hardened in body and spirit. The Wildmother often visited him in dreams or moments of prayer, guiding him as the wind guides the seed to take root. The dichotomy of her domain and her love was later seen in the burgeoning faith and oath from companion Fjord Stone, who took up her tenets with a warrior's oath.

Caduceus, moved by Fjord's journey, made him his own symbol of the Wildmother. There could be no more fitting symbol for two men caught in the torrential rain of chaos and crisis, and, from that deluge, grew.

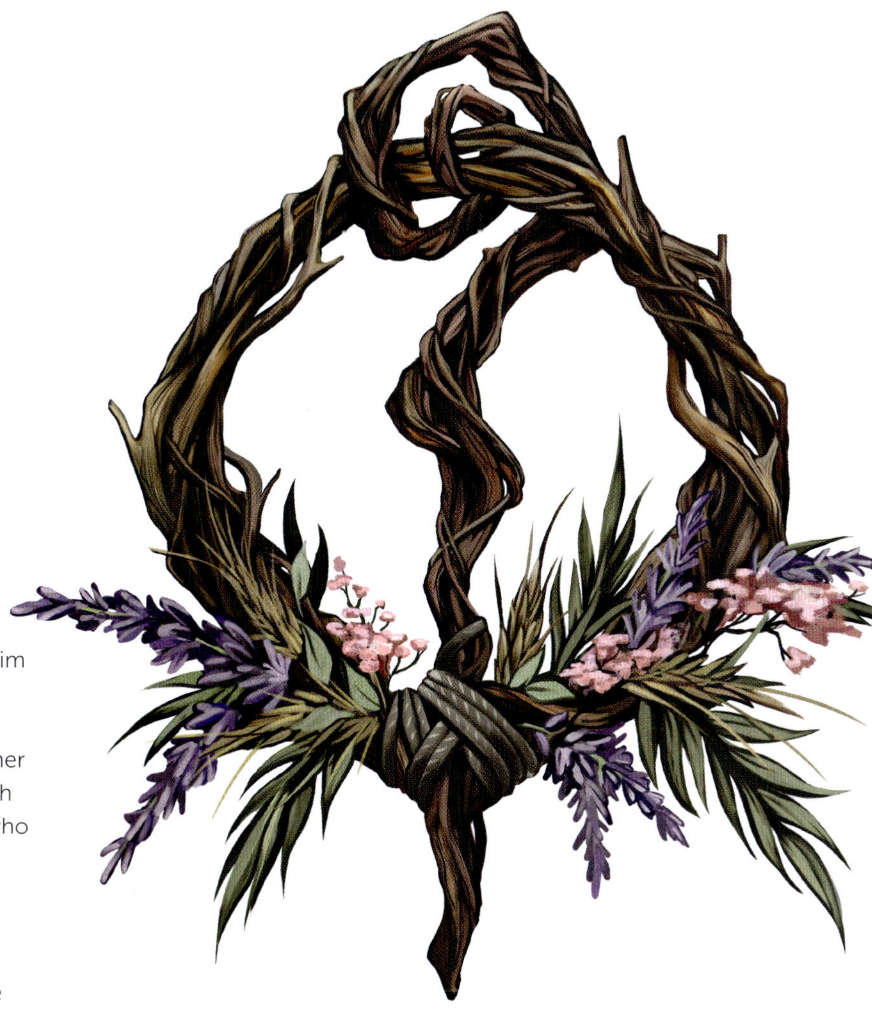

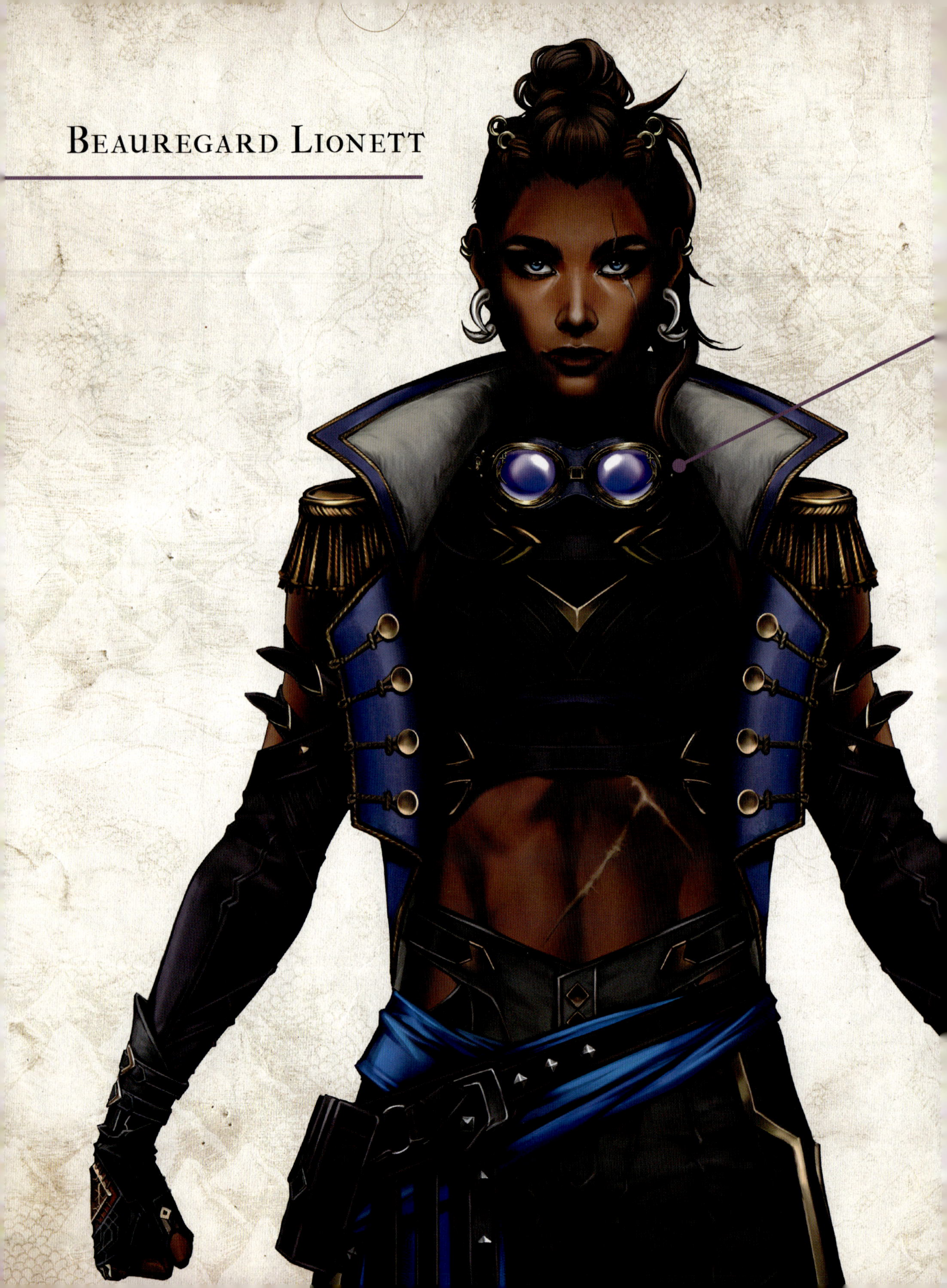
BEAUREGARD LIONETT

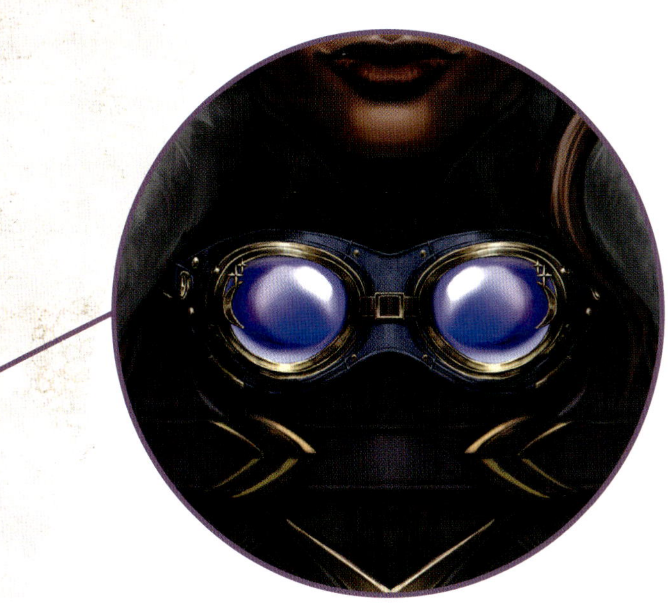

"You understand I cannot divulge the secrets of my order, yes? Very well. Attempt to wheedle information at your own peril, songstress.

Now, my pupil. Yes, I am very proud. Her path toward Expositor is hers to discuss, but from my observations, it is one that she eventually embraced. Even after learning of the truth of her time in the monastery, of the betrayal of Zeenoth, Beauregard Lionett came to understand that she could do more good from within than beating her fists against the walls from outside the mechanism of hierarchy.

That is something that some come to the teachings with, but more often than not, the true transformation begins when they start taking seriously not the studies but themselves. To know you can do good, you must believe you *are* good. To know you can enact serious change, you must take yourself seriously, your mission. To give your heart to the teachings, you must open the door to your own heart, and then, yes, keep that door open. Through pain and heartache, loss and fury. Every sorrow you invite through the door of your heart helps as much as it hurts.

Expositor Lionett has torn the hinges off that door, and I'm proud of her; even I still have trouble with that from time to time. But her time with the Mighty Nein gave her a family to share the burden of such a heart. And friends to share in joy, when it arrives—or, more often, when it is fought for. And Beauregard is a hell of a fighter."

—Tallulah Fontaine, in conversation with Expositor Dairon of the Cobalt Soul, interviewed while undercover in Emon

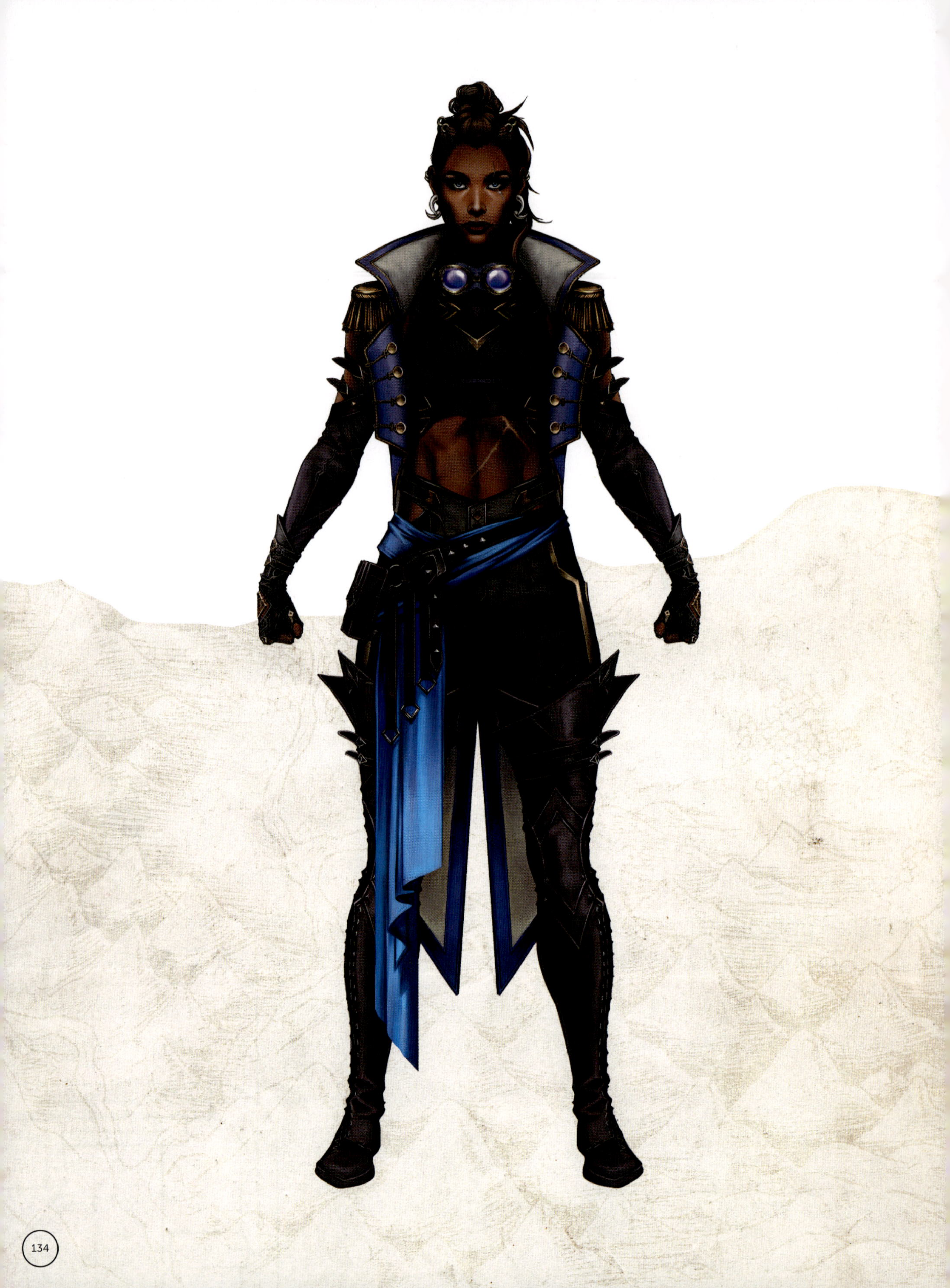

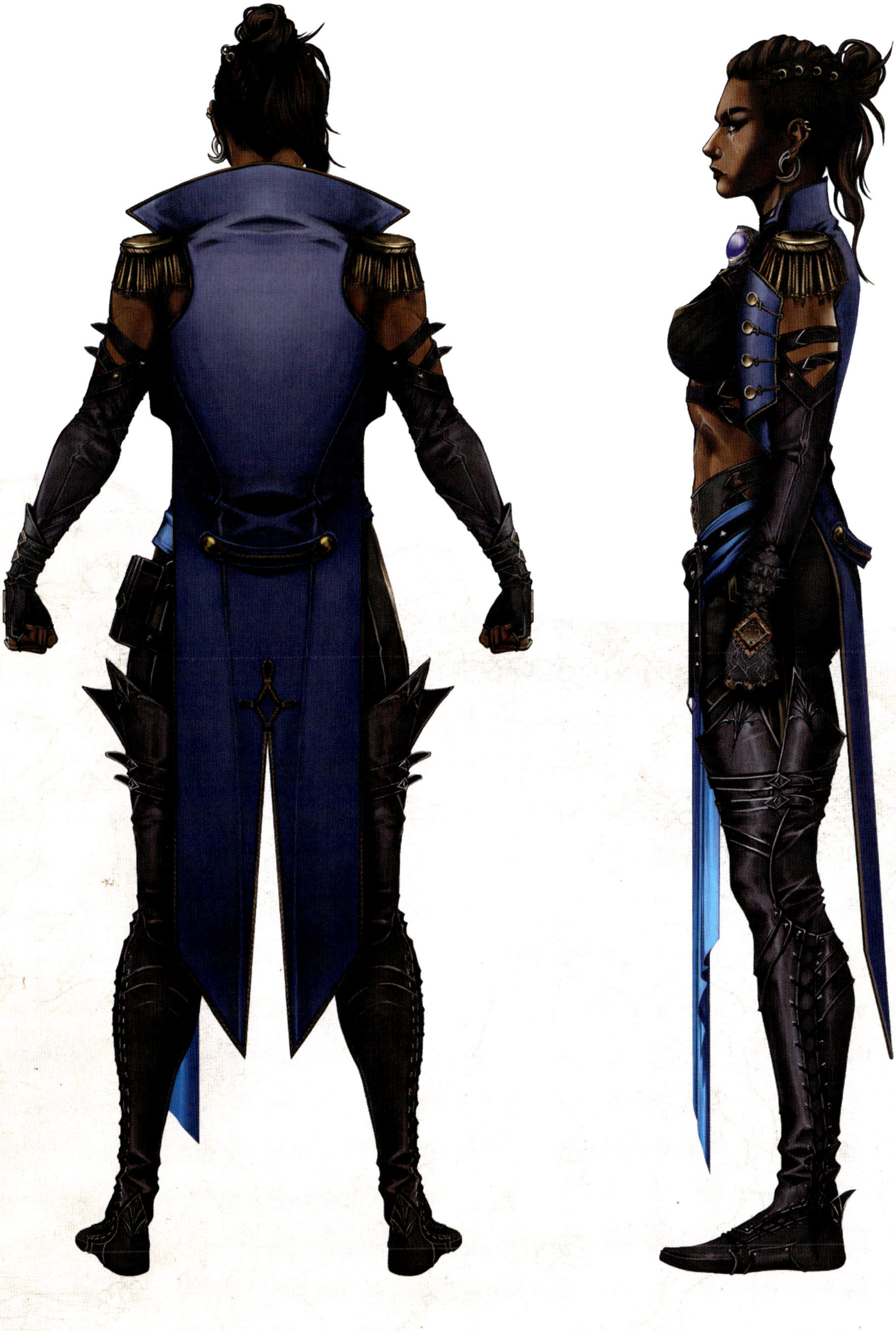

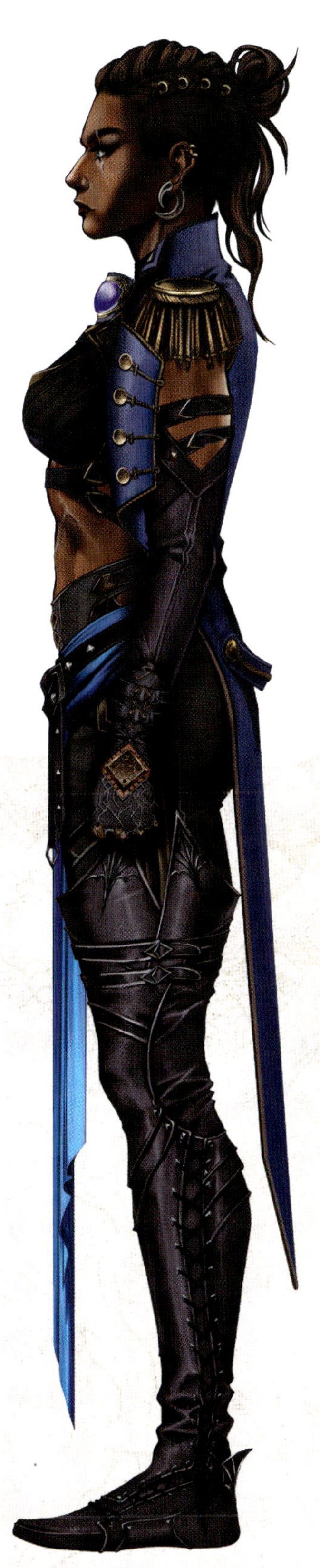

Boots of the Vigilant

These black and indigo boots were taken from a defeated Kryn operative found in the sewers of Zadash following a failed attempt to steal back a Luxon Beacon for his dynasty. The echo knight, bereft of gear and health, was soon killed by agents of the Empire, and the Mighty Nein left with both his magic items and the sought-after Luxon Beacon. Using the inherent time/space manipulation of dunamancy, these boots afforded great alacrity to the operative Beauregard Lionett, making a quick warrior even faster in the pitch of battle.

"As swift as shadows cast from light
Faster than the arrow's flight
My blood, my life, for ruler Bright
Thus the creed of the Echo Knight."

—Oren Keth'Kaylis, a reading from the "Oath of Echoes," made when an echo knight is sworn in

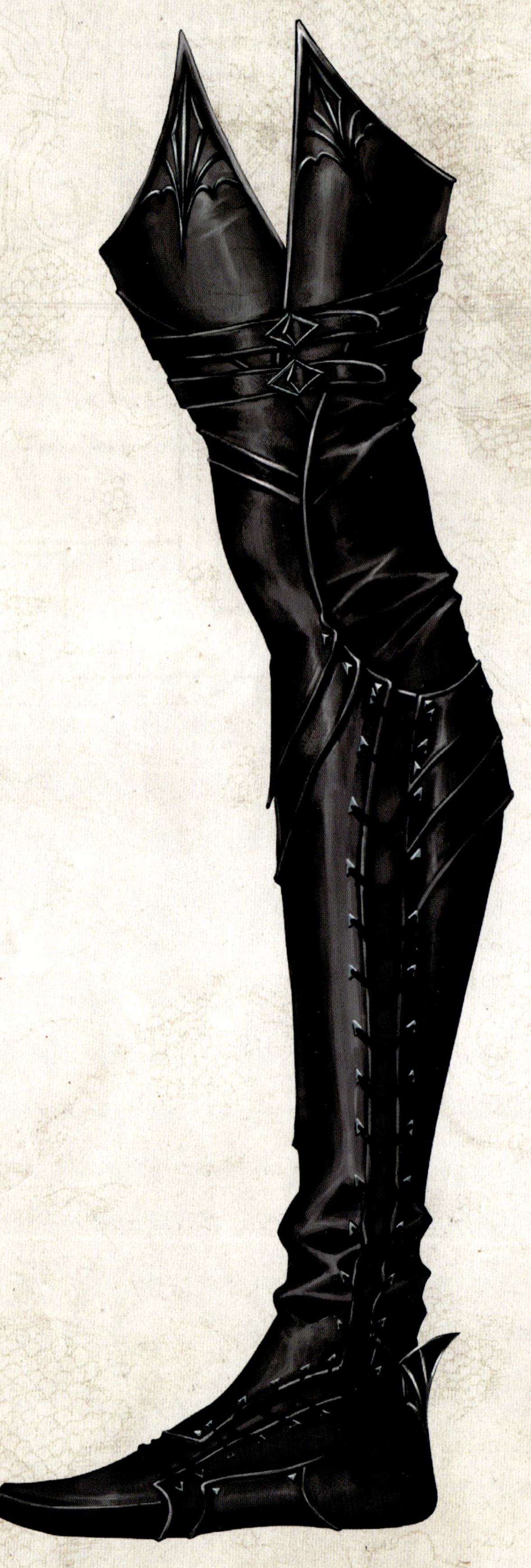

Headband of Intelligence

Found in the depths of the Halls of Halas, also known as the Archmage's Bane, this beautiful silver circlet was stored in one of many arcane warehouses scattered throughout the ancient archmage's demiplane. Under assault from a mageslayer golem, Beauregard found this in the wreckage, whereupon she took her already bright mind to nigh-impossible heights. Nestled on her brow, her increased intelligence combined with her precise strikes and keen insight made her an even deadlier weapon not just for the Mighty Nein but for the interests of the Cobalt Soul at large.

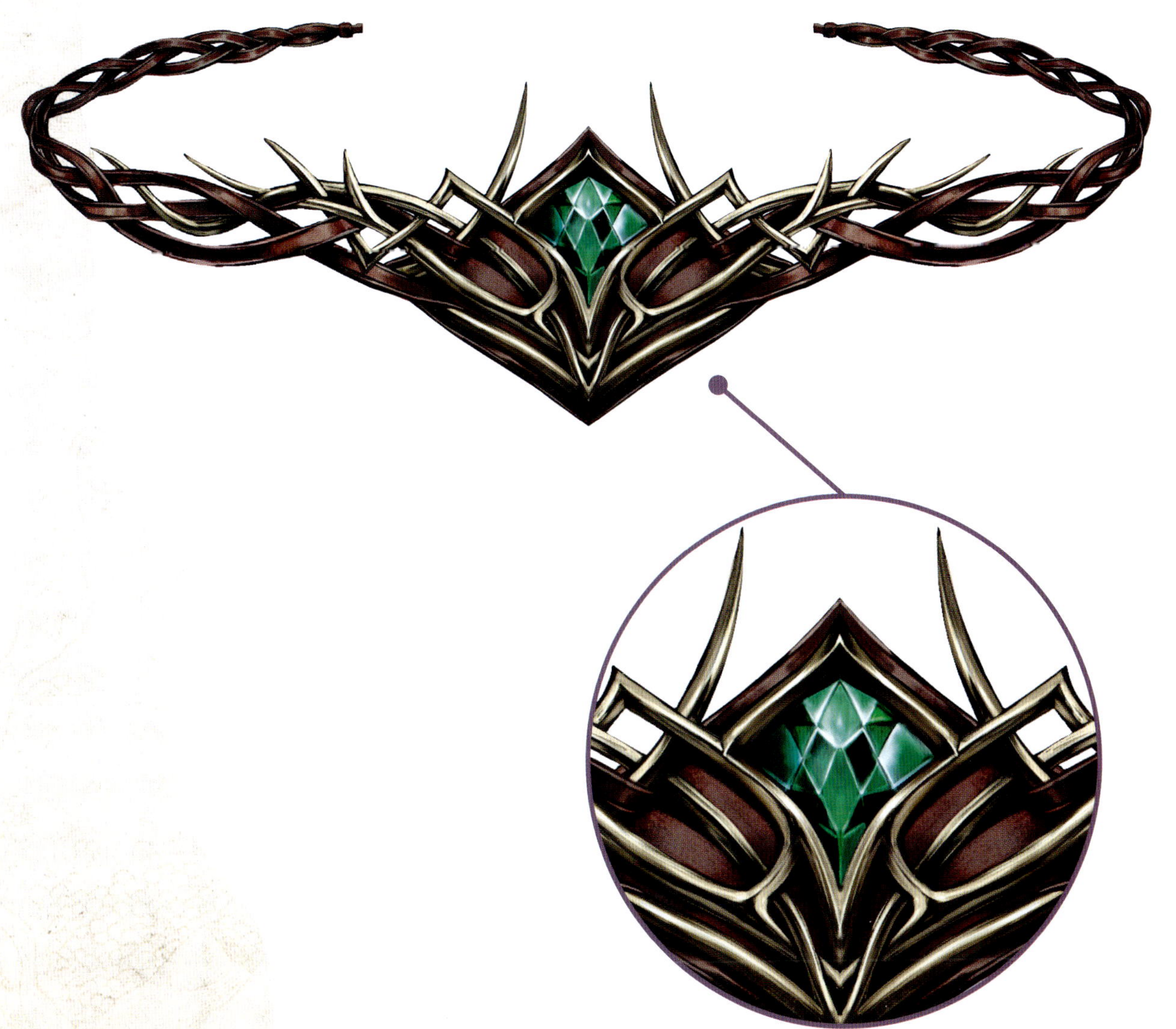

Maelstrom Gloves

These gloves were originally worn by a powerful demon as he emerged from a planar tear in an underground cavern in Asarius, a city deep in the heart of Xhorhas. The fiend used these in conjunction with powerful magic and two cunning fiends, an incubus and a succubus, to attempt the death of the Mighty Nein. But in his defeat, these gloves went to the most martial of the group. With the power of lightning now at her fingertips and the ability to extend her martial prowess over a distance, Beauregard, a growing weapon of the Cobalt Soul, became even more adept.

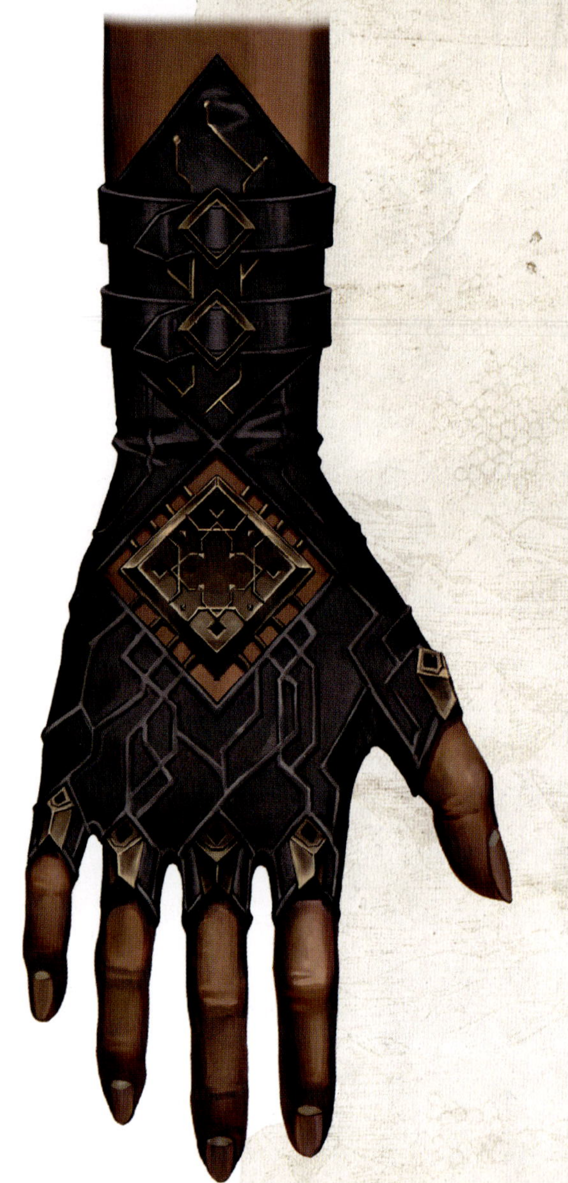

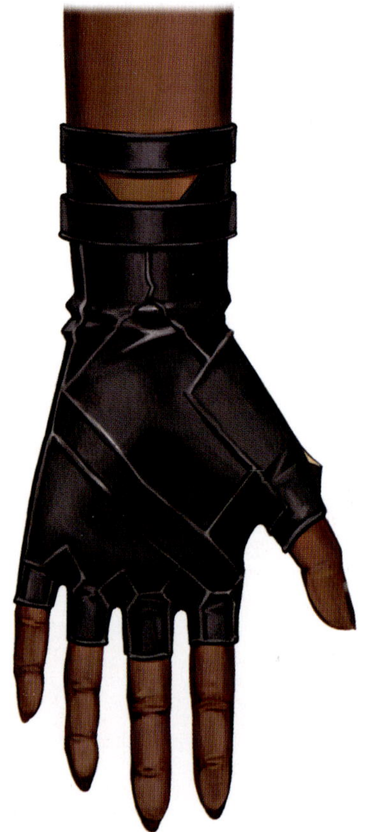

"That which injures the demons of the Abyss will eventually be embraced, for what is pain to a fiend but education. Such are the weapons of the Outer Realms built, for what hurts a fiend even a little will make a mortal wish they were dead."

—Oren Keth'Kaylis

Goggles of Twilight

As one of the few members of the Mighty Nein without the ability to see in the dark, Beauregard found a pair of enchanted lenses in the mines near Alfield, off a dead priest of Yeenoghu. With the Goggles of Twilight, Beauregard was able to see in the dark perfectly, enabling even stealthier approaches and ease in pitch-black night. These Goggles stayed with her for her entire time with the Nein. The only time she shared them with other members of the Nein who lacked such vision was when she was granted temporary boons by the Somnovem, one of which was the ability to see in the dark. When those boons faded with the defeat of Lucien, she returned to her use of the Goggles of Night.

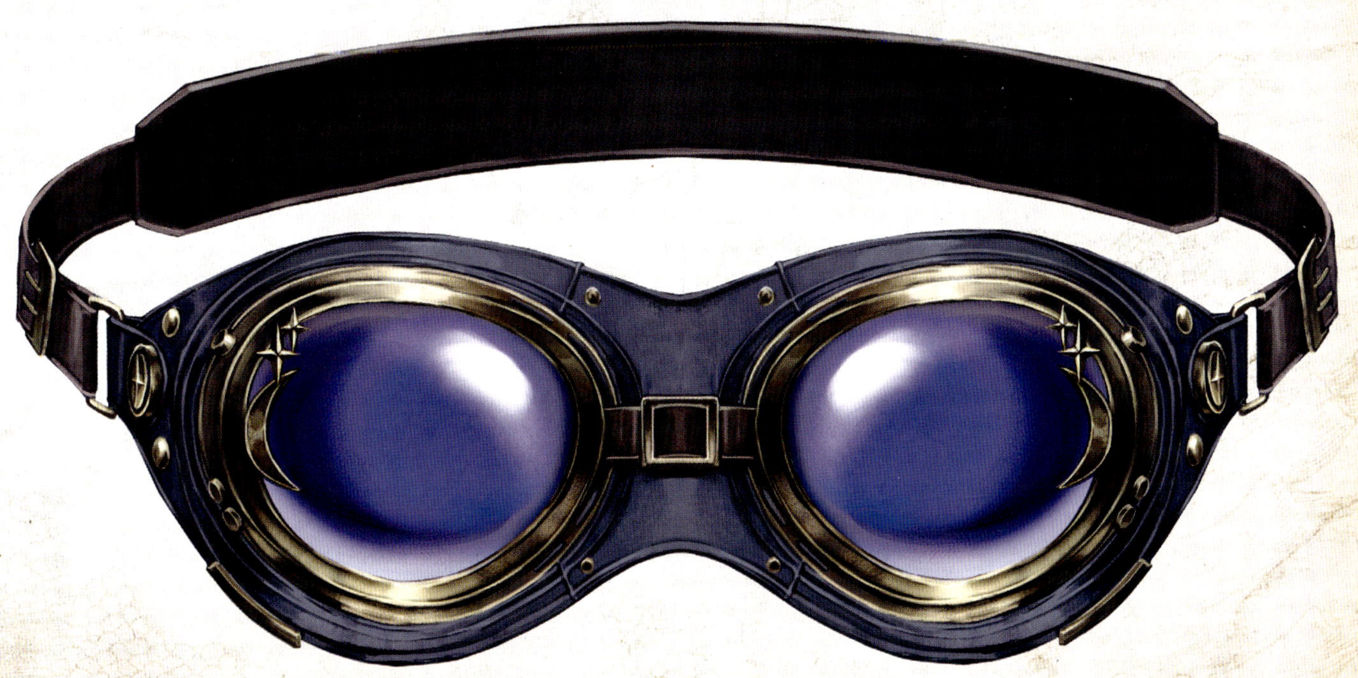

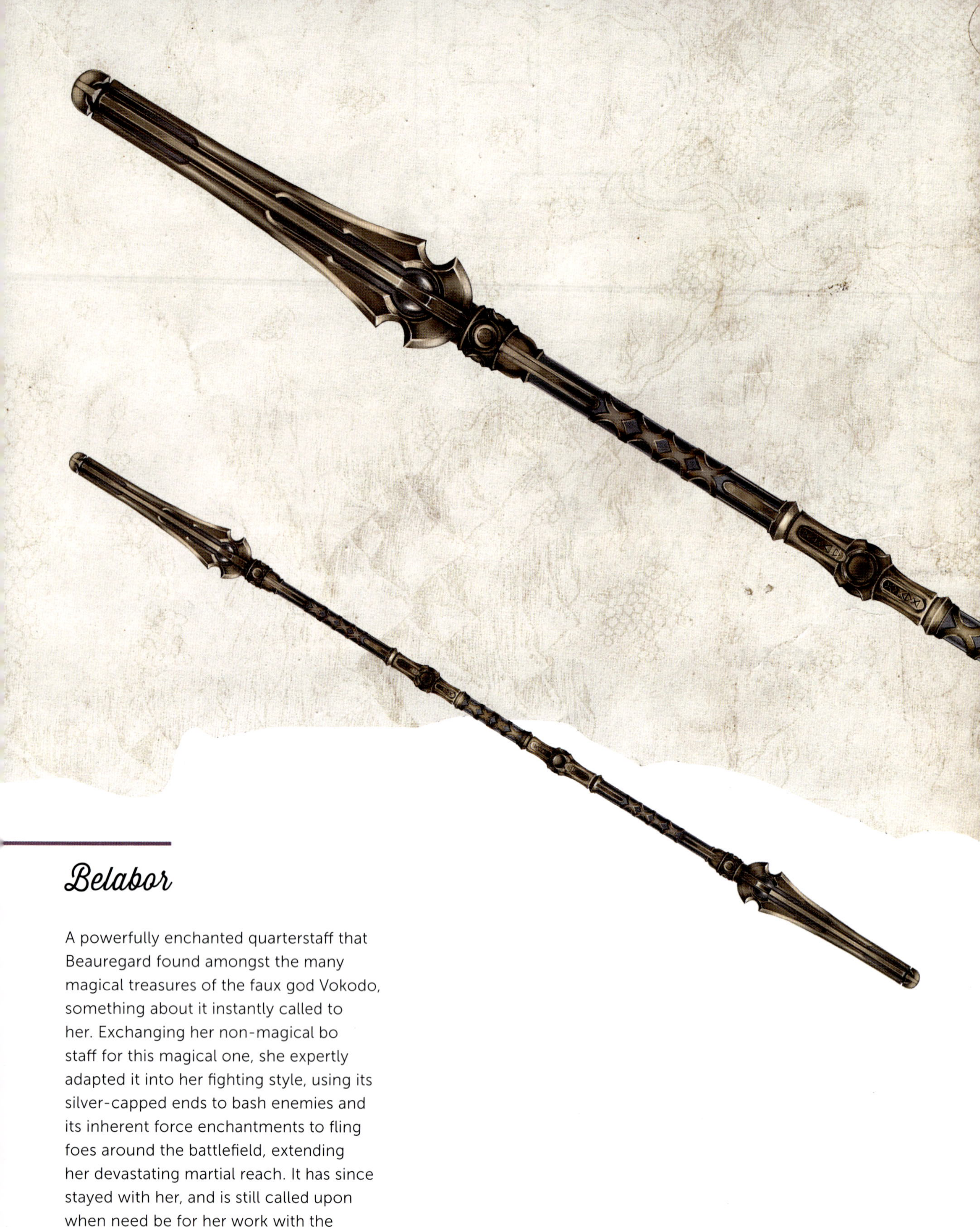

Belabor

A powerfully enchanted quarterstaff that Beauregard found amongst the many magical treasures of the faux god Vokodo, something about it instantly called to her. Exchanging her non-magical bo staff for this magical one, she expertly adapted it into her fighting style, using its silver-capped ends to bash enemies and its inherent force enchantments to fling foes around the battlefield, extending her devastating martial reach. It has since stayed with her, and is still called upon when need be for her work with the Cobalt Soul.

"Ours is an art of motion. Of stillness. And of every single moment between one and the other. How we navigate those moments, how we choose to spend the currency of motion to pay the price of actions, is much of what we will study here. And make no mistake, what we do is an art. Balletic steps of precision. Threading movement through foes. The musicality of muscle, eye, and spirit. Ours is an art that unites body, mind, and soul. And it all begins with this: a single breath."

—Recorded at the Cobalt Soul of Rexxentrum, recited by Archivist Orpho Arabel

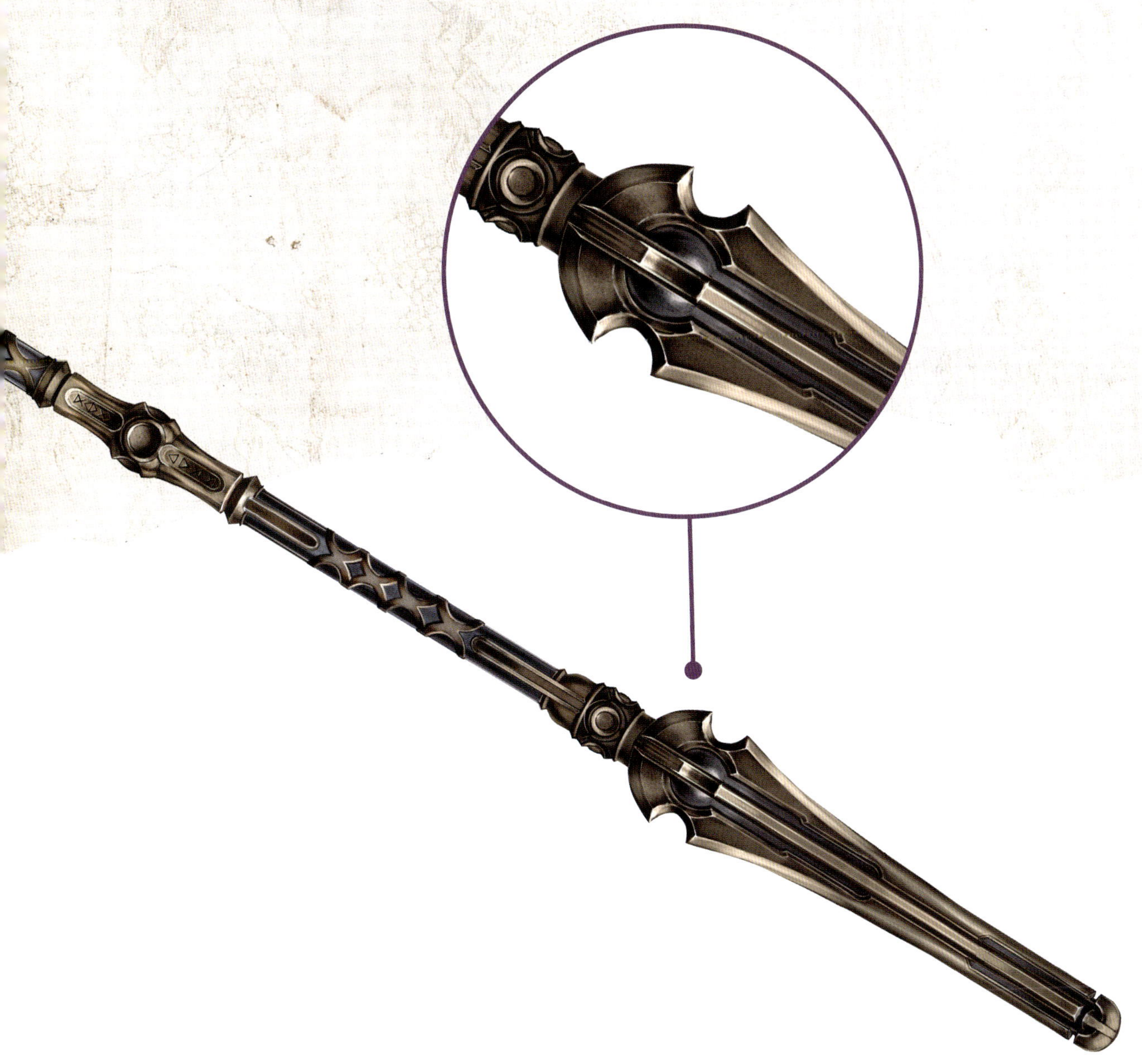

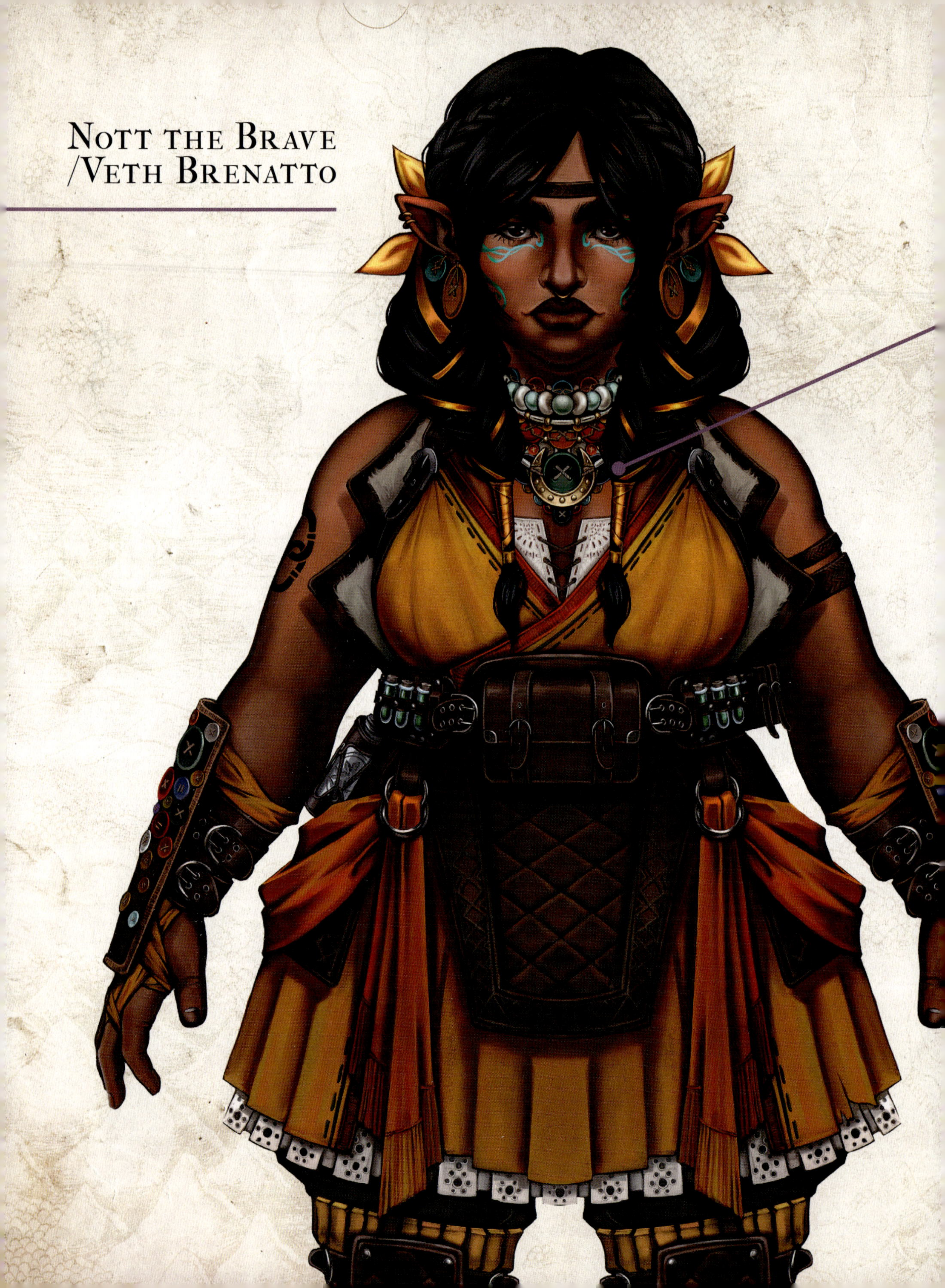

Nott the Brave /Veth Brenatto

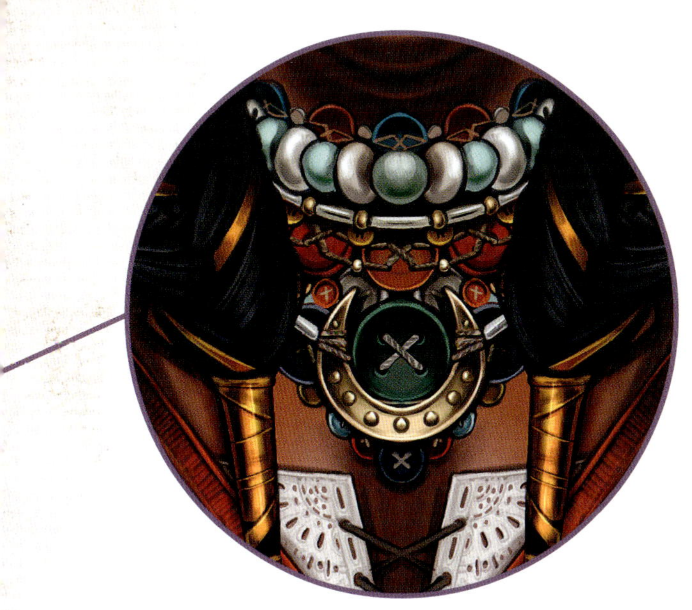

"As a fellow green gal, I feel close to the story of Veth Brenatto, who for a while, hid behind a different name. Nott the Brave is who emerged from the forests of Felderwin, but it was Veth Brenatto who gave herself to the goblin hoard and bought her husband and son enough time to escape. It was Nott the Brave suddenly in a body that was not hers, feared and seen as monstrous, just as much as it was Veth Brenatto who could not bear to call herself thus as a goblin.

While she's in her transformed state, we have to remember this, friends: Nott never stopped being Veth, and when she became a halfling once more, Veth didn't let go of Nott. Being a goblin taught that halfling sharpshooter things she never could have learned, and a life as a halfling gave that goblin things to live for when all she wanted was to dive into a sea of booze and never surface. Yes, it was a curse that made Veth into Nott. And yes, a spell returned her to the body she knew was always hers. But magic one way or the other cannot account for the bravery, the skill, and the massive heart that belonged to both women, and as the stories say, no magic ever took that away from her. Both of her."

—Tallulah Fontaine

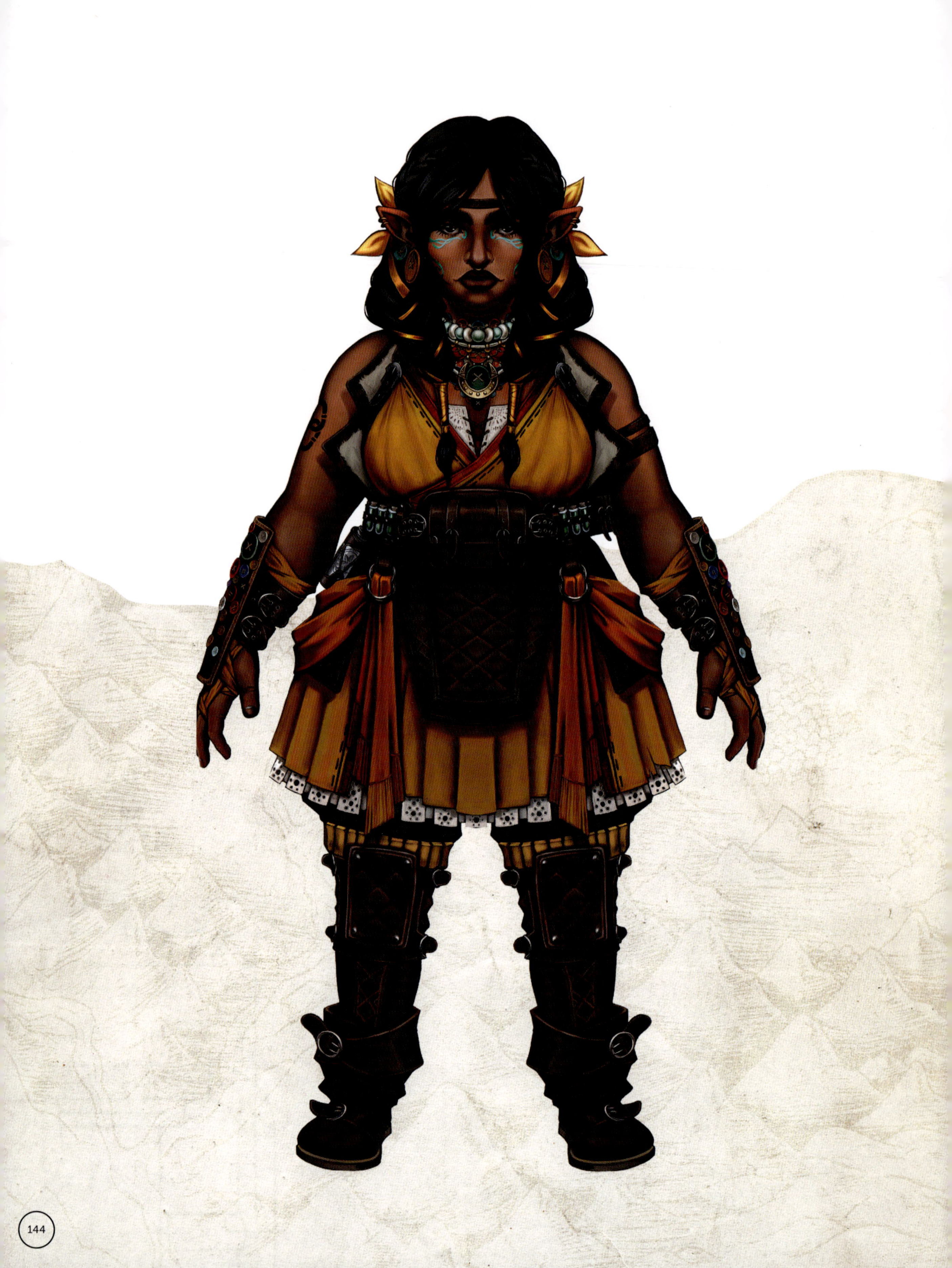

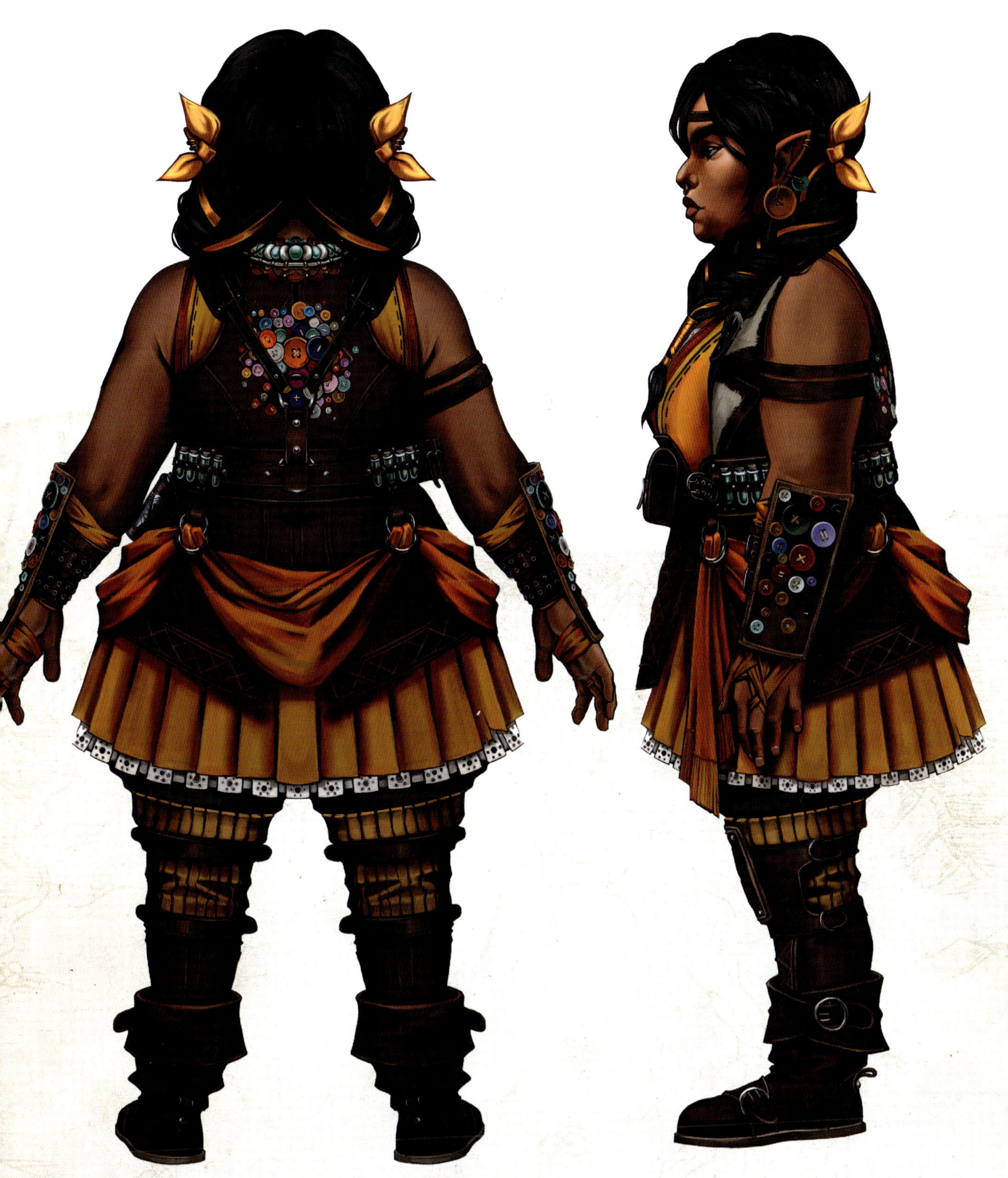

Doll Half-Mask

Nott the Brave found that when she affixed the mask, the bottom half of a ceramic doll's face, to the lower half of her face, with her hood up, the once halfling could at least pass somewhat for her true self. And though the mask made it slightly easier to appear in public, it didn't keep Nott from being caught when she tried to nab something shiny—which was often.

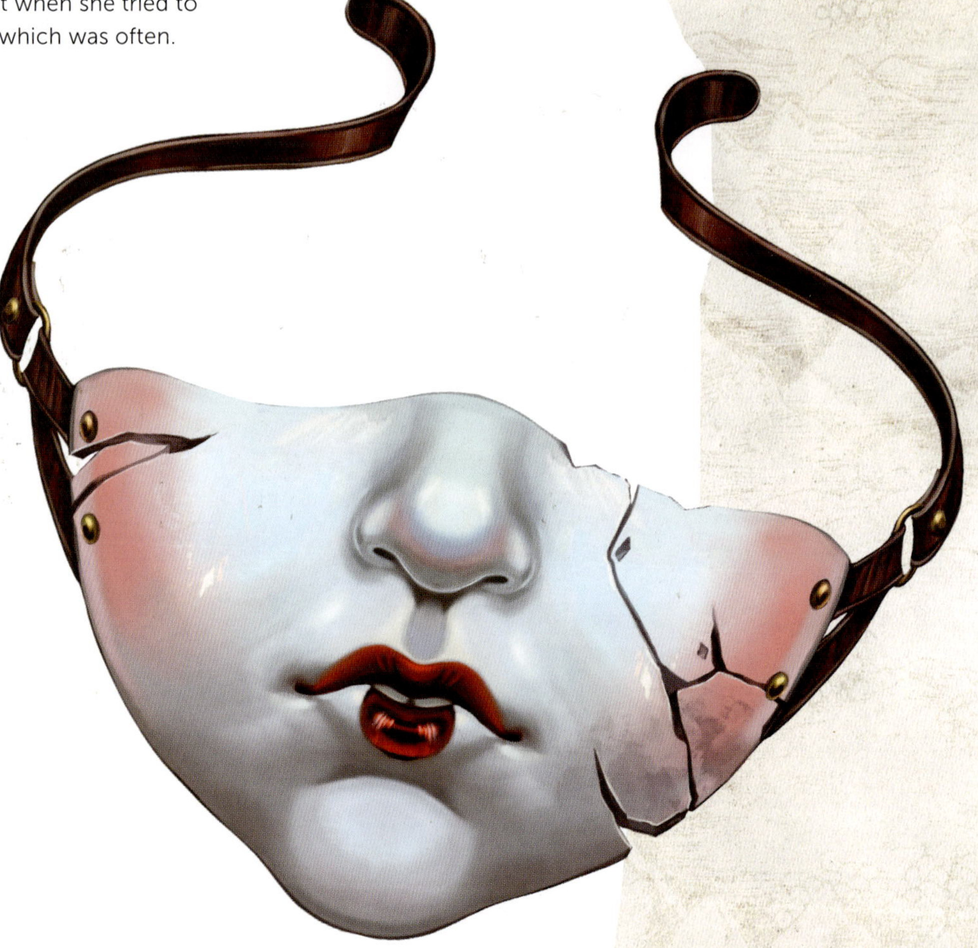

"Sometimes that which we choose to hide within can become the very thing keeping us from ever venturing out."

—Oren Keth'Kaylis

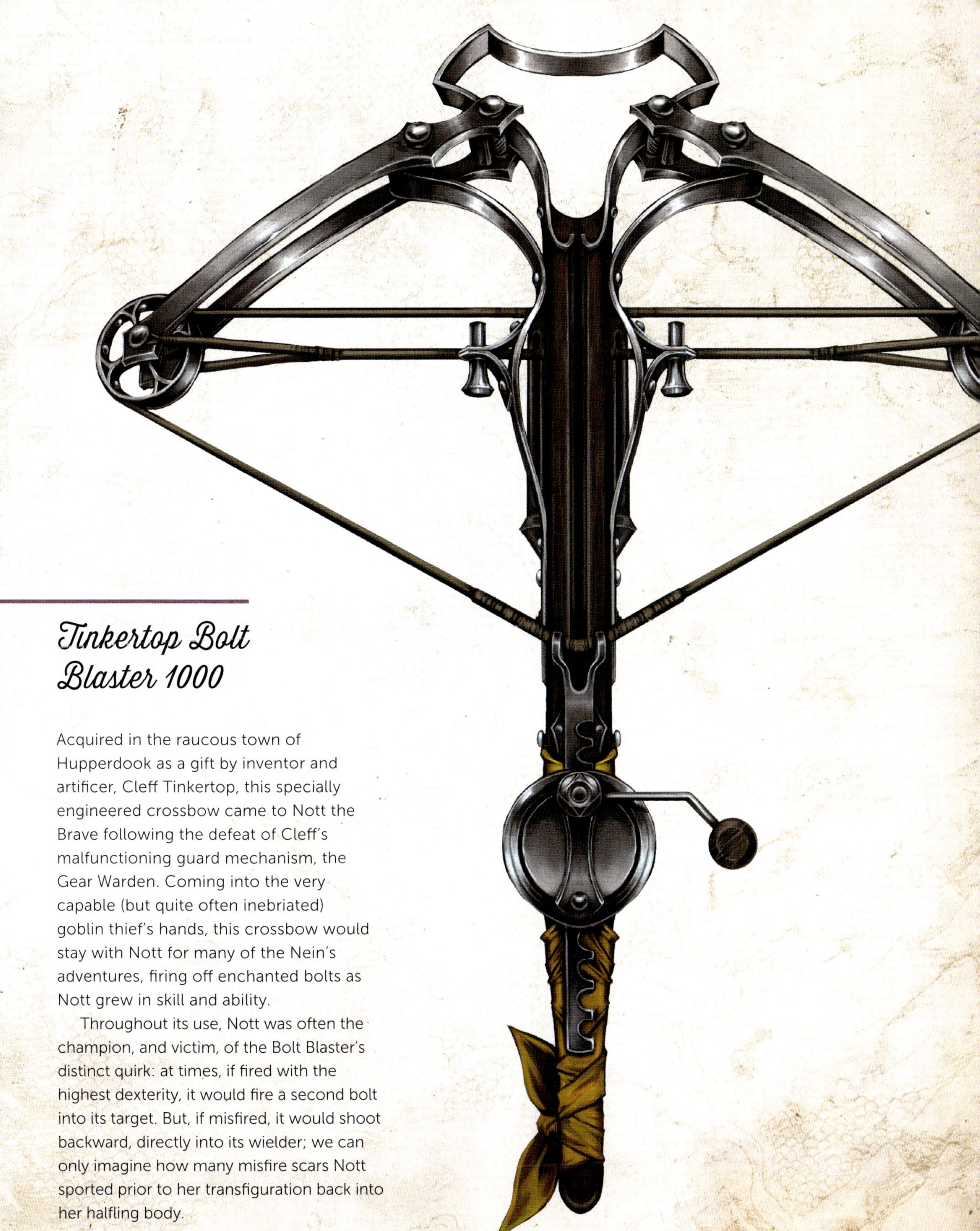

Tinkertop Bolt Blaster 1000

Acquired in the raucous town of Hupperdook as a gift by inventor and artificer, Cleff Tinkertop, this specially engineered crossbow came to Nott the Brave following the defeat of Cleff's malfunctioning guard mechanism, the Gear Warden. Coming into the very capable (but quite often inebriated) goblin thief's hands, this crossbow would stay with Nott for many of the Nein's adventures, firing off enchanted bolts as Nott grew in skill and ability.

Throughout its use, Nott was often the champion, and victim, of the Bolt Blaster's distinct quirk: at times, if fired with the highest dexterity, it would fire a second bolt into its target. But, if misfired, it would shoot backward, directly into its wielder; we can only imagine how many misfire scars Nott sported prior to her transfiguration back into her halfling body.

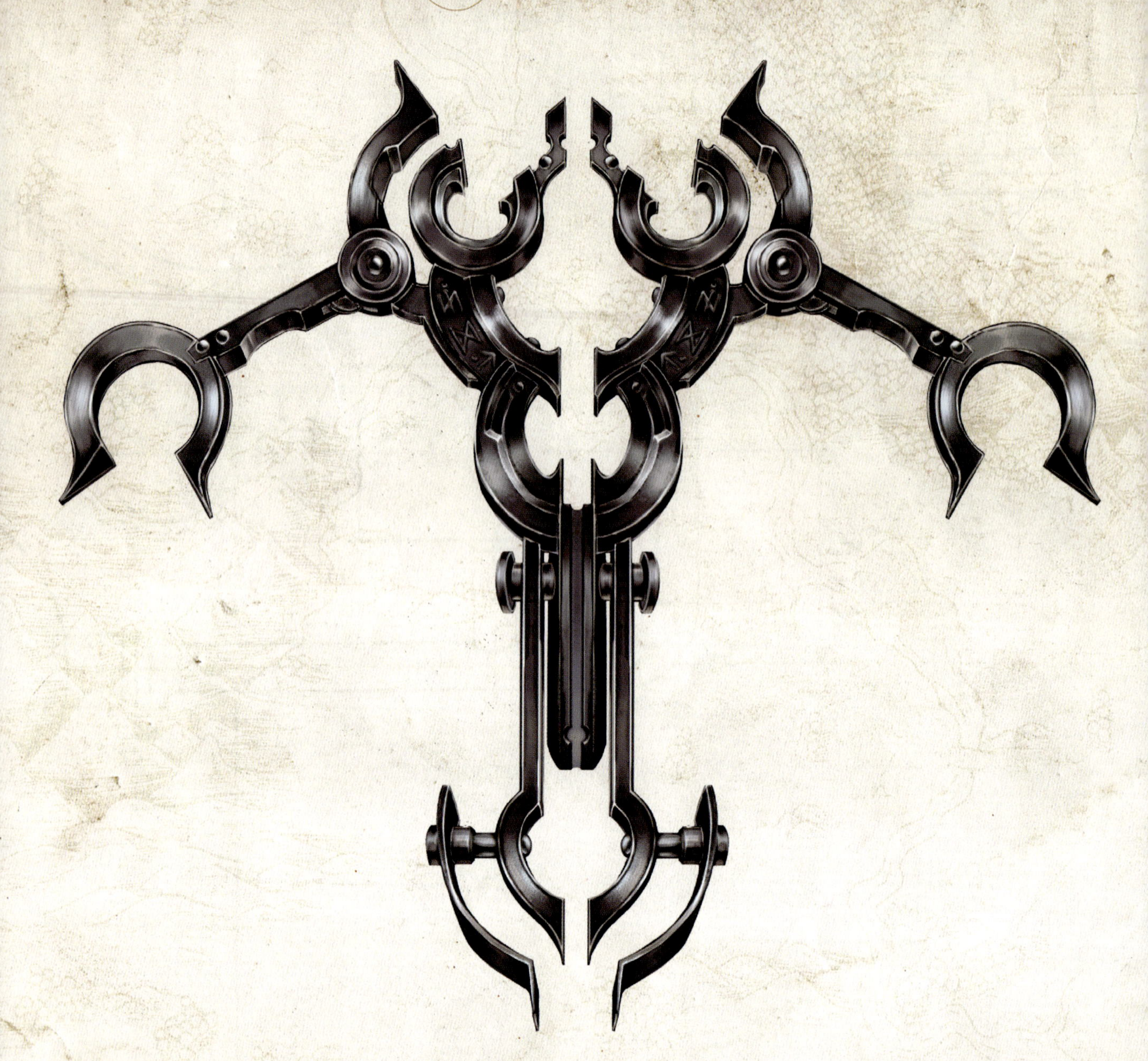

Aeorian Security Cannon

A sleek, gunmetal gray crossbow found in the depths of the Genesis Ward, this high-tech crossbow possesses no string, instead using gravitational runes inscribed along its shaft and bow-arc to hold a bolt in place before firing it off at great speed. Veth immediately took to it, trading her Tinkertop Bolt Blaster 1000 for this security cannon, the name of which they learned from a dead soldier in the room.

Unlike the Tinkertop model, this Aeorian Security Cannon possessed a boon upon a misfire—she could call the bolt back and try again in a split-second window of time. Veth took this security cannon with her throughout the rest of her time with the Nein in Cognouza, and to this day still possesses the ancient arcane weapon—though she must keep it hidden from her curious son, Luc.

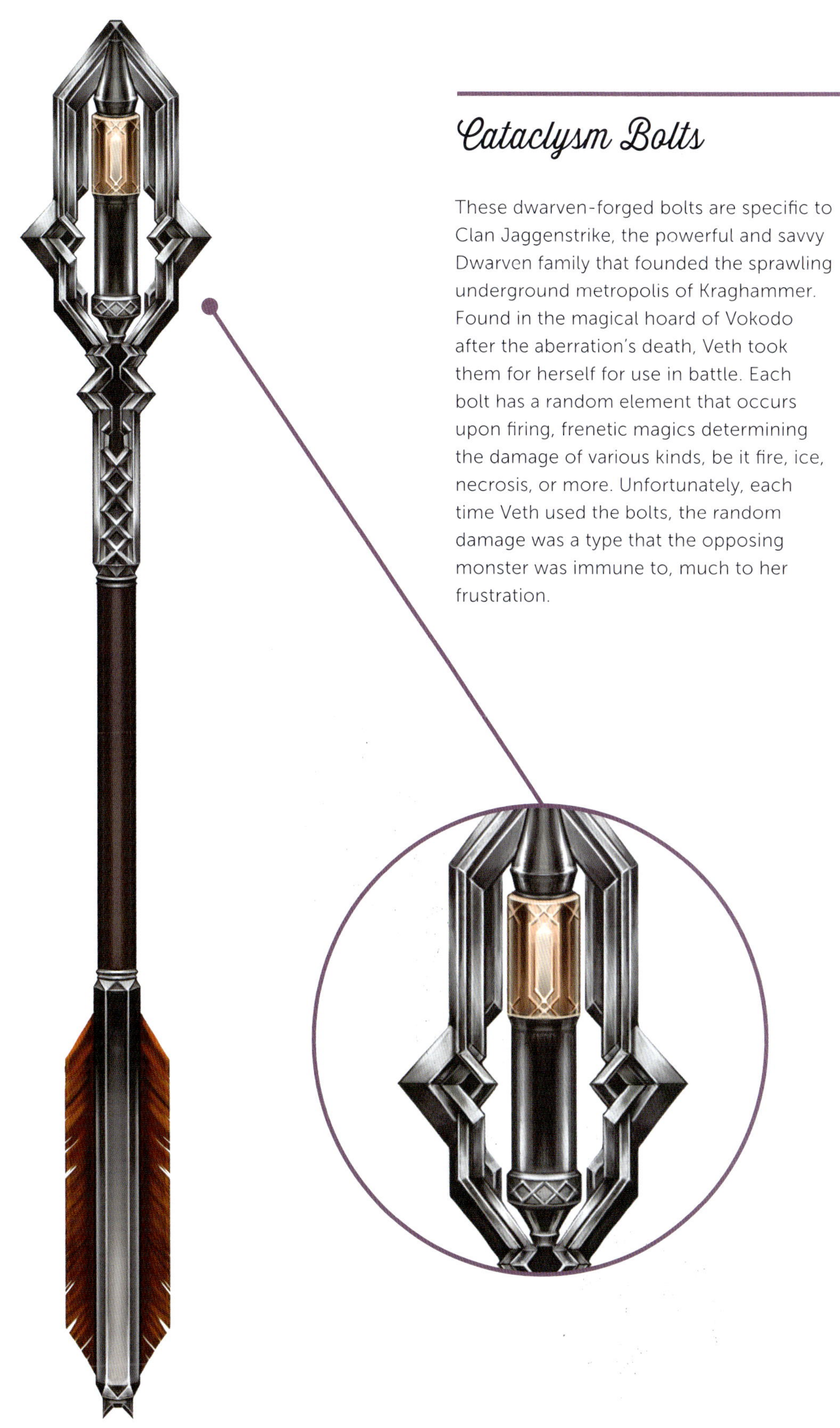

Cataclysm Bolts

These dwarven-forged bolts are specific to Clan Jaggenstrike, the powerful and savvy Dwarven family that founded the sprawling underground metropolis of Kraghammer. Found in the magical hoard of Vokodo after the aberration's death, Veth took them for herself for use in battle. Each bolt has a random element that occurs upon firing, frenetic magics determining the damage of various kinds, be it fire, ice, necrosis, or more. Unfortunately, each time Veth used the bolts, the random damage was a type that the opposing monster was immune to, much to her frustration.

Dagger of Denial

This beautiful silver dagger was also found in the Mighty Nein's time traversing the terrifying King's Cage, a prison that held back the Crawling King and kept his undying servant, the Laughing Hand, bound. One of the many rooms along the way was covered from wall to wall in mirrors, whose reflections began to crawl out of the glass and pull the Nein into their realm. The literal key to leaving was this stiletto, found embedded within a statue of an angel in this mirror trap. Taking it with them, Nott used its enchantment to seal passages from intruders, who could not open the way without the dagger. It stayed on Nott's person until Fjord renounced his pact, whereupon Fjord took it for himself to wield in the interim.

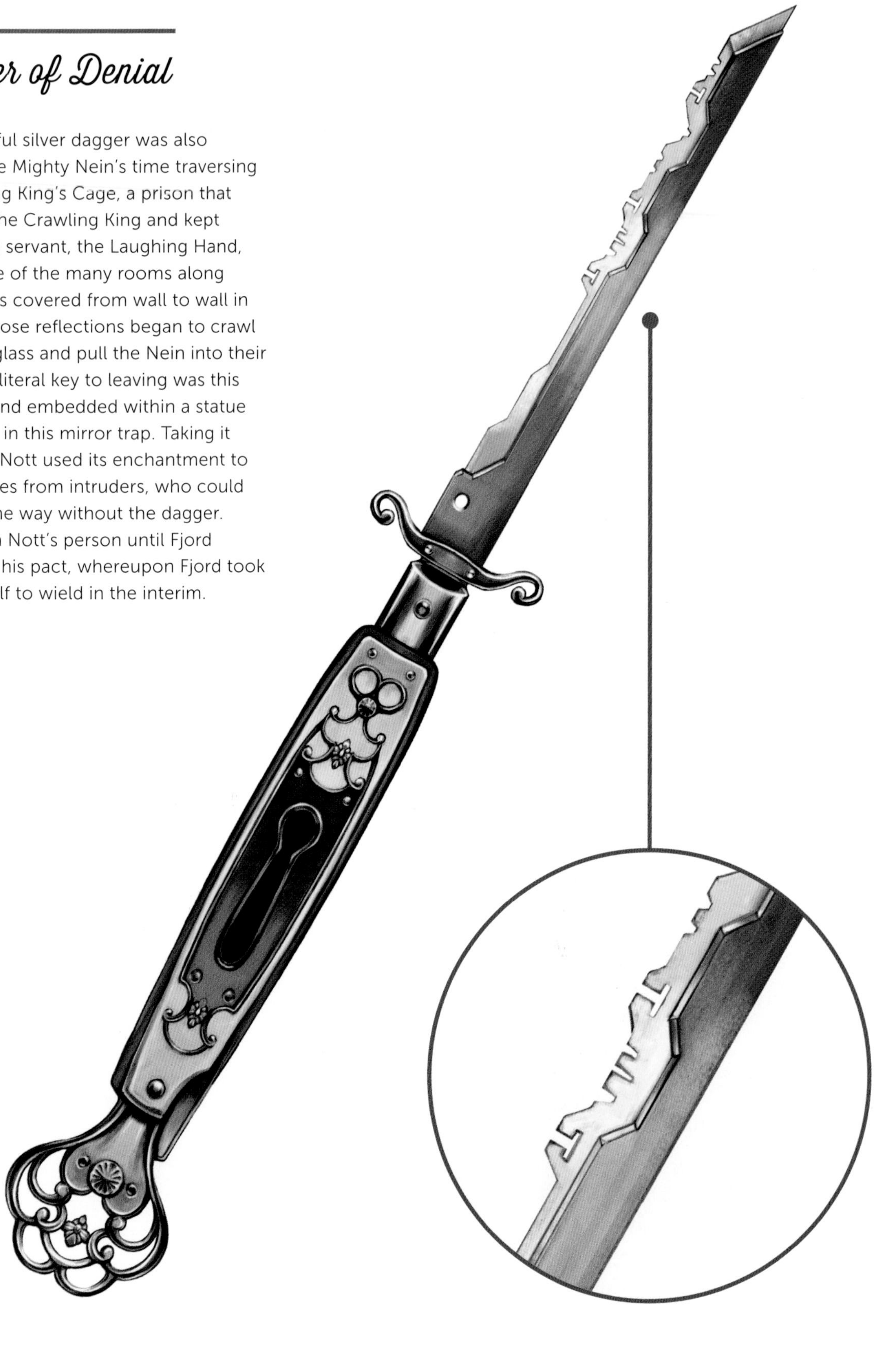

"When in doubt, rely on math: add fire to powder, multiply it by a factor of 'should we be doing this,' subtract the amount of time until you are caught, then divide your assailants in half. The Fluffernutter is, what we call in the business of survival, a real godsdamned gamble."

—Tallulah Fontaine

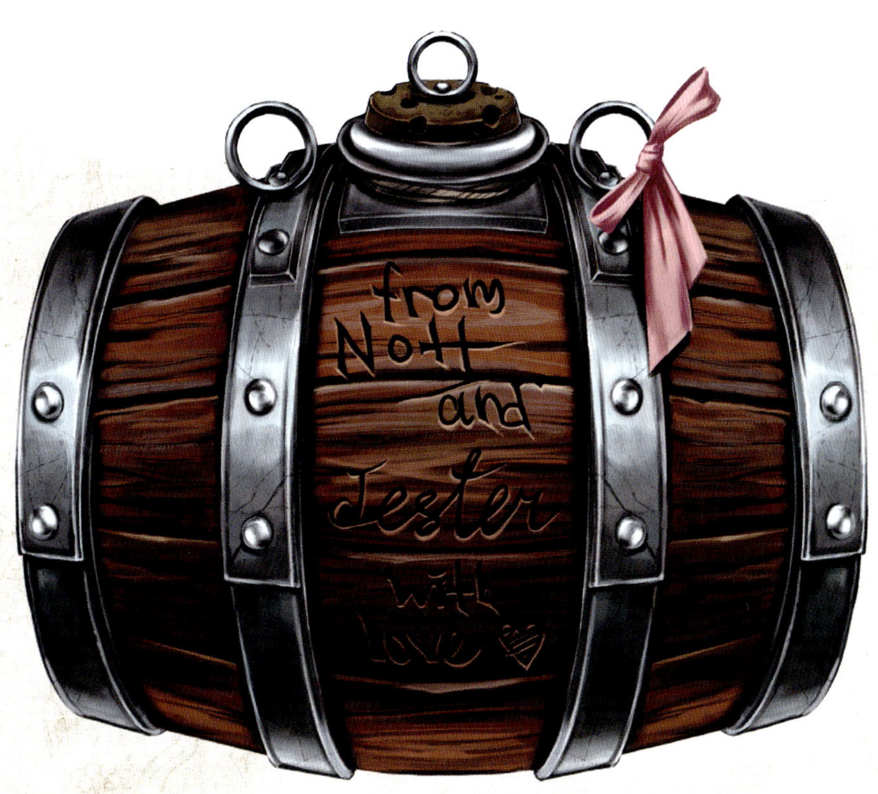

Fluffernutter

Sometimes, adventuring is doing the best with what you have while under duress. With a miniature keg of black powder, an explosive bolt in a crossbow, and being pursued by dozens of murderous lizard cultists, Nott the Brave and Jester invented a type of combustible that would make even the Terrible Tinkerer of Tal'dorei blush at its power. When the so-called Fluffernutter is sought as an option, it usually means you've burned through every other tactic on your list and need to roll the dice.

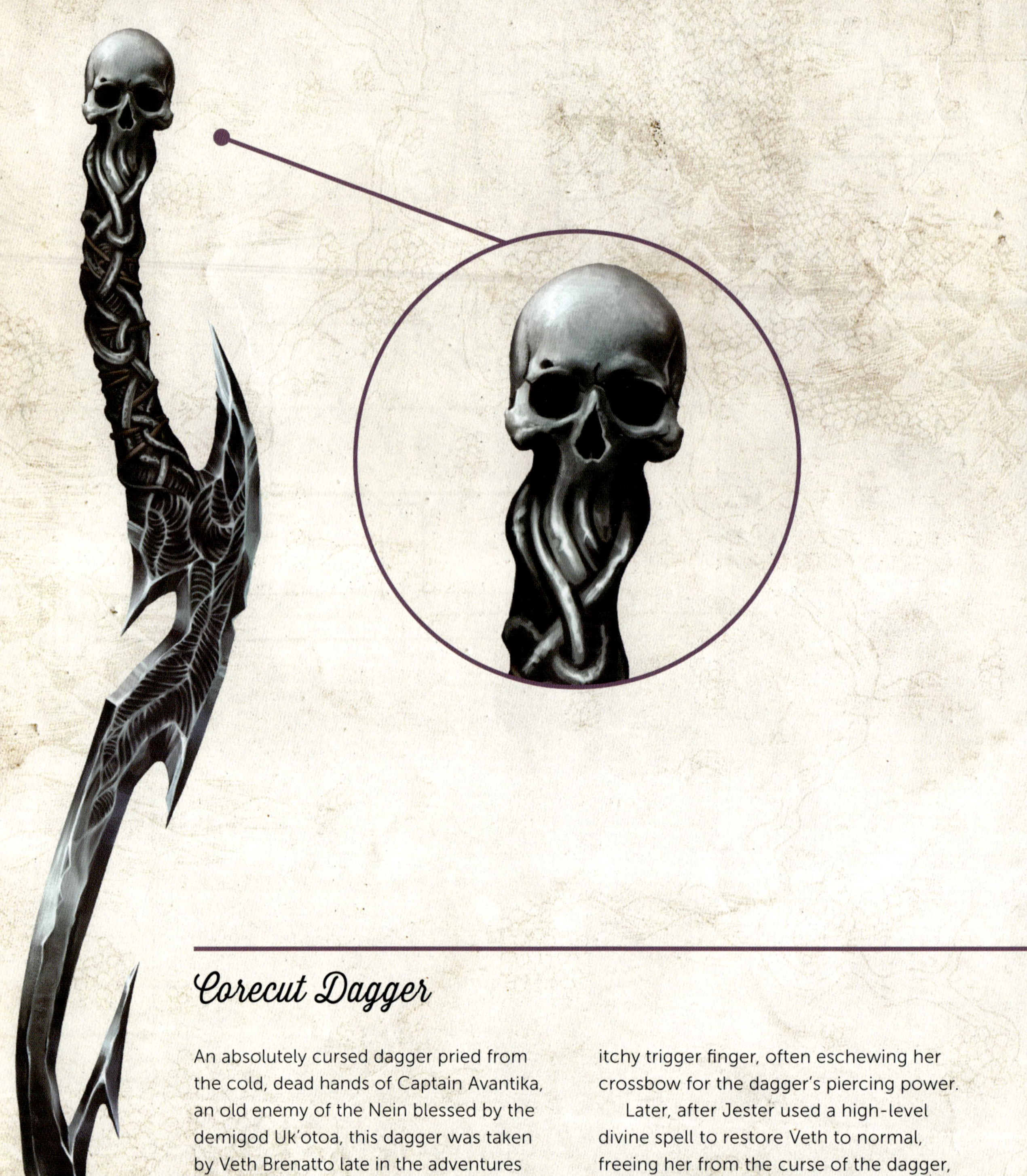

Corecut Dagger

An absolutely cursed dagger pried from the cold, dead hands of Captain Avantika, an old enemy of the Nein blessed by the demigod Uk'otoa, this dagger was taken by Veth Brenatto late in the adventures of the Nein, becoming a melee weapon she utilized for a time. Though she kept the truth of the dagger to herself, it didn't escape the notice of the Nein that while wielding the Corecut Dagger, Veth became (even more) paranoid (even more) anxious, and developed (even more) of an itchy trigger finger, often eschewing her crossbow for the dagger's piercing power.

Later, after Jester used a high-level divine spell to restore Veth to normal, freeing her from the curse of the dagger, it was discovered that not only did the dagger's curse compel the wielder to never part with it, it also stole their vitality to damage foes, at the risk of ending their life. Once her mind was restored, the dagger was discarded; one can only hope Veth learned her lesson.

"Demons do not just live across the myriad layers of the Hells. They can be found in the grip of a weapon, within the minds of the despairing, at the bottom of bottles. The most insidious keep us from seeing the truth, if they can keep our minds as hazy as possible. Only demons benefit from our pain, and sometimes, our pleasure."

—Oren Keth'Kaylis

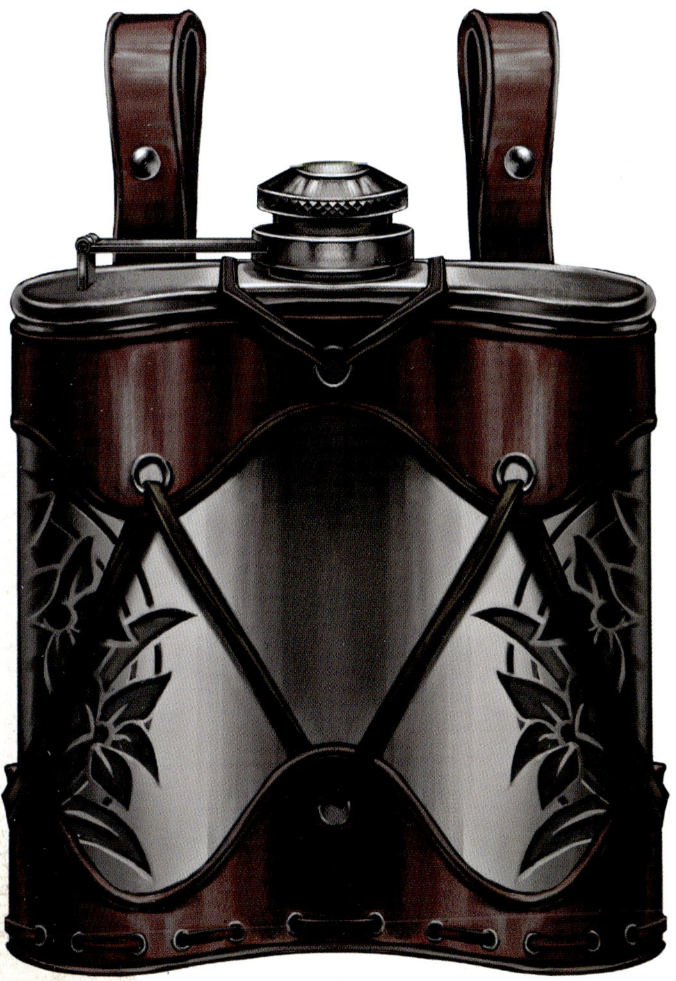

Flask of Perpetual Booze

Though this was a minor magical item, it was one that would go on to have great effect on Nott the Brave. Nott paid the enchanter Pumat Sol of the Invulnerable Vagrant to enchant a platinum flask, to have an endless supply of whiskey for her consumption whenever she felt the urge. This flask landed Nott in more trouble than not, but it continued to stay on her person for much of the Mighty Nein's initial time together, though she entrusted it to Yasha when she decided to work through her alcoholism. As Veth Brenatto, she passed the flask first to Beau, then off to the newly christened Kingsley Tealeaf, a gift as he embarked on a third chance for life. Rumor has it she commissioned another, this time with a sparkling rosé.

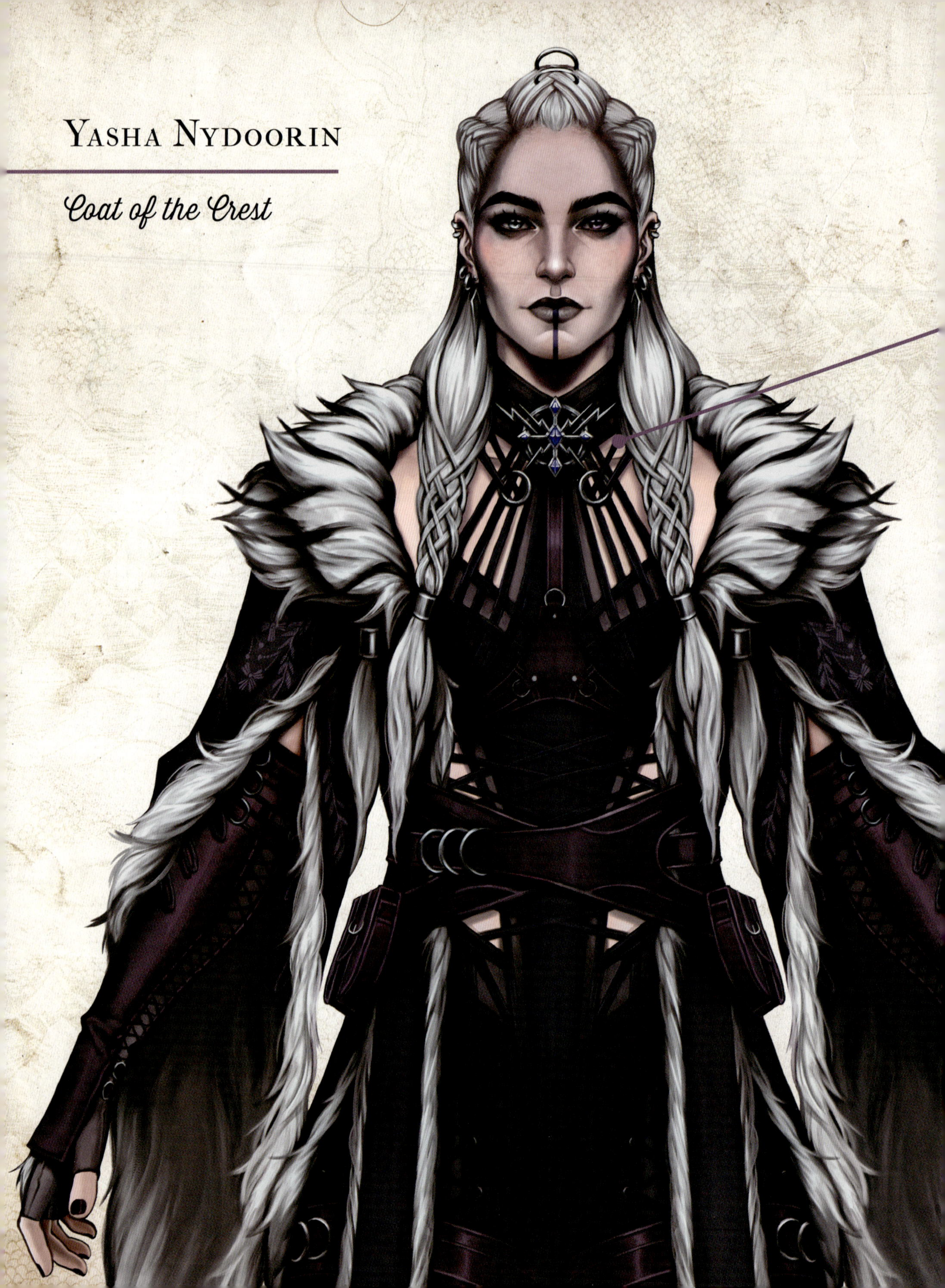
YASHA NYDOORIN
Coat of the Crest

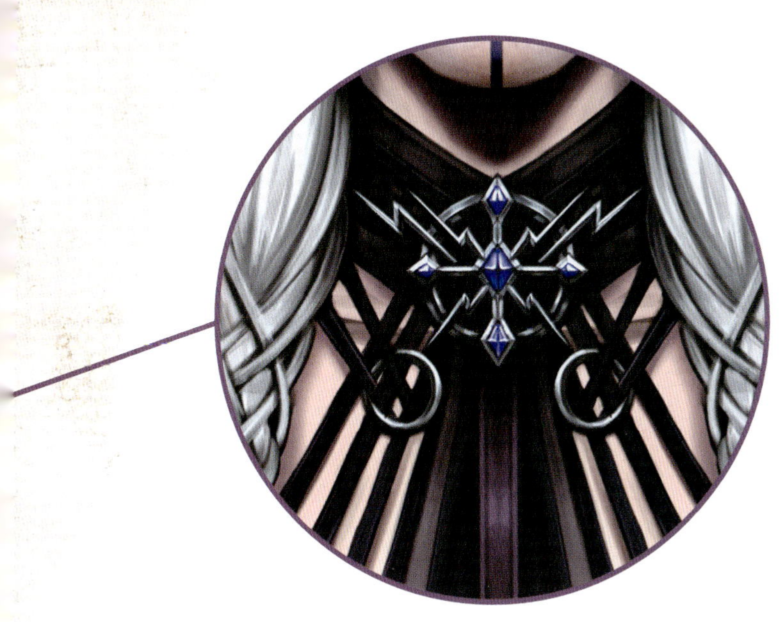

One of several magic items found in the hoard of Vokodo on the island of Rumblecusp, this stylish and striking coat ultimately ended up in the hands of resident warrior, Yasha Nydoorin. Not often a fan of armor of any kind, Yasha took this to a tailor in Rexxentrum, the capital of the Dwendalian Empire, to have it updated to a style that felt more her. Sporting a sleek, black coat into battle, Yasha used the Coat of the Crest to absorb and halve certain kinds of damage throughout her time in Aeor and into the astral plane in pursuit of Cognouza and the Somnovem.

"Life in the clan of Dolorav is not one of comfort. It is not one of warmth, nor kindness freely given. Yasha Nydoorin, adopted child of the Skyspear herself and destined for great battle, was not given the gift of a comfortable upbringing and that which she had she earned through blood, sweat, and yes, tears. Even after she fled the clan and the tragedies both committed and beheld, Yasha lived a hard life. Furs and weapons and pitfires in the dark nights of Wildemount. I can only imagine the hardship of her time with the devil, Obann.

It would be a long time, after the circus, after the on and off again time with the Nein, before Yasha would begin to let herself be comforted. Some of that was material, such as the beautiful and enchanted Coat of the Crest, which kept her warm and battle ready. But most of it was mental and emotional, as the love and warmth and care of her new chosen family began to finally break through the armor she'd been forced to construct all those years ago.

Though she is one of the most fierce of the Nein, Yasha Nydoorin has one of the largest, and most fragile, of hearts. And to see her finally cherish it, and let herself enjoy the love and comfort of her family, brings warmth to this old archivist."

—D'Rishk Dawnscale

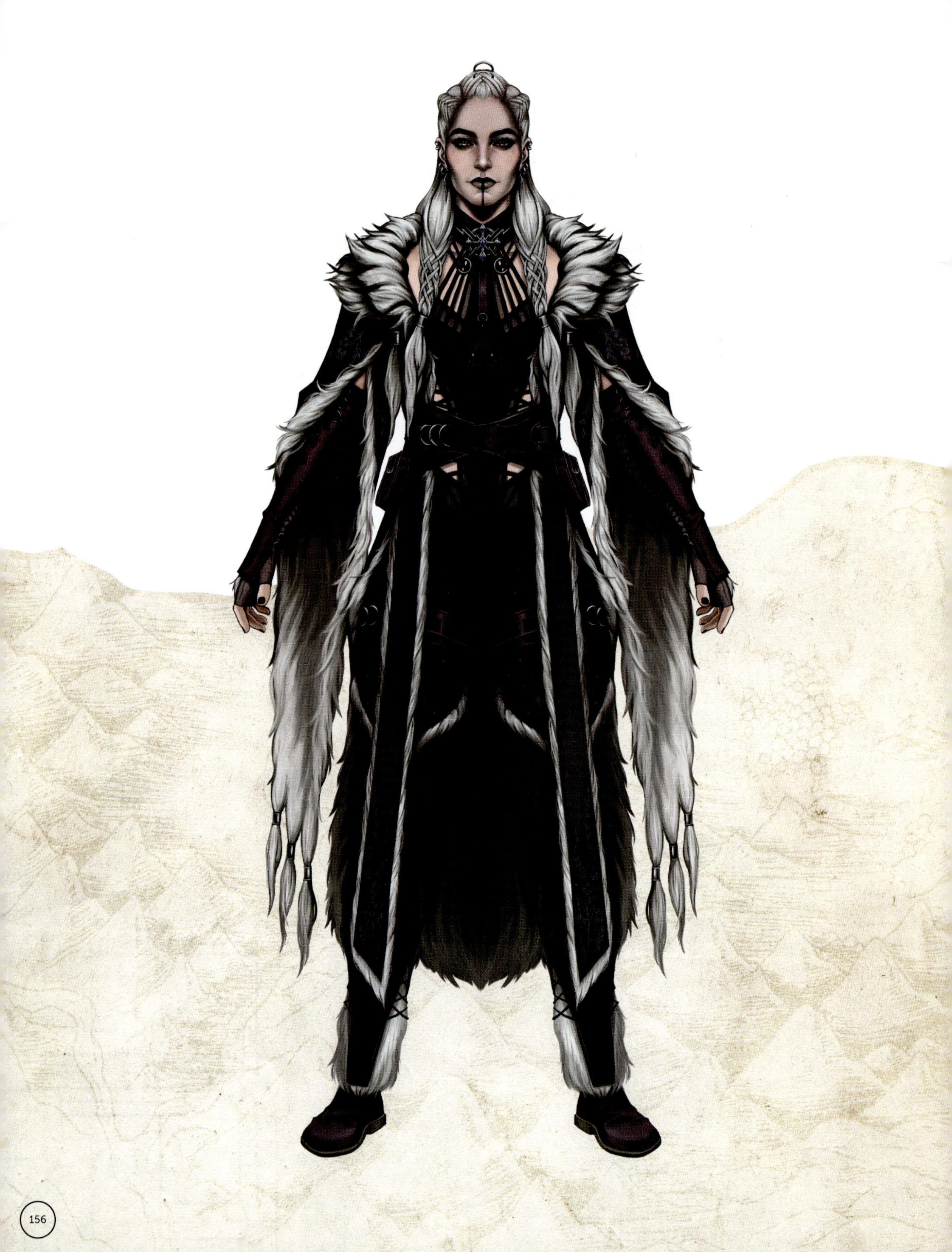

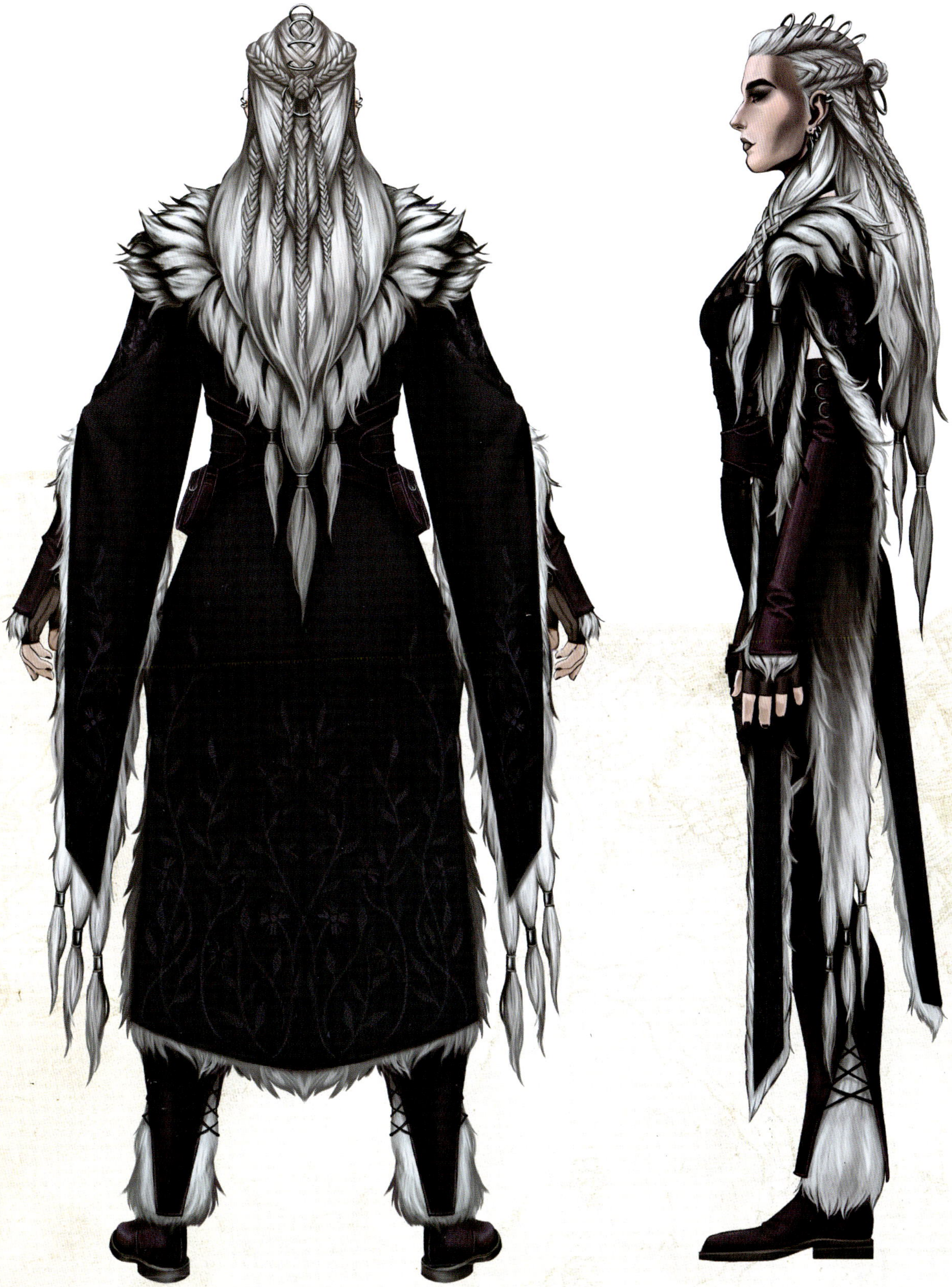

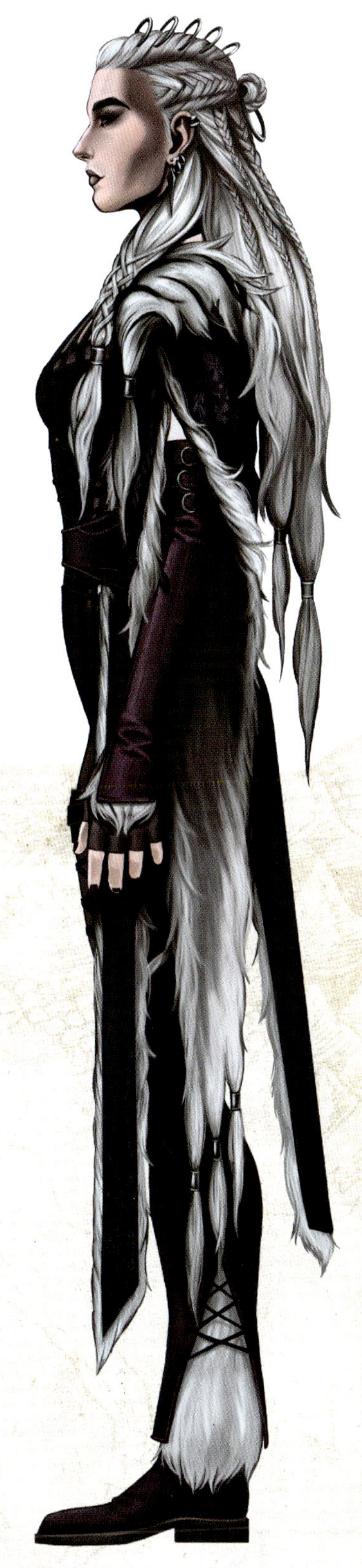

Tuskborn Breastplate of Reprisal

A breastplate of heavy, dark iron, its most striking feature are the two massive horns that curl out from the center of it, clearly indicative of its fiendish origin. Worn by Yasha when she was taken by the insidious charm of Obann, this breastplate served her for some time, even after she was freed from his control. Eventually, as she came to understand her own guilt and shame, she was able to give up this piece of armor for the Coat of the Crest, relinquishing it, and thankfully never learning the darker secrets at the heart of this fiendish wrought armor.

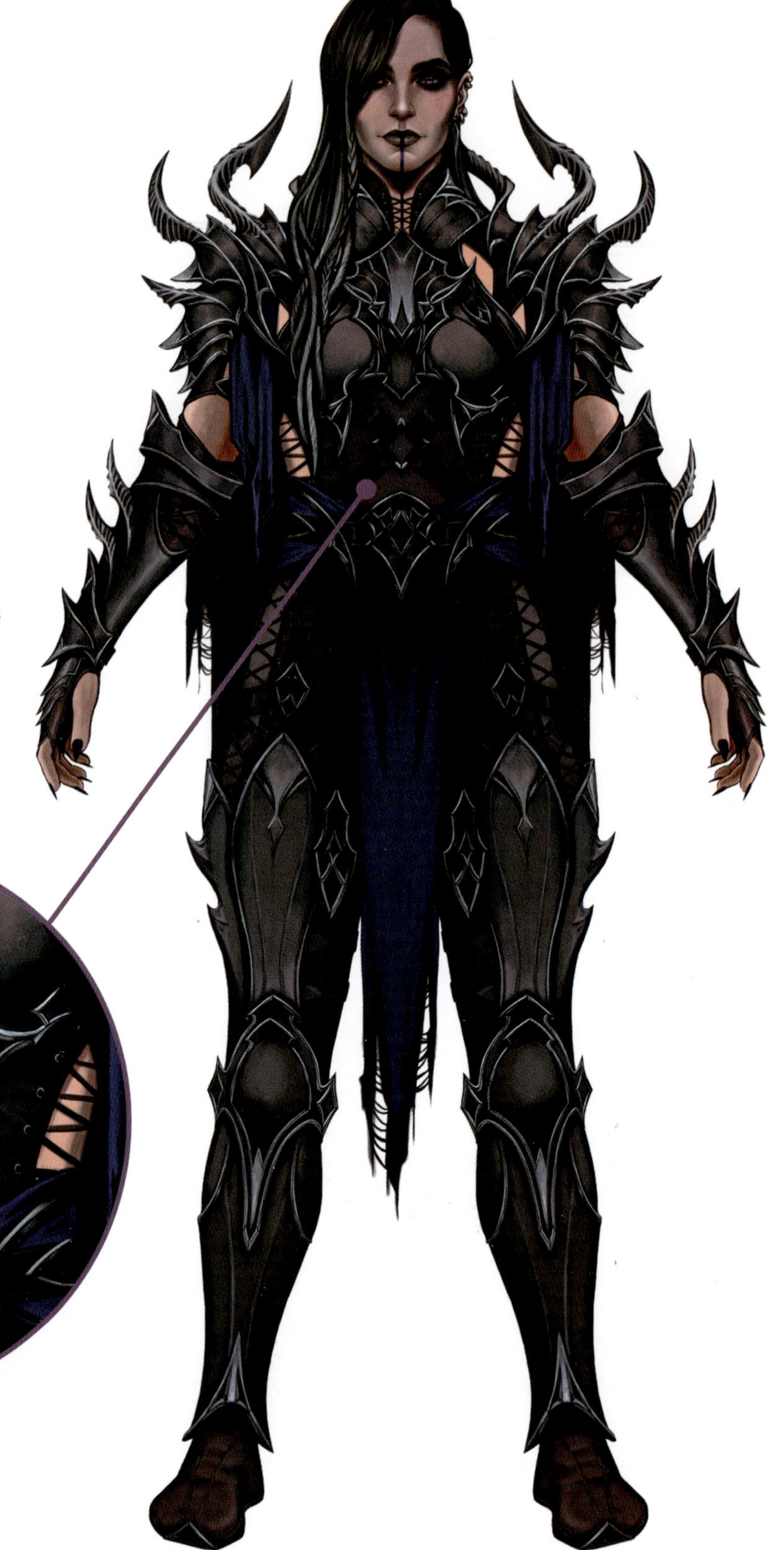

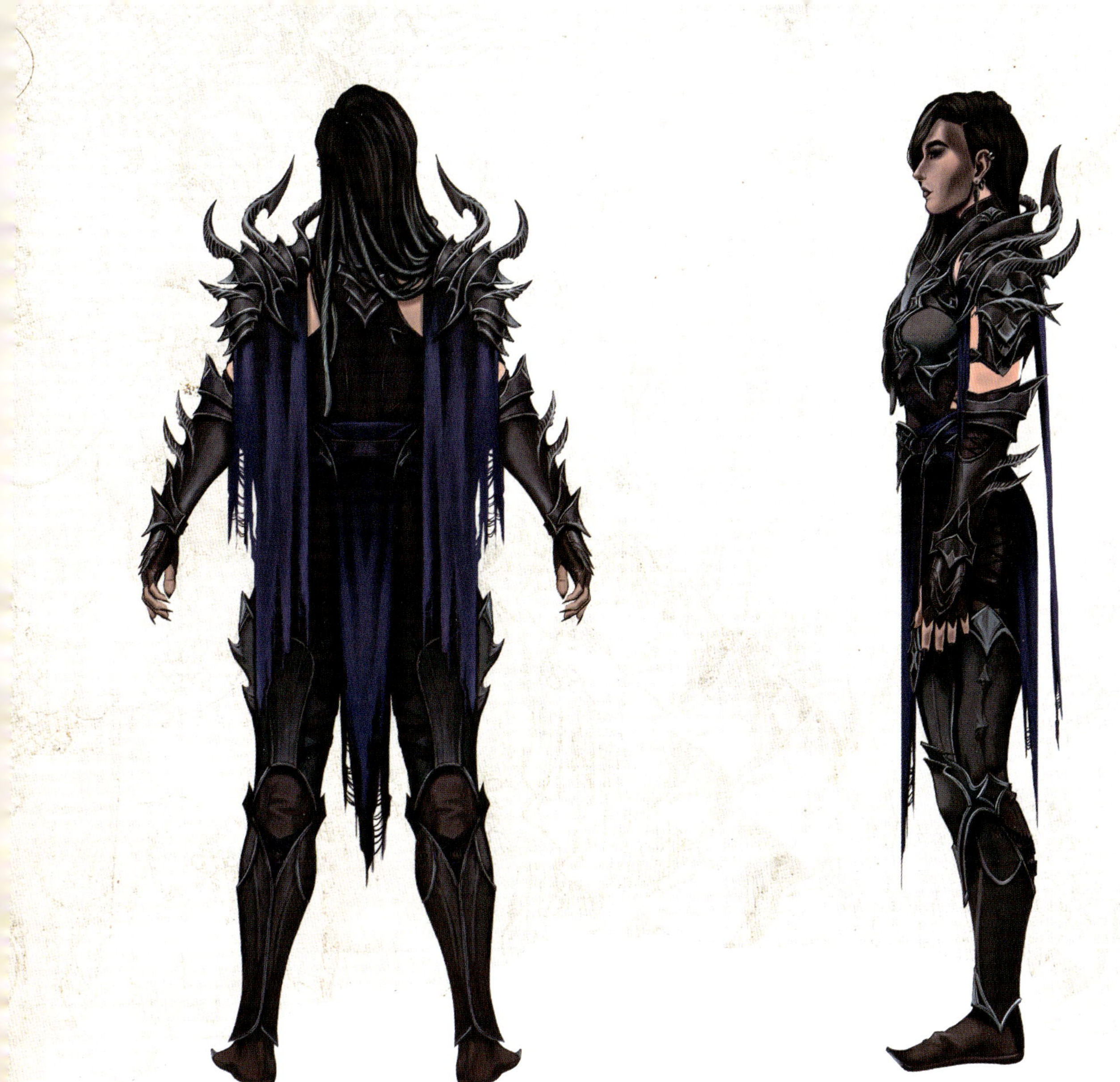

"We had word from some Lens scouts when this particular piece of armor adorned the infamous Orphanmaker of the Dolorav clan. At the time, we had little intel to inform her allegiance with the fiend Obann (see "Angel of Irons" file for more information). Now, having been given a firsthand account from the Shadowhand, corroborated by our agents within the Empire, we understand that this armor was selected and given to the Orphanmaker as a sign and signal to other fiendish powers that she was under the protection of, and controlled by, Obann. Clearly of infernal design, we're hoping to locate its whereabouts for study, as there was most certainly some sort of cursed property to it. But one thing is clear: While under the control of that fiend, the Orphanmaker seemed a very devil herself."

—Oren Keth'Kaylis

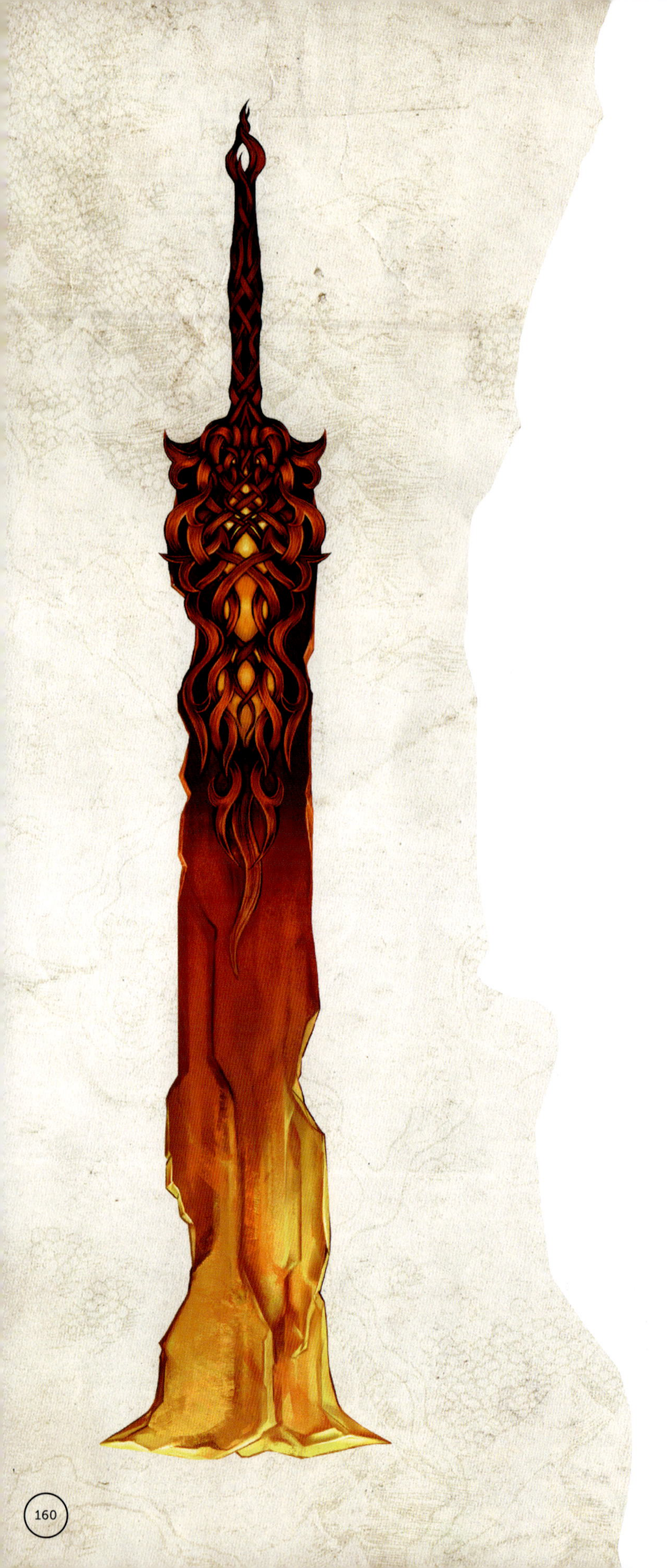

Scaldsaber

A massive, glowing-red cleaver-like blade, the Scaldsaber was a gift from Lady Kima when Yasha wisely returned her greatblade, Sacred Retribution, following the downfall of the Somnovem and Lucien's misguided takeover. An exemplar of the highest order, Lady Kima has acquired over the years many different blades for many different purposes; seeing the great fury and fire within Yasha's soul, Kima gifted her with this, a greatsword that ignites on contact with the air, infusing every fearsome strike with literal fire power.

In the time since Scaldsaber has been in her care, Yasha has used it happily against the brief release of Uk'otoa, as well as the demonic entity Omentis, after it terrorized the town of Blumenthal following the Red Moon's Rise. In the hands of such a capable warrior, Scaldsaber sings with every burning swing.

"There is little question as to where the blade came from; the screams of vengeance coming out of the village of Oshinik-Ka can be heard even in Rosohna. Some great-grand-someone's legacy has been despoiled, and so forth. However, if they would like to go and take back some beaten, heavy, rusted, and I believe corroded length of iron from an acclaimed champion of the Stormlord, they may certainly be my guest."

—*Oren Keth'Kaylis*

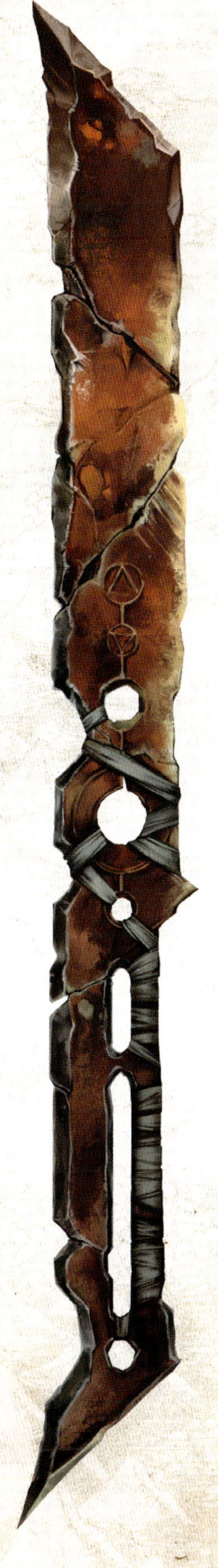

Skingorger

There has never been a greatsword that Yasha Nydoorin didn't love and wasn't loath to give up. As she never had a need for a shield, Yasha could concern herself more with the weapons she chose to wield on the battlefield. Taken in battle, this rusty greatsword had no hilt, just two wrapped places at the bottom to hold it. But with an ability to exhaust the body at the cost of more ferocious attack, it was not a blade easily put aside. Often Yasha had her pick of weapons, deciding which she'd fight with on a day-to-day basis between Skingorger, Magician's Judge, and later, Sacred Retribution.

"I found this within an old Aeorian text, recovered from one of the many sites in Eiselcross. It appears to be some sort of judicial code by which the mageocracy survived. It is burnt from spellfire and I've only translated half from ancient draconic, but it reads:

'Aye and should the Runic Parliament decide ye life forfeit, by the fell stroke of steel shall ye be judged. Let not magic hold back the swift blow of justice, let the greatblade sever mind from body as it severs spell from soul. Let none who would usurp the mage-state of Aeor live to cast again.'"

—D'Rishk Dawnscale, quoting from a partially destroyed tome, "The Codices of Conduct, IV"

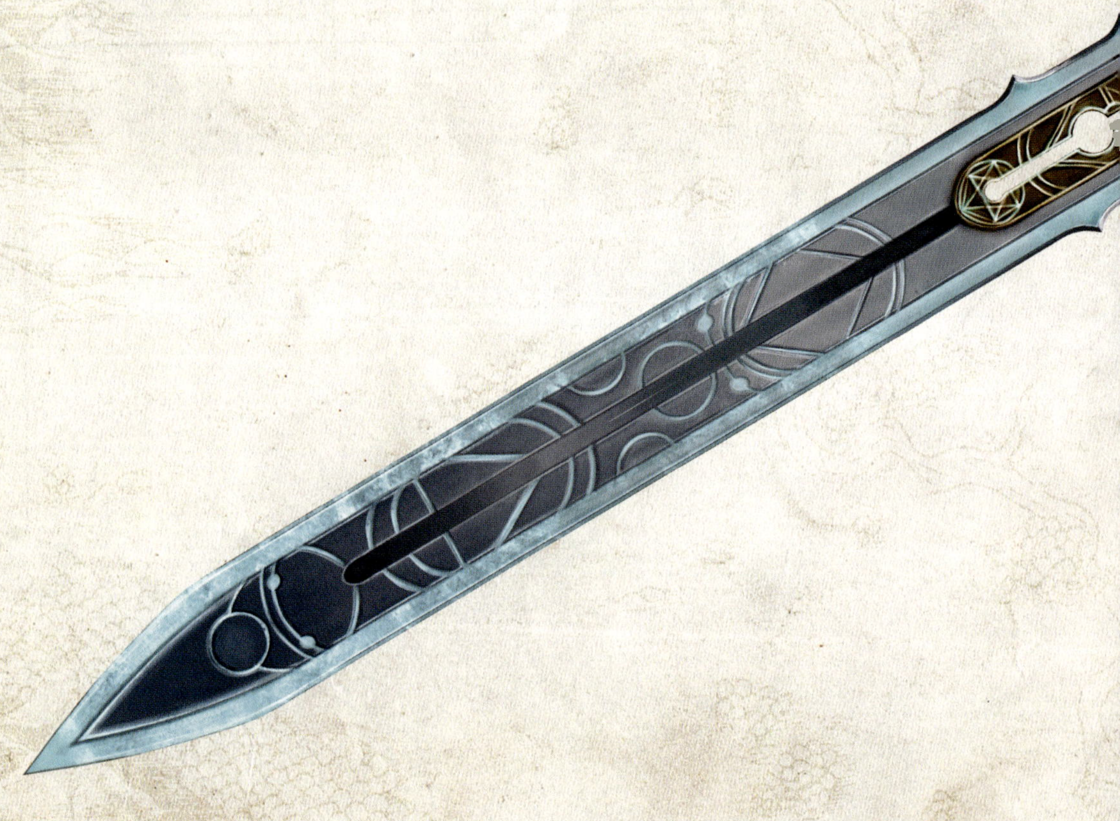

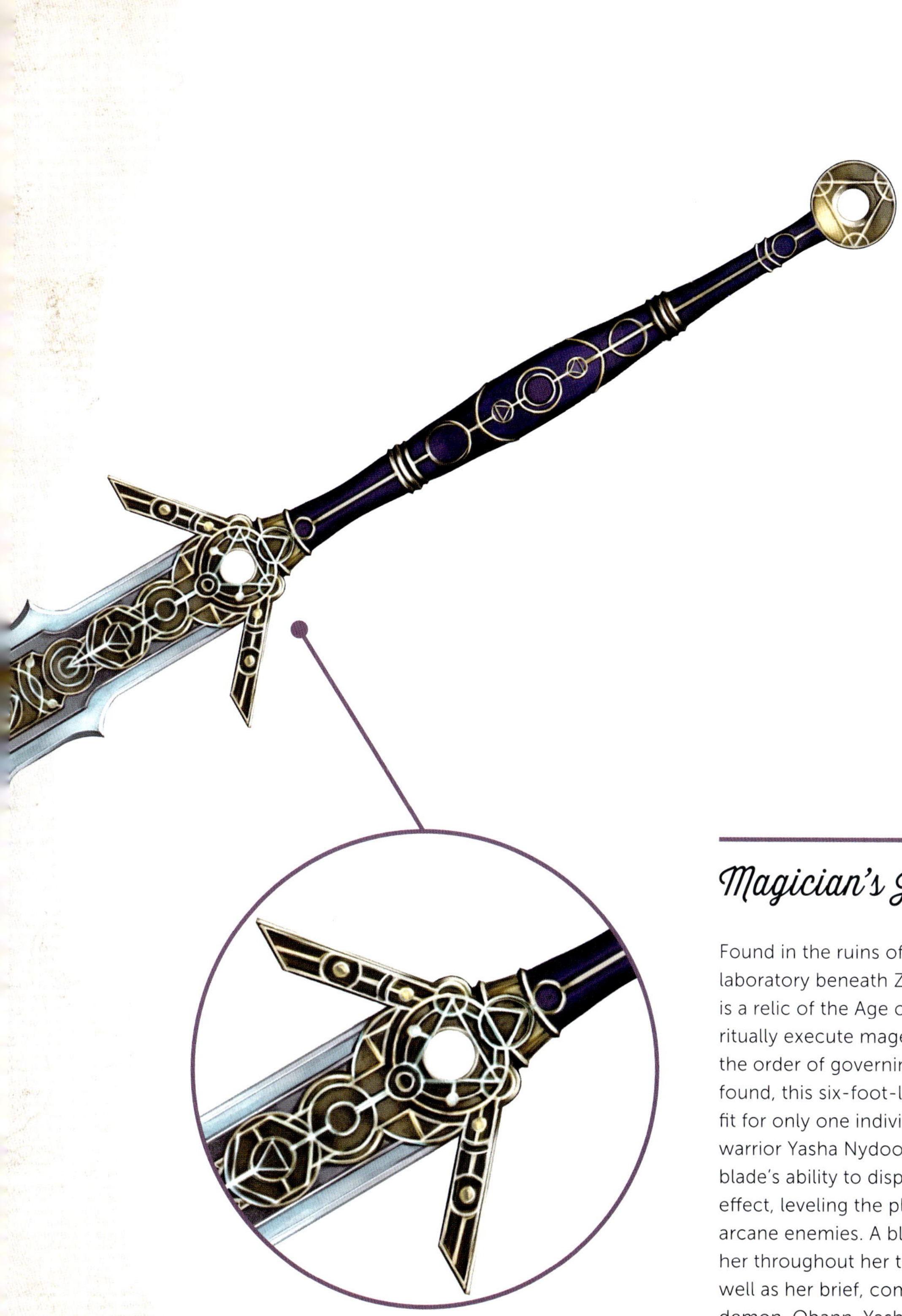

Magician's Judge

Found in the ruins of an old arcane laboratory beneath Zadash, this weapon is a relic of the Age of Arcanum used to ritually execute mages who went against the order of governing bodies. When found, this six-foot-long greatsword was fit for only one individual, the mighty warrior Yasha Nydoorin, who utilized the blade's ability to dispel magics to great effect, leveling the playing field against arcane enemies. A blade that she kept with her throughout her time with the Nein, as well as her brief, compelled return to the demon, Obann, Yasha temporarily traded this to the Lady Kima of Vord, exemplar wife to Archmage Allura Vysoren, in order to use her sacred blade as they pursued the Tombtakers into Cognouza.

"It is not lost on me, an archivist, how much we look for history's arrow in the stroke of a pen, the strike of a chisel, the swish of a painter's brush. But I think we cannot discount the arc of a blade either, especially such a legendary weapon as the Sacred Retribution, wielded by Lady Kima of Vord, passed into the hands of Yasha Nydoorin. A blade that swept through the flames and poison and cold of the Chroma Conclave in Tal'Dorei, and fought against the undead of the Whispered One during the Attempted Resurrection, was passed into the hand of she who faced down the wondrous horrors of Aeor and the ghosts of the Age of Arcanum and saw battle against the Somnovem of Cognouza deep within the Astral Sea.

As much as we of the Cobalt Soul Archives may never experience violence or battle as others have, we have just as much of an appreciation for what these weapons and their wielders can tell us about our history, and the future they defend."

—D'Rishk Dawnscale

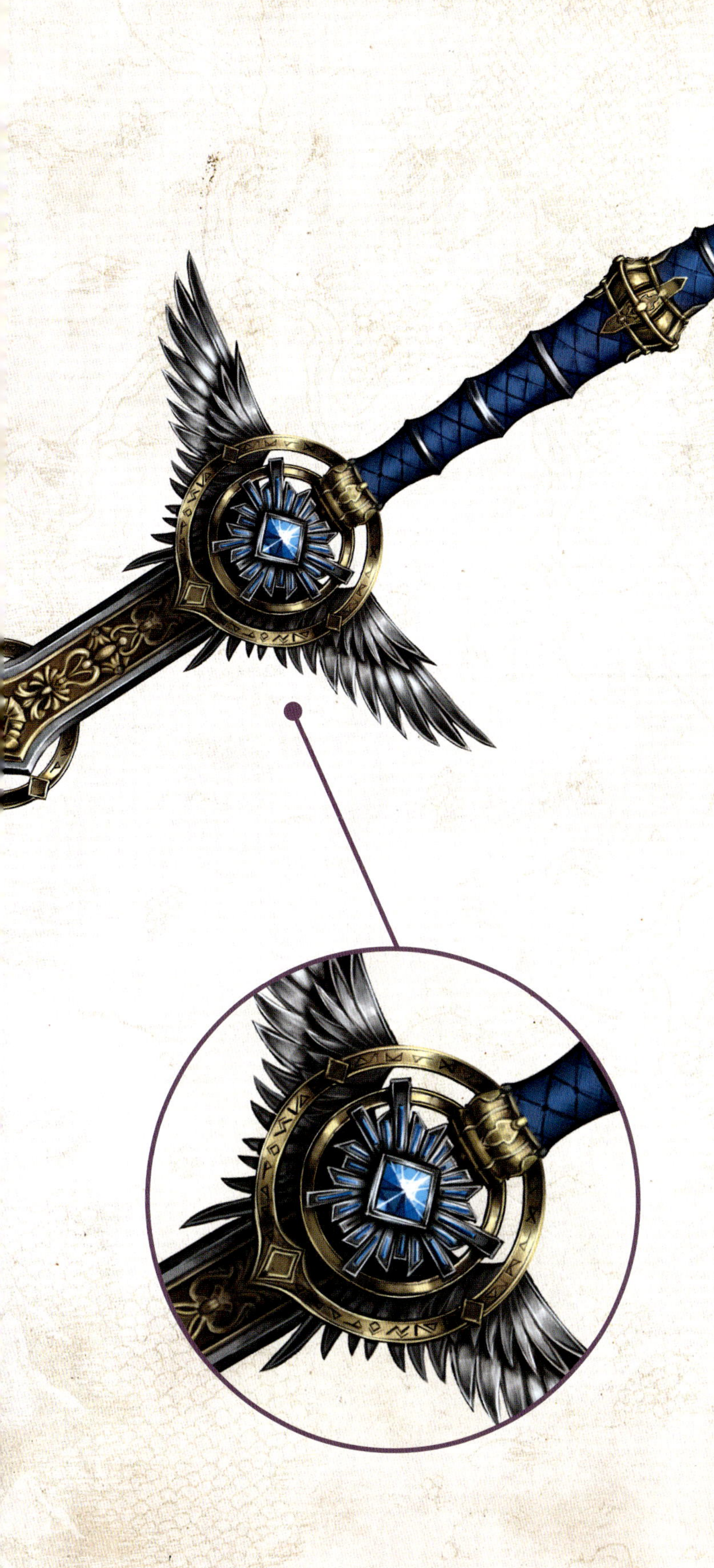

Sacred Retribution

As the severity of the threat the Somnovem posed began to crystallize, especially as the mad machinations of Lucien and his Tombtakers became apparent, the Mighty Nein sought help from Archmage Allura Vysoren of the Arcana Pansophical and her wife, Lady Kima of Vord. When it was determined they wouldn't join the Nein, Allura lent her staff to Caleb Widogast, and Lady Kima, begrudgingly, lent her Sacred Retribution greatsword to Yasha, holding Magician's Judge in its place as a loan. One of the preeminent weapons an exemplar can wield, inscribed with celestial runes, brimming with holy devastation for fiends and undead, it found a strong home in the hands of Yasha.

Though a champion of the divine herself, the Stormlord made Yasha prove her worth before being able to bear such a holy weapon. She brought it to bear against the Somnovem and Lucien's attempt to wrest control of the sentient city of Cognouza. Reportedly, it has been returned to Lady Kima, who gave back Magician's Judge, and another blade, the Scaldsaber, in recompense.

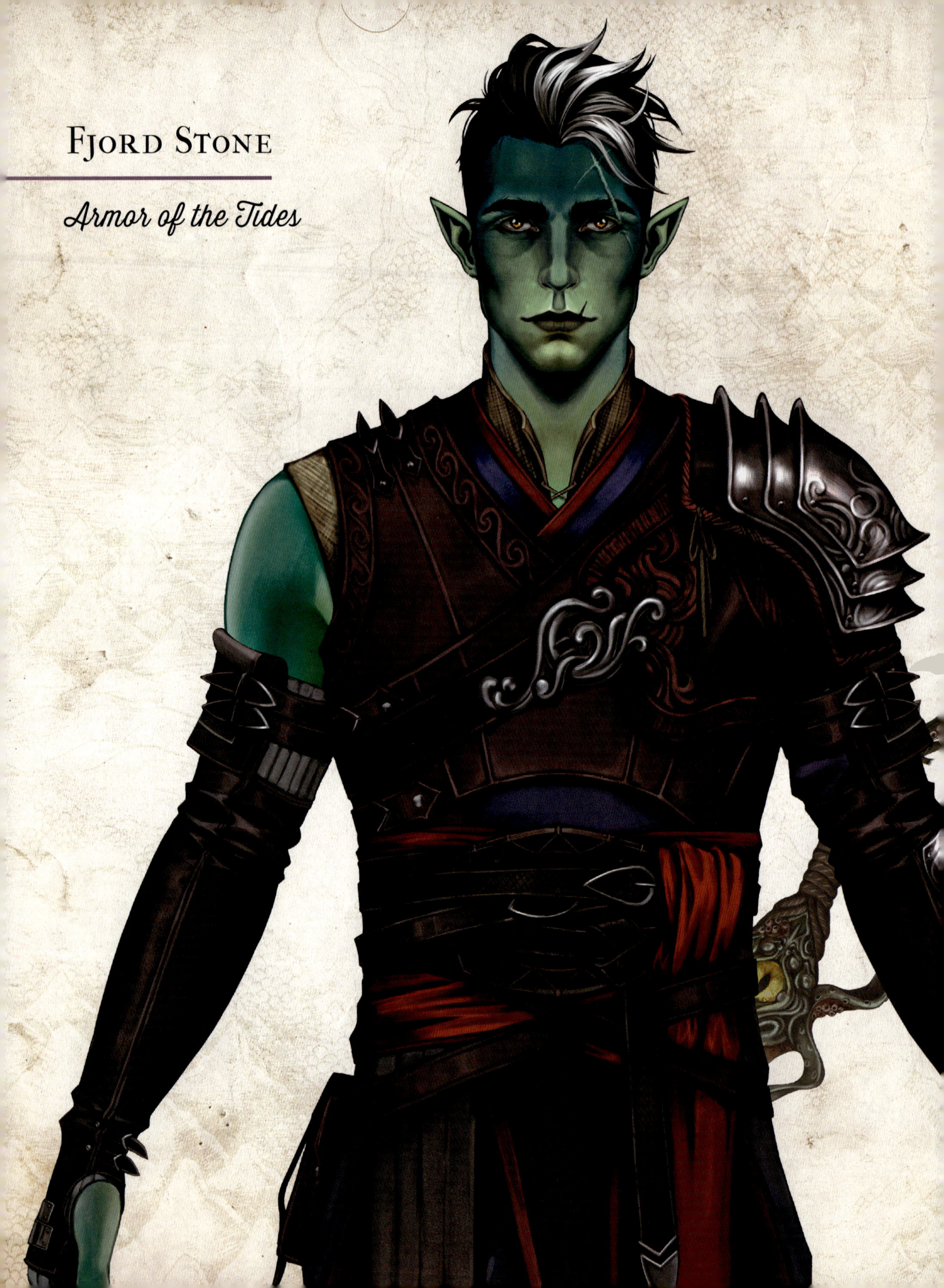
Fjord Stone
Armor of the Tides

A signature piece of armor early in Fjord's adventuring life with the Mighty Nein, this Armor of the Tides was originally found in the sewers of Zadash. When the truth of its enchantment was discovered, Fjord had a keen interest in transferring it to his original armor, cobbled together from his own days at sea. With the help of enchanter and magical shopkeeper Pumat Sol, he was able to lift the enchantment of the Armor of the Tides and meld it into Fjord's original protection, granting him equal speed in the water as on land, and the ability to take his unconscious body to the surface, something he wished he'd had earlier in his life.

The armor would eventually become moot once Fjord gained an eldritch invocation that gave him the same abilities, but for those early few months with the Nein, this armor and its enchantments gave this seafaring swordsman just that much more confidence out on the water.

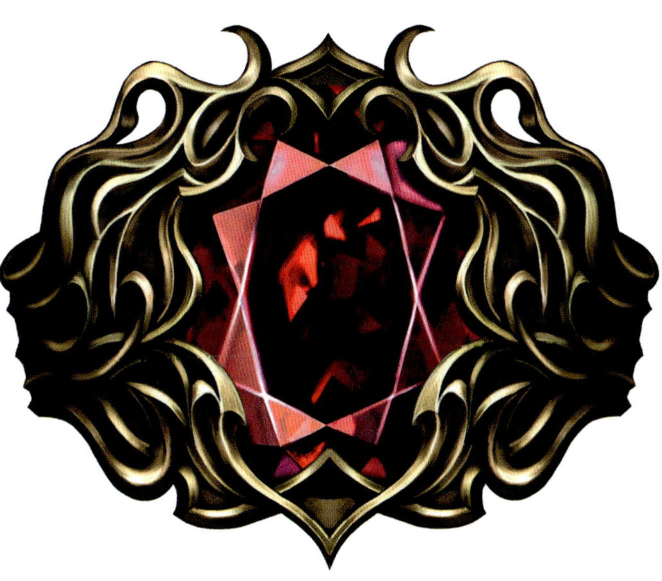

Ring of Fire Resistance

One man's item they forgot to pick up in a magic shop is another man's treasure. Or at least that's what Fjord thought when he found a handy enchanted ring of elemental resistance in a magical pawn shop in Nicodranas. Knowing the true destructive power of fire, thanks to watching Caleb for months, Fjord purchased the ring for a hefty sum, as it was meant for a member of the influential Sutan family and cost much to make. Even though he tried to sell it later, only to discover it wasn't worth as much as he spent, it's a good thing he kept it around.

As his relationship with Jester found its sea legs, he gifted her the ring, wishing to keep her safe from the harm to come in Aeor and, later, Cognouza. And indeed, as the transformed form of Lucien, the Neosomnovem, rained down fireballs on the party, Fjord's purchase kept his newly beloved safe from the flames. Though it didn't do much good for Fjord, he can be happy for what he spent, for if Jester is safe, that's all that matters in the end.

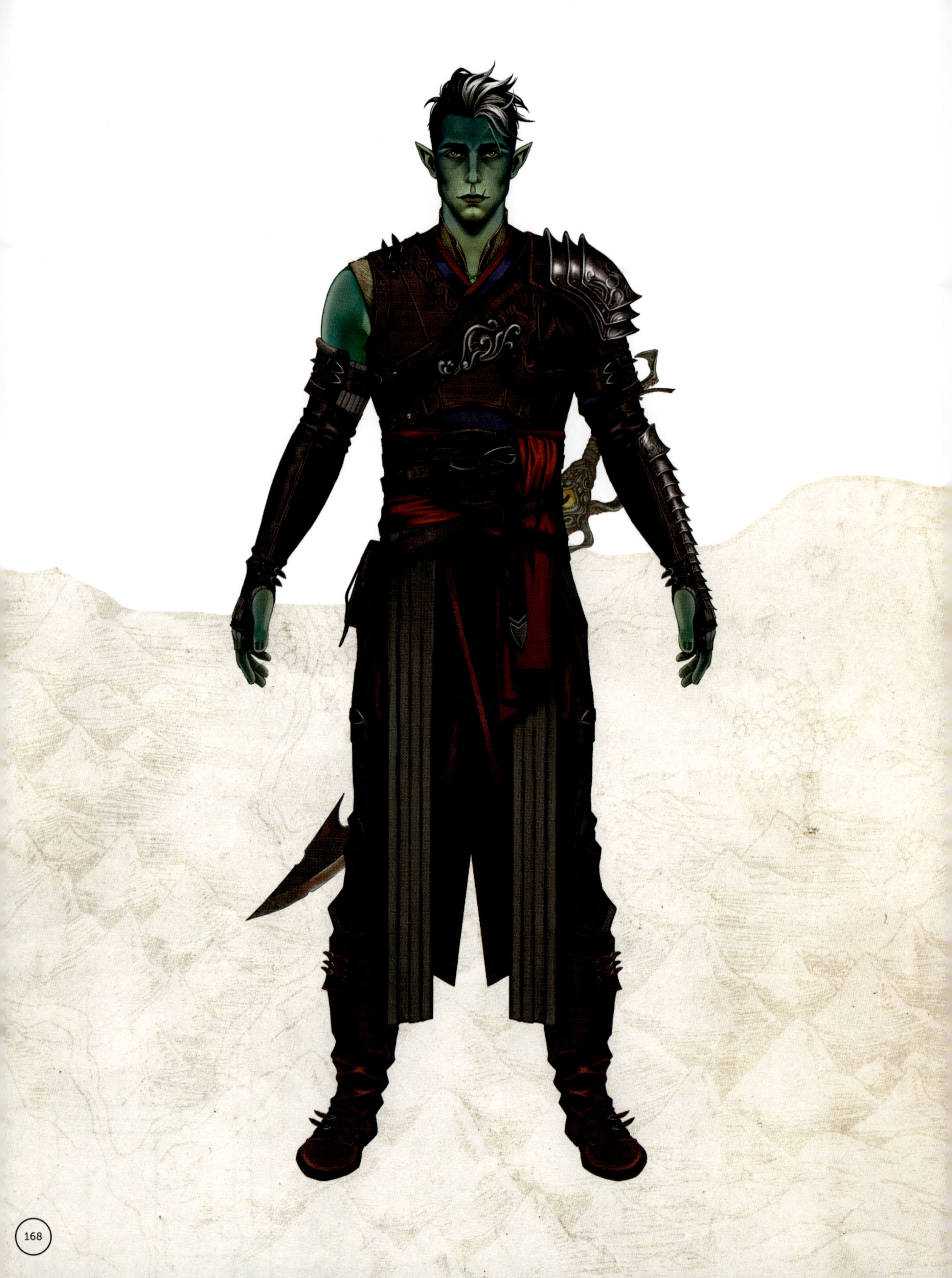

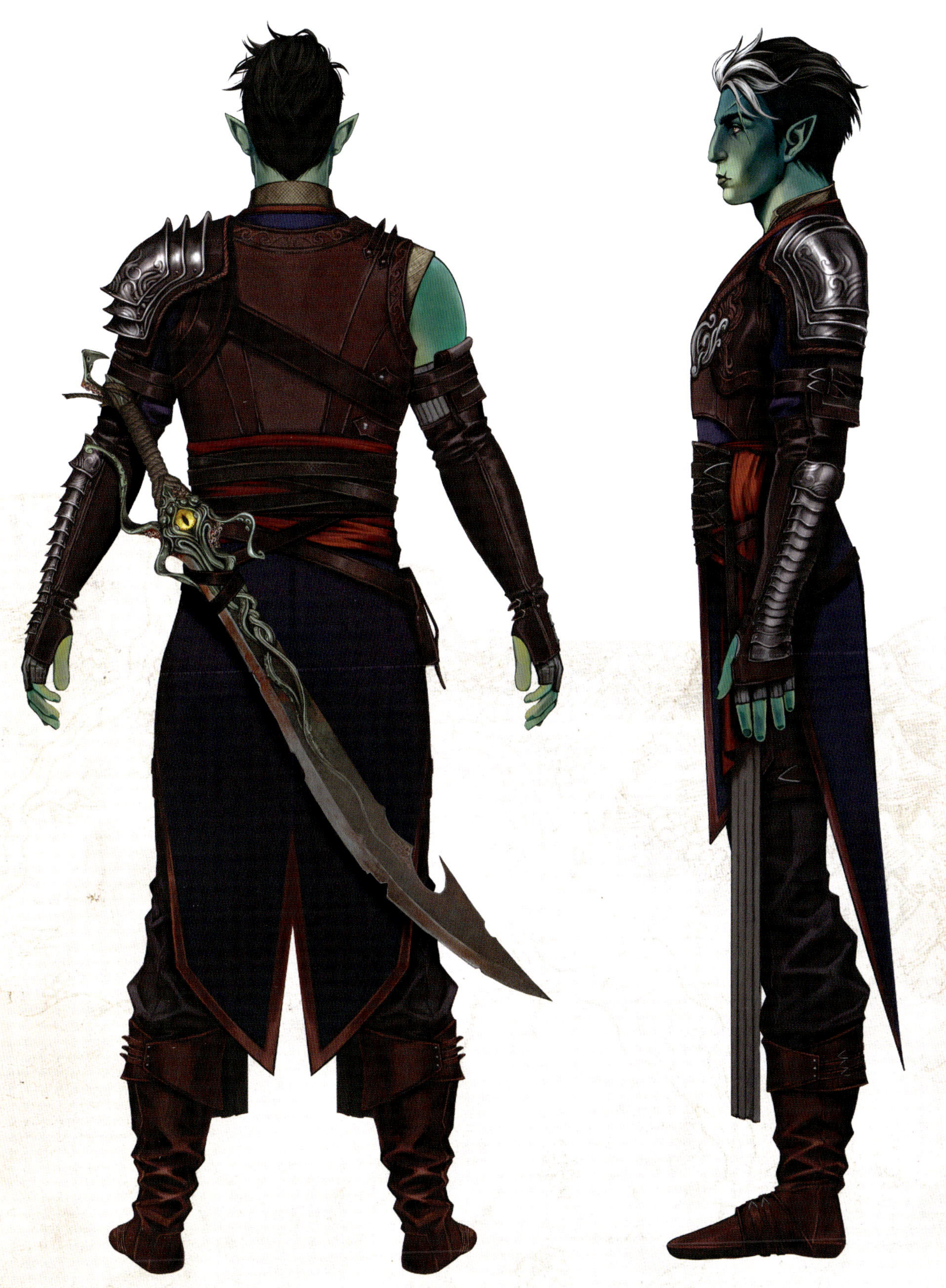

Sword of Fathoms

Fjord Stone used to be a normal sailor until the day his ship was sabotaged at the hands of his rival and crewmate, Sabian. With the explosion of the Tide's Breath, Fjord was thrown into the sea, drifting into the depths, unable to save himself. Something in the deep responded. When Fjord came to, he found himself alive on an island somewhere in the Lucidian Ocean, and in his hand, a beautiful barnacle-encrusted falchion, dripping with seawater. Unbeknownst to Fjord, he entered a pact with the eldritch entity Uk'otoa, a demigod trapped within the ocean following the Calamity.

As the strength of his pact grew, so too did the blade. Fjord learned to summon it at will and used his connection to Uk'otoa to consume the magical properties of other weapons. It changed appearance when Fjord consumed a Cloven Crystal, one of the three keys to unlocking Uk'otoa's prison, with a single, yellow eye appearing in the hilt. Though the blade served him for the first half of his time with the Nein, Fjord eventually threw the Sword of Fathoms into a volcanic forge after Uk'otoa's increasingly volatile insistence on being freed, severing his pact and losing his magic in the process. Other versions of the Sword of Fathoms would later appear in the various hands of Uk'otoa's other champions as they hunted Fjord for the Cloven Crystals to secure their demigod's freedom.

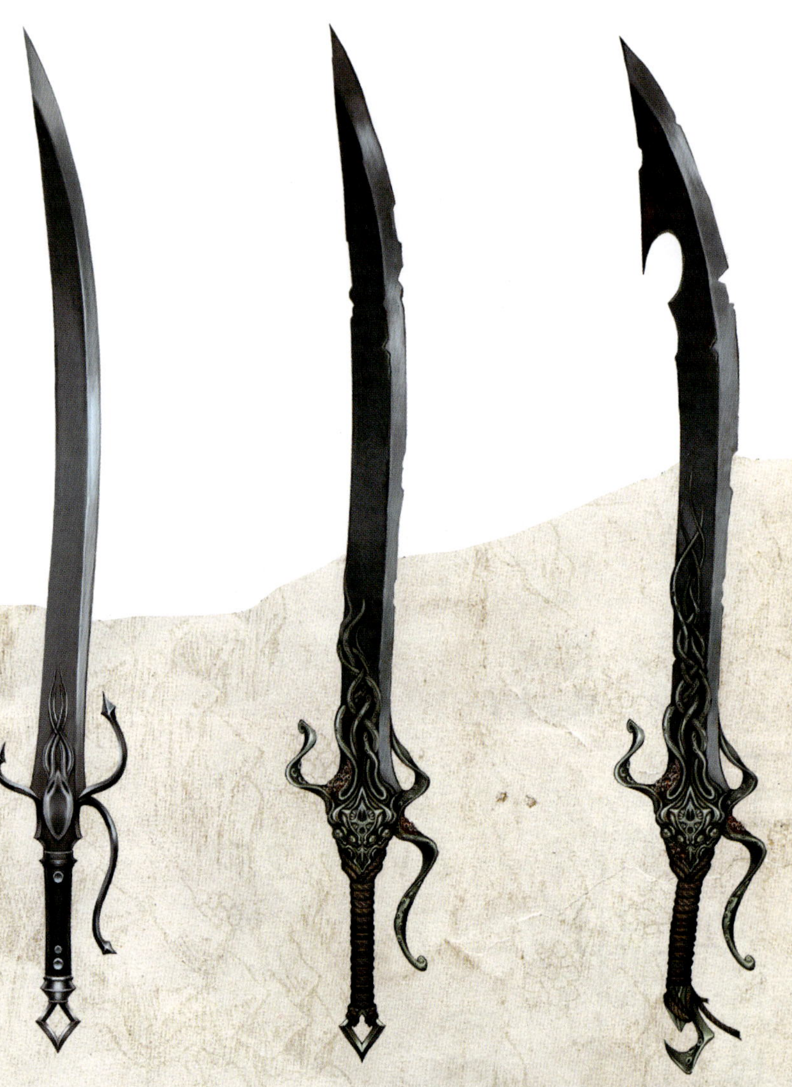

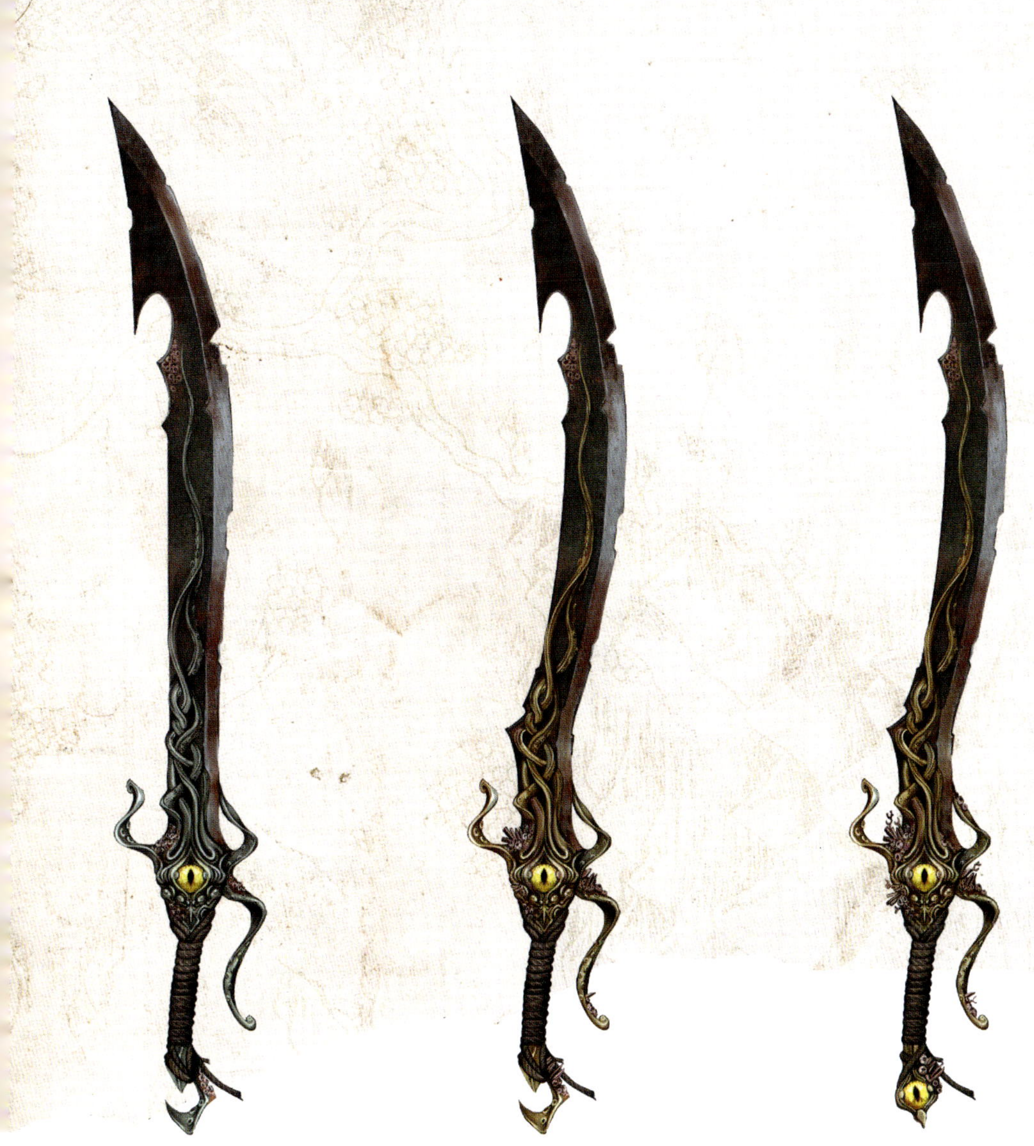

"The form of a dark magus's pact has been of fascination to me for some time. One might think that in a personal relationship with an entity gifting you magic, the sign or symbol of your partnership would be exclusive to you and you alone. And yet, as we can see in these reports ranging from Nicodranas to Port Zoon, up and down the coast, those taken in by the Leviathan of the Deeps all report the same boon: a blade of barnacles, dripping with seawater, its steel sharp as coral. Each bears a weapon that looks as though it emerged from ocean bedrock fathoms below only yesterday.

I have texts still to consider, but one thing is clear: The emblem of the golden eye is the same on every hilt, no matter the soul Uk'otoa has ensnared. Through the Sword of Fathoms, it seems, he can do more than watch your movements: He can witness the very world he wishes to rule over."

—D'Rishk Dawnscale, oral recording for work-in-progress "Elder Beings of Exandria, Volume II"

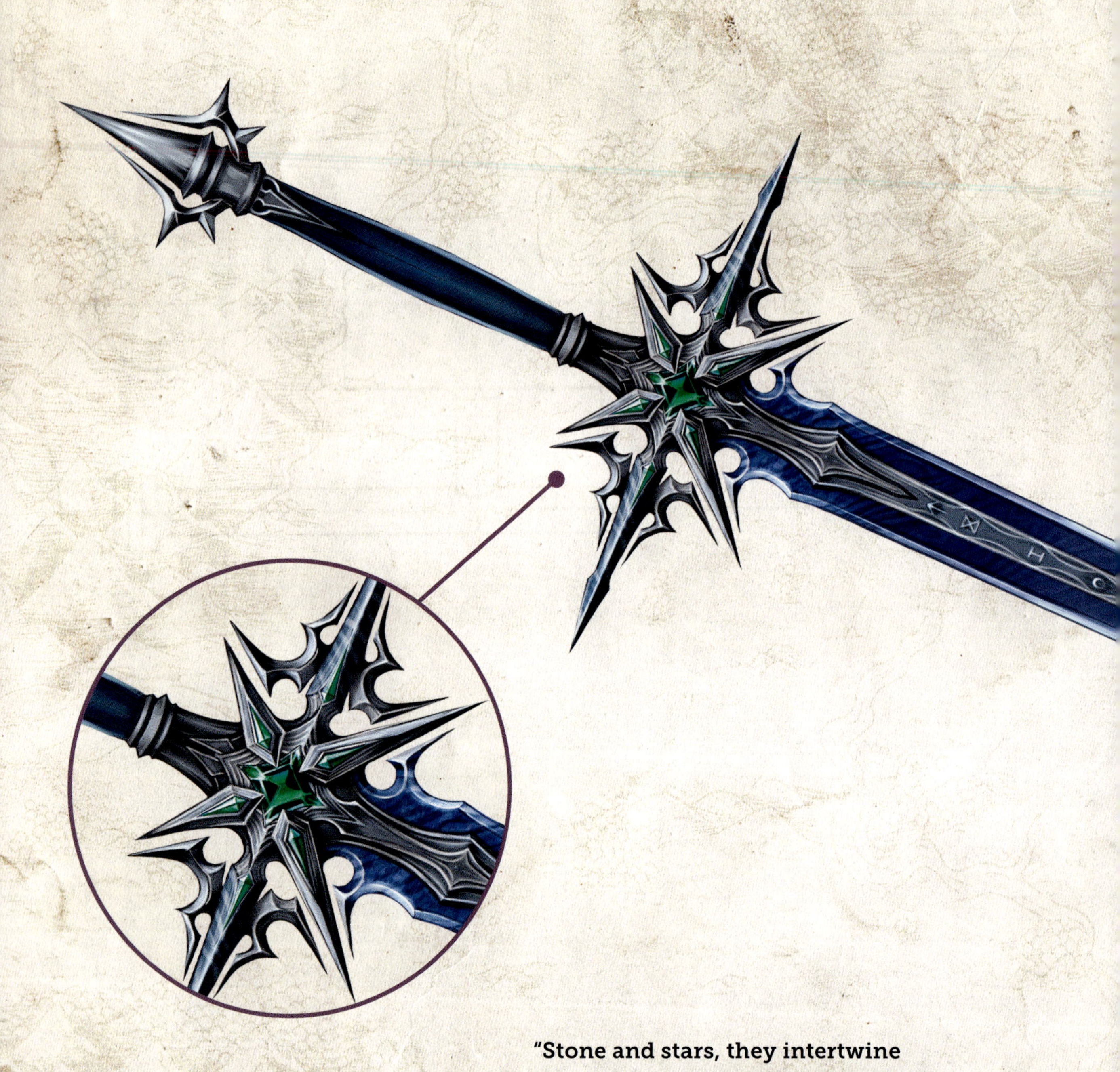

"Stone and stars, they intertwine
As warming sun grows emerald vine
Let justice bloom from blade divine
Evil burns from Dwueth'var's shine!"

—Tallulah Fontaine, Stanza VI of "Galas Var aer Nothe: Light of Evil's Bane," elvish epic on the creation of the Star Razor

Dwueth'var the Star Razor

When two halves of a mythic sword are sundered to either end of a continent, it must be divine mandate that brings them back together. With one half of the blade recovered from shopkeeper and ally Pumat Sol, and the other bargained for by an arcanist in service to the Bright Queen, the Mighty Nein reforged this Vestige of the Moonweaver and the Wildmother in the northern city of Uthodurn, after a harrowing trial to claim a magical mineral, iceflex, for its reforging. Destined for Fjord Stone after his pact renunciation with Uk'otoa, he took the new blade and became devoted to the Wildmother, oathsworn to her cause. Star Razor was used for the remainder of the Nein's time together, growing alongside Fjord as he came into his own as an exemplar, culminating an exalted state with the slaying of the undead Captain Avantika.

To this day, Fjord still uses the combined power of earth and stars to defeat legendary evils, protect the seas, and defend the peoples of Exandria.

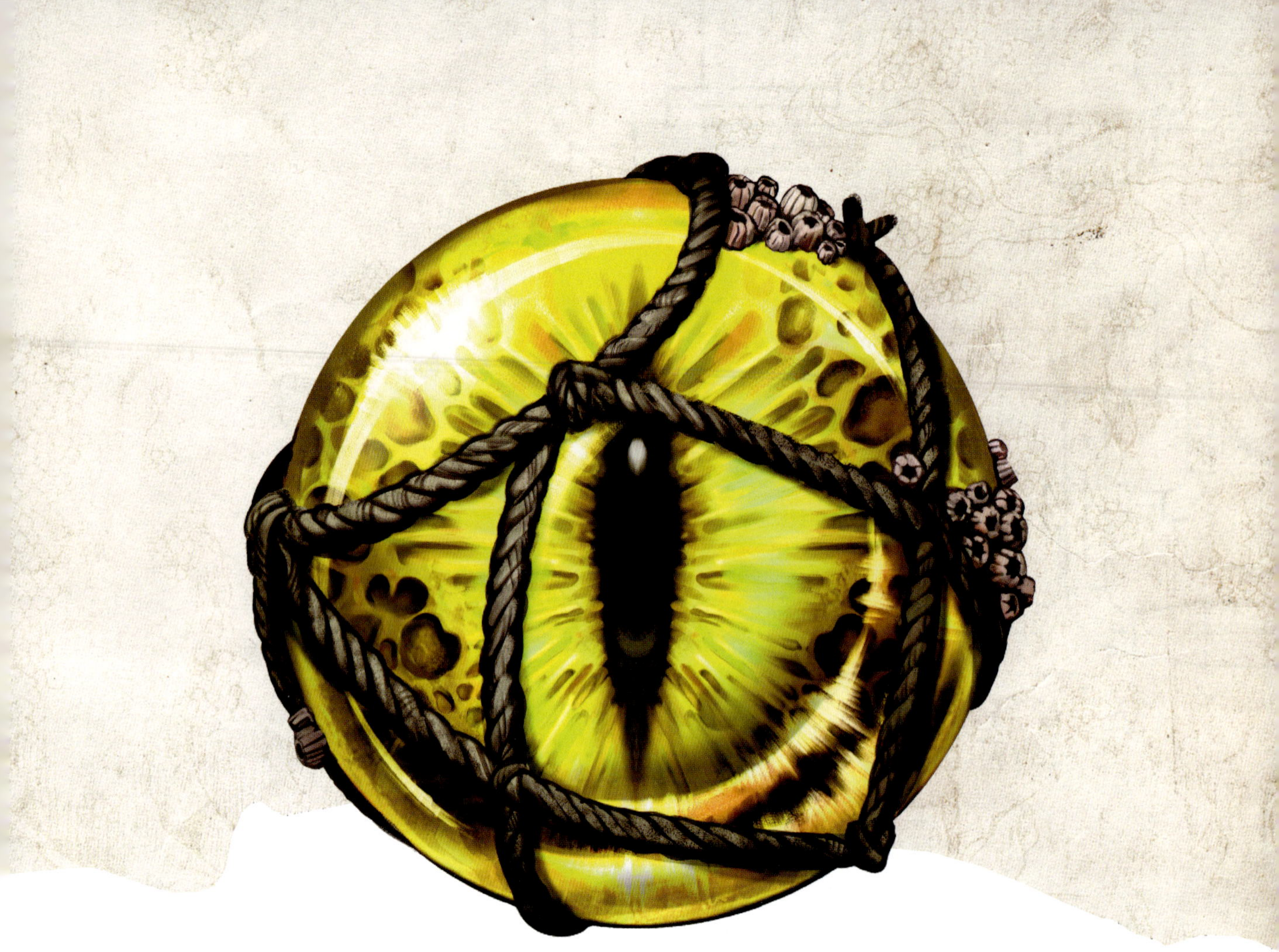

Cloven Crystal

Three stones, each glowing with a thin vertical pupil of yellow, slit like a serpent's eye, mark these three legendary keys to the prison of demigod Uk'otoa. Created when the serpent was punished and imprisoned at the end of the Calamity, they were scattered throughout the ocean depths, sealed away and guarded. Visions of these crystals are sent to followers of Uk'otoa to find and return them to three scattered temples across Wildemount, to free him and bring about his reign. When one of his followers does so, Uk'otoa bestows them with new blessings and spells, usually themed around the control of water. Captain Avantika, a true believer of Uk'otoa, unsealed the first lock with her crystal, and Fjord unlocked the second in the depths of the Gravid Archipelago to gain more of Uk'otoa's power.

When Fjord truly began to question his pact, he determined the third crystal, already absorbed into his person, must be kept from the Leviathan. However, by doing so, he made himself a target of the serpent's wrath several times, the final of which led to the taking of the third crystal and the unlocking of the final key. Following the calamitous release of Uk'otoa and his subsequent resealing by the Mighty Nein, three new crystals were made. This time, Fjord disposed of and hid them immediately, ensuring Uk'otoa stayed sealed.

Glove of Blasting

Found on the dead body of a cursed priest, this magical item came first to Caleb by way of Fjord in an exchange, with Fjord gaining his signature Armor of the Tides from the mage. With the Glove of Blasting, a gauntlet that enables its wearer to shoot off multiple beams of flame at once, Caleb added another elemental-based magic to his growing repertoire of signature spells that invoke fire. The gauntlet changed hands throughout the adventure, ultimately landing back in the hands of Fjord after he renounced his pact with Uk'otoa. This item, in addition to others, gave him more options in combat until such time as he was taken in by the Wildmother, his source of magic renewed.

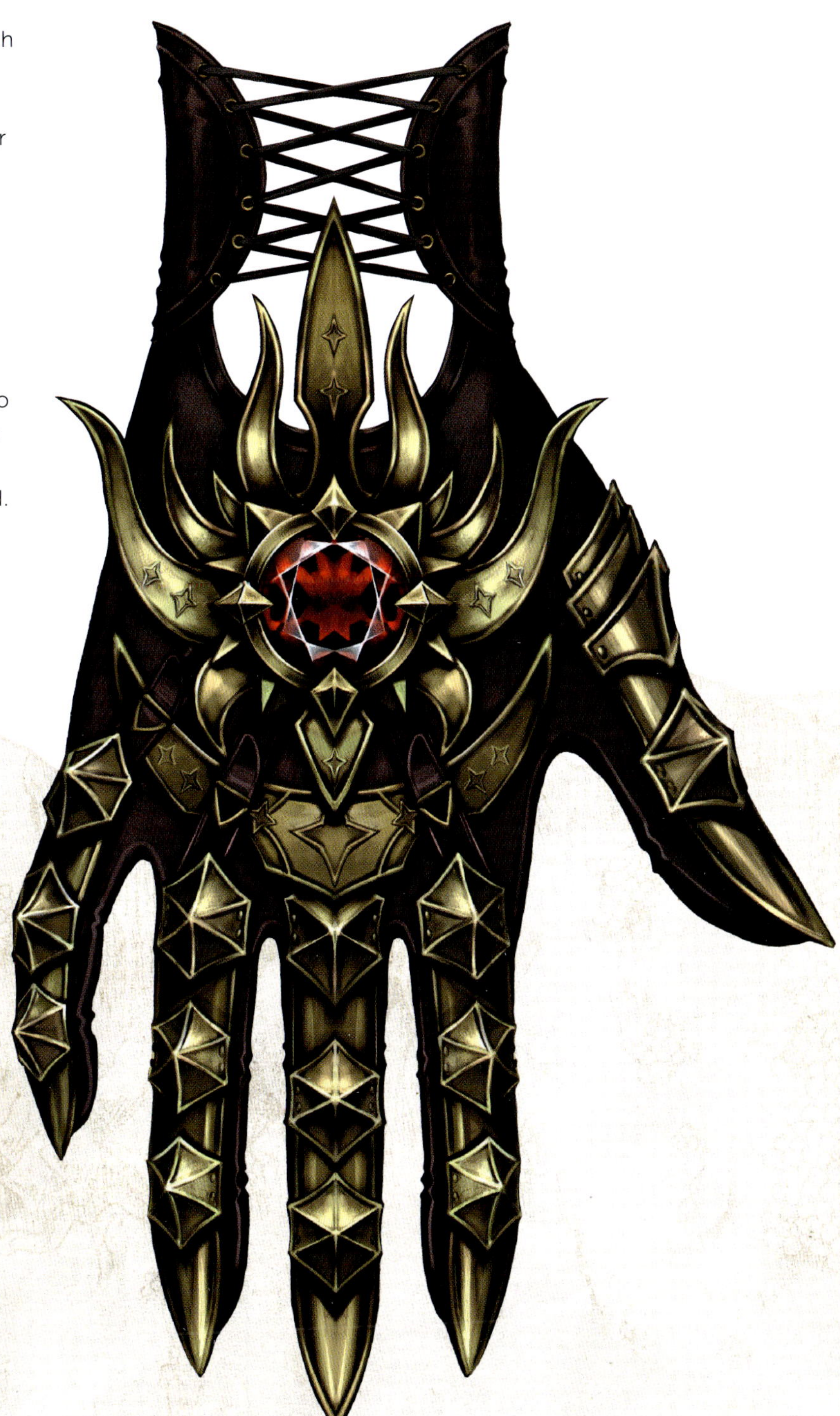

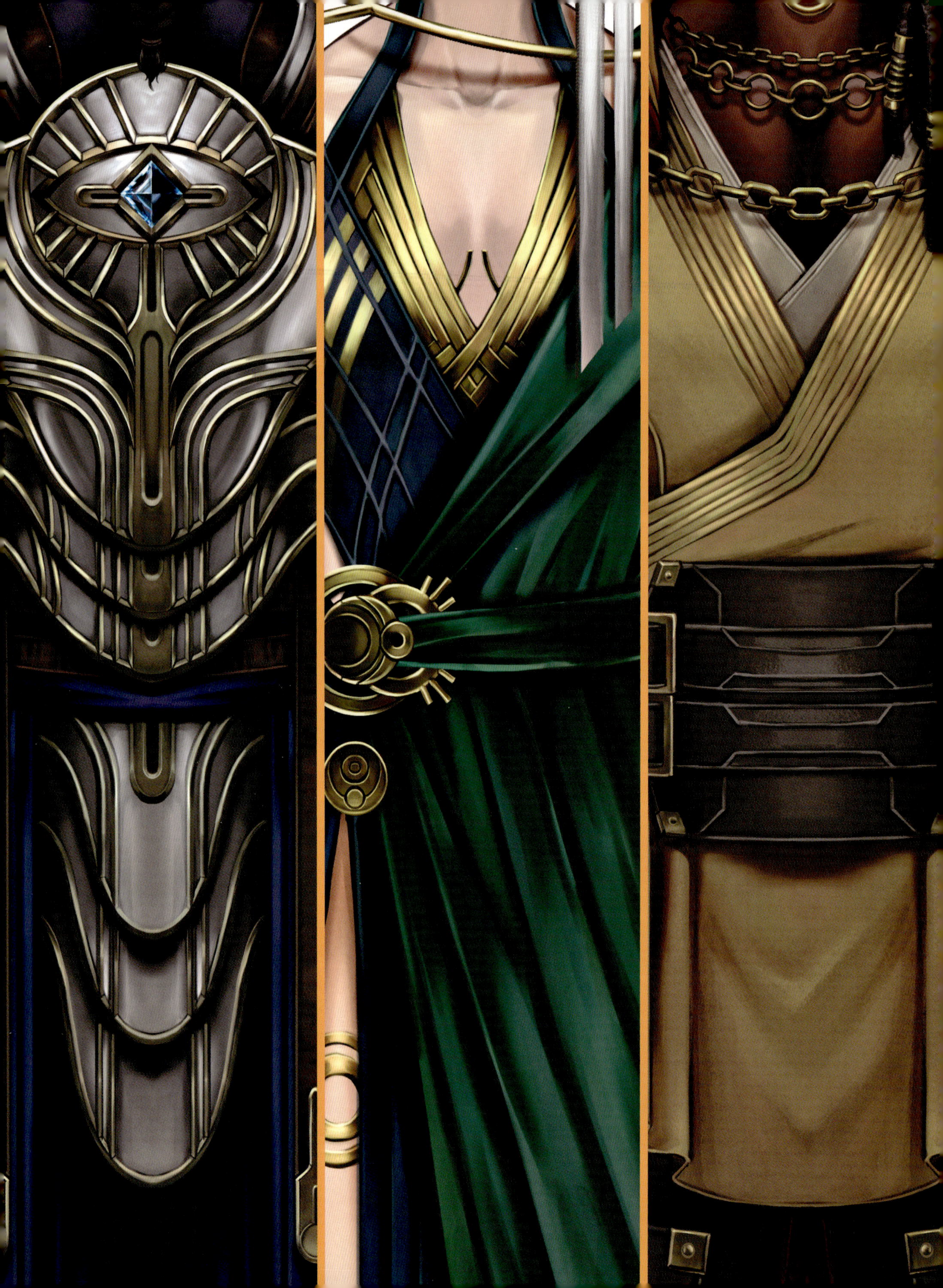

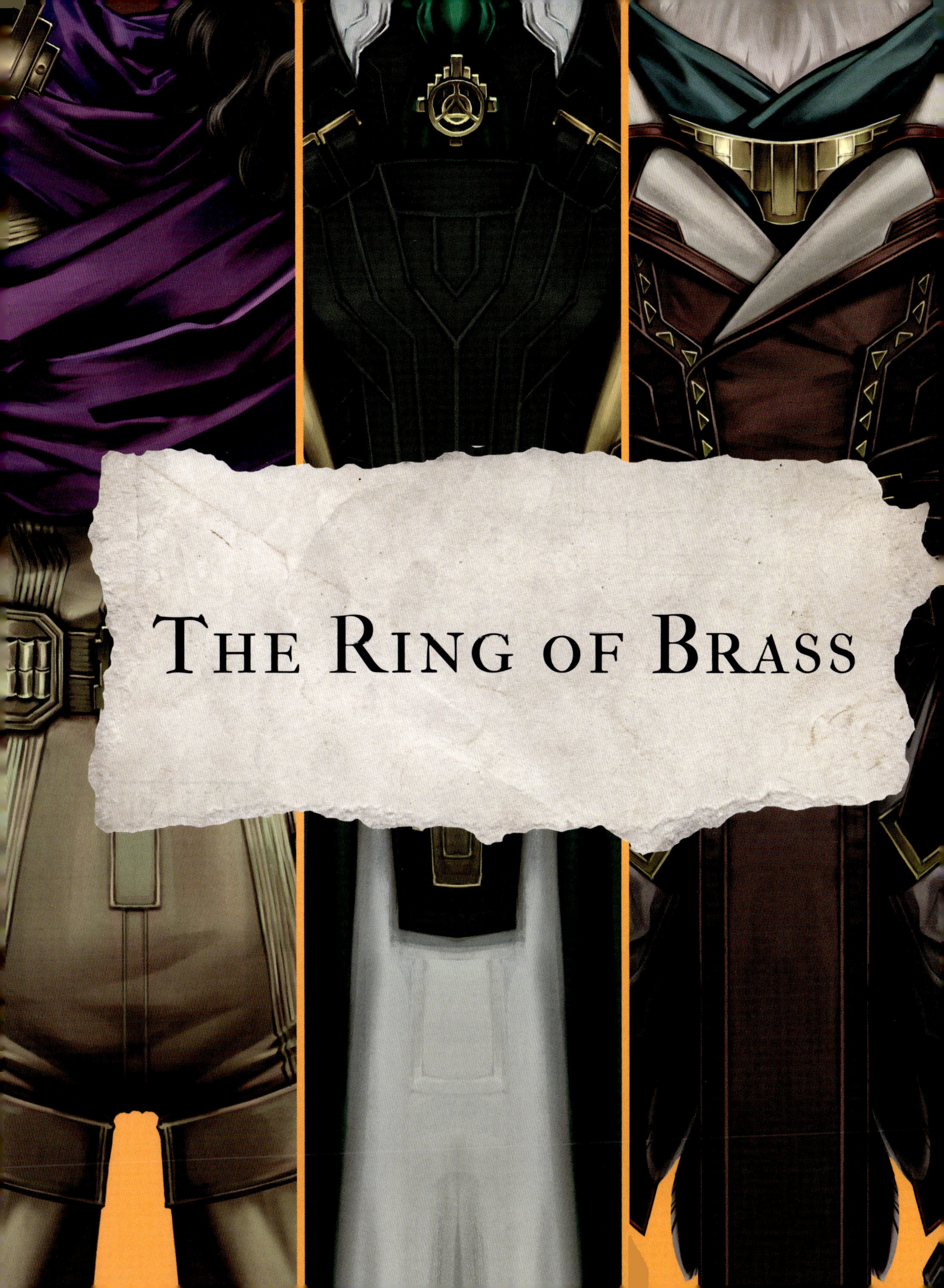

The Ring of Brass

The Ring of Brass

"We know little of the flying nation-states that lived and thrived in the Age of Arcanum. What we know of Aeor, we know because we have wrenched history from its carcass in the far north. Lathras has just been a name over the centuries. And Avalir, said to be the most beautiful, we are only just learning of; what history remains, remains because of a dedicated alliance of leaders and heroes within the City of Crowns. And it should be no surprise who it was that saved what remained, in the end, when the immense inferno of the Calamity began. Gold is bright, but it is soft; it gives under pressure. Silver shines, but it is conducive; the hand that holds it determines its strength and what it does. But brass! Beautiful, sturdy brass. A metal that is only made by the joining of other elements; a metal that can endure the heat. A metal that only weakens when it is corroded, weakened from the outside in. It is no surprise that it is the Ring of Brass who kept Avalir alive, even after all these years. It is simply a sorrow that so few know it."

—D'RISHK DAWNSCALE, "SUCH GREAT HEIGHTS: A NEW TREATISE OF THE SKY CITIES OF EXANDRIA"

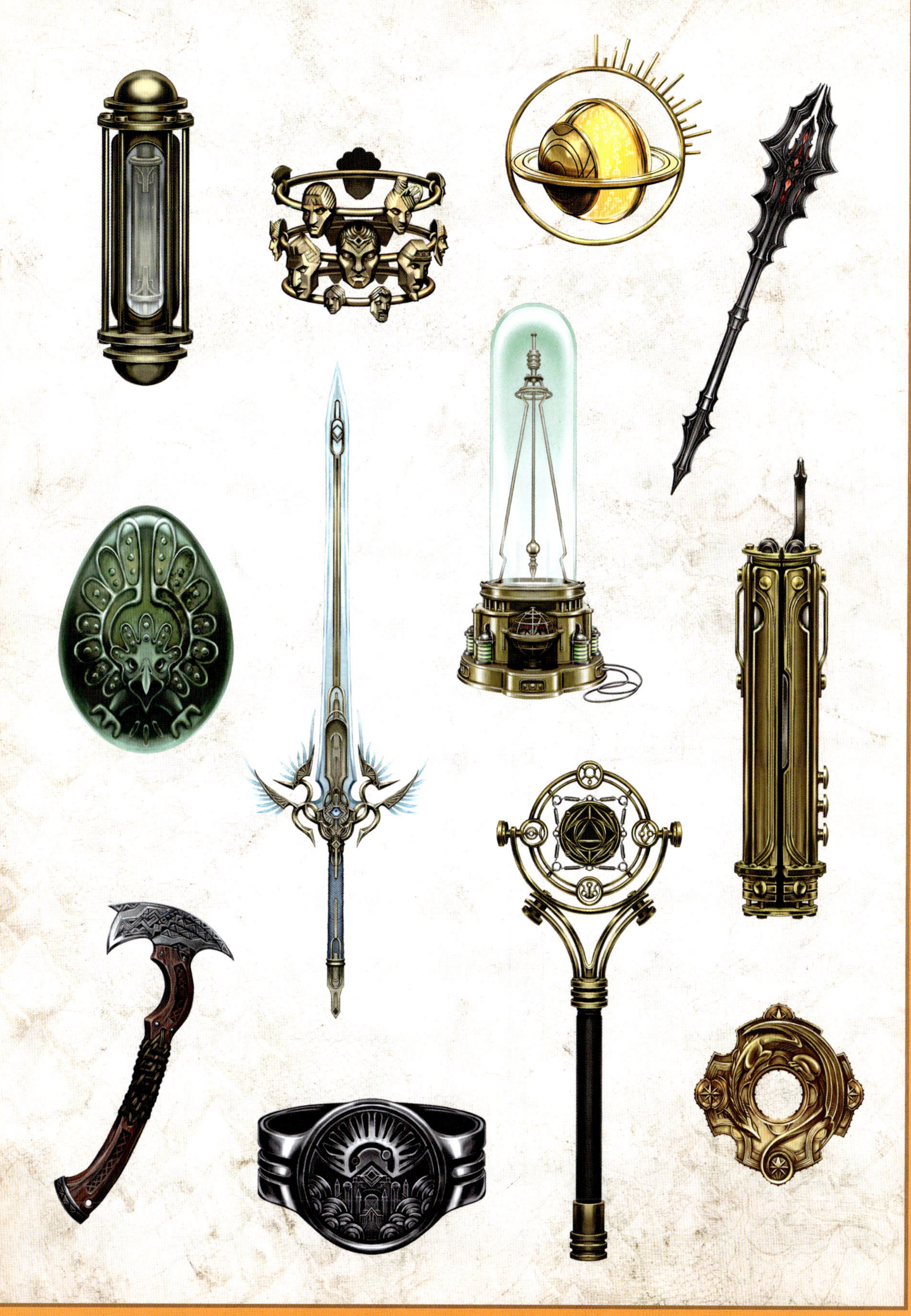

Zerxus Ilerez

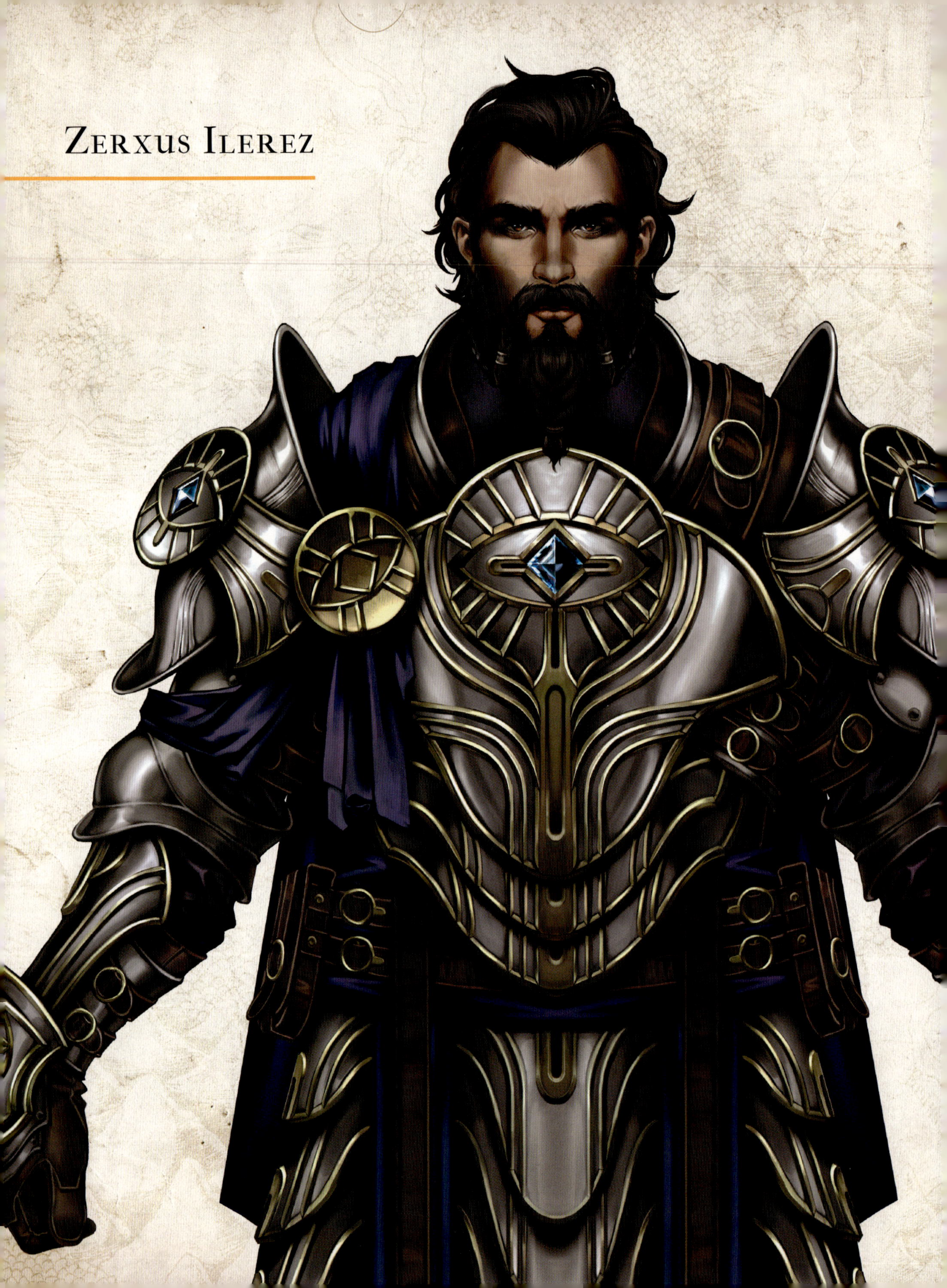

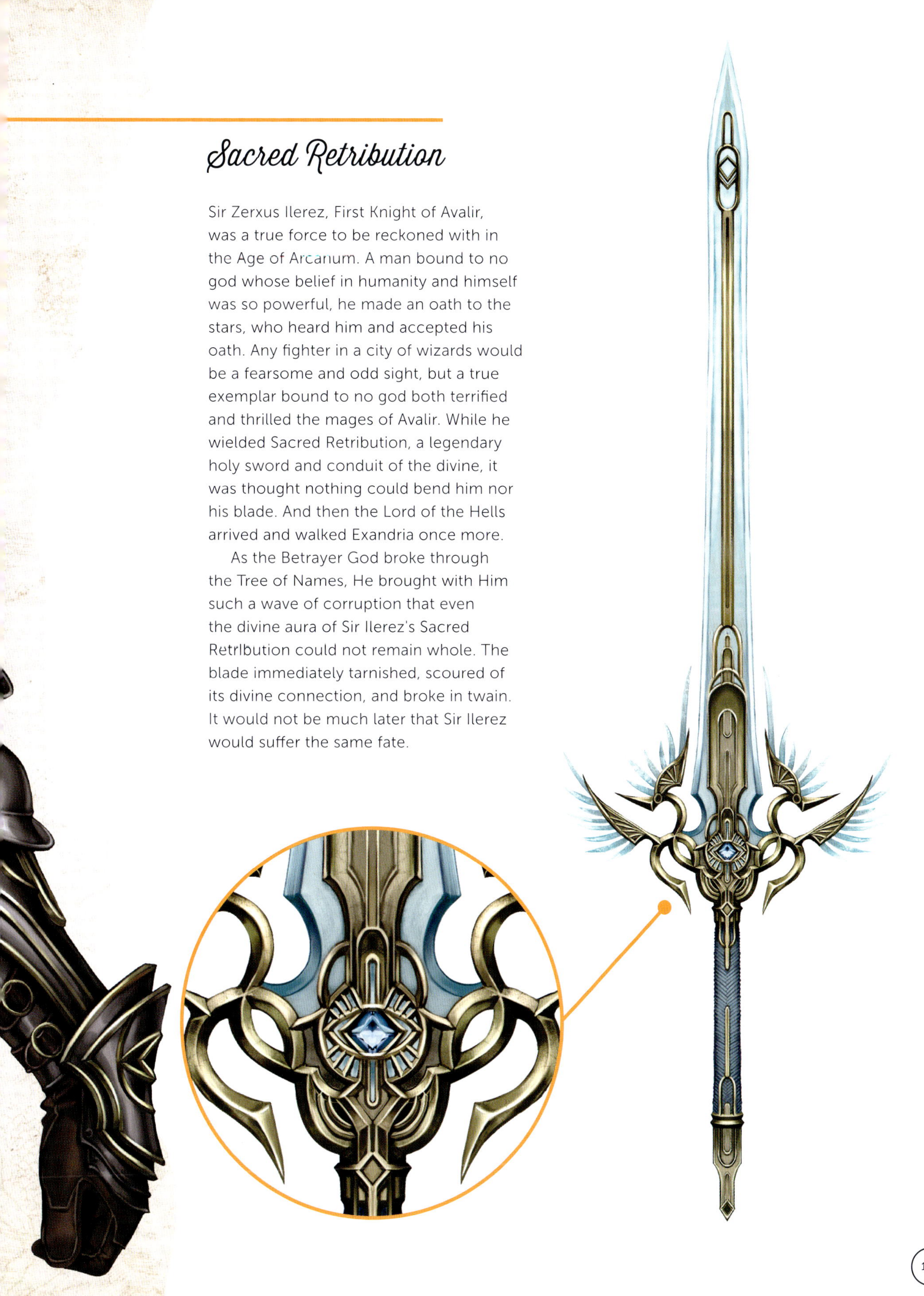

Sacred Retribution

Sir Zerxus Ilerez, First Knight of Avalir, was a true force to be reckoned with in the Age of Arcanum. A man bound to no god whose belief in humanity and himself was so powerful, he made an oath to the stars, who heard him and accepted his oath. Any fighter in a city of wizards would be a fearsome and odd sight, but a true exemplar bound to no god both terrified and thrilled the mages of Avalir. While he wielded Sacred Retribution, a legendary holy sword and conduit of the divine, it was thought nothing could bend him nor his blade. And then the Lord of the Hells arrived and walked Exandria once more.

As the Betrayer God broke through the Tree of Names, He brought with Him such a wave of corruption that even the divine aura of Sir Ilerez's Sacred Retribution could not remain whole. The blade immediately tarnished, scoured of its divine connection, and broke in twain. It would not be much later that Sir Ilerez would suffer the same fate.

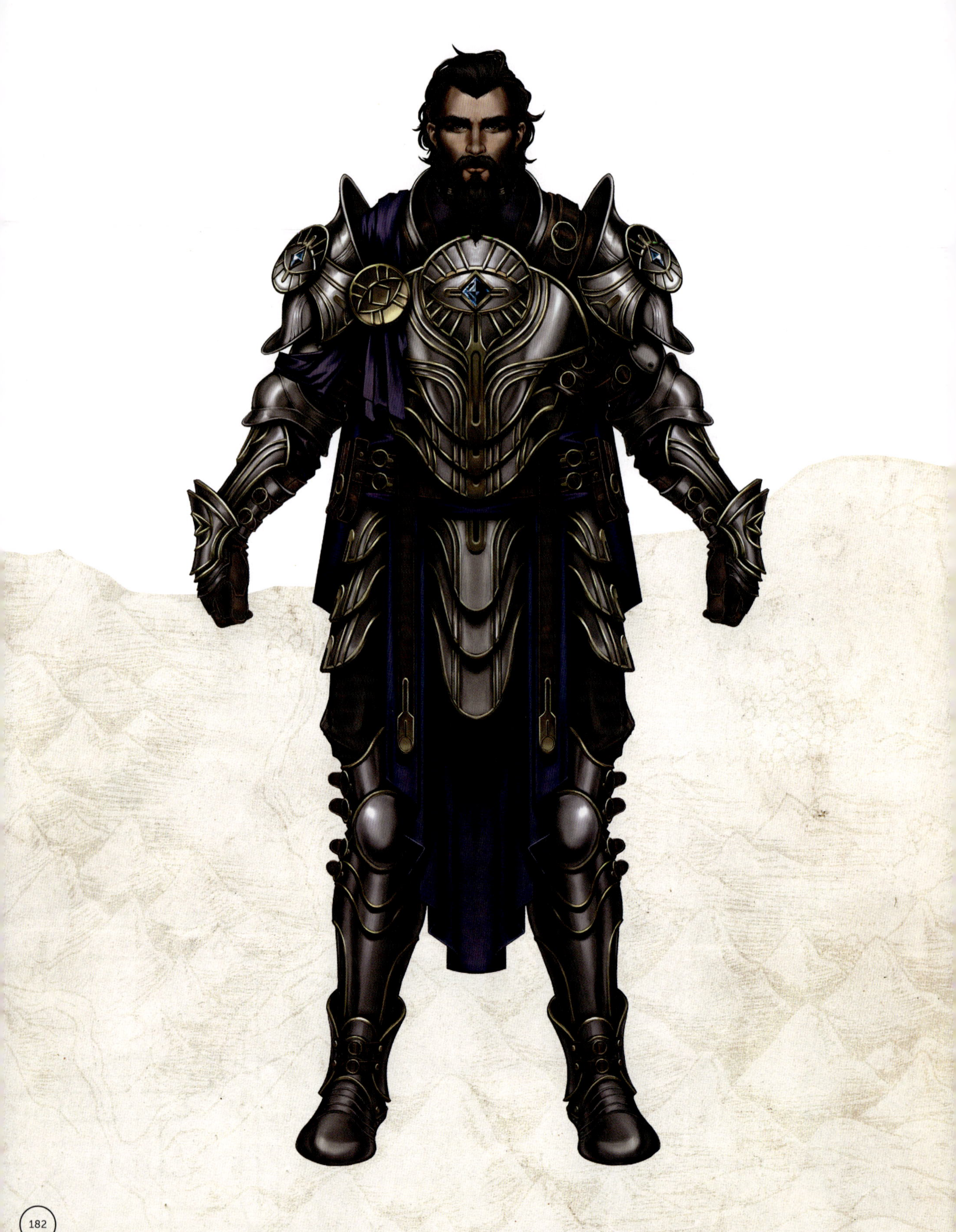

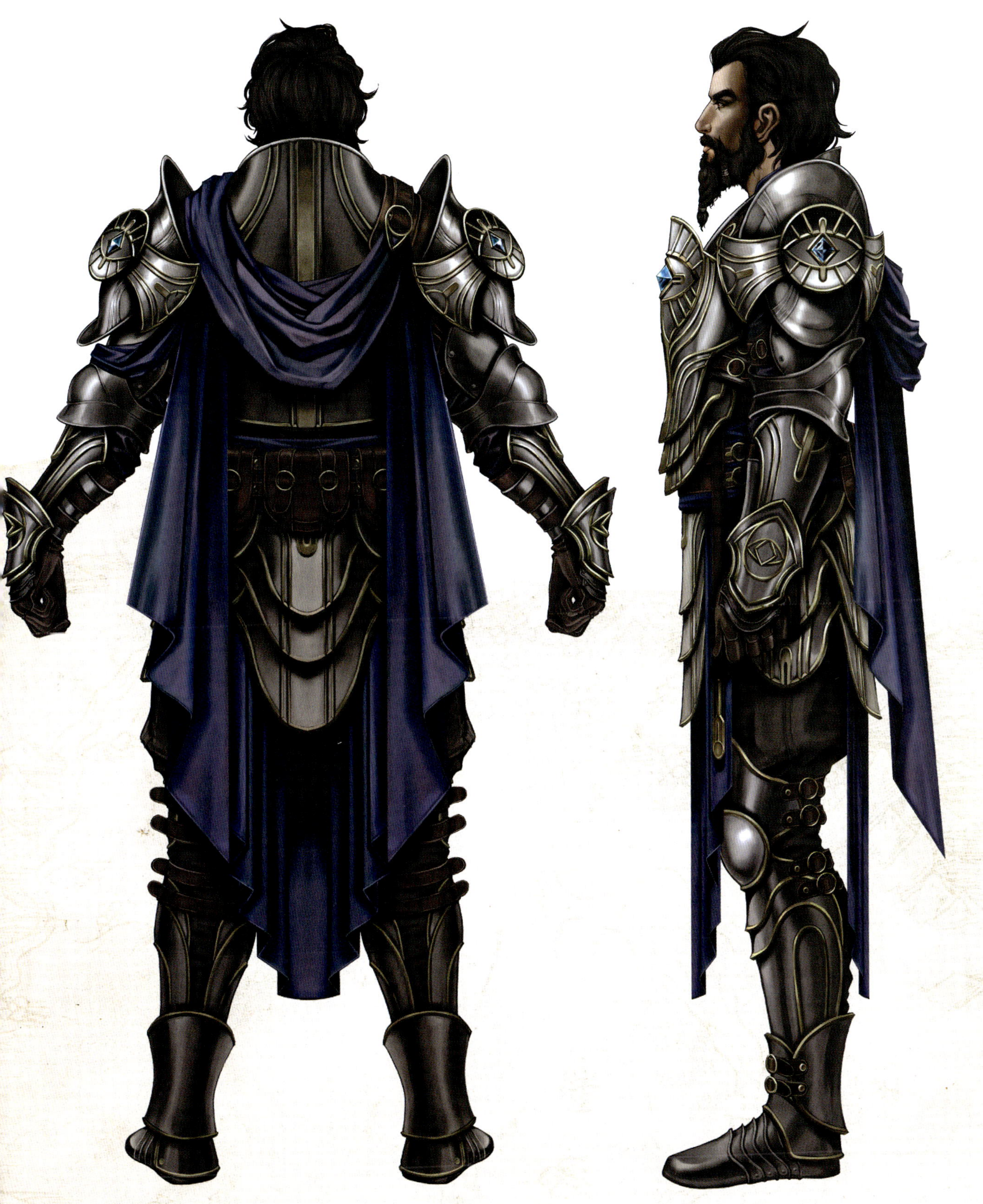

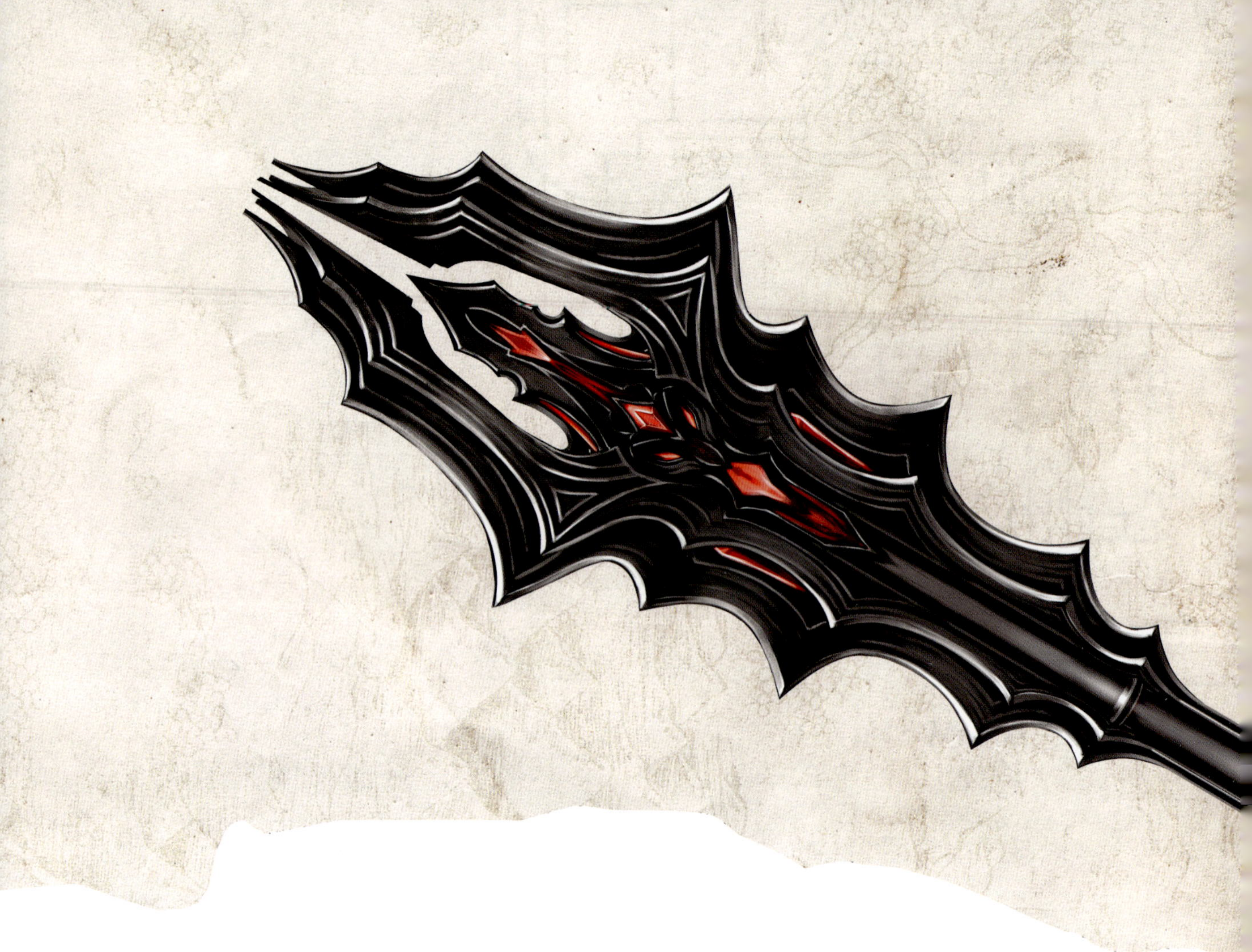

"To this day, it is uncertain as to the fate of Sir Ilerez, the fabled knight of Avalir. He gave his soul to protect Exandria, and for that, we must remain grateful. But in the centuries after, through Calamity, through Divergence, there has been very little record of Sir Ilerez on the Material Plane. One would think the wielder of such an important Vestige of the Hells would be on the frontlines, enacting his Lord's agenda. And yet, given Sir Ilerez's history, his temperament, and his very character, it would not surprise me to know that the Lord of the Hells keeps him close at hand. Not because, if given the chance, the damned knight would attempt to free himself from the chains he allowed himself to be bound in, no. But because keeping the soft, familiar light of Exandria's stars from he who loved them most probably brings the Lord of the Hells joy unending. If Sir Ilerez remains whole, mind unbroken after all these years, one hopes he someday finds freedom. Or at the very least, enough redemption to save his soul from its fiery fate."

—Oren Keth'Kaylis, "A Catalog of Fiends, Major and Minor, Expanded Edition"

Mace of the Black Crown

The Lord of the Hells offered Sir Ilerez an impossible choice, and to his credit, Zerxus did not balk but chose. In the frozen moment in which He emerged, the Lord of the Hells choked the soul from a fiend known as Xartaza and used it to bring the Mace of the Black Crown into being. A black iron weapon embedded with a ruby at its top and encrusted throughout, the gems glow with flame, the weapon itself smoking with malice around its head, like a crown. Along the handle, the fiendish contract the Lord of the Hells offered Sir Ilerez awaited his grasp. And when Zerxus, choosing his son, Exandria, and hope, took that handle, it began to magically write his fate into the black iron handle.

A last-moment gamble brought back Archmage Vespin Chloras's mind long enough for him to interrupt the contract and amend it, giving Zerxus until dawn before the contract went into effect. Zerxus used those precious hours to see his son one last time, evacuate Avalir and Toramunda, and help hold off Vespin long enough for Laerryn to enact her plan. In his corporeal death, Zerxus burst into flames, and along with the mace he wielded, burned away to nothing, his soul bound for the Hells.

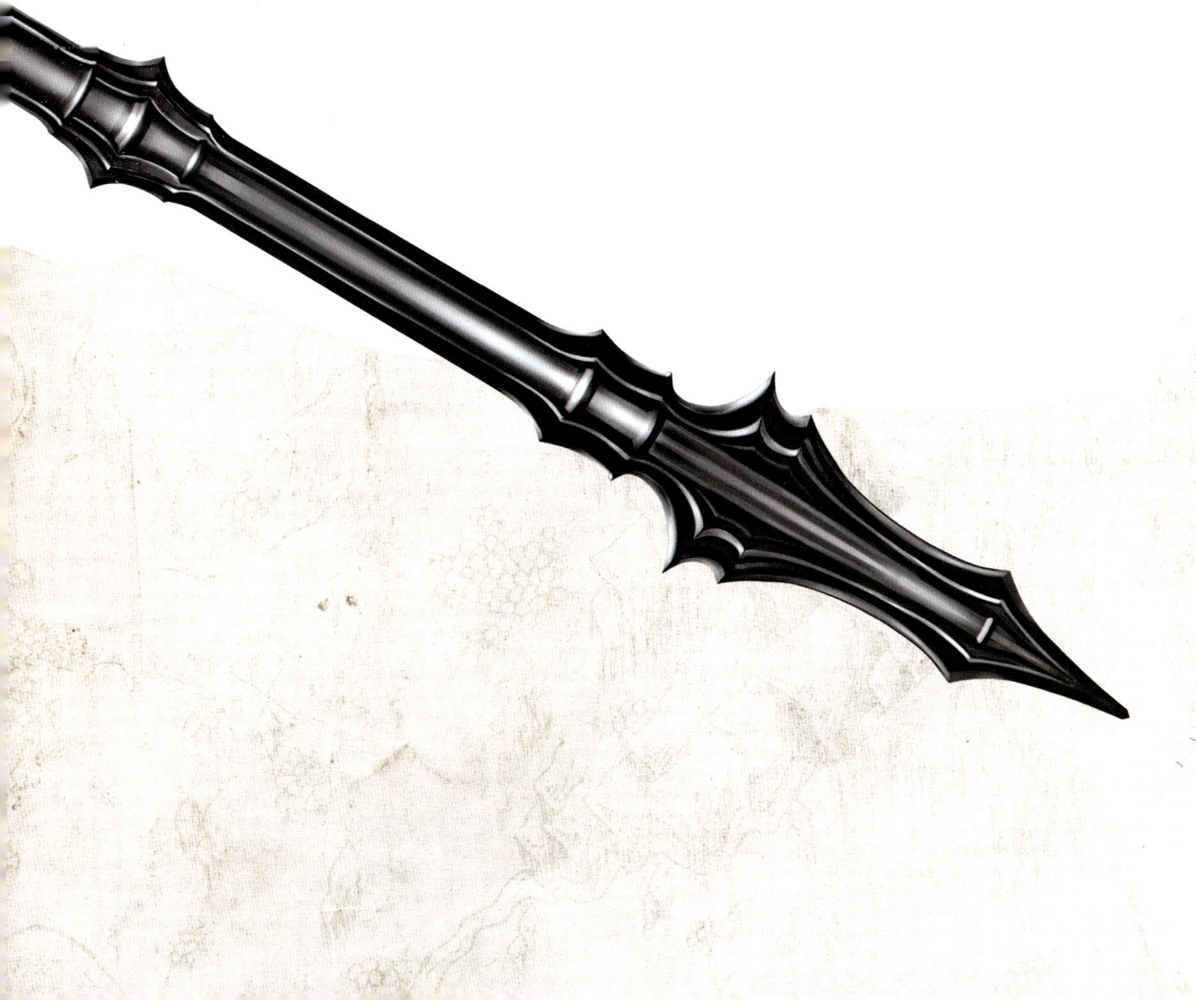

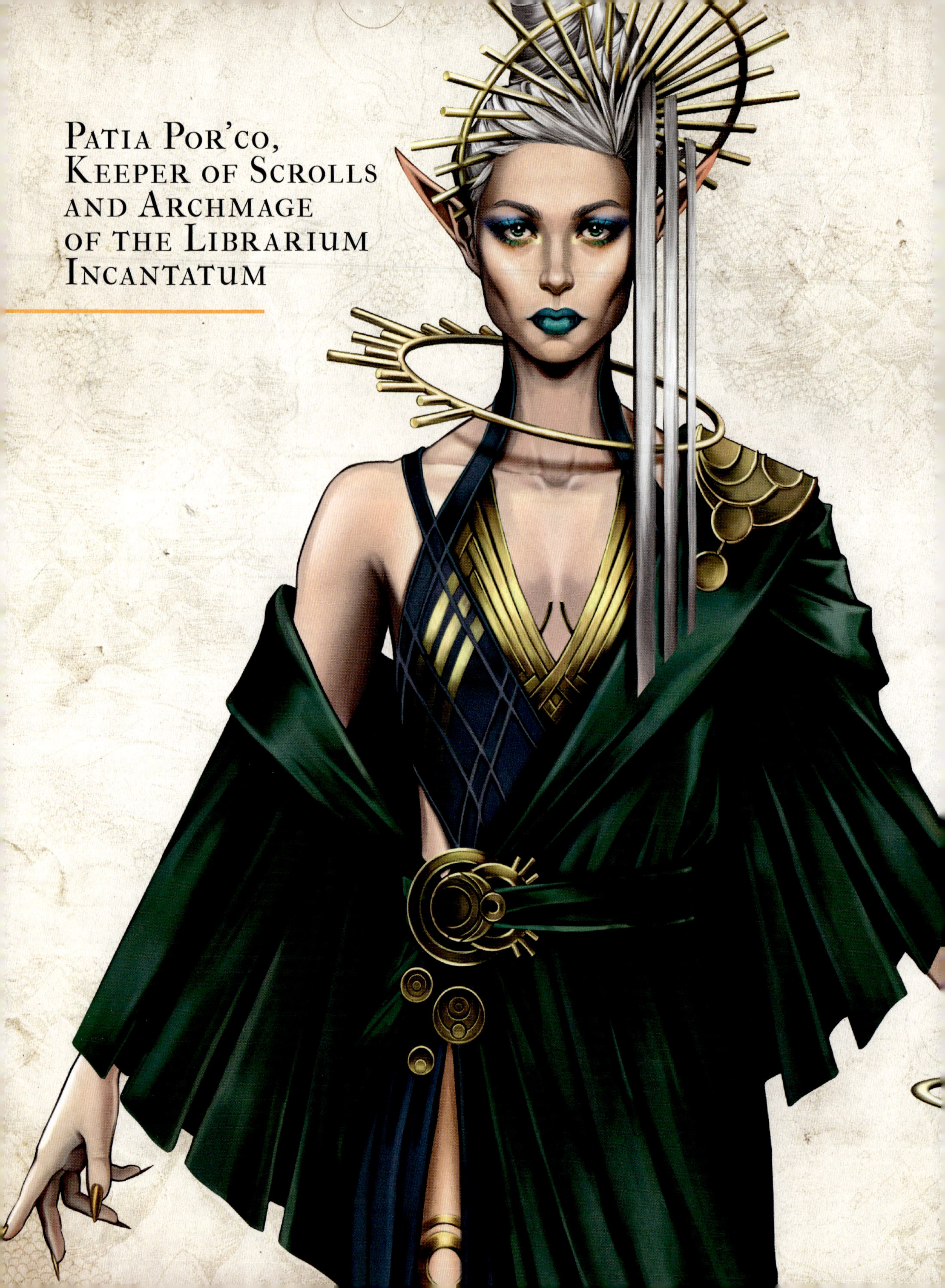

Patia Por'co, Keeper of Scrolls and Archmage of the Librarium Incantatum

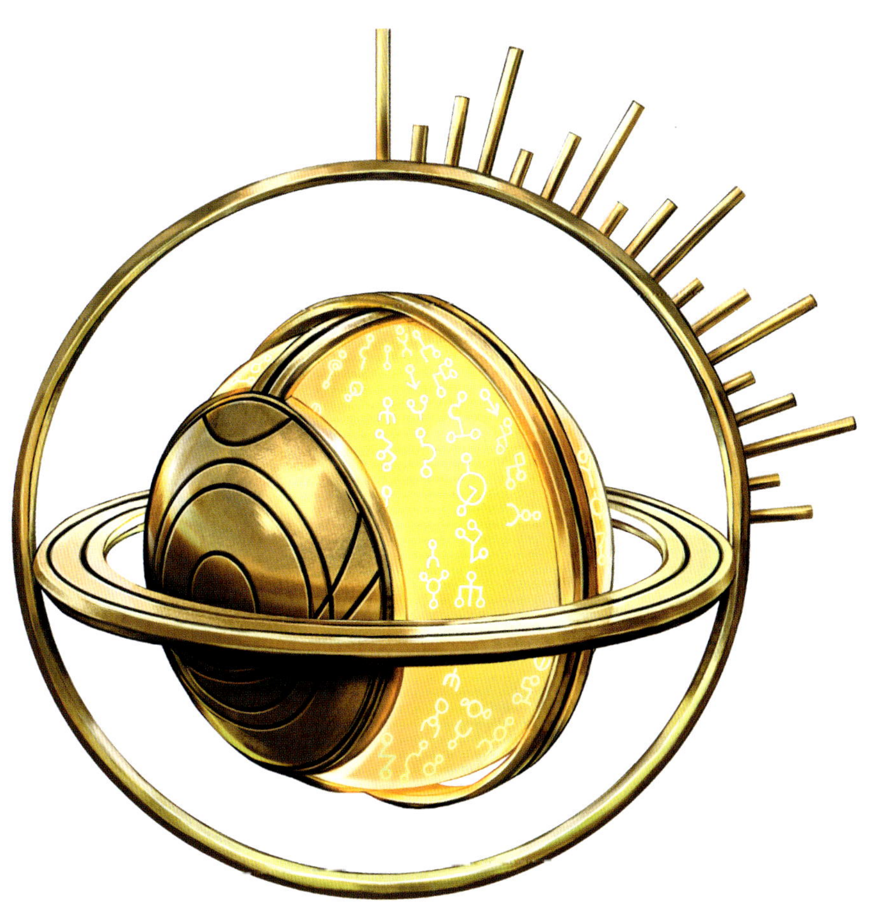

Sphere of Power

Granddaughter to the founder of Avalir, Archmage Imyr Por'co, Patia carried on his legacy as a powerful mage, using her vast intellect, social standing, and legacy to become Keeper of Scrolls for the entire library of spells within the city. As such, a simple staff would not be enough to house the enormity of spells at her disposal. Instead, a Sphere of Power was crafted, utilizing a recursive tesseract function within to house the many, many spells of the Librarium Incantatum. Housing not just the spells of the Age of Arcanum, Patia also spent much time housing the vast and varied tomes, papers, notes, blueprints, and research of note, so much so, that by the end of her prodigious life, her Sphere of Power contained nearly every bit of knowledge within Avalir.

As the doom of Avalir came upon Patia and she recognized just how much she had given to the city of her grandfather (including a recently severed arm), the idea of legacy loomed. And realizing what was about to happen and what would be lost, Patia took her Sphere of Power, full of the history of Avalir, and knew it was her turn to give to someone else. She teleported the Sphere to Maya, Cerrit's daughter, recently escaped and far from the continent of Domunas. With all she had learned now safe, Patia went forth toward her doom, ready to give the rest of herself to safeguard Exandria. To this day, no one can say exactly where her Sphere is, though numerous rumors abound.

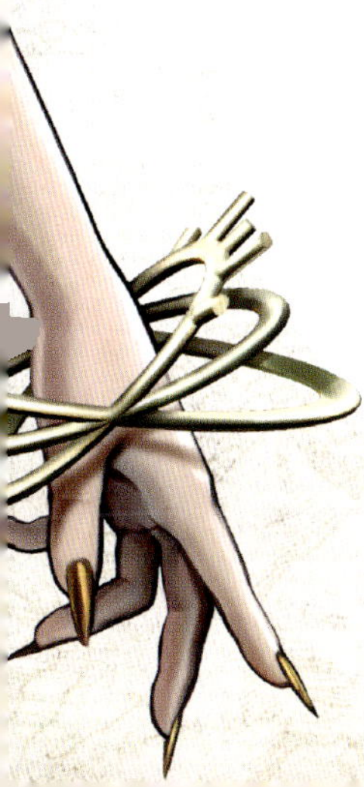

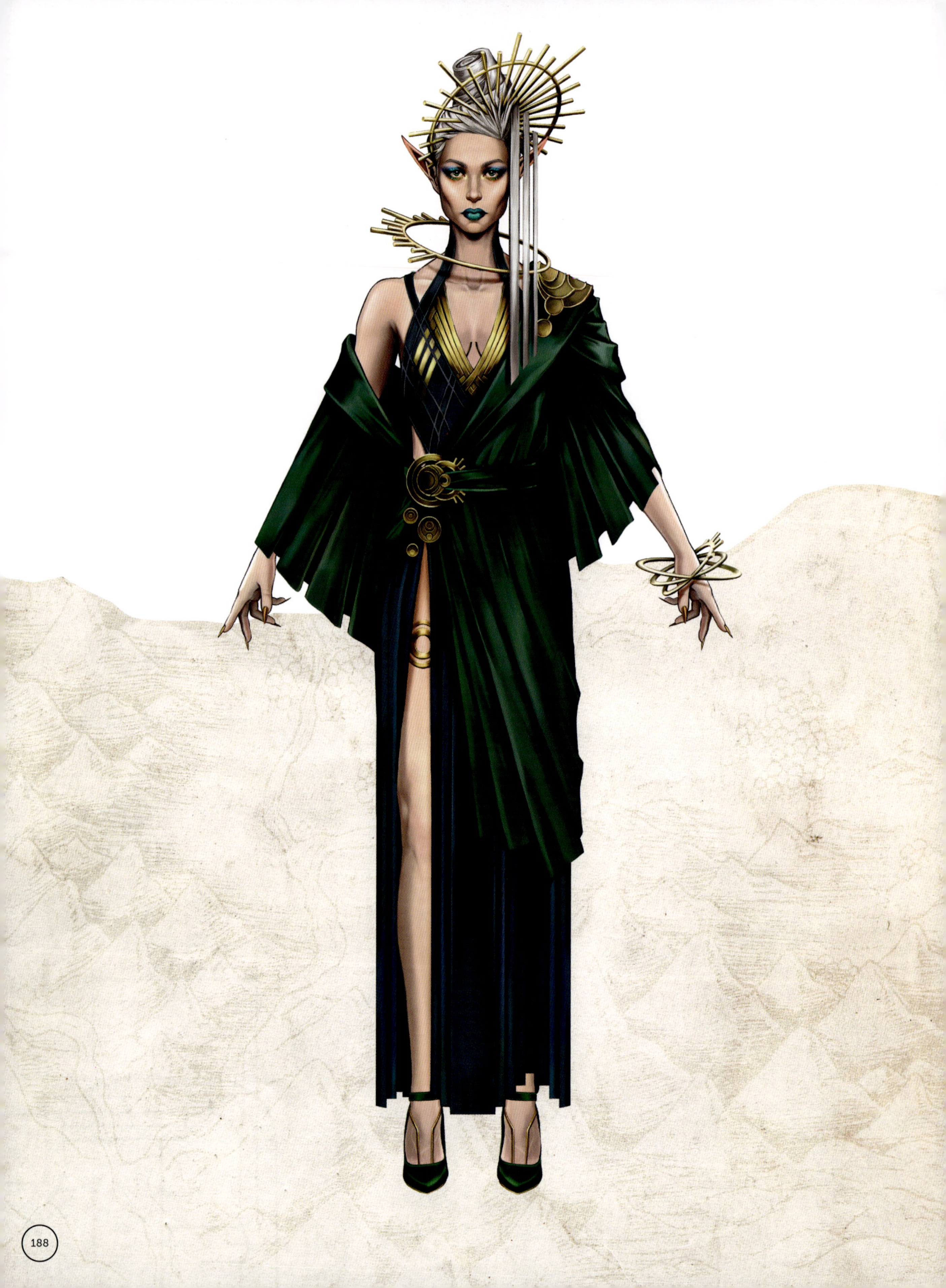

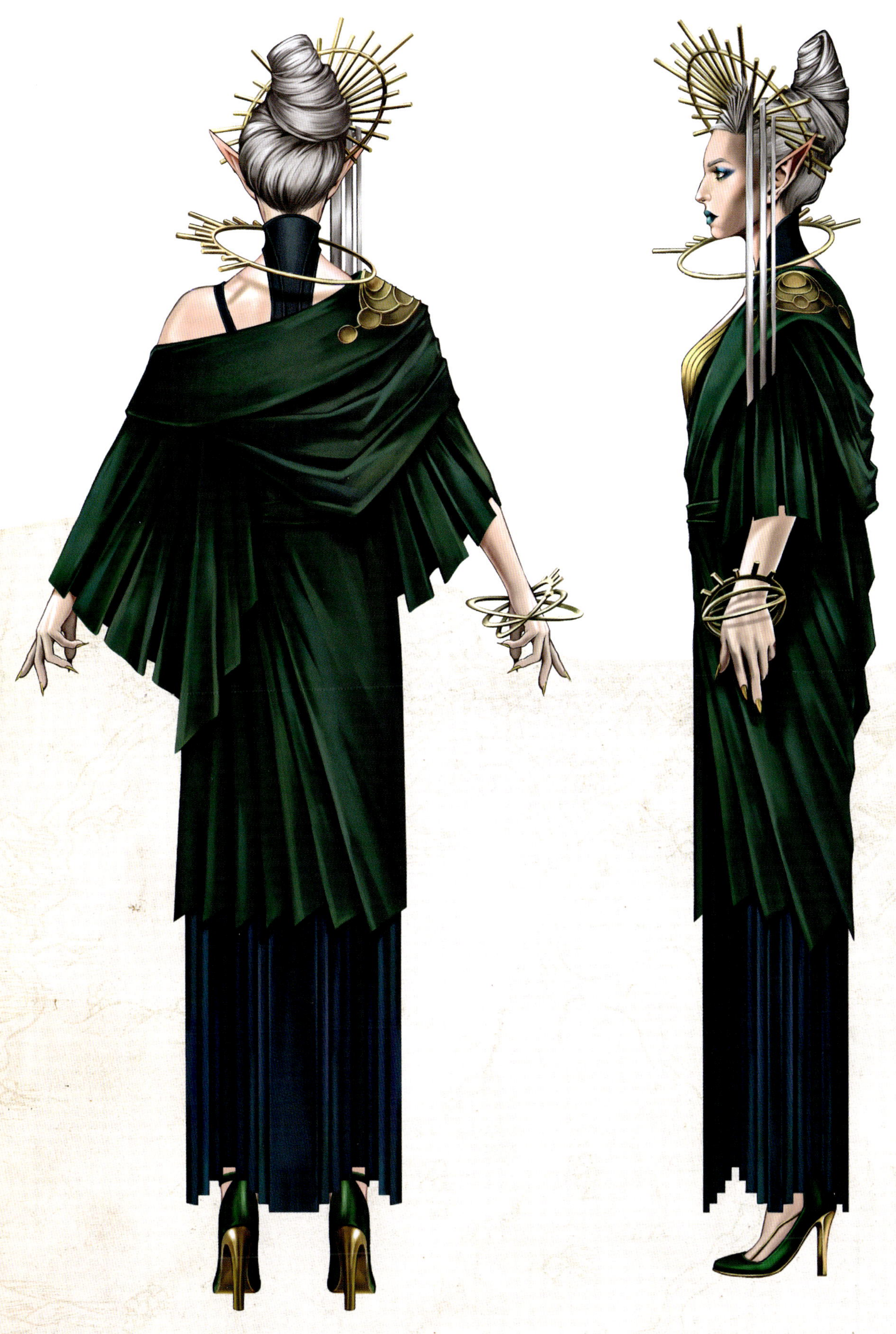

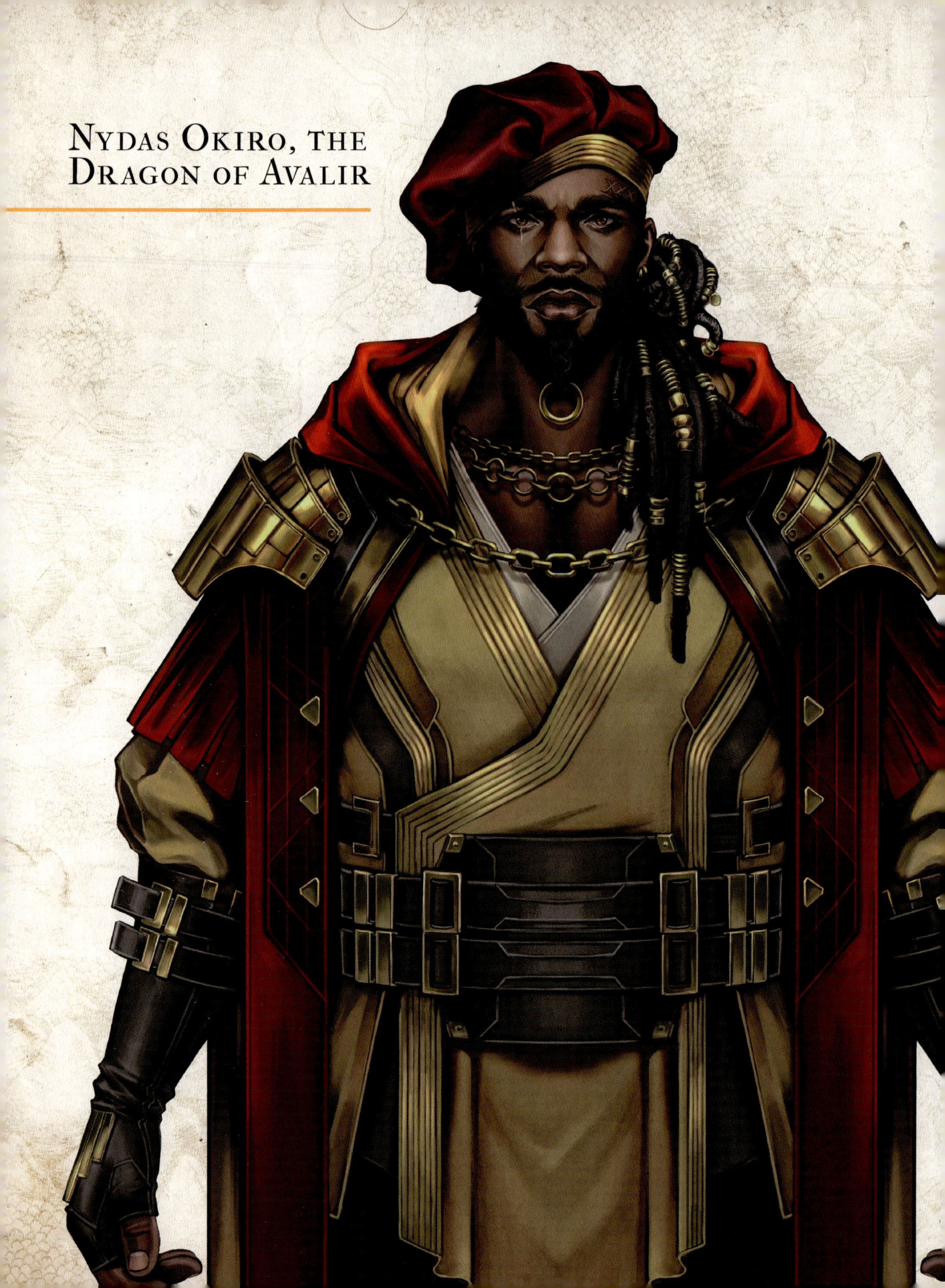

Nydas Okiro, the Dragon of Avalir

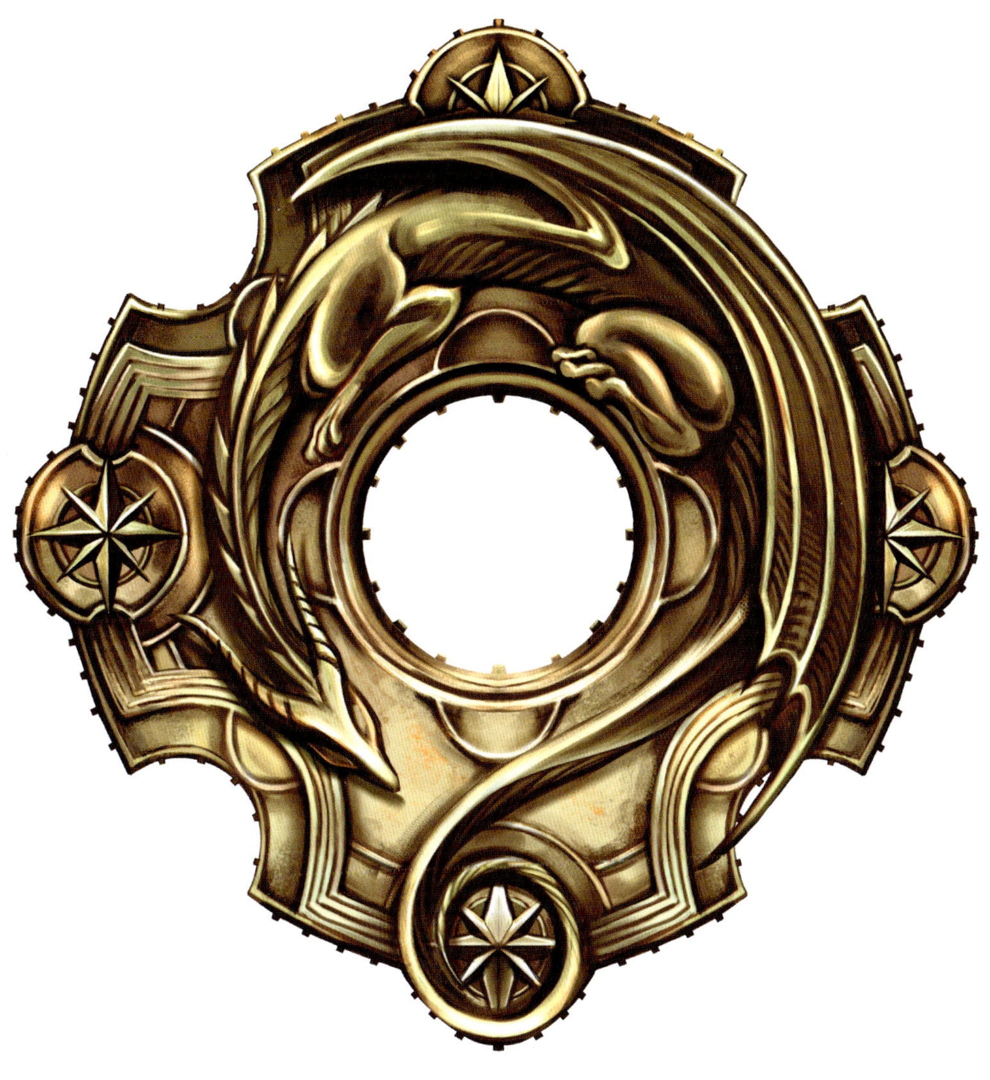

Coin of Sha'korzhan

Every time a newly chosen Guildmaster of the Golden Scythe began their tenure, they were gifted this one treasure and told to use it in time of greatest need. Nydas Okiro, final Guildmaster of the Golden Scythe, was given this gold coin; though he didn't know he'd be its last bearer, it is fitting that the first and last dragons of Avalir met their end together. On the fateful night of Avalir's doom, Nydas called forth the ghost of the gem dragon Sha'korzhan from within the coin, and as one, both dragons defended the city from the clutches of the rampaging K'nauthi as they flooded the city. In their final act of protecting Avalir, the two stood against the undead Vespin Chloras and the corrupted automatons known as Taxmen, war machines invented by Nydas himself.

Together, they worked to give the Architect Arcane time enough to foil the plans of the Lord of the Hells. As Sha'korzhan's spirit dissipated into the ether and Nydas lay dying, let it be said that neither's memory would ever be mocked again, but celebrated by those who knew their final sacrifice, the dual dragons of Avalir.

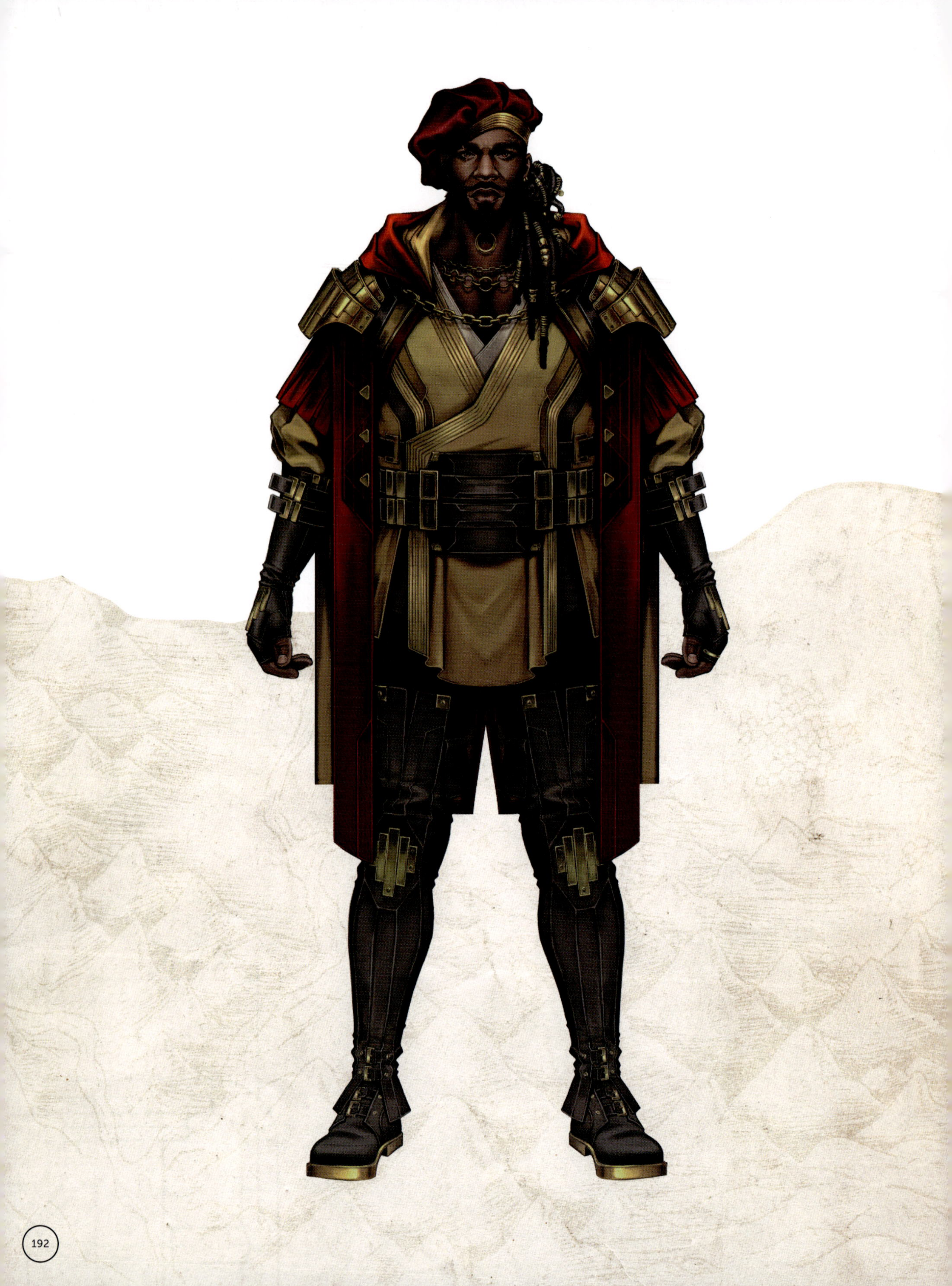

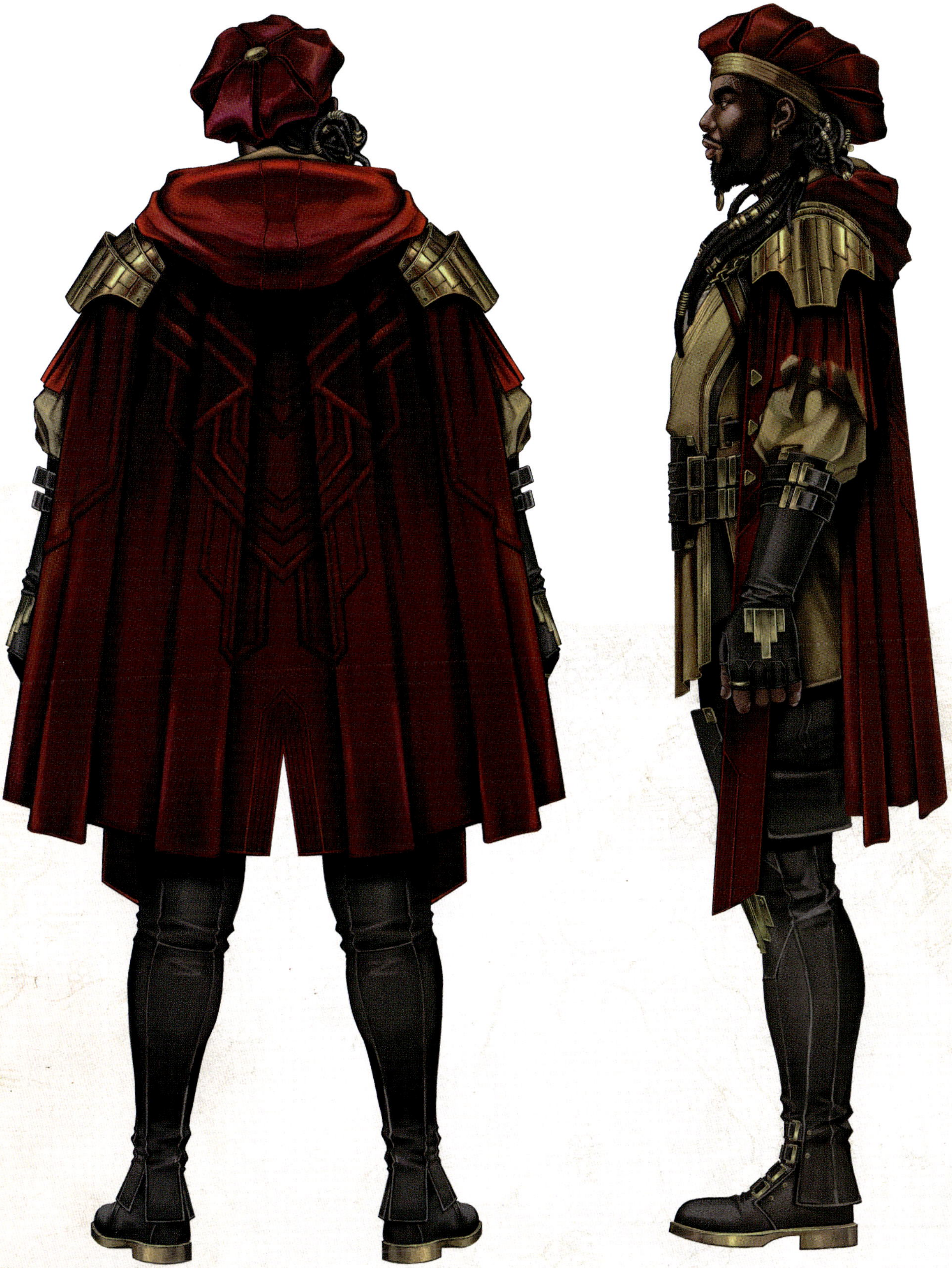

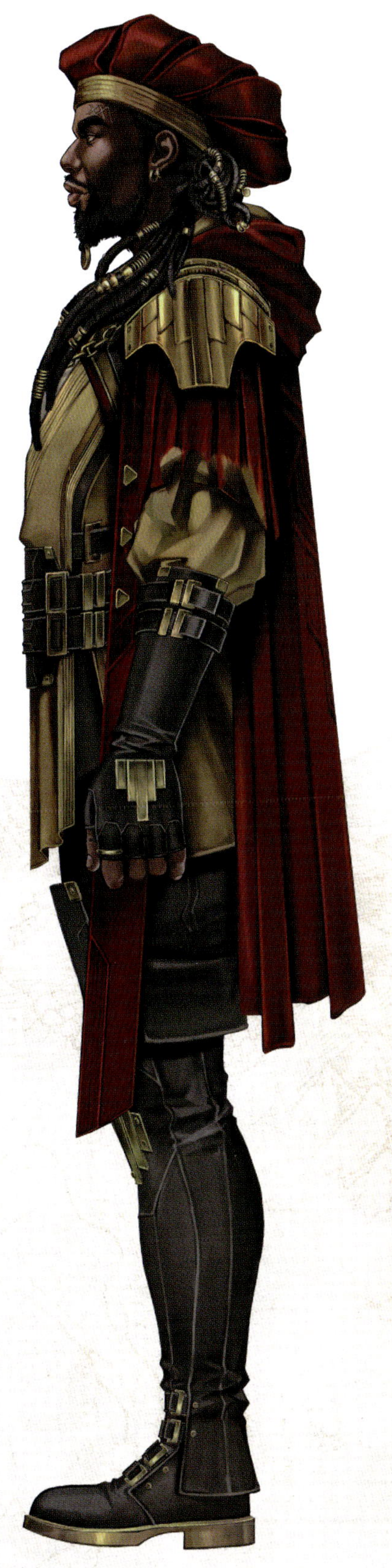

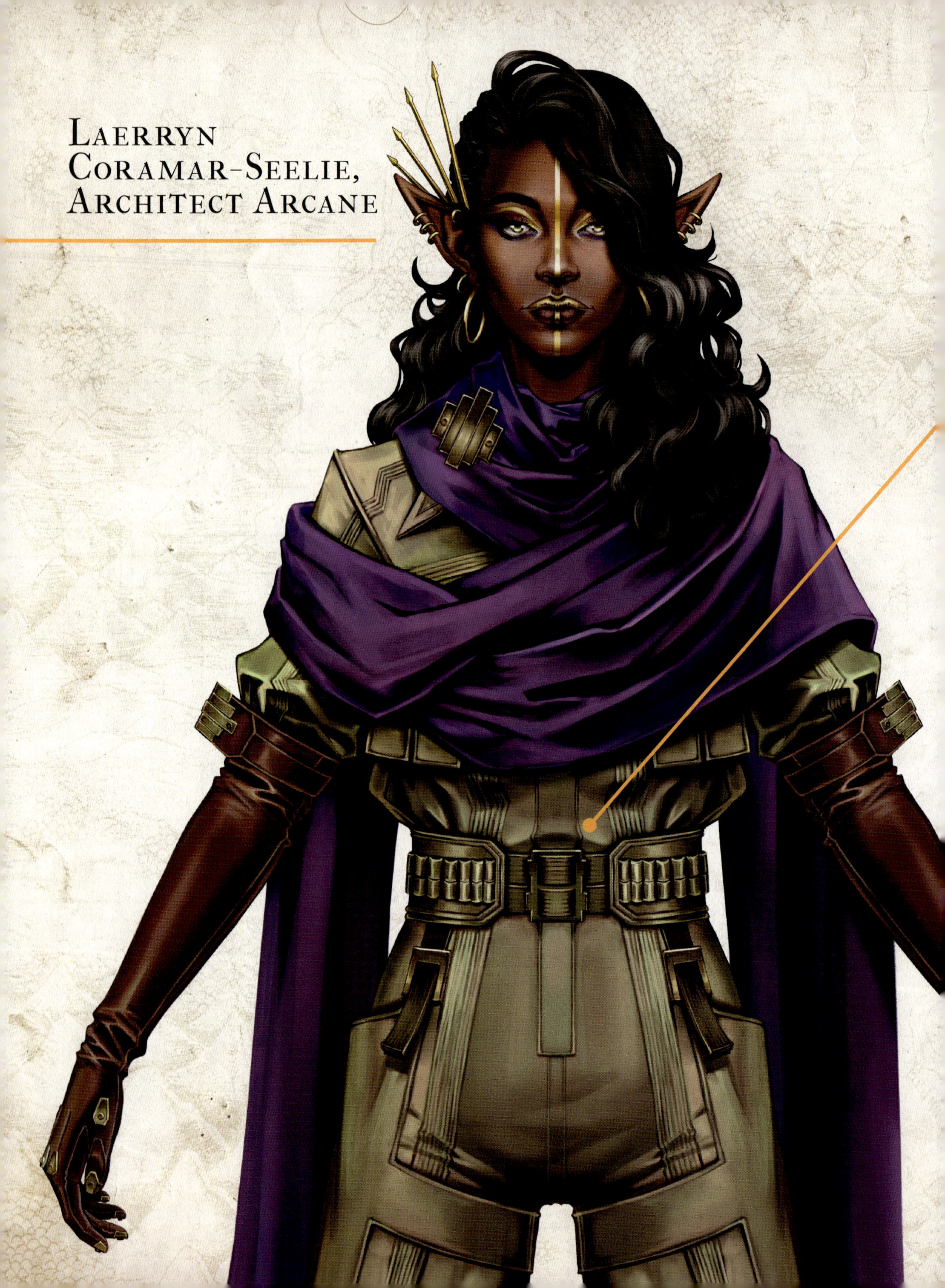
Laerryn
Coramar-Seelie,
Architect Arcane

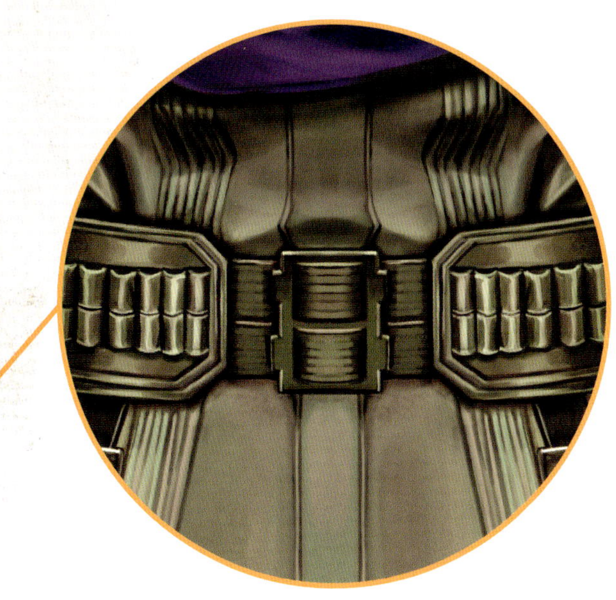

"The Architect Arcane was of great assistance this afternoon as I checked the Eldritch Batteries against the coming Convergence of Leylines. No more than a handful of moments went by before she saw, diagnosed, and fixed the issues besieging the internal capacitors of arcane conversion, and the quarter-bell had yet to even toll past the hour before she asked with her signature curtness if there was anything else I desired her assistance with. I chortled and said that with her speed and intelligence, it is as though she was blessed by the Archeart themself.

I must admit surprise when she burst out laughing, uproariously, even wiping away a tear in good humor. 'Oh yes,' she had said, 'they wish they could take all the credit. No, my friend, what you see is what you get, and what you get is all me, always.'

And then her Ring of Masks buzzed, she conversed for a moment, and then bid me farewell. Such a shining example of Avalir's progress and an exemplar of intelligence, she is most correct: Laerryn Coramar-Seelie is entirely herself and is herself the sole architect of all she has. And what she has is Avalir, and we are, thank the gods, lucky that we have her, too."

—Oren Keth'Kaylis, documenting a burned piece of parchment pulled from a stasis bubble in the Shattered Teeth

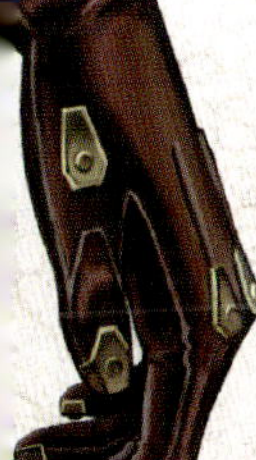

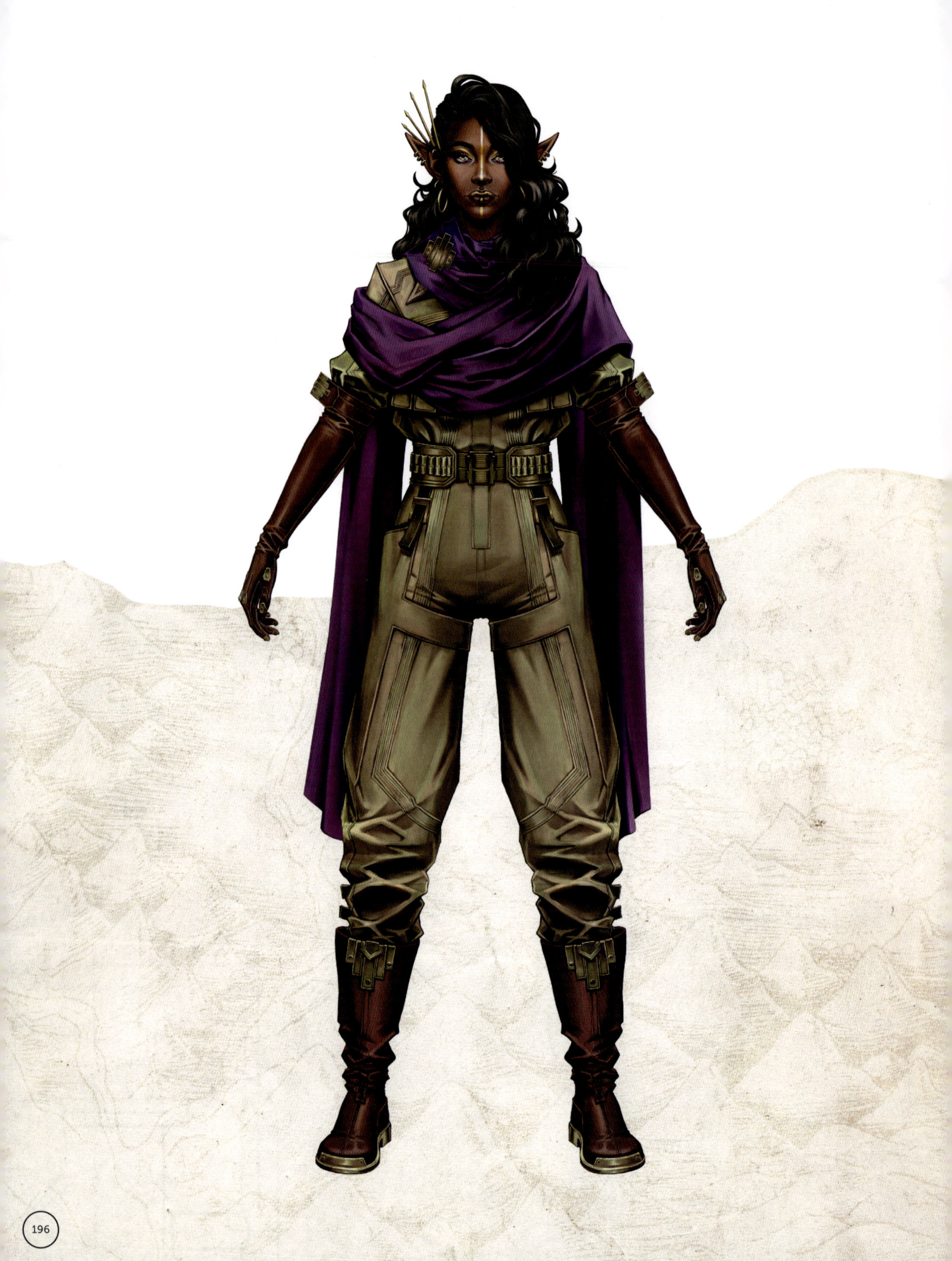

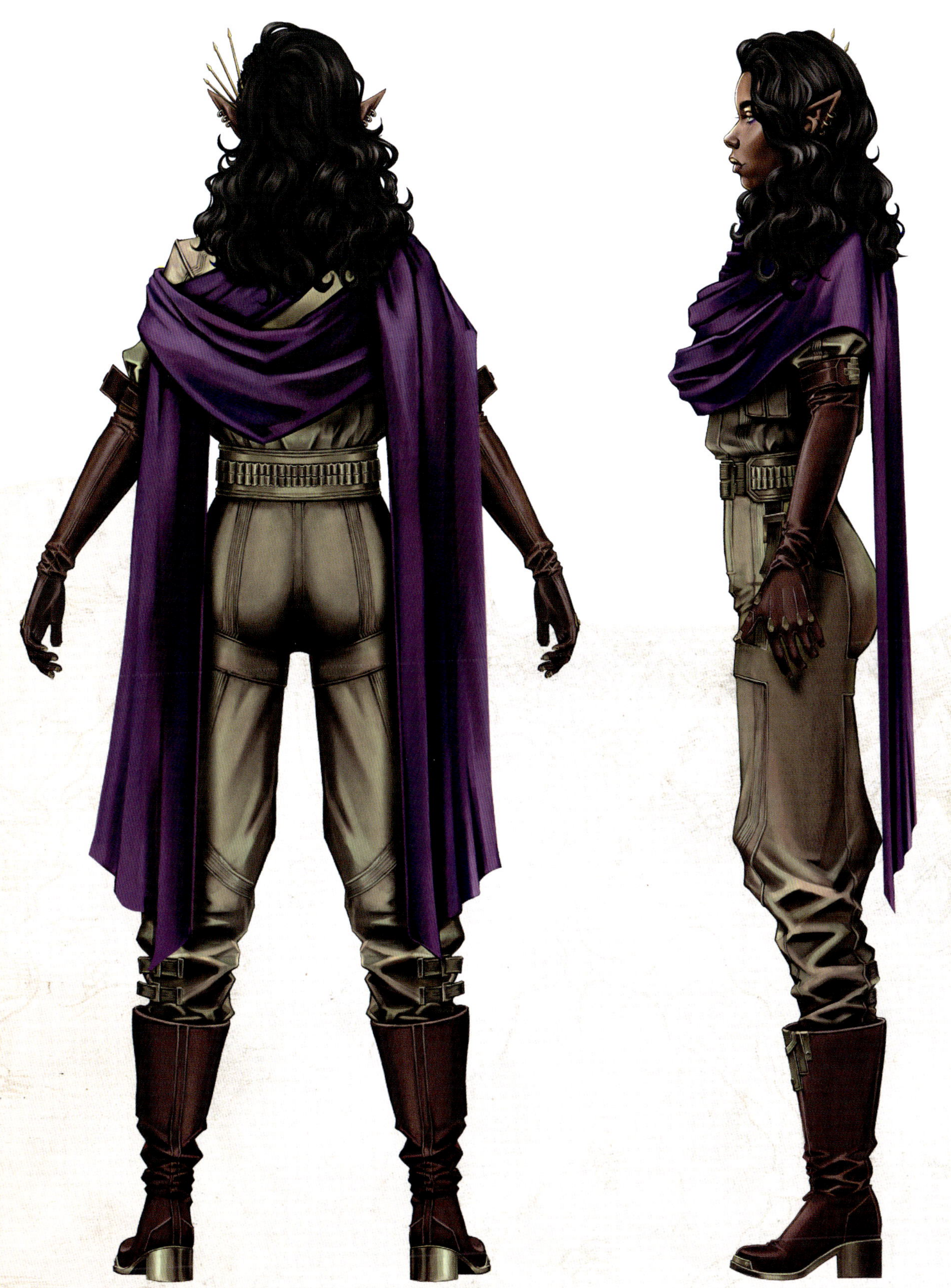

Ring of Masks

One of the many innovations of the Age of Arcanum that eased the annoyances of everyday life, a Ring of Masks was an invention meant to establish communication with various peoples in an instant. This small bracelet of intricate glass and ceramic masks had mirrors with their counterparts, to be activated when the wearer called upon you. For the Architect Arcane of the City of Avalir, her own Ring of Masks had a number of high-ranking colleagues throughout the city, including Akami Rowe, the Guildmaster of the Navigator's Guild; Calum Staffwright, her second-in-command; Dweomer, her aeormaton personal assistant; and many more. For private communications, Laerryn preferred the telepathic bond she shared with the Ring of Brass to share sensitive information.

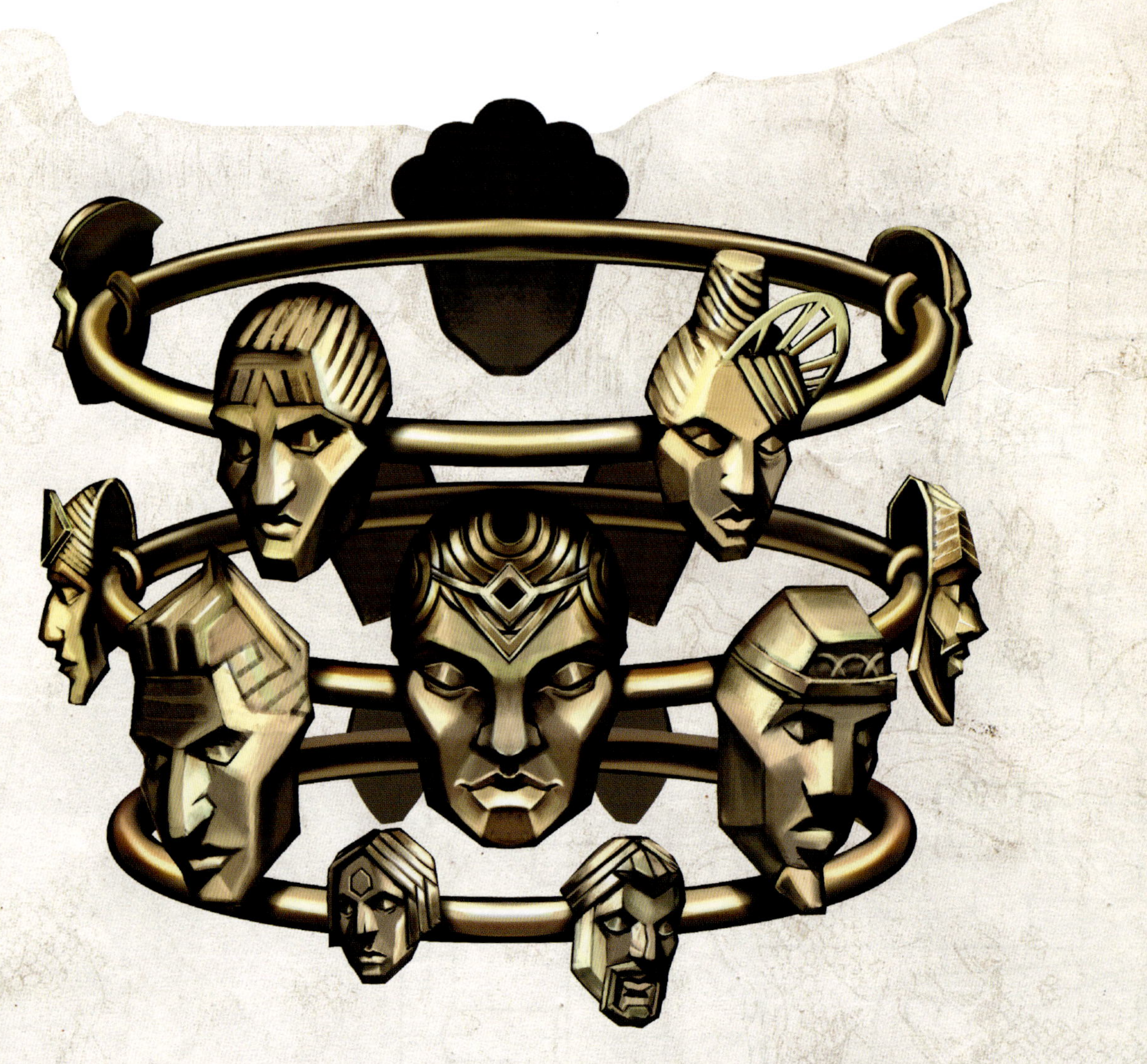

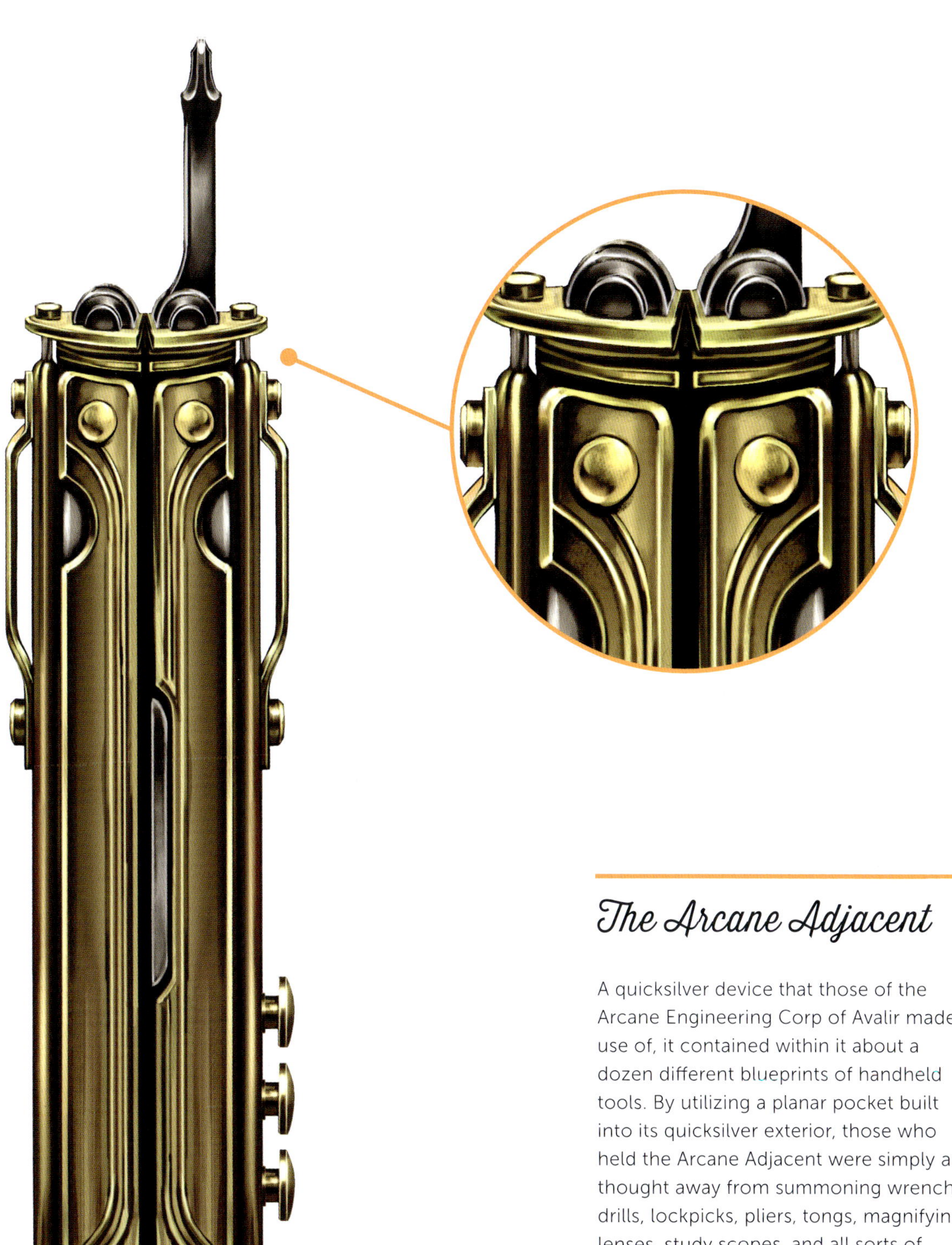

The Arcane Adjacent

A quicksilver device that those of the Arcane Engineering Corp of Avalir made use of, it contained within it about a dozen different blueprints of handheld tools. By utilizing a planar pocket built into its quicksilver exterior, those who held the Arcane Adjacent were simply a thought away from summoning wrenches, drills, lockpicks, pliers, tongs, magnifying lenses, study scopes, and all sorts of engineering tools to be used at any given time. In Laerryn's final stand before Vespin Chloras, she taught all future arcane engineers that when the chips are down and spell power is precious, sometimes a massive wrench says everything one needs to say.

Astral Leywright

Laerryn Coramar-Seelie worked every day of her life to benefit the peoples of Avalir. A brilliant, ambitious engineer with a dream of freeing her city and its citizens from the whims of the divine, she spent seven years building the Astral Leywright. This massive and intricate arcane device was a large platform of thousands of intricate runes, built beneath a swinging central pendulum that gathered ether and arcane energies to fuel its purpose. Built deep within the heart of Avalir, in the Meridian Labyrinth, this mighty arcane engine could harness and wield the leylines of Exandria. It would be the final key to unlocking transplanar travel for the mortals of Exandria, of which the City of Crowns would be the first and quite possibly the only metropolis to do so.

However, as the doom of Avalir came upon Laerryn and the Ring of Brass, she realized her Leywright, powerful enough to withstand the immense power of the leylines during an Apogee Solstice, was the only way to prevent the return of two primordial titans. The emergence of the titans would ensure victory for the Betrayer Gods, according to an oracle. As Laerryn and the Ring of Brass made their way to the Leywright, she undid a lifetime of work to rewrite the purpose of the Leywright. It would now send Ka'Mort, Empress of Earth, and Rau'Shan, Emperor of Fire, through the planes, rending their forms and diffusing them across all of existence.

With her dying breaths, under assault from Vespin Chloras, reunited with her husband, and surrounded by her friends, Laerryn reengineered her dream to save the world and succeeded. The continent of Domunas was well and truly shattered, Avalir gone in moments, but because of her intellect, her bravery, and her Leywright, Exandria lived.

"So much was destroyed in the Calamity. When they say that in the Age of Arcanum, great workings of magic were indeed possible, well . . . they were correct. And even though we have only begun to uncover just a fraction of Laerryn Coramar-Seelie's research, even just this minuscule amount of information is enough to cement her status in Exandria's long history of the arcane. Through the design and theoretical purpose of the Astral Leywright, we see the seeds of modern-day abjuration, enchantment, teleportation, planar theory, leyline manipulation, and those are just the beginning! Avalir's final Architect Arcane had dreams beyond even the scope of this Age, and the Astral Leywright was her final dream made manifest.

That she was willing to destroy her dream so that all Exandria could live . . . it makes my heart pause, to feel the weight of that choice. It is this researcher's deepest wish that someday we can repay that debt, and possibly make her final dream come true."

—D'Rishk Dawnscale

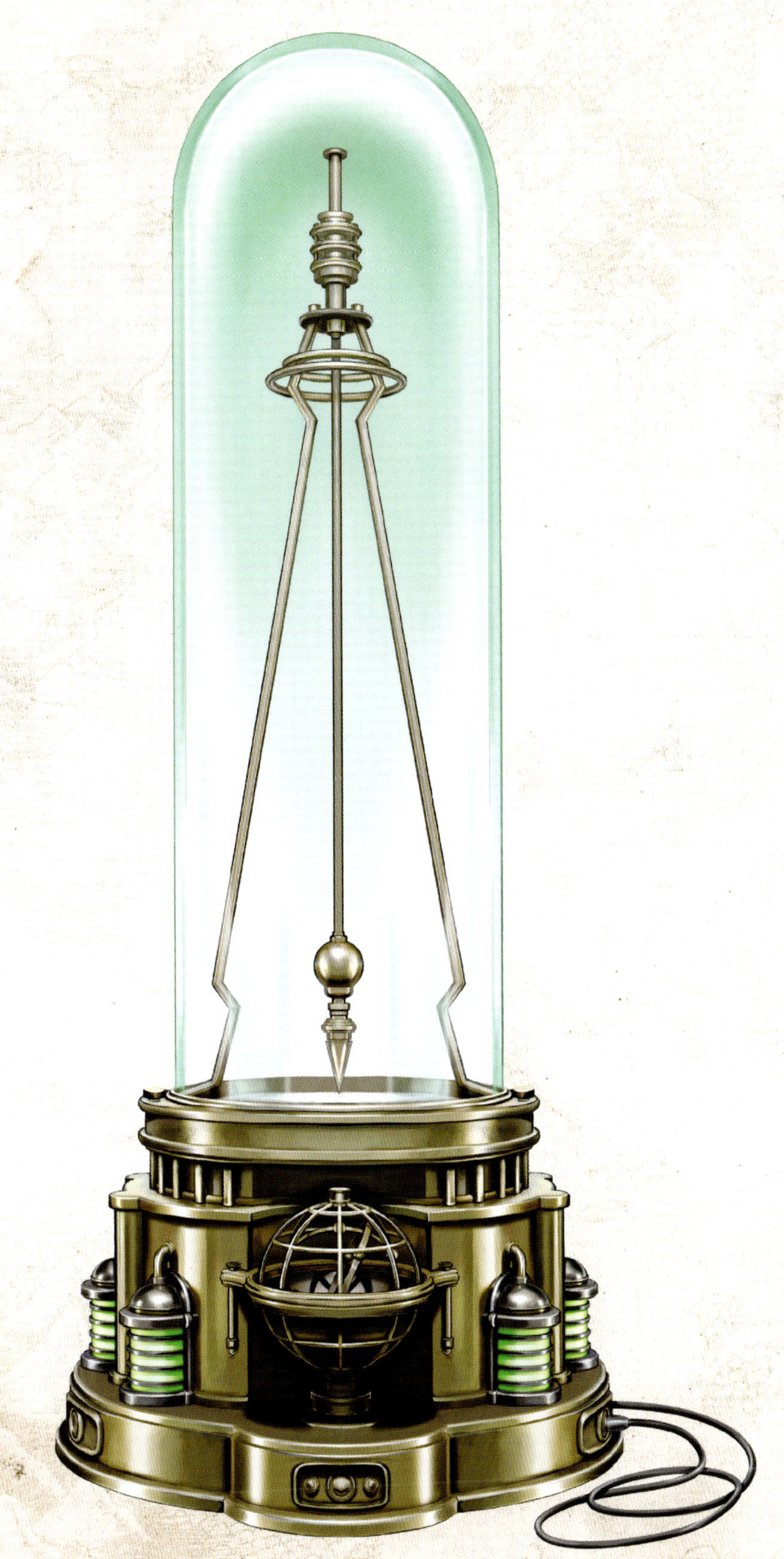

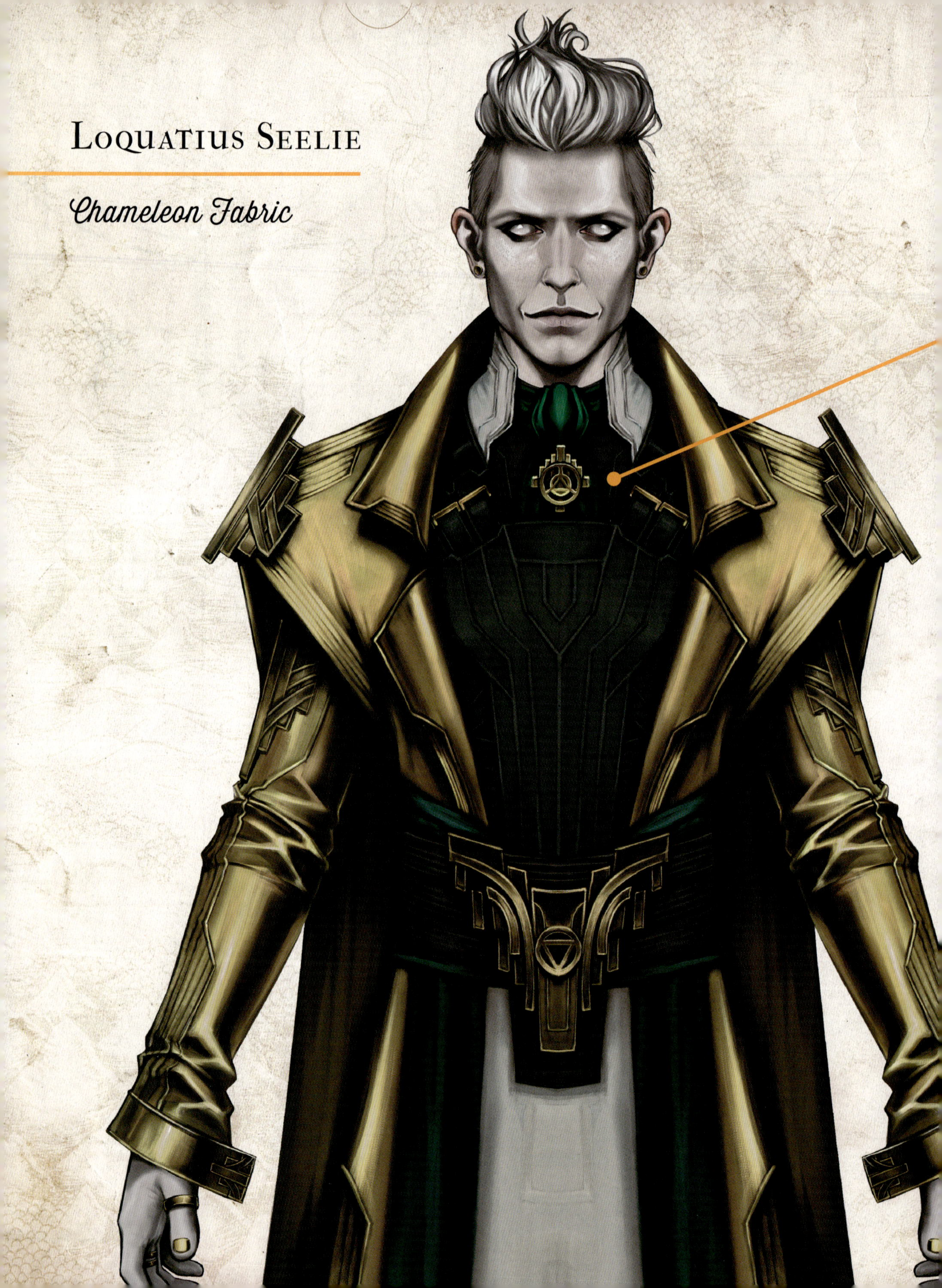

Loquatius Seelie

Chameleon Fabric

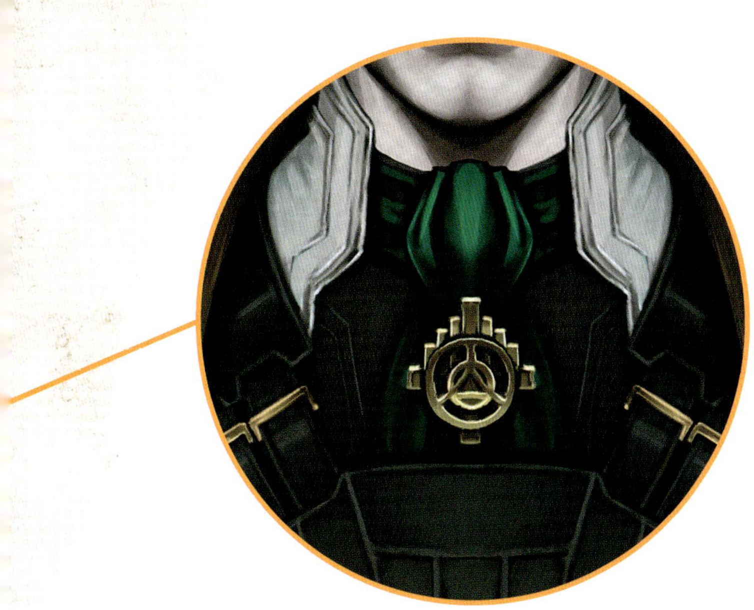

"Headed to a swanky soiree of sorcerous students and didn't bring your best robes? Running late to a laissez-faire afternoon of laconic lounging and don't have time to change out of your work clothes? That's why we recommend Kozhak's Chameleon Fabric, whose change you can believe in! Take what you're wearing and turn it inside out. If it's good enough for the Voice of the City, it's certainly good enough for you!"

—Old broadcast from Loquatius Seelie, recovered

Being a changeling on the go, and asked to go to every which function you shake a wand at, Loquatius Seelie quickly learned in his day job that even taking a few minutes to change into different attire several times a day was really eating into his agenda. With the Chameleon Fabric, he was able to finally find a set of clothes that morphed and changed as fast and as easily as he did. Though the clothing was not very protective, let it never be said that Mr. Seelie was not the height of fashion.

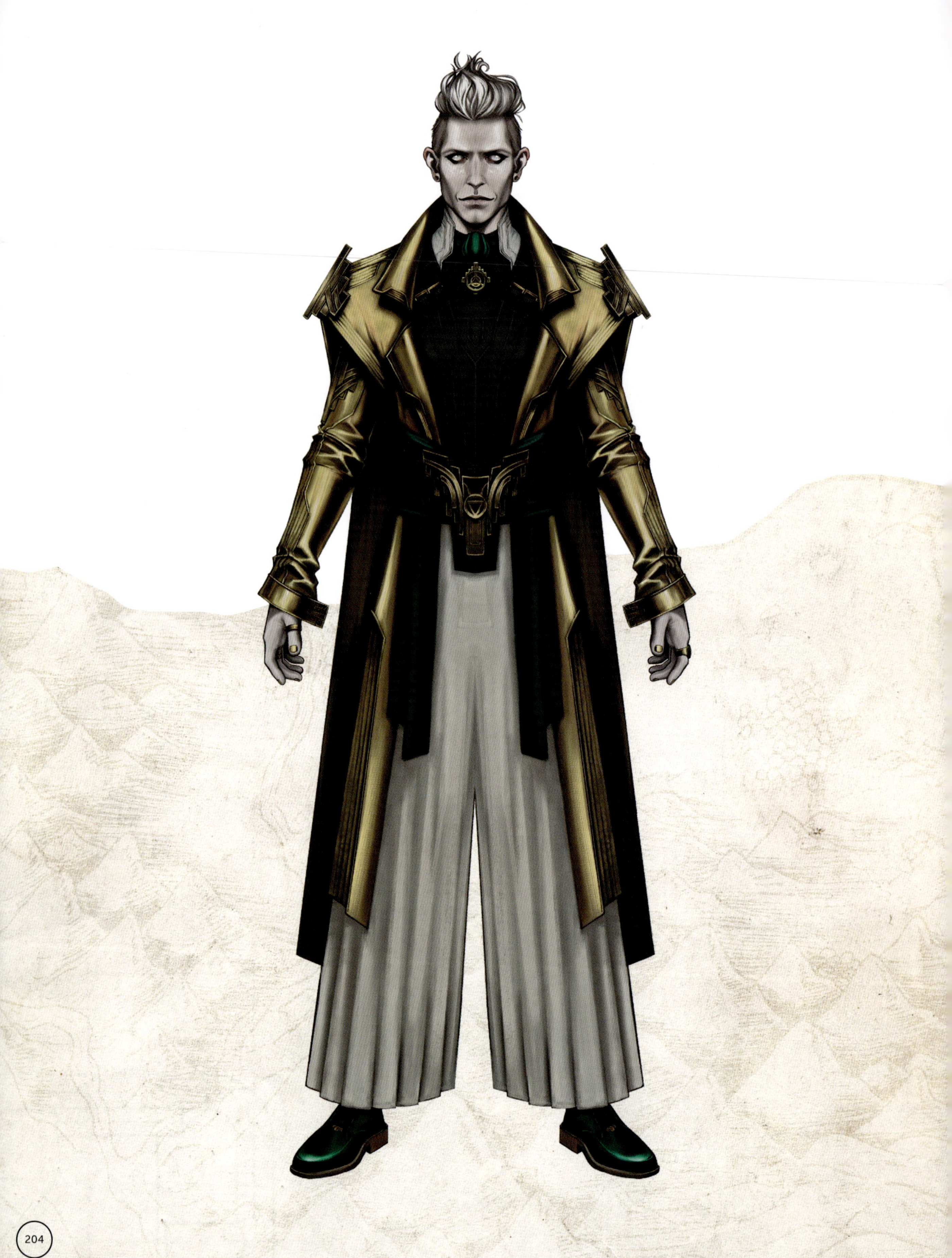

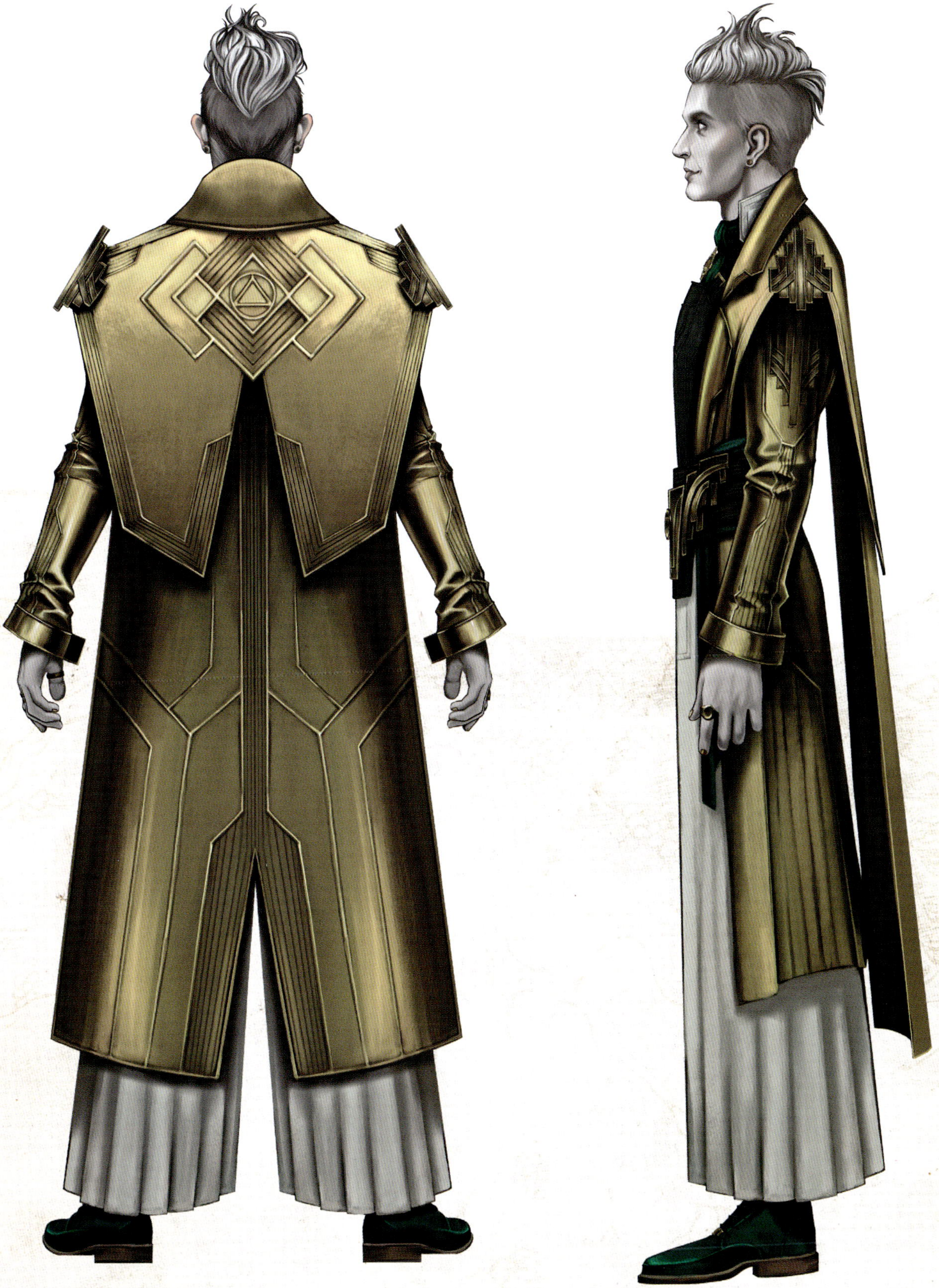

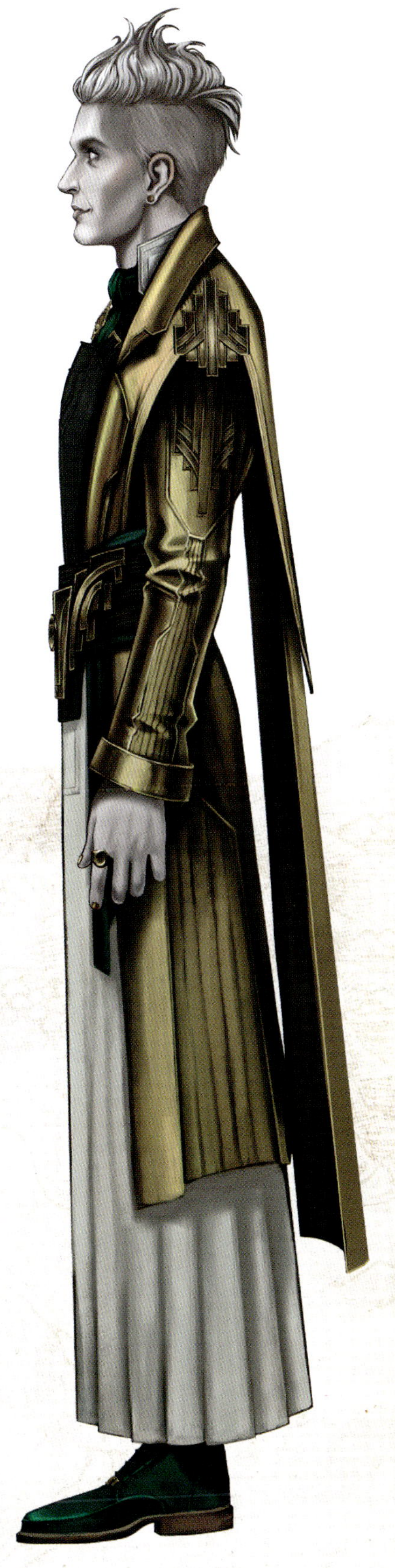

Pneumatic Sending Tubes

Though he could change his appearance in the blink of an eye, replicating himself was still beyond Loquatius's ability. And as one of the beating hearts of the Herald's Tome, Avalir's premiere home for news, Loquatius needed to be able to pass off information as quickly as possible. Like the veins of such a heart, he worked to create a series of pneumatic tubes that he and his other heralds could utilize, firing them off to certain people in the city at mostly safe speeds. If they ever hit anyone or damaged property, the legal team of the Herald's Tome can comfortably say, no, they did not.

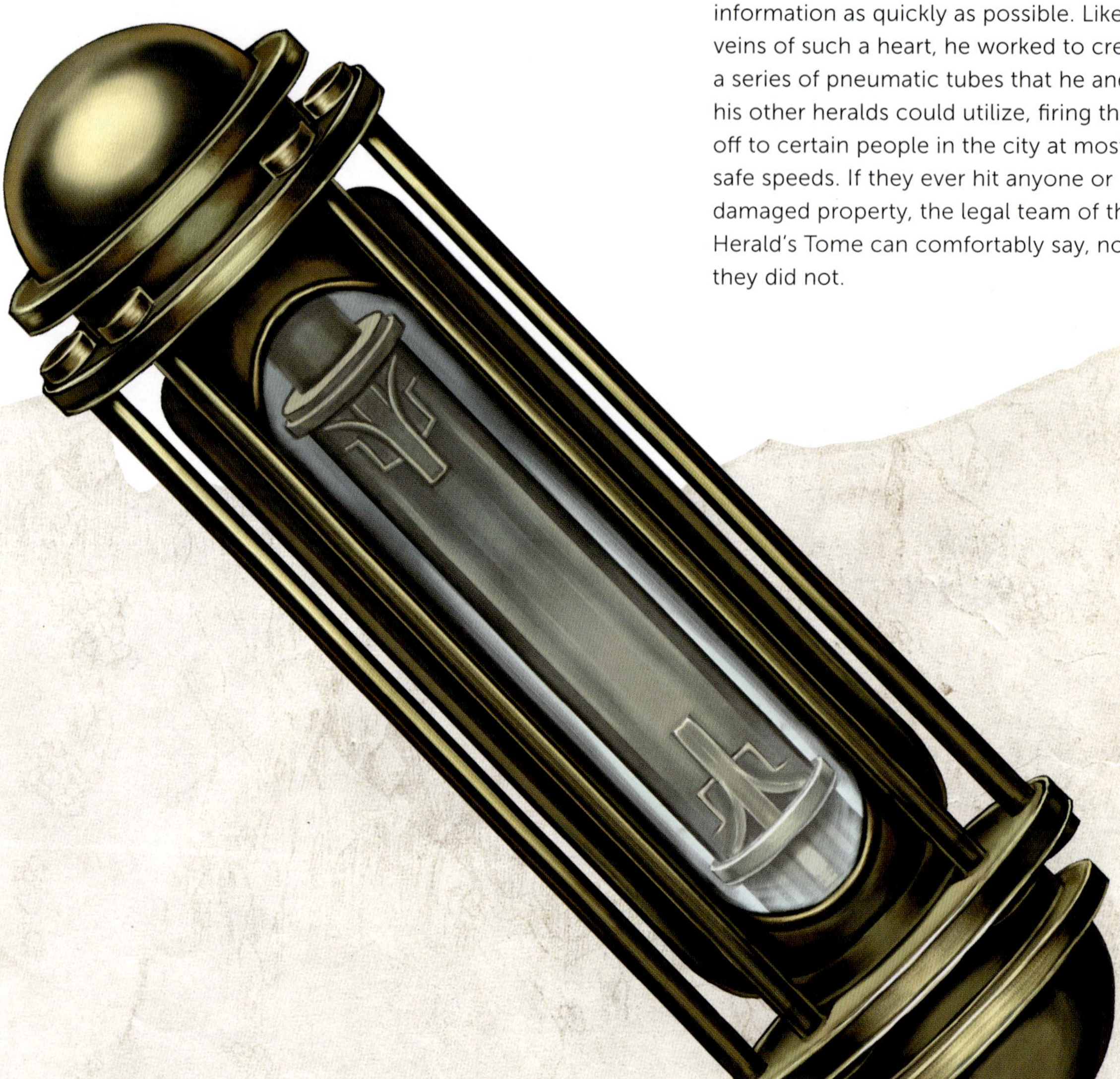

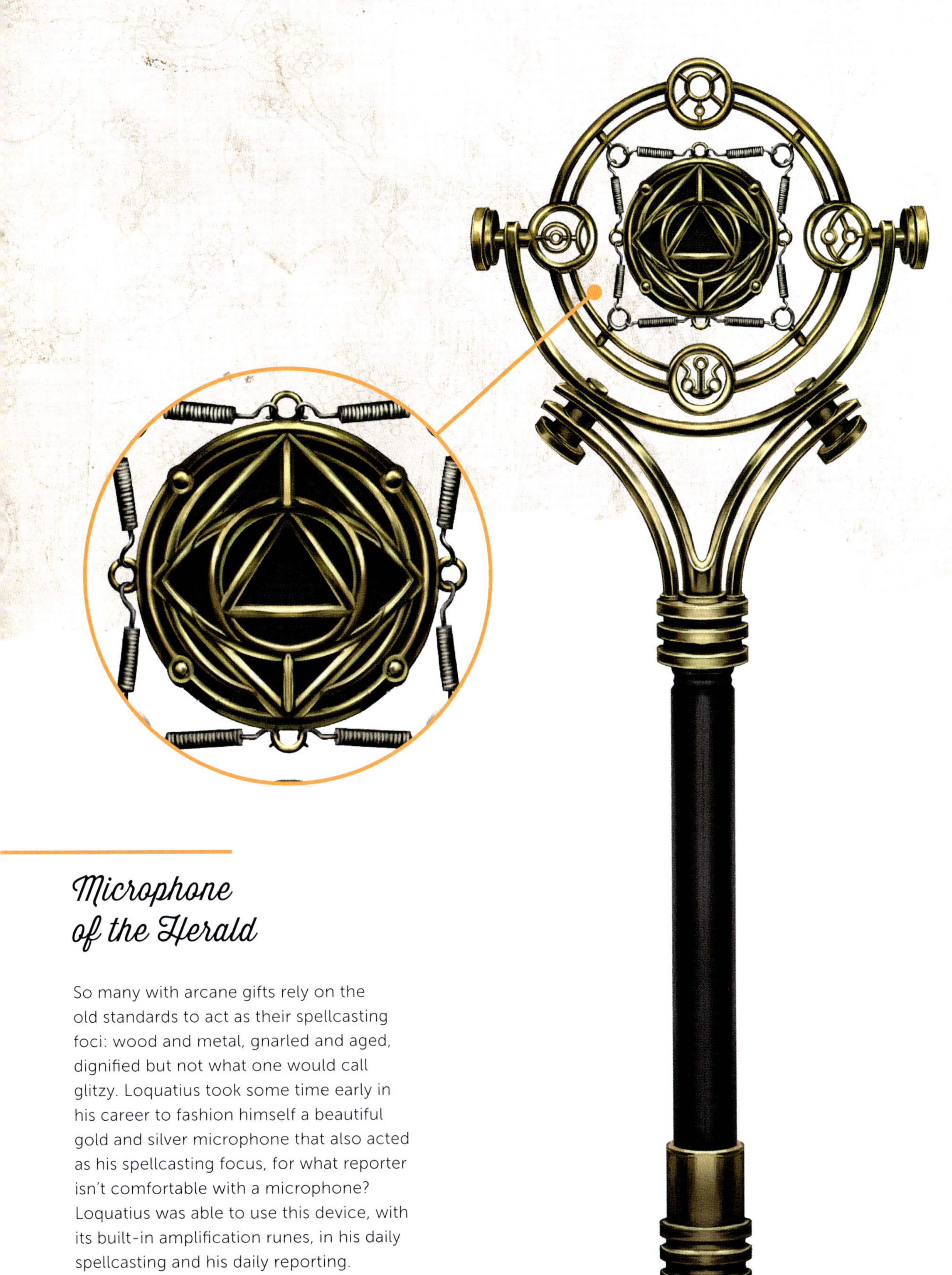

Microphone of the Herald

So many with arcane gifts rely on the old standards to act as their spellcasting foci: wood and metal, gnarled and aged, dignified but not what one would call glitzy. Loquatius took some time early in his career to fashion himself a beautiful gold and silver microphone that also acted as his spellcasting focus, for what reporter isn't comfortable with a microphone? Loquatius was able to use this device, with its built-in amplification runes, in his daily spellcasting and his daily reporting.

Cerrit Agrupnin

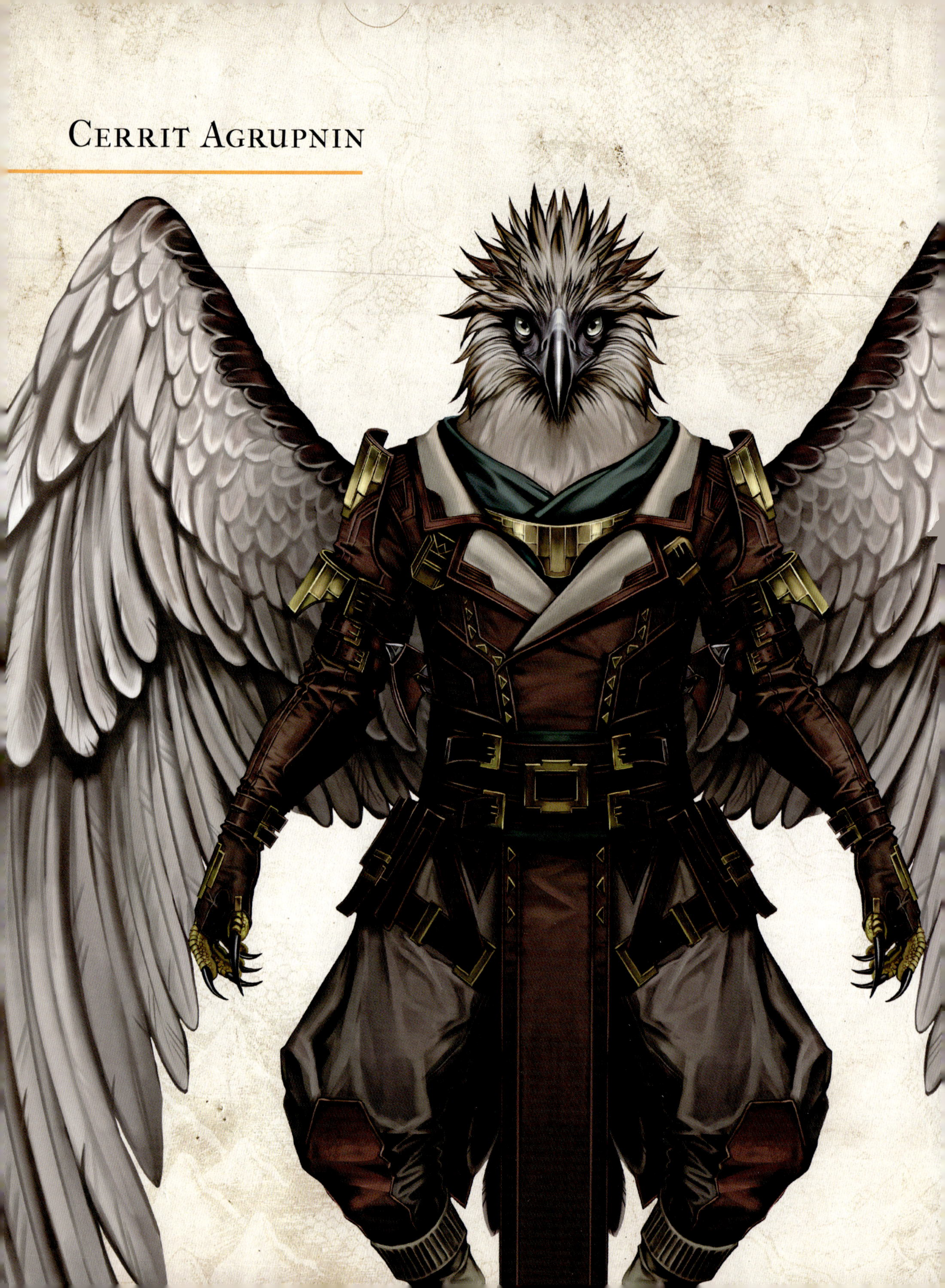

"With this ring, our eyes become Avalir's. Through them, may we see the truth. And if we do not see it, let us find it; in every sweep of shadow, beyond every cloud, through every spell, no wall nor door nor enchantment nor heart will keep us from the truth. Let us hear the truth in those we meet, and through our actions, may the City of Crowns be kept aloft, safe and secure. I close my eyes as myself for the last time. And when I open them once more, Sightwarden I shall be for the rest of my days."

—D'Rishk Dawnscale, "Oath of the Eyes of Avalir," recovered from a descendant's keepsake in Eiselcross

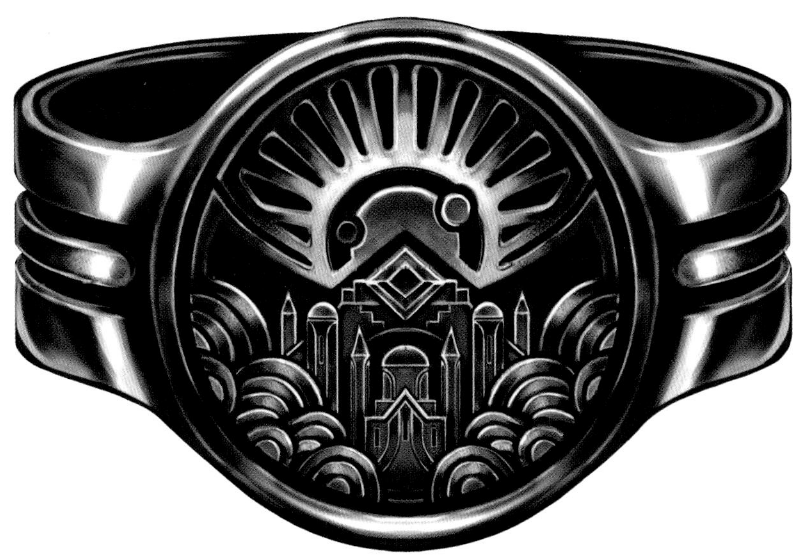

Ring of Honor

A silver ring with a vision of Avalir, this item was crucial for the Eyes of Avalir to do their duty in a city of the arcane, where magic can muddy the waters of truth. There were very few that could lie with such dexterity as to bypass the enchantment on the ring, which had a powerful enchantment on it meant to detect if someone within earshot was lying. Ironically, one of those beings was Cerrit's ally, Loquatius Seelie.

Cerrit used the ring often across his long career as Sightwarden, discerning the truth and seeking it. In the end, though, truth was the one thing he couldn't hide, as his children caught him lying before he sent them to safety. With his ring aglow, lit up in his own deception, Cerrit had a moment of realization: sometimes, however painful, the lie was needed.

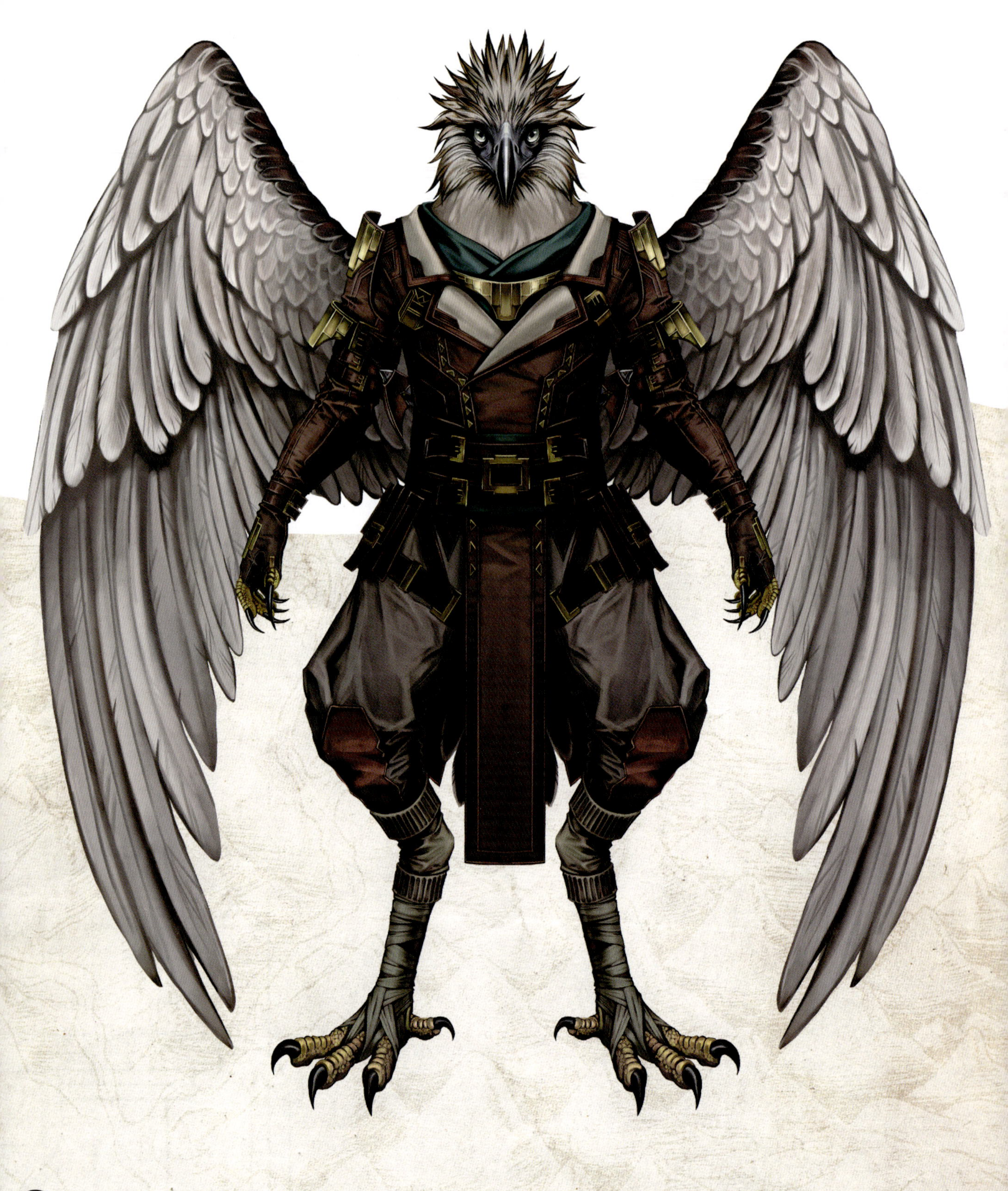

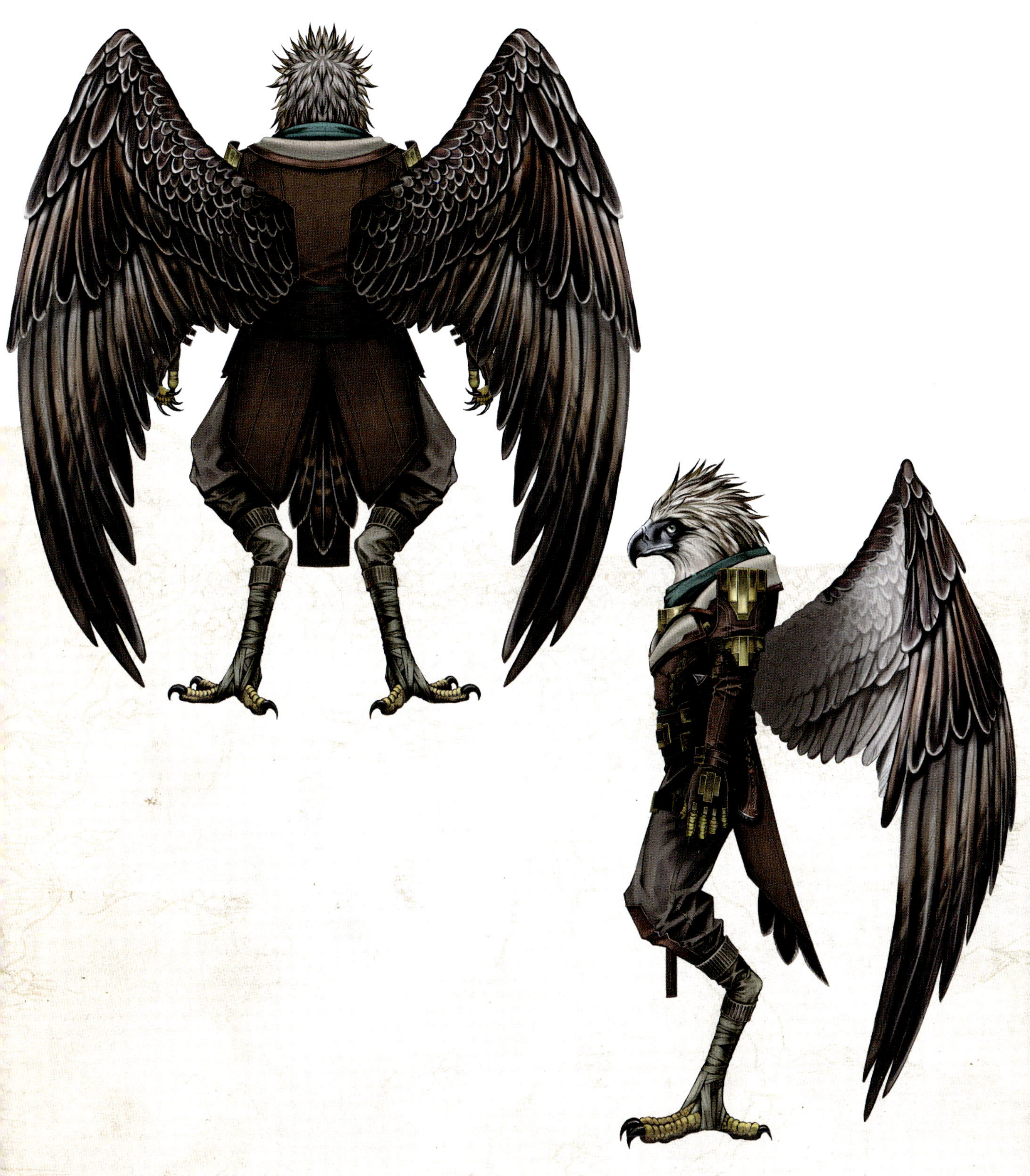

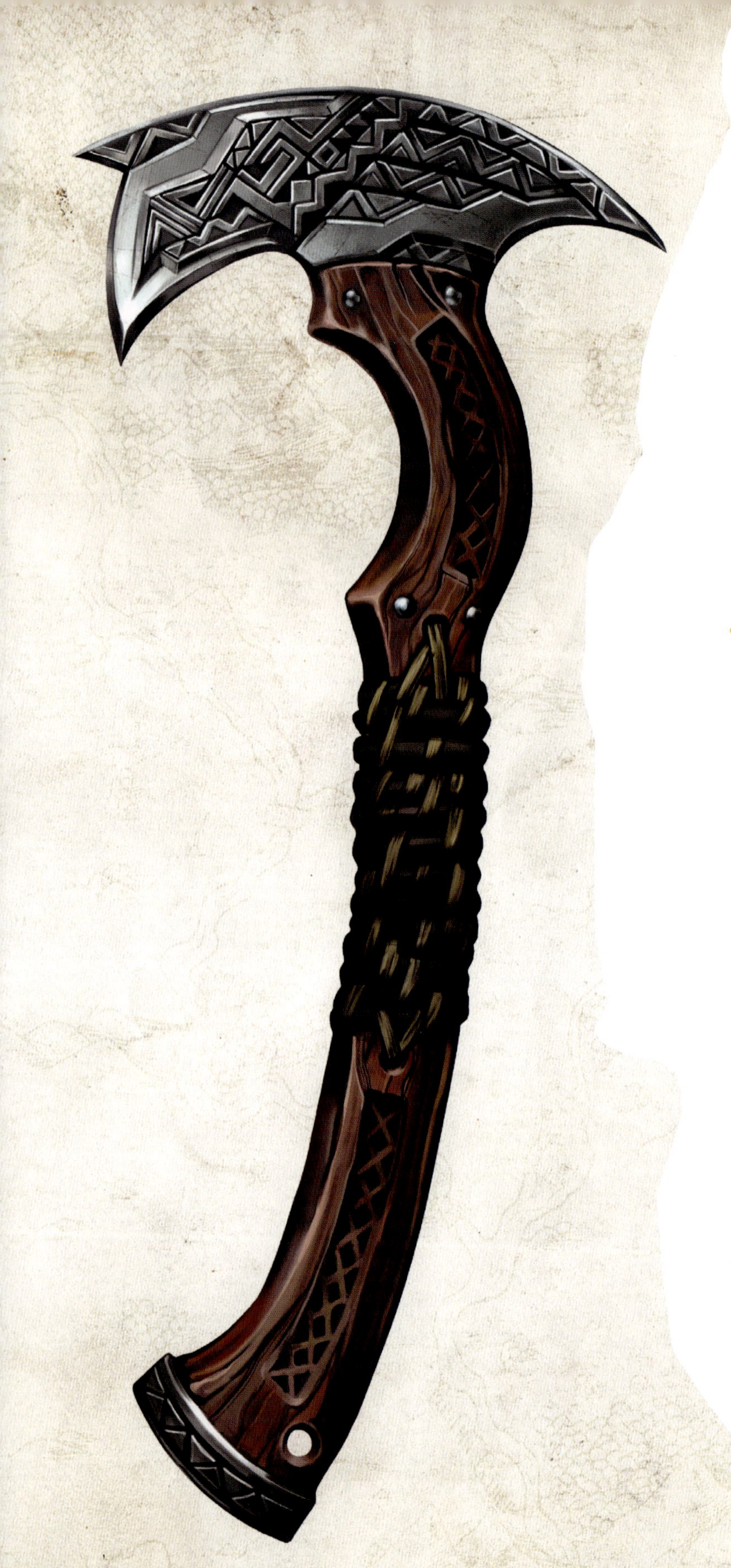

Twin Hawks

If anyone ever caught an unwanted glimpse of these weapons, chances were they were the last things you'd ever see. Cerrit's "hawks" were two razor-sharp tomahawk axes kept in a holster beneath his wings, hidden from sight. As he had already trained extensively in hand-to-hand combat, feats of stealth, and combatting mages, the final aspect of Cerrit's training was weapons expertise, for when joint locks, nerve pinches, and grappling wouldn't do. In the hours preceding the doom of Avalir, these twin hawks drank their fair share of blood and ichor, used in Cerrit's final act of defense of the city. Their last act was to halt the advance of the undead Vespin Chloras, moments from annihilating Laerryn, and with a final swipe of their razored edge, decapitating the puppet-mage of the Lord of the Hells.

Message Stones

These small, enchanted stones are used in conjunction between two parties. Though Cerrit had his telepathic bond with the Ring of Brass, and a sending stone to communicate with his partner within the Eyes of Avalir, the sending stone he used most frequently was the one he gave to his family, namely, his son, Kir, and his daughter, Maya. Invoking the use of code names to communicate, often regardless of his father's working hours, Kir would call his father to report on the goings-on of his sister. In the end, the sending stone allowed Cerrit, his children and wife, Wrayne, to share one last conversation before the doom of Avalir. This conversation inspired Cerrit's final flight from the City of Crowns and his safe return to his family.

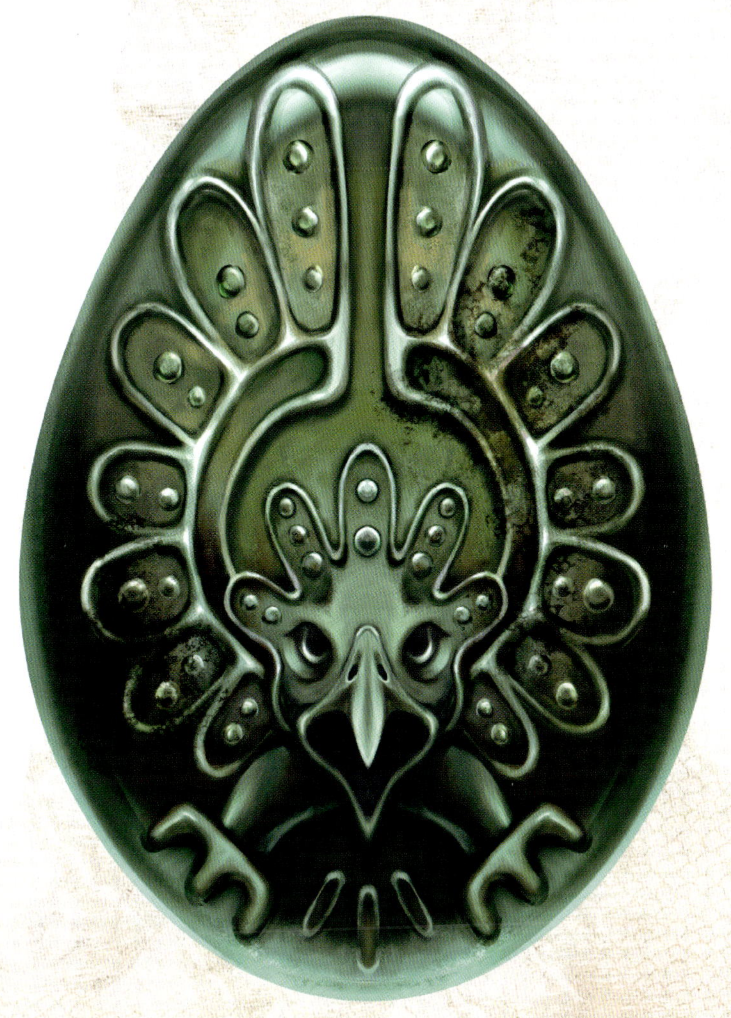

About the Author

Martin Cahill is a writer living just outside of New York City. He's the author of *Audition for the Fox*, a novella from Tachyon Publications, and was a contributor to *Critical Role: Vox Machina - Stories Untold*. Martin was a 2022 Ignyte Awards nominee for Best Short Story and a graduate of the 2014 Clarion Writers' Workshop. He has published fiction with *Reactor*, *Clarkesworld*, *Lightspeed Magazine*, and many more. His story "Godmeat" appeared in *The Best American Science Fiction & Fantasy 2019,* and he was one of the writers on *Batman: The Blind Cut* from Realm Media. Martin also writes, and has written, book reviews, articles, and essays for Tor.com, Catapult, Ghostfire Gaming, Book Riot, Strange Horizons, and the Barnes and Noble Science Fiction & Fantasy Blog.

About the Illustrator

Ana Fedina, also known as Anafi, is a concept artist working primarily in the video game industry. She began her journey studying academic arts and design, then later on moved on to freelancing and working in-house for various video game projects. With her experience designing characters for games, Ana has decided to dip her toes into the world of tabletop in recent years. Combining her love for various cultures, fashions, and character stories, she is ready to take up any design challenge, be it the regal heroes of old or gothic villains. In her free time she likes to play with her cats, participate in D&D games, and draw suspiciously way too many elves.

About Critical Role

Critical Role is one of the fastest-growing independent media companies in the world, starting as a roleplaying game between friends and evolving into a new kind of organization dedicated to storytelling, community, and imagination. As Critical Role continues to expand the unique universe it has created, with complex stories set in an ever-evolving world, it also continues to create more ways for fans to experience the brand, including both fiction and nonfiction books on the *New York Times* Best Sellers list, comic books, graphic novels, collectibles, tabletop and roleplaying games, podcasts, live events, and a critically acclaimed animated series, *The Legend of Vox Machina*, airing exclusively on Amazon Prime Video. Additionally, Critical Role has launched two major initiatives: an official 501(c)(3) non-profit, the Critical Role Foundation (CRF), and a tabletop game publishing company, Darrington Press. With an original cast of award-winning veteran voice actors who are also co-founders of the company, including Matthew Mercer, Ashley Johnson, Marisha Ray, Taliesin Jaffe, Travis Willingham, Sam Riegel, Laura Bailey, and Liam O'Brien, Critical Role is committed to ensuring anyone can discover its stories, characters, and community. For more information on Critical Role go to www.critrole.com.

CRITICAL ROLE:

Founders: Laura Bailey, Taliesin Jaffe,
Ashley Johnson, Matthew Mercer,
Liam O'Brien, Marisha Ray,
Sam Riegel, Travis Willingham

Lore Keeper: Dani Carr

Licensing Brand Associate: Niki Chi

Licensing Manager: Shaunette DeTie

RING OF BRASS CAST:
Luis Carazo, Aabria Iyengar, Lou Wilson

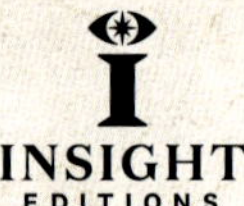

PO Box 3088
San Rafael, CA 94912
www.insighteditions.com

Find us on Facebook: www.facebook.com/InsightEditions
Follow us on Instagram: @insighteditions

2025 © Gilmore's Glorious Goods LLC. All Rights Reserved.
Critical Role, Vox Machina, Mighty Nein, Bells Hells, character names, associated logos, and images are all trademarks of Critical Role LLC.

Published by Insight Editions, San Rafael, California, in 2025.

No part of this book may be reproduced in any form without written permission from the publisher.

ISBN: 979-8-88663-553-9

Publisher: Raoul Goff
SVP, Group Publisher: Vanessa Lopez
VP, Creative: Chrissy Kwasnik
VP, Manufacturing: Alix Nicholaeff
Editorial Director: Mike Degler
Art Director: Catherine San Juan
Designer: Lola Villanueva
Editor: Sadie Lowry
Editorial Assistants: Audrey Salo and Jeff Chiarelli
Managing Editor: Nora Milman
Senior Production Manager: Greg Steffen
Strategic Production Planner: Lina s Palma-Temena

Text by Martin Cahill
Illustrations by Ana Fedina

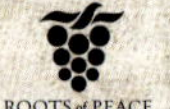

REPLANTED PAPER
Insight Editions, in association with Roots of Peace, will plant two trees for each tree used in the manufacturing of this book. Roots of Peace is an internationally renowned humanitarian organization dedicated to eradicating land mines worldwide and converting war-torn lands into productive farms.

Manufactured in China by Insight Editions
10 9 8 7 6 5 4 3 2 1

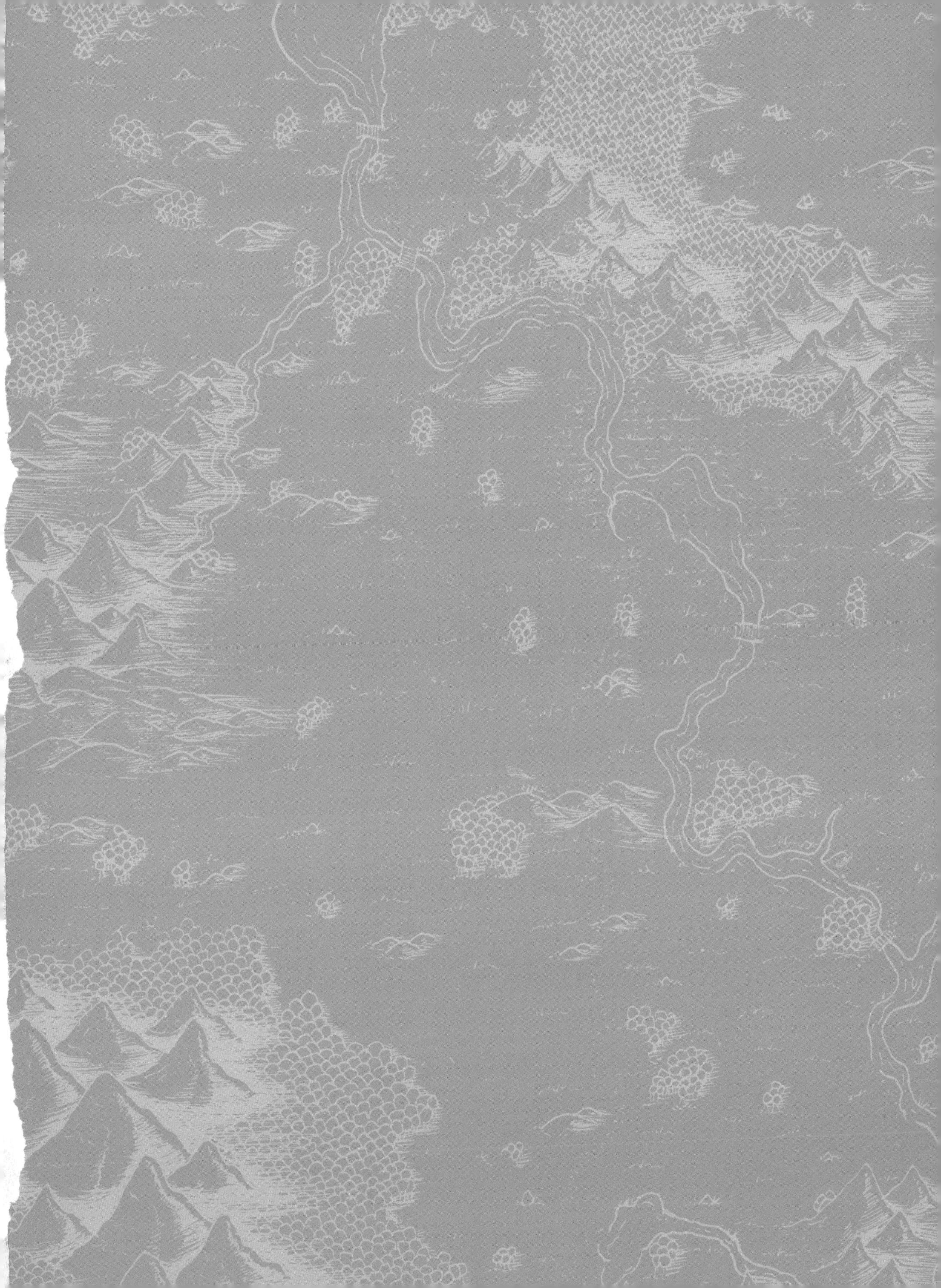